Destructive Organizational Communication

Destructive Organizational Communication brings together highly respected communication and management scholars to examine the destructive communicative processes in organizations. Going beyond descriptions of various types of organizational communication, this volume explores how we might live and work together in a way that organizes our endeavors more humanely. Each problelm-focused chapter examines a specific aspect of destructive organizational communication, reviews existing theory and research about that communicative form, and outlines its consequences and associated harms.

Contributors explore such key issues as workplace bullying, incivility, sexual harassment, and the destructive potential of teams and communication technologies. The volume's central focus is on social interactions and meaning systems that organize in destructive ways—ways that constitute abusive, oppressive, harmful, or exploitative organizational environments.

The insights provided herein make a valuable contribution toward understanding harmful communication processes in the workplace. This book is an excellent resource for scholars studying destructive organizational communication, managers dealing with hostile workplaces, organizational members trying to understand their current experiences, and instructors of graduate and upper-level undergraduate classes in organizational studies.

Pamela Lutgen-Sandvik (Ph.D. Arizona State University) is an Assistant Professor in the Department of Communication and Journalism at the University of New Mexico. She teaches and researches in the area of organizational communication. Her current research includes the issues of workplace bullying and employee emotional abuse, particularly the impact of abuse at work on targets and the ways in which employees resist bullying.

Beverly Davenport Sypher (Ph.D. University of Michigan) is Associate Provost for special initiatives at Purdue University. In addition to her administrative appointment, she is a Professor in the Department of Communication. Prior to this appointment, Sypher was a Senior Fellow in the Office of the Provost at Virginia Tech University, Divisional Dean for the social sciences at the University of Kansas, and Chair of the Department of Communication at the University of Kentucky. Dr. Sypher is President-Elect of the Organizational Communication division of the National Communication Association, and has served on the Board of Directors of the International Communication Association. She has received the highest honors for teaching at the Universities of Kansas and Kentucky, and by the National Communication Association. Sypher has also been the principal investigator on more than $6 million in grants and served as the Director of the Dean's Scholars Program at the University of Kansas.

Communication Series
Jennings Bryant/Dolf Zillmann, General Editors

Destructive Organizational Communication

Processes, Consequences, and
Constructive Ways of Organizing

Edited by
Pamela Lutgen-Sandvik
University of New Mexico

Beverly Davenport Sypher
Purdue University

Routledge
Taylor & Francis Group

NEW YORK AND LONDON

First published 2009
by Routledge
270 Madison Ave, New York, NY 10016

Simultaneously published in the UK
by Routledge
2 Park Square, Milton Park, Abingdon, Oxon OX14 4RN

*Routledge is an imprint of the Taylor & Francis Group,
an informa business*

© 2009 Taylor & Francis

Typeset in Gill Sans and Sabon
by Swales & Willis Ltd, Exeter, Devon
Printed and bound in the United States of America
on acid-free paper by Walsworth Publishing Company, Marceline, MO

Library of Congress Cataloging in Publication Data
Destructive organizational communication: processes,
consequences, and constructive ways of organizing/edited by
Pamela Lutgen-Sandvik, Beverly Davenport Sypher.
p. cm.— (communication series)
Includes index.
1. Communication in organizations. 2. Bullying in the workplace.
3. Work environment. I. Lutgen-Sandvik, Pamela. II. Sypher, Beverly
Davenport.
HD30.3.D474 2009
658.3'04—dc22
2008048439

ISBN 10: 0–415–98993–0 (hbk)
ISBN 10: 0–415–98994–9 (pbk)
ISBN 10: 0–203–92855–5 (ebk)

ISBN 13: 978–0–415–98993–0 (hbk)
ISBN 13: 978–0–415–98994–7 (pbk)
ISBN 13: 978–0–203–92855–4 (ebk)

For our children:
Jeannette and Joseph
Ford and Sloan

Contents

Contributors

Brenda J. Allen (Ph.D., Howard University) is an Associate Dean in the College of Liberal Arts and Sciences and Professor in the Department of Communication at the University of Colorado Denver. Her research and teaching areas are organizational communication, diversity, group communication, and computer-mediated communication.

Janell C. Bauer (M.A., University of the Pacific) is a Ph.D. student in the Department of Communication at the University of Colorado at Boulder. Her research focuses on the organization of grief in the workplace.

Natalya N. Bazarova (M.S., Cornell University) is a Ph.D. student in the Department of Communication at Cornell University. Her research interests are in the areas of communication and technology, social cognition, group dynamics, and research methods.

Beverly A. Bondad-Brown (M.A., Columbia University) is a Ph.D. student in the Department of Communication at the University of California, Santa Barbara. Her research interests include the use of new media technologies, media enjoyment, and mass media effects.

Patrice M. Buzzanell (Ph.D., Purdue University) is a Professor and the W. Charles and Ann Redding Faculty Fellow in the Department of Communication at Purdue University. Her research specializes in gendered constructions of career, leadership, and work-life issues.

Stanley Deetz (Ph.D., Ohio University) is a Professor of Communication in the Department of Communication and Director of Peace and Conflict Studies at the University of Colorado. His work focuses on corporate governance and communication processes in relation to democracy, micropractices of power, and collaborative decision making.

Debbie S. Dougherty (Ph.D., University of Nebraska-Lincoln) is an Associate Professor in the Department of Communication at the University of Missouri-Columbia. Her scholarship focuses on power in the workplace, particularly as it pertains to sexual harassment, emotions, and mergers and acquisitions.

Mohan J. Dutta (Ph.D., University of Minnesota) is an Associate Professor in the Department of Communication at Purdue University. His scholarship centers on health communication, public relations, and mass media.

Andrew J. Flanagin (Ph.D., University of Southern California) is a Professor in the Department of Communication at the University of California, Santa Barbara. His research focuses on how communication and information technologies structure and extend human interaction, with particular emphases on processes of organizing and information evaluation and sharing.

Bernadette M. Gailliard (B.S., American University) is an M.A. student in the Department of Communication at the University of California Santa Barbara. Her research investigates the experiences of traditionally underrepresented groups in organizations and the implications for such processes as assimilation and identification.

Matthew J. Gill (Ph.D., Purdue University) is an Assistant Professor in the Department of Communication Studies at Eastern Illinois University. His research interests include organizational trust, workplace incivility, and worklife quality and how organizations interact with society through social responsibility and corporate sponsorship.

Jody Jahn is an M.A. student in the Department of Communication at the University of California, Santa Barbara. Her research interests include vocational anticipatory socialization, and organizational assimilation and socialization in high reliability organizations.

Paul Kang (M.A., University of California, Santa Barbara) is a Ph.D. student in the Department of Communication at the University of California, Santa Barbara. His research focuses on small group communication, particularly how emotion, time, and interaction influence group development.

Loraleigh Keashly (Ph.D., University of Saskatchewan) is an Associate Professor in the Department of Communication and Academic Director for the graduate program in Dispute Resolution at Wayne State University. Her research and consulting focus on conflict and conflict resolution at the interpersonal, group, and organizational levels and the nature, effects, and amelioration of emotionally abusive and bullying behaviors in the workplace.

Lorraine G. Kisselburgh (Ph.D., Purdue University) is an Assistant Professor in the Department of Communication at Purdue University.

Her research and teaching interests lie at the intersections of organizations, technology, and difference to include marginalized voices in
organizations; cross-cultural and gendered constructions of science,
technology, and engineering work and careers; and the social structure
and discursive construction of privacy.

Andrea P. Lewis (Ph.D., Arizona State University) is an Assistant Professor
in the Department of Communication at Northern Illinois University.
Her research currently focuses on how sexuality is organized at and
through work.

Kristen Lucas (Ph.D., Purdue University) is an Assistant Professor in the
Department of Communication Studies at University of Nebraska-
Lincoln. Her research focuses on dignity in the workplace, particularly
as it applies to blue-collar workplaces and stigmatized careers.

Pamela Lutgen-Sandvik (Ph.D., Arizona State University) is an Assistant
Professor in the Department of Communication and Journalism at the
University of New Mexico. Her research centers on organizational
communication, specifically the topics of workplace bullying, employee
emotional abuse, and positive organizational communication.

Dennis K. Mumby (Ph.D., Southern Illinois University, Carbondale) is a
Professor and Chair of the Department of Communication Studies at
the University of North Carolina, Chapel Hill. His research focuses on
the relationships among discourse, power, gender, and organizing.

Gary Namie (Ph.D., University of California, Santa Barbara) and **Ruth
Namie** (Ph.D., California School of Professional Psychology) are consultants whose work focuses solely on workplace bullying in the United
States and Canada. The Namies (workplacebullying.org) are mentors
for targeted workers, authors of self-help material (*The Bully At Work*,
2003), researchers, co-founders of the Workplace Bullying Institute
(Bellingham, WA), organizational consultants and trainers (Work Doc-
tor®, Inc,), and advocates for anti-bullying legislation.

Joel H. Neuman (Ph.D., University at Albany, State University of New
York) is an Associate Professor of Management and Organizational
Behavior and Director of the Center for Applied Management in the
School of Business at the State University of New York, New Paltz. His
research and consulting activities focus on workplace aggression and
violence, workplace bullying, and the use of collaborative inquiry
within the participative action research process.

Katy Pearce (M.A., University of London) is a Ph.D. student at the
University of California, Santa Barbara. She studies issues of cultural
differences in innovation.

Jeffrey Pfeffer (Ph.D., Stanford University) is the Thomas D. Dee II Professor of Organizational Behavior in the Graduate School of Business at Stanford University. His research interests include organizational behavior and theory, human resource management, evidence-based management, and unconventional wisdom about management.

Robyn V. Remke (Ph.D., Purdue University) is an Assistant Professor of Communication in the Department of Intercultural Communication and Management at the Copenhagen Business School. Motivated by questions of social injustice, she studies alternative forms of organizational structures, gendered identity in the workplace, and how organizational members respond to and resist irrationality in public service organizations.

David R. Seibold (Ph.D., Michigan State University) is a Professor of Communication in the Department of Communication and Director of the Graduate Program in Management Practice (College of Engineering) at the University of California, Santa Barbara. His interests include group communication and interpersonal influence, organizational communication, and applied communication.

Suchitra Shenoy (M.A., Pittsburg State University) is a Ph.D. student/doctoral candidate in the Department of Communication Studies at Purdue University. Her research interests include, among others, the intersections of gender, race, class, and society in constructing career discourses in contested work spaces, and the negotiation of multiple identities across occupations and organizations, as informed by historical and contemporary contexts such as globalization.

Patricia M. Sias (Ph.D., University of Texas-Austin) is a Professor of Communication in the Edward R. Murrow School of Communication at Washington State University. Her research centers on workplace relationships, coworker friendships, developmental processes, and dialogue and collaboration.

Beverly Davenport Sypher (Ph.D., University of Michigan) is a Professor of Communication, the Susan Bulkeley Butler Chair for Leadership Excellence, and an Associate Provost at Purdue University. Her research focuses on quality of worklife issues including civility in the workplace, technology, and health communication.

Sarah J. Tracy (Ph.D., University of Colorado-Boulder) is an Associate Professor and Director of the Project for Wellness and Work-Life in The Hugh Downs School of Human Communication at Arizona State University-Tempe. Her research expertise lies in organizational communication and qualitative methods, with particular focus on issues of emotion labor, burnout, identity, workplace bullying, dirty work, and work-life transitions.

Vincent Waldron (Ph.D., Ohio State University) is a Professor of Communication in the Department of Communication Studies at Arizona State University West and Faculty Research Director for ASU's *Osher Lifelong Learning Institute*. His research addresses problematic communication situations in work and personal relationships.

Joseph B. Walther (Ph.D., University of Arizona) is a Professor in the Department of Communication and Professor of Telecommunication, Information Studies and Media at Michigan State University. His research focuses on the interpersonal dynamics of communication via computer networks, in personal relationships, work groups, and educational settings.

Stacey M. B. Wieland (Ph.D., University of Colorado, Boulder) is an Assistant Professor at Villanova University. Her research focuses on how organizational and societal discourses surrounding work and life regulate identity construction.

Preface

Communication constitutes organizing and organizations. It is the explicit as well as the often unrecognized meanings and values of language-in-use and the associated symbols, messages, interactions, relationships, networks, and larger discourses that constitute *organizations as communication*. Destructive communication is that form of interaction that demeans, exploits, oppresses, or abuses others. Abusive workplaces are characterized by destructive communication practices that are both apparent and seemingly transparent. Destructive communication ranges from subtle forms of incivility such as rolling of the eyes, profanity, and demeaning remarks to more intense forms such as verbal aggression, workplace bullying, desk rage, and even physical assault. This book explores a number of destructive communicative processes, and the systems of meaning that drive those processes, that make organizational life unhealthy, unproductive, painful, and at times unbearable.

This volume brings together communication and management scholars from multiple perspectives to forward current understandings, explore ways to integrate theory and practice, and to identify areas for more constructive ways of organizing. It is a cooperative effort by scholars who have long been interested in exploring, critiquing, and exposing destructive practices at work and those committed to advancing supportive, healthy, and communal organizations. Each author or group of authors examines a specific aspect of destructive organizational communication, reviews current research about that communicative form or ideology, outlines its consequences and associated harms, and suggests fruitful possibilities for building constructive and supportive workplaces. Some chapters review and critique existing work, some report new research findings, some offer case studies, and some provide insightful critiques of things as they are in abusive workplaces. This book provides rich resources for scholars studying destructive organizational communication, managers dealing with hostile workplaces, organizational members trying to understand and change their current experiences, and instructors of graduate and upper-level undergraduate classes in organizational studies who are looking for original and provocative contributions to their seminars. Although we have not explicitly created the book to serve as a textbook, the various topics and proposals put forth by authors are easily accessible for upper-level undergraduate and graduate students in the areas of organizational studies, business and management, and communication. As such, the volume could readily serve as content for a class on destructive organizational communication that we hope finds its way to the lists of organizational communication and management courses traditionally offered.

Managers and researchers alike should be particularly interested in the forms of destructive communication, its harmful consequences, and the processes likely to produce potential solutions for decreasing and eventually replacing destructive communication with much healthier practices that improve employee well-being, instill pride and dignity in one's work and workplace, increase morale, enhance teamwork, and propel productivity.

Understanding the potential consequences of failing to address these issues will also be of particular interest to anyone in positions to provide leadership for what will and will not be tolerated in terms of workplace communication and the work that must be done to protect employees' faces and health by creating workplaces with a soul. Similarly, readers will find explanations for hostile work environments and see that experiences shared by reportedly three-fourths of the workforce are shared by numerous others. They will also find ways to navigate these landmines to prevent destructive practices that undermine workers and workplaces. We hope these chapters spark new ideas for research and encourage new scholars to join this emerging and important dialogue.

Acknowledgements

This book is the result of many people's efforts from a wide variety of institutions, colleagues, and professionals. First, we wish to thank the Dean of the College of Arts and Sciences at the University of New Mexico (UNM) for funding this project. A Junior-Faculty Summer Research Grant provided resources for the first editor to give considerable time to this project, time that was essential for the project's completion. Second, we wish to thank Linda Bathgate and Kerry Breen at Routledge/Taylor & Francis for their unconditional support during the entire project. Thanks to their proficiency, patience, and guidance, editing this volume was pleasant and rewarding. Finally, we wish to acknowledge the support of the Department of Communication and Journalism at UNM and the Department of Communication Studies at Purdue University.

Pamela Lutgen-Sandvik
Beverly Davenport Sypher

Introduction

*Pamela Lutgen-Sandvik and
Beverly Davenport Sypher*

Although organizational life can be a place to find and forge important relationships, craft and nurture a valued identity, and experience a deep sense of accomplishment, it can also be the source of trauma and stigmatization, emotional and psychological pain, and workloads that grind down even the toughest workers. Organizational discourse and meanings that serve certain interests at the expense of others are noteworthy, particularly when these result in human and organizational damage. Increased demands at work and the accompanying "pressure cooker" environments created by those demands mark communication at and about work in increasingly negative ways. The destructive side of organizational communication is evidenced through incivility, harassment, and abuse of power, among other things. In such environments, individual and organizational drives for control, power, or capital usually outweigh human concerns. Moreover, injustice and incivility often underscore communicative interactions and illegal, unethical, and reprehensible interactions sadly become the norm. Destructive interactions at work, in which people are harmed, workgroup communication deteriorates, and trust and cooperation decline, are of central importance and are the issues the authors explore in this volume. Although this volume provides accounts of mostly American workplaces, there are a number of studies that point to a growing epidemic of workplace incivility in Europe as well. Many such instances are cited throughout the book.

We have gathered some of the finest scholars and practitioners in the fields of communication and management to present these ideas. All are experts in their fields and bring an accumulation of decades-long research and practice built around social change in organizations to their respective contributions. Each chapter examines a particular communication phenomenon or cluster of related phenomena by outlining the contributing processes and consequences to organizations and organizational members. Given the complexity of organizational life, many—even most—of these topics overlap, intersect, and influence each other; our collective efforts to separate them into discrete phenomena is simulated. Nonetheless, such an approach is useful for exploring ideas, naming organizational experiences, and making sense of organizational life. The book, however, goes beyond simply describing different types of organizational communication problems. Each problem-focused chapter ends with how we might live and work together in ways that organize our endeavors more humanely. In this vein, the final four chapters focus solely on constructive approaches to organizational communication. As such, in addition to extending what we know about destructive discourses, this book also adds to a growing body of research roughly categorized as positive organizational scholarship (e.g., Cameron, Dutton, & Quinn, 2003).

For the most part, the book has a communication-as-constitutive perspective. This position assumes that communication is more than the unproblematic exchange of information between senders and receivers. Rather, most authors view communication as a system of historical discourses and day-to-day interactions that create, recreate, and, transform shared realities to which future interactions respond. That is, communication does not merely describe or occur within already formed organizations; it generates and regenerates organizations through multiple interactions.

Organizational communication is how we think and talk about organizations: the ways in which communication constitutes organizing and organizations, the often unrecognized meanings and values of current language-in-use, and the associated symbols, messages, interactions, relationships, networks, and larger discourses that comprise organizations. In addition to a communication-as-constitutive perspective, the book underscores that the communication that organizes human endeavors is never value-neutral or value-free. Rather, the meanings and messages of human interaction carry and perpetuate far-reaching histories and ideologies—histories that typically benefit some groups at the expense of others. And power is always a dynamic inherent to these meanings, one that often works at a tacit, non-conscious level for those negotiating everyday organizational activities and interactions.

In what follows, we introduce the central themes of the book and the topics clustered around each theme. In the first theme, "Forms of Destructive Communication," authors explore some of the painful processes in organizations and introduce an idea that runs through subsequent chapters: Organizations are hotbeds for emotions, emotional anguish, and social interactions that evoke feelings of humiliation, powerlessness, rage, and despair. Waldron opens this section by exploring the communicative aspects of emotional tyranny and drawing the readers' attention to verbal and nonverbal tactics, interactive processes, and the discourse of workplace emotion. Lutgen-Sandvik, Namie, and Namie review the history and key findings of workplace bullying research, a persistent and harmful form of mistreatment comprised of numerous patterned negative interactions that feel intimidating, insulting, or exclusionary. Closing out this section, Gill and Sypher explore the various forms of workplace incivility that range from subtle acts of rude and discourteous behaviors to the more intense forms of verbal aggressiveness and interpersonal injustice that diminish both interpersonal and organizational trust. Of particular note is the more destructive effect of persistent low-intensity uncivil discourse as compared to less common but more intense and egregious acts. They remind us that, much like domestic partner abuse, less intense incivility repeated over time may do more to damage relationships and organizational well-being than previous studies to date have suggested.

The second theme, "Cultural and Organizational Pressures," investigates other forms of destructive communication as well as some of the deeper cultural meanings that drive these destructive patterns. Tracy opens this section with a critical review of the stress and burnout literature that she hopes will assist employees dealing with burnout, managers trying to prevent burnout, and academics who want to study burnout. Wieland, Bauer, and Deetz then present the cultural, economic, and historical discourses that contribute to careerism, the devotion to career success, typically at the expense of personal lives, ethics, and personal integrity. Kisselburgh and Dutta end this section with an insightful treatment of the larger culturally situated notions of incivility and a reminder that norms and values about what is appropriate and destructive (or not) must be examined in light of cultural ideologies and histories. They heighten our awareness of the conformist assumptions embedded in mostly Western treatments of civility and examine the issues of silences, erasures, and absences to make their point.

The third theme, "Difference and Discrimination," takes a close look at the painful experiences of diversity, in particular, workers' experiences when they are different from the implicit models to which they are tacitly compared (and found wanting). The authors review and critique the history and ideologies sustaining racism, sexism, and homophobia and present the current manifestations of these in organizational life. Sias opens this section by looking at the painful experiences of social ostracism and shunning by important others at work. She examines difference in general and discusses why some employees become outcasts and others "incasts" or important members of social networks. Allen follows this with a historical and cultural examination of racial discrimination in organizations. She focuses on the importance of the workplace and the classrooms as critical contexts for addressing racism and understanding assumptions about context, power, communication, and identity in these settings and processes. Lewis presents a timely examination of the issues that lesbian, gay, bi-sexual and transsexual (LGBT) employees encounter in organizations and the destructive potential for painful communication involved when these workers face social stigmatization. In particular, she unmasks the implied values of heteronormativity operating in many organizations and outlines the damage embedded in this set of value assumptions. Dougherty closes this section with a discursive approach to understanding sexual harassment, one she argues provides a particularly rich lens through which to view gendered processes. She discusses the social character of sexual harassment and the communicative processes that structure gender relations, how we come to know who men and women should be and how they should behave, and how we define their proper roles in society.

The fourth theme, "Technology and Teams," examines two rapidly emerging processes in organizations, the burgeoning use of both electronic communication technologies and team structures. Flanigan, Pearce, and Bondad-Brown open this section with an extensive look at the different types and forms of communication technology in modern organizations and their potential to be used in negative ways. They examine the detrimental aspects of electronic technology use in organizations by introducing five types of destructive activities in this realm. Bazarova and Walther also look at the harmful potential for communication technology but focus in particular on how social interactions among virtual team members can erode due to attributions of blame. This piece is a provocative exploration that weaves together the well-known ideas of attribution with the use of new communication technologies and team structures. Extending an exploration of teams, Seibold, Kang, Gailliard, and Jahn present a comprehensive, multilevel review of teams and teamwork. This chapter effectively reviews team research and the individual, dyadic, subgroup, group, organizational, and environmental factors contributing to what they call the "dark side" of teams.

The final section, "Perspectives for Constructive Organizing," moves toward a series of more encouraging pieces regarding organizational life dealing with resiliency, humor as resistance, aggression-reducing interventions, and developing communal organizations. Buzzanell, Shenoy, Remke, and Lucas open up the emancipatory possibilities of reframing adversity by coalescing findings from a number of contexts—job loss, organizational irrationalities, and disease and disability management. They explore the different ways that people have transformed debilitating work-related experiences into resources of resilience and personal strength. Mumby, in a delightful departure from conventional academic prose, explores humor and organizing and addresses the ways in which humor can serve to puncture, undermine, and destabilize systems of organizational power. He specifically makes the case that Kersten's (2005) *The Art of Demotivation*, as an example of "resistance leadership," radically intervenes in mainstream management theory by articulating its own theory of management that is simultaneously deeply parodic of "management thought" itself. Keashly and Neuman recount a long-term participatory action research project with the U.S. Veterans Affairs that effectively reduced aggressive communication through teaching organizational members basic communication skills. This piece is an encouraging illustration of how small, well-focused communicative interventions can sometimes produce significant, enduring improvements. We end with Pfeffer's chapter on building communal organizations (reproduced with the permission of Palgrave McMillan). He describes the U.S. business movement away from the conception of organizations as communities and what may have produced this change. He provides ideas for building on the workplace as community.

It is our hope that this volume speaks to issues of concern for organizational scholars and professionals. It is a cooperative effort that opens a dialogue among communication and management scholars that explores destructive communication in organizations and addresses the central issues and concerns regarding these phenomena.

References

Cameron, K. S., Dutton, J. E., & Quinn, R. E. (Eds.). (2003). *Positive organizational scholarship*. San Francisco: Berrett-Koehler.

Kersten, E. L. (2005). *The art of demotivation*. Austin, TX: Despair, Inc.

Part I

Various Forms of Destructive Organizational Communication

Chapter 1

Emotional Tyranny at Work

Suppressing the Moral Emotions

Vincent Waldron

> I felt angry—humiliated and betrayed. [I] felt like I had been stabbed in
> the back, with no way to defend myself or explain my position. Because
> of the audience, I probably would not have confronted the senior man-
> agement person in this meeting, even if time permitted .... He forever
> damaged my credibility. (Adapted from Waldron, 2000, p. 67)

Raul,[1] a middle manager at a large American banking firm, was criticized
by his boss pointedly, unexpectedly, and most bothersome to him, very
publicly. Indeed, this incident occurred during Raul's presentation before
a monthly gathering of senior managers and Raul's own staff. His recol-
lection bristles with an emotional intensity seldom associated with the
workplace. Nonetheless, Raul's report is surprisingly typical of those I
have collected from employees working in a wide variety of organizational
settings. As Raul sees it, the disrespectful treatment he received from his
boss was *designed* to embarrass him, to "put me in my place," to send a
forceful message to an up-and-coming subordinate about who was really
in charge. Undeniably, many veteran employees readily recall similar
instances of what I have come to call *emotional tyranny*—the use of emotion by powerful organization members in a manner that is perceived to be
destructive, controlling, unjust, and even cruel.

Emotional tyranny is sometimes a strategic ploy of an individual bent on
acquiring or maintaining power. At other times it is a collective exercise,
perpetrated by a cast of cooperating organization members. But emotional
tyranny also emerges as an *unintended* consequence of organizational
structures, values, and practices. It is by no means commonplace, but it
often yields harmful and lasting effects on individuals, relationships, and
organizations. Even years later, Raul feels a certain bitterness, and he has
learned to be "careful about whom to trust." This highly emotional event
was a negative turning point in what was already a strained supervisory
relationship. Dispirited by this and similar instances of emotional abuse,
Raul began searching for an organization with a more supportive culture.

When he finally left the bank, Raul took with him expertise developed through several years of apprenticeship and an intercultural savvy developed as one of the bank's few Hispanic managers.

In this chapter I explore the *communicative* aspects of emotional tyranny. In doing so, I draw the reader's attention to verbal and nonverbal tactics, interactive processes, and the discourse of workplace emotion. As with any brand of tyranny, communication is simply one element, albeit an important one, of a larger destructive process. But by necessity I spend relatively less of this limited space on the important political, occupational, and economic factors that can encourage powerful people to wreak emotional havoc. I also note that some emotions are undeniably intrasychic, biologically-grounded experiences (e.g., a fearful reaction to heights). Nevertheless, my work is concerned with the decidedly *social* aspects of emotion. Those taking a social constructionist view of emotion call our attention to the intersection of emotion, language, and normative behavior (Averill, 1983). From this perspective, emotional experiences such as embarrassment or shame or anger are reactions to violations of moral codes, by ourselves or by those who share our communities. The language of affect is also of interest to social constructionists because we frequently use emotion words and phrases to communicate our moral sensibilities. Consider such phrases as these, reported by various employees: "I couldn't be proud of the hurtful things I said that day," or "I was so angry at the way I was disrespected by the new employees," and "He got to work closely with the boss, and I was incredibly jealous of him."

This chapter is grounded in workers' experiences of emotional tyranny—anger, pride, indignation, and other "moral emotions"— collected through surveys, interviews, and the author's observations (Waldron, 1994, 1999, 2000, 2003; Waldron & Kelley, 2008; Waldron & Krone, 1991). They were shared by probation officers, factory workers located in a rural southern community, data entry and supervisory staff at a large urban bank, a large sample of service workers, state employees from three agencies, and members of human service organizations serving unemployed persons and those living with AIDS. Where illustrative (and prudent), I also draw from my own experiences working at a large state university where rapid change, limited oversight, and the centralization of power have created conditions ripe for emotional tyranny. Because of the focus of this volume, I address most extensively those emotional experiences that involve encounters with more powerful employees (one of the most common of emotional experiences reported in my own studies).

After a brief review of how theorists have conceptualized emotion at work, this chapter examines work relationships as sites of emotional abuse. The "moral" emotions are described and the practices of emotional tyrants are examined, with particular emphasis on their emotional weaponry, communicative tactics, and efforts to manipulate the cultural values that shape the emotional dimensions of work. Finally, drawing from Weiner (2006), I argue that emotional tyranny can be fruitfully conceptualized as an effort to control the moral infraction–cognitive assessment–emotional communication cycle.

Emotion at Work: A Brief Introduction

Historically, emotion was considered by management theorists to be a relatively blunt force—the fear by which workers might be motivated or the subjective sense of satisfaction reported by the happy employees of well-run companies. So, for early organizational theorists, the study of emotion was subjugated to larger concerns for employee motivation or job satisfaction, what Miller and colleagues classified as "emotion toward work" (Miller, Considine, & Garner, 2007). But in recent decades, the study of emotion at work has become nuanced and rich. A turning point was Arlie Hochschild's (1983) publication of *The Managed Heart*, a seminal analysis of the labor performed by airline attendants and other service employees. Drawing from earlier fieldwork (Hochschild, 1979), her book described in vivid detail the performance of what she called *emotional labor*. Hochschild observed that for many service workers, emotion is not simply a reaction to work, it *is* the work. When emotion *is* work, emotional performances are dictated by management, taught through training, and enforced through surveillance techniques, such as customer satisfaction surveys (*"Was your server cheerful at all times?"*) and "secret shopper" programs.

For these reasons, emotional labor often produces inauthentic emotion. Hochschild's (1983) airline attendants were expected to *fabricate* such emotions as cheerfulness, to *repress* their anger at obnoxious customers, and to *transmute* one emotion, such as fear, into another, more acceptable one, such as sympathy. As such, emotional laborers learn *feeling rules*. Some of these regulate how emotion is communicated. *"Never get angry with a customer,"* is a familiar example. Other rules guide *interpretation*. They help employees know what counts as organizationally-legitimate emotional experiences. Statements like, *"Wipe that smile off your face,"* and *"That is nothing to be proud of,"* instruct employees (and children) in the emotion rules of working life (Waldron, 1994). Interestingly, these kinds of directives are doubly communicative in that they are also messages about the rules of emotional communication. More interesting still, they often draw their force from their emotional tone. As will be discussed, lower-power workers are sometimes intimidated or shamed into compliance with community codes of behavior, including those concerning the expression of emotion.

Building on Hochschild's contributions, researchers extended the study of emotional displays to convenience store clerks (Sutton & Rafaeli, 1988) and Disneyland employees (Van Maanen & Kunda, 1989). It quickly became evident that some work was authentically emotional by its very nature, including that performed by criminal investigators and detectives (Rafaeli & Sutton, 1991; Stenross & Kleinman, 1989), 911 operators (Tracy & Tracy, 1998), and corrections officers (Tracy, 2005). As this literature developed theorists argued that unremitting emotional labor and the dissonance workers experienced between *felt* emotion and role-required *expressed* emotion could have harmful consequences, including identity loss, stress, and burnout (Ashforth & Humphrey, 1993; Morris & Feldman, 1996). Some feminist scholars argued that simplistic conceptions of workplace emotion are a legacy of patriarchal assumptions that dichotomize emotion and reason (Myerson, 2000). More recent reviews of the emotion-related scholarship (Briner, 2004; Fineman, 2000) broaden and deepen our understanding of organizational emotion as a cultural and relational phenomenon. For example, the notion of *bounded emotionality* (Mumby & Putnam, 1992) describes the balancing of individual needs for authentic and spontaneous emotional expression, with relational requirements and organizational control (Martin, Knopoff, & Beckman, 2000). Workplace emotion is now understood as a phenomenon that flows across organizational boundaries—one deeply connected to domestic life and the practices of the larger popular culture (Waldron, 2000).

One theme that has emerged in my more recent work (Waldron, 2000; Waldron & Kelley, 2008) and that of others (e.g., Harlos & Pinder, 2000) involves its connection to issues of relational morality and justice. The narratives workers tell about intensely emotional events are often relational morality tales (Miller et al., 2007). Even those workers who perform emotionally daunting roles (probation officers, social workers, prison guards) rarely cite their tasks in these narratives. Instead they describe disloyal coworkers, disrespectful supervisors, cold-hearted peers, inequitable relationships, and other relational threats. Abuses of relational power are the subject of some of the most alarming, emotionally painful, sometimes chilling, accounts.

Organizational Relationships as Sites for Emotional Abuse

Organizational relationships are, for at least four reasons, unique contexts for the study of emotional communication. First, power differences abound in workplace relationships. Leaders are empowered to make evaluations, bolstering or threatening a member's work identity through recognition or criticism. Interactions with leaders can be risky; success or failure is linked with economic risk and career consequences. For that reason, it is not surprising that certain kinds of work interactions are tinged with the emotion of fear. As just one example, the traditional reluctance of employees to be the bearers of bad news can be attributed in part to fear of the consequences (Wagoner & Waldron, 1999). But supervisors too may approach these interactions with trepidation, sometimes hesitating to deliver negative feedback for fear of the emotional toll it may take on the worker or the relational harm it may cause (Larson, 1989). Fear, frustration, and rage often appear in narratives about supervisory abuses of power. Hopeless despair or burning indignation may be the emotional reaction to repeated and persistent misuses of power.

Second, workplace encounters can be excruciatingly public, as they are frequently witnessed by an audience of peers, customers, or supervisors. The quote beginning this chapter is testimony to the feelings of embarrassment that compound difficult work interactions. Raul's feelings will only be intensified as he contemplates the working of his organization's informal communication network. Witnesses will share his fate in whispers as they gather around the office water cooler. Indeed, who has not been tempted to pass along rumors of a coworker's humiliation at the hands of an emotionally-insensitive boss, the coworker who "lost it" during a tense meeting, or perhaps, the unsettling sight of an employee brought to tears by a nasty coworker or customer? Workplace emotion buzzes along the communicative corridors of nearly every organization, changing in intensity and form as it goes, sometimes building a collective feeling of outrage, excitement, despair, or confidence. This kind of *second-order* emotional reaction, linked only tenuously to the original encounter, tells us that organizational emotion is not only witnessed by a public, it is also created *through* a public's interactions.

A third unique feature of organizational emotion is its enmeshment in work roles. The performance of emotion is simply *expected* from the occupants of many work roles. Inspiring teachers are expected to produce emotionally arresting lectures; police officers must project a sense of emotional calm under the most stressful of circumstances; competitive athletes work themselves into a frenzy of excitement; on cue, campaigning politicians display their feelings of compassion, moral outrage, and patriotic pride, hoping to make a connection with emotionally-perceptive voters. These emotional performances are familiar and well-documented (Ashforth, Kreiner, & Fugate, 2000), but less appreciated are the more subtle emotional performances that sustain typical work relationships. Success in this arena is evaluated frequently, both formally and informally. Team members who fail to appear sufficiently enthusiastic may be subtly sanctioned by coworkers who question their commitment. A newly promoted manager may be "brought down to earth" by the biting comments of less favored employees, especially if he or she appears *excessively proud* at this good fortune. Those who flatter the new boss with obsequious emotional displays may themselves be subject to unflattering labels—"brownnoser" and "pet poodle" are among those reported in surveys.

Finally, a unique thing about emotion at work is, interestingly enough, its failure to be bounded by the workplace. The joys and disappointments of our larger lives come to work with us, and emotions we experience at work follow us home. Although "a professional" may be encouraged to check these boundary-crossing emotions at the office door, this is sometimes impossible. In fact, emotional behavior is more likely to be overlooked if coworkers know, for example, that an employee is in the midst of an "emotionally-messy" divorce. However, recognizing that any type of communal arrangement requires some degree of emotional constraint, workers strive to "keep things under control," to "put a lid on it," even on the most trying days. Unedited venting and emotional exhaustion can be the unattractive alternatives to this collective attempt at emotional censorship. Emotions repressed at work, however, are sometimes displaced. At home, family members may become the unwitting targets of suppressed anger. Other emotions may be displaced as well. Family members are usually safer audiences for expressions of envy at coworkers, fear of abusive supervisors, and indignation over unjust practices. However, habitual displacement may lead to emotional fatigue among family members and supportive friends. They may learn to carefully edit work-related discussions to avoid another round of emotional dumping. In this way, emotional tyranny in the workplace indirectly controls our private conversations and personal relationships.

All of this is to say that the emotional landscape of workplace relationships is a complicated but interesting terrain. One reason emotional work experiences resonate so soundly is that they mark the dimensions of work about which we care the most. In particular, they draw attention to the relational practices that we consider right and those we consider wrong.

The Moral Emotions

In his model of social motivation and justice, the motivational psychologist Bernard Weiner (2006) envisions a prominent place for what he calls the "moral emotions." The model is helpful in understanding how emotions and communication are linked to relational justice (or injustice) at work. With Averill (1983; see also Waldron, 1994), Weiner sees anger and similar emotions as reactions to moral transgressions. "Anger is an accusation or a value judgment following from the belief that another could and should have done otherwise" (p. 35). For example, the obligation to do one's fair share is an integral part of the moral code for most workers in most organizations. The perception that a coworker is consistently failing to perform his or her share of the work on a group project may yield a rising sense of *anger* in coworkers. As anger builds, coworkers may be motivated to take such corrective actions as asking for more help, recruiting peers to pressure the "lazy" worker, and ultimately, complaining to the boss. On the other hand, if colleagues perceive that the coworker's poor performance is due to uncontrollable external factors (an overwhelming workload) they may feel *sympathy* rather than anger. As a moral emotion, sympathy may lead them to redress injustice by looking beyond the coworker's personal moral failure to the larger context. They might ask the boss to reassign some of their coworker's tasks or simply accept the injustice for a longer period of time.

A Typology of Moral Emotions

In work settings, the list of moral emotions is extensive. Most are other-directed, but some are primarily self-oriented (e.g., shame), and others are chiefly directed toward larger social systems (e.g., indignation). Table 1.1 lists selected emotions and the social actions or conditions to which they refer. A quick perusal gives a sense of how clearly these emotions mark violations of personal and relational morality, although they clearly serve other functions as well, and how they might motivate corrective responses. For example, the experiences of emotional *shock* or *outrage* often arise when an organization member blatantly violates taken-for-granted moral codes. We are shocked when a trusted colleague is caught stealing from the company or when a loyal peer engages in "backstabbing" political behavior.

Table 1.1 Moral Emotions and their Social Referents

Emotion	Social Referents
Admiration	Success of deserving others
Anger	Hurtful or immoral behavior committed by others
Embarrassment	Acts that reveal moral failures or create an appearance of moral failure
Envy	Desire for the qualities, possessions, or accolades possessed by others
Guilt	Responsibility for wrong doing
Humiliation	Threats to dignity; dehumanizing behaviors
Humility	Exposure to transcendent moral forces
Indignation	Ire at the unfairness of a social situation or system
Jealousy	One's rightful role in relationships is threatened by rivals
Outrage	Fury aroused by the offensive acts of others
Pride	Personal or group accomplishments; recognition by valued others
Regret	Having hurt others or made a serious mistake
Resentment	Sustained or acute ill-treatment of others
Scorn	Someone or something held in contempt
Schadenfreude	Shame experienced by another brings joy to the self
Shame	Disgraceful, unworthy, or dishonorable behavior
Shock/Surprise	Unexpected moral violations by others
Sympathy	Pain or distress of another brings feelings of pity or sorrow

In addition to simply marking moral violations, emotions may stimulate change. When employees feel *shame* after flouting legitimate organizational rules, they may be motivated to pledge improved behavior in the future. Expressing shame is an acknowledgement of the work community's existing moral codes and possibly a precondition if one hopes to rejoin it. Relational obligations are enforced by emotions like *guilt, jealousy, scorn,* and *embarrassment.* Organizations often cultivate extreme identification in members by involving them in closely-knit work teams, encouraging workplace "bonding" through social activities, and using relationship metaphors ("We are all just one big family here"). It is an easy matter then to elicit guilt from those who "let down the team" or "share the family secrets." Loyal members may feel scorn for those who violate the relational code.

Jealousy arises from perceptions that one's rightful place in a valued relationship is threatened. Coworkers who are the recipients of special attention from the boss or inequitable rewards may be the subject of this emotion. Alternatively, eliciting embarrassment can be a way of exerting power in work relationships or "leveling the field." For example, factory workers in the mid-south reported that newly promoted shop foremen sometimes took advantage of workers, embarrassing them on the shop floor by mimicking their accents and taunting them (Waldron et al., 1993). Convinced that these former peers had gotten "too big for their breeches," workers conspired to "humble" them through embarrassing practical jokes or by intentionally slowing production. In other contexts, workers sometimes experience *humility* as a positive experience wrought by the existence of larger moral forces. For instance, a social worker reported that she was "humbled by the goodness" of colleagues who worked long hours at low pay to care for extremely ill AIDS patients. In the case of the shop foremen, however, humility was an emotional experience reluctantly acquired.

Communicating the Moral Emotions

Figure 1.1 depicts relationships between organizational morality, emotion, and communication as a cycle. Emotion is triggered (Step 1) by a perceived infraction—a behavior that potentially threatens the moral codes governing relationships in a particular organization. For current purposes, we will assume the act is one of sharp criticism, that the actor is a supervisor, and that the observer/recipient is a member acting under the supervisor's direction. According to the model, the member assesses the act's morality (Step 2) before experiencing emotion (Step 3). The employee may think criticism is morally justified in the context of this supervisory relationship (e.g., perhaps he or she violated a well-known safety policy). If so, the felt-emotion may be a negative and self-oriented one like shame or remorse. In deciding whether to express the emotion (Step 5), the member makes an assessment of risk (Step 4). Will expressing shame cause harm to the self or put a valued relationship at risk? Or would it have potentially beneficial effects? Expressing shame *could be* beneficial, as it assures the supervisor that the employee understands the prevailing moral codes and feels disappointment at failing to conform to them. This expression may lead the supervisor to modify the original act ("Well, I may have been a bit too harsh. I just wanted to make sure you stay safe at work"). This act may trigger a new round of moral assessment, felt-emotion, and so on.

In contrast, the employee may conclude that the act of criticism violated codes of relational morality because it was unduly harsh, delivered in public, or unfairly directed at a single violator of the rules. In such cases, the felt-emotion may be other-directed anger or perhaps system-directed indignation. The expression of these emotions to the supervisor will, most likely, be edited to comply with prevailing norms of relational respect. The emotion may be suppressed, directed elsewhere (for similar thoughts on "displacement," see Kassing, 2007), or transmuted into a more acceptable linguistic form ("I am *proud* of my record in the past, and I am sure this won't happen again").

Practicing Emotional Tyranny

The practice of emotional tyranny involves the use of power to intervene in the cycle presented in Figure 1.1. I first consider the various communicative tools used by powerful people for manipulating the moral emotions.

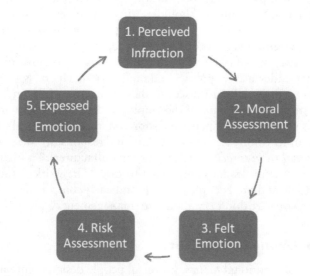

Figure 1.1 Communication of the moral emotions.

A Short Course on Emotional Weaponry

Emotion is subject to manipulation at several levels of communication. At the level of *nonverbal display*, powerful people utilize the intensity, duration, and intermittence of emotional displays. For instance, an emotionally-abusive boss may express emotions at high volume, for unusually long periods of time, in unpredictable bursts, and ever-changing hues. These behaviors are violations of normal emotional conduct, but power differences may prevent the censoring of such behavior. In fact, these displays may consolidate power by making others feel intimidated, confused, or humiliated. Sharon, a staff assistant at a university, describes an emotionally tyrannical boss:

> My boss would rant and rave, like a nutcase, really. Then he would be nice as can be for a few days. Then, out of the blue he would be embarrassing me or saying hurtful things. I never knew what to expect, so I would come to work on pins and needles. Everyone else was that way too—never quite sure of what to say or do.

At the level of *emotional language*, powerful people can use emotion words or phrases in ways that are harmful in a work context. Some emotional language is often *appropriated*, taken from contexts in which it might be benign or even positive, and used to cast dispersions on the character of employees. In my studies, workers have been described as "too eager and excited," "shameless," "emotionally under-carbonated," "grumpy," "wimpy," "fearless," "lacking personal pride," "explosive," and as having a "chip on her shoulder." In some cases, these emotional labels are used to discredit those who have good reason to be emotional. The "grumpy" employee was one who was deeply concerned that his government agency was failing to perform its designated function (safety inspections) under a new political administration. His boss (a political appointee) used the label to discount these concerns while finding fault with the emotional make-up of the employee. In many cases, emotional language is used to suggest perceived shortcomings in the moral character of workers or to "motivate" desired behavioral responses. "We don't need any *emotional train wrecks* here at [auto manufacturer]," a highly dedicated engineer/team leader complained to me. "The work is tough, the hours are long, and tired people get mean and nasty. But you don't let it get to you, and you sure don't *cry* about it to management."

Tactics of Emotional Tyrannists

At the level of emotional *tactics*, powerful people design communication that elicits or changes emotional responses (see Table 1.2). These include

Table 1.2 Tactics of Emotional Tyrannists with Discourse Examples

Tactic	Exemplar
Betrayal	"I put my heart into the job because my boss liked me and believed in me. But after he got promoted I got nothing but coldness. He stabbed me in the heart."
Blackmail	"I (stupidly) told my boss about a crush I had on a coworker. He threatened to tell if I didn't show a good attitude. Maybe joking…but he enjoyed the threat."
Deflecting	"He basically told us it was not his fault [that people haven't been paid on time]. We all should be mad at the contractor. He dodged responsibility."
Discounting	"[The Dean asked], 'Why did you care so much about the staff evaluations? All I care about is the faculty. We really don't need to be so emotional.'"
Embarrassing	"She criticized me right on the floor, in front of my customers (two were my friends)! My face went red, and I ran for the bathroom."
Faking	"The HR person could really pretend like she was sincere when we brought up a grievance—like she cared and was all worried. But it was an act, a joke really."
Grinding	"After a while I got tired of the everyday anger control issues. She snipped and yelled and wore me down over time. I finally left (which is what she wanted)."
Guilting	"Because I was super-dedicated back then, they could guilt me into anything. I'd stay late because they would make me feel disloyal or selfish for going home."
Intimidating	"I was told I would pay a huge price if I went public with the problem. Basically, they scared me into conformity."
Exhorting	"[My boss] was like a preacher at church, getting us all whooped up and excited about the company and our sales. But we found out it was all BS. The company didn't care about us, and the bosses made all of the money. We were used."
Orchestrating	"This guy [team leader] was threatened by me. So he went around spreading rumors that I wasn't working hard and thought I was too good to work. Before I knew it people resented me."
Reframing	"You think poor sales are no big deal? This is an embarrassment to me."
Ridiculing	"When I see my servers cry, I know they aren't ready for prime time. Crying doesn't make customers happy and babies don't get tips. I say, buck-up!"
Shaming	"After I complained, they made me feel like I was being selfish, like I was more important than everybody. Just because I wanted them to follow the [curriculum development] process rather than just rush it through."
Silencing	[A college told me] "Sure I am disgusted … and I think the policy is stupid. But keep my name out of it. I have already had my head chewed off in too many meetings (by university administrators)."
Vanquishing	"Wipe that smile off your face and don't let me see it again!"

such varied activities as emotional *blackmail*, false concern (*faking*), using emotion to wear down resistance (*grinding*), redefining the emotional experience of others (*reframing*), and simply *vanquishing* emotions from the work place. Of course, there exist many others. At my university, the implementation of a complicated new computer system was by all accounts badly bungled. One unfortunate result was that some (largely low-level) employees received reduced paychecks, or none at all, for several pay cycles. Employees expressed concern, then alarm, then frustration, then anger, and finally burning resentment as their plight went unacknowledged by leaders. After remaining mute about the problem for weeks (i.e., dismissing the emotional urgency expressed by employees and many of their supervisors), the President's office finally responded by blaming the contractor and the Human Resources Department (*deflecting*), claiming that the administration had been highly concerned all along (*appropriation* of employee emotion), and arguing that the administration had "no choice" but to implement the computer change because the old system was defunct and essentially in danger of self-destructing. This last tactic seemed designed to cultivate *sympathy* for the beleaguered administration. At the same time, administrative rhetoric implied that employees were selfish to complain about their personal losses in light of the organization's eminent destruction at the hands of a decrepit computer. Not surprisingly, this *shaming* tactic was met by considerable indignation at what appeared to be emotional manipulation.

Emotional Tyrannist's Shaping of Processes and Culture

At the level of communication *processes*, powerful actors manipulate procedures, structures, and behavior sequences to manipulate emotions. Familiar examples are the sales rallies designed to "whoop up" enthusiasm for new products and initiation rites that humiliate new members and cultivate their emotional connection to senior leaders (one purpose of military basic training). In other examples, management trainees may be subjected to a variety emotionally-demanding exercises and simulations (e.g., mock interviews; working in teams on a time-limited tasks) to "test their mettle," "toughen their hides," and assess their performance "under fire." I have noted previously that organizational actors sometimes work collectively to "pull off" emotional performances that benefit themselves at the cost of others (Waldron, 2000). In one courtroom, I observed a defense attorney and prosecutor collaborating to create the appearance of "elaborate concern" for a teenage defendant and his family, only minutes after belittling him in an "offstage" conversation.

Finally, at the level of *culture*, powerful members communicate organizational and occupational values, prescriptions, and understandings that give meaning to emotional experiences of members. At this level, leaders indicate the emotions they expect from members (e.g., enthusiasm for innovation), the emotional connections they condone or prohibit (e.g., rules on employee romance), and the emotional tenor pervading whole spheres of organizational life (e.g., "get serious about safety" or "we work hard and play hard"). This culture-shaping capacity facilitates emotional tyranny in indirect but powerful ways. Members who are deeply socialized into a culture may experience strong and negative emotions when they detect hints of deviance or change. For instance, Rita described her early experiences working as a probation officer in a male-dominated organizational culture. As she described it, her coworkers were angry and disdainful, convinced that a female had no place in their field. They made her life an "emotional hell," not because she was a poor performer but because a *female* probation officer simply did not conform with cultural expectations. She reported:

> My coworkers harassed me because they did not want to work with a woman. They criticized and demeaned me [in front of clients and peers]—anything to make me feel bad. This went on for eighteen months. I should have told them to get off my back and filed a grievance. I felt humiliated and angry. I wanted to strike out and hurt them; instead, I attempted suicide.

Rita's case is obviously extreme, but it does suggest the smothering effect of emotional norms as enforced by veteran coworkers. Rita's harassment was due, in part, to a cultural belief that women were too emotionally "soft" to handle hardened parolees. Ironically, her presence elicited highly-emotional responses from coworkers. But, she did not directly express her negative emotional experiences to managers, probably because she believed her emotional distress was not culturally "legitimate." Rita's emotional experiences could have been valued as warning signs of a dysfunctional culture and indicators of relational wrongdoing. Unfortunately, within this cultural context her coworkers (and perhaps Rita) interpreted these as signs of personal weakness.

Manipulating the Moral Infraction–Assessment–Communication Cycle

As I have argued, emotions can serve important moral functions in organizational settings. Emotional tyranny involves, in large part, the use of power to distort the process of moral evaluation presented in Figure 1.1. I have already illustrated that powerful people enjoy considerable liberty in producing and demanding emotional behavior. In some cases, as when a boss unloads a venomous emotional attack on an employee, the display itself is an unjust act (Step 1). As Weiner (2006) and so many others have noted, the emotions we feel when confronted by a potentially immoral action, whether or not it is an emotional one, are dependent on the attributions we make. Was it intentional? Was the actor aware of the relevant moral standards? Was the behavior under his or her control? Emotional tyranny is practiced through the manipulation of these attributional assessments. For example, supervisors may impose "special" emotional standards, which deem their emotional outbursts to be acceptable after all, citing perhaps the emotional rigors of leadership. The actor is relieved of the need to feel guilty for violating the standards of emotional decency, and observers are compelled to accept this explanation. Alternatively, a leader can manipulate the kinds of accomplishments that "justify" feelings of pride or admiration, indicating, for example, that workers who generate large revenues have "more to be proud of" than those who follow ethical practices or safety standards.

Employees' moral assessments shape their felt emotions. If the staff assistant mentioned above believes the boss was intentionally abusive, the felt emotion (Step 3) is likely to be anger or indignation. If the abuse is attributable to external circumstances, or if an employee has been convinced that leaders have a "right" to such behavior, the felt emotion may be less negative or even sympathetic. However, as I have suggested earlier, tyranny at this stage can be exercised more directly through tactics designed to elicit fear, jealousy, shame, and other feelings.

The decision to express emotion can involve a calculated risk. What are the potential positive and negative consequences of expressing emotion in this work relationship within this work culture? Emotional tyranny figures here as well, as informal (and sometimes formal) company procedures discourage employees from expressing felt emotions like indignation (even when it is justified by moral failure), conveying emotional distress (even when it is produced by unreasonable work conditions), or sharing fears (in the form of bad news or moral reservations). Emotional tyrants discount such expressions, shame those who use them, deflect them elsewhere, or simply repress them. As indicated in Figure 1.1, these acts of emotional abuse are also evaluated as potential moral infractions, and the cycle starts again. As power is exerted through repeated cycles, employees can become emotionally exhausted, numb, mute, or alienated. Their moral sensibilities may become dulled. Emotions may be directed outside the organization, internalized as stress, or (in extreme cases) expressed dysfunctionally in physical violence.

Conclusions

Although I do not want to be overly dramatic, or should I say, *too emotional* about it, the practices of emotional tyrants are undeniably harmful. Power brings with it the capacity to manipulate the emotional resources of individuals, relationships, and whole organizations, and even family members and friends who are only indirectly connected to the workplace. This harm comes to individuals in the form of psychic and physical distress, burnout, and even damaged careers. When emotional manipulation is the norm, relationships with powerful others can become less authentic, more guarded, ethically-compromised, and anxiety ridden. I have suggested too that emotions are a kind of moral barometer in the workplace. Their suppression can sometimes dull the moral sensibilities of leaders and members alike. Finally, the failure to create legitimate channels for the expression of strongly felt negative emotion can encourage certain employees to choose physical violence and other dehumanizing means of expression.

Powerful people should feel a heightened responsibility to engage in responsible emotional behavior. They simply enjoy more opportunities for abuse, and their communication "carries more weight." But I hurry to add that emotional abuse can be practiced by the less powerful and those who aspire to power. I also caution that practices perceived to be emotionally abusive are not always so. The following narrative was shared by Garth, a 24-year-old telecommunications employee who, upon reflection, seems to recognize the themes of emotional immaturity, misperception, envy, and dehumanization of his supervisor.

> I had worked at a telecom company for several years and considered myself one of the best telemarketers in the company. I thought that I had earned an interview to reach a higher position in management, by way of example. All of my coworkers considered me a gentleman, hard worker, and talented salesman. I was eager to go to work every day, perform well, and listen to my managers on a daily basis. When I did finally get the interview, I thought I had delivered a good speech to get the job. A week later I was devastated to hear that another employee, who was inferior to my skills, got the job! I got jealous and depressed, and it reflected on my behavior. I started to disrespect my managers by mouthing off rather than just going along with things. I felt betrayed by the company and cared less about getting fired. I started showing up late to work with a bad attitude about everything until I eventually just quit. Later I heard (from a coworker) that the company had me next in line for any manager job that would be available. I realized that my stupidity got me nowhere and made me lose an opportunity.

When faced with emotional tyranny, employees may have any number of constructive responses (also see Lutgen-Sandvik, 2006; Tracy, 2005). For example, they can develop emotionally-supportive relationships with peers, seek authentic emotional experiences outside of work, and use therapy as a means of expressing and recovering authentic feelings. In cases where moral infractions are acknowledged by a transgressor, the releasing of negative emotion through a process of forgiveness may be appropriate. Many workers describe a positive process of "emotional toughening," which allows them to withstand occasional acts of abuse. More important than thick-skinned workers, are organizational leaders who choose to avoid the tactics of emotional manipulation. If emotions are important indicators of the moral state of an organization, our most successful leaders may be those who monitor them most carefully.

Notes

1 Raul is a fictional name, as are all of those presented in this chapter. To further protect informants, identifying details have been omitted or modified. Quotes have been edited to preserve continuity, eliminate redundancy, and improve readability. In all cases, I have labored to preserve the meaning intended by the speaker.

References

Ashforth, B. E., & Humphrey, R. H. (1993). Emotional labor in service roles: The influence of identity. *Academy of Management Review, 18*(1), 88–115.

Ashforth, B. E., Kreiner, G. E., & Fugate, M. (2000). All in a day's work: Boundaries and micro role transitions. *Academy of Management Review, 25*(3), 472–491.

Averill, J. R. (1983). Studies on anger and aggression. *American Psychologist, 38*(11), 1145–1160.

Briner, R. B. (2004). Themed book reviews: Emotion and organizations: A decade of development. *Human Relations, 57*(10), 1333–1362.

Fineman, S. (2000). An emotion agenda. In *Emotion in organizations* (2nd ed., pp. 216–224). Thousand Oaks, CA: Sage.

Harlos, K. P., & Pinder, C. (2000). Emotion and injustice in the workplace. In S. Fineman (Ed.), *Emotions in organizations* (2nd ed., pp. 255–276). Thousand Oaks, CA: Sage.

Hochschild, A. R. (1979). Emotion work, feeling rules, and social structure. *The American Journal of Sociology, 85*(3), 551–575.

Hochschild, A. R. (1983). *The managed heart: Commercialization of human feeling*. Berkeley, CA: University of California Press.

Kassing, J. (2007). Going around the boss: Exploring the consequences of circumvention. *Management Communication Quarterly, 21*(1), 55–75.

Larson, J. R. (1989). The dynamic interplay between employees' feedback seeking strategies and supervisors' delivery of performance feedback. *Academy of Management Review, 14*(3), 408–422.

Lutgen-Sandvik, P. (2006). Take this job and ... : Quitting and other forms of resistance to workplace bullying. *Communication Monographs, 73*(4), 406–433.

Martin, J., Knopoff, K., & Beckman, C. (2000). Bounded emotionality at the body shop. In S. Fineman (Ed.), *Emotion in organizations* (2nd ed., pp. 115–139). London: Sage.

Miller, K. I., Considine, J., & Garner, J. (2007). "Let me tell you about my job": Exploring the terrain of emotion in the workplace. *Management Communication Quarterly, 20*(3), 231–271.

Morris, J. A., & Feldman, D. C. (1996). The dimensions, antecedents, and consequences of emotional labor. *Academy of Management Review, 21*(4), 986–1010.

Mumby, D. K., & Putnam, L. I. (1992). The politics of emotion: A feminist reading of bounded rationality. *Academy of Management Review, 17*(3), 465–486.

Myerson, D. E. (2000). If emotions were honoured: A cultural analysis. In S. Fineman (Ed.), *Emotion in organizations* (2nd ed., pp. 167–183). London: Sage.

Rafaeli, A., & Sutton, R. I. (1991). Emotional contrast strategies as means of social influence: Lessons from criminal interrogators and bill collectors. *Academy of Management Journal, 34*(4), 749–775.

Stenross, B., & Kleinman, S. (1989). The highs and lows of emotional labor: Detectives encounters with criminals and victims. *Journal of Contemporary Ethnography, 17*(4), 435–452.

Sutton, R. I., & Rafaeli, A. (1988). Untangling the relationship between displayed emotions and organizational sales: The case of convenience stores. *Academy of Management Journal, 31*(3), 461–487.

Tracy, S. J. (2005). Locking up emotion: Moving beyond dissonance for understanding emotion labor discomfort. *Communication Monographs, 72*(3), 261–283.

Tracy, S. J., & Tracy, K. (1998). Emotion labor at 911: A case study and theoretical critique. *Journal Applied Communication Research, 26*(4), 390–411.

Van Maanen, J. V., & Kunda, G. (1989). Real feelings: Emotional expression and organizational culture. In L. L. Cummings & B. M. Staw (Eds.), *Research in organizational behavior* (Vol. 11, pp. 43–104). Greenwich, CT: JAI Press.

Wagoner, R., & Waldron, V. R. (1999). How supervisors convey routine bad news: Face-work at UPS. *Southern Communication Journal, 64*(2), 193–210.

Waldron, V. R. (1994). Once more with feeling: Reconsidering the role of emotion in work. In S. A. Deetz (Ed.), *Communication yearbook 17* (pp. 388–416). Thousand Oaks, CA: Sage.

Waldron, V. R. (1999). Communication practices of followers, members, and protégés: The case of upward influence tactics. In M. Roloff (Ed.), *Communication yearbook 22* (pp. 251–299). Thousand Oaks, CA: Sage.

Waldron, V. R. (2000). Relational experiences and emotions at work. In S. Fineman (Ed.), *Emotion in organizations* (2nd ed., pp. 64–82). Thousand Oaks, CA: Sage.

Waldron, V. R. (2003). Relationship maintenance in organizational settings. In D. Canary & M. Dainton (Eds.), *Maintaining relationships through communication: Relational, contextual, and cultural variations* (pp. 163–184). New York: Lawrence Erlbaum.

Waldron, V.R., Foreman, C., & Miller, R. (1993). Managing gender conflicts in the supervisory relationship: Relationship definiction strategies used by women and men. In G. Kreps (Ed.), *Sexual harassment: Communication implications* (pp. 234–256). Cresskill, NJ: Hammond Press.

Waldron, V. R., & Kelley, D. (2008). *Communicating forgiveness*. Newbury Park, CA: Sage.

Waldron, V. R., & Krone, K. J. (1991). The experience and expression of emotion in the workplace: A study of a corrections organization. *Management Communication Quarterly, 4*(3), 287–309.

Weiner, B. (2006). *Social motivation, justice, and the moral emotions: An attributional approach.* Mahwah, NJ: Lawrence Erlbaum Associates.

Chapter 2

Workplace Bullying
Causes, Consequences, and Corrections

*Pamela Lutgen-Sandvik, Gary Namie, and
Ruth Namie*

Adult bullying at work is shockingly common and enormously destructive. In an in-depth analysis of 148 organizations worldwide, "workplaces evidencing bullying on a relatively routine basis [made] up 49% of the total analyzed" (Hodson, Roscigno, & Lopez, 2006, p. 391). U.S. studies also suggest alarming prevalence rates. During any given 6 to 12 month period up to 13% of workers are bullied on the job; this increases significantly when counting those bullied at any time during their careers (30%, Lutgen-Sandvik, Tracy, & Alberts, 2007; 37%, Namie, 2007). These numbers translate to millions of workers: "According to the Bureau of Labor Statistics (U.S. DOL) 146 million Americans were employed in July 2007. An estimated 54 million Americans have been bullied at work using the 37% rate" (Namie, 2007, para. 4).

This chapter reviews the current literature regarding the history of bullying research, the factors associated with bullying onset, its consequences or effects, and various avenues for prevention and intervention. Following conventions in bullying research we refer to those bullied as *targets* and bullies as *actors*, *bullies*, or *perpetrators*.

Workplace bullying is repeated, health-harming mistreatment that takes one or more of the following forms: verbal abuse; offensive conduct and behaviors (including nonverbal) that are threatening, humiliating, or intimidating; or work interference and sabotage that prevent work from getting done. Numerous negative interactions that feel intimidating, insulting, or exclusionary constitute this phenomenon. Targeted workers typically believe it is an intentional effort to harm, control, or drive them from the workplace. There is no question that the experience is deeply traumatic and stigmatizing (Lutgen-Sandvik, 2008) and marks the severe end of the employee-abuse continuum (Namie, 2003b). Bullying can involve persistent supervisory abuse of subordinates (most common), coworkers "ganging up" on colleagues, or in rare occasions "bullying up" when subordinates abuse a higher-level organizational member (Einarsen, Hoel, Zapf, & Cooper, 2003). Table 2.1 outlines the verbal and nonverbal negative acts associated with bullying.

Table 2.1 Actions/Interactions Associated with Workplace Bullying

1 Rudeness, discourteousness, lack of regard, condescending/patronizing attitude
2 Derogatory remarks, name calling, insulting/offensive remarks about personal life or attributes
3 Explosive outbursts (yelling, screaming, swearing), angry tone of voice, temper tantrums
4 Threats (job loss, physical harm, retaliation); coercion, intimidation
5 Withholding needed information/materials; sabotaging work
6 Aggressive eye contact or facial expression (grimacing, glaring, staring); hostile body language (finger snapping/pointing, foot stomping, fist shaking)
7 Being humiliated, ridiculed, put down in front of others, public embarrassment
8 Having statements/requests ignored, having opinions belittled
9 Excluded from workplace camaraderie, avoided, isolated, treated as nonexistent, silent treatment
10 Interrupted, cut off when speaking, not allowed to speak for/defend oneself
11 Insulted, use of sarcasm, made fun of, object of jokes at target's expense
12 Flaunting status/power, reminding of control and authority
13 Gossip, talking behind back, rumor mongering, slandering
14 Throwing something, slamming doors, slamming things down, damaging property
15 Physical assaults, physical harm, danger of physical harm
16 Excessive, continued criticism
17 No work given or given meaningless, humiliating, insulting work tasks; assigned impossible tasks/deadlines
18 Unfairly/wrongly accused, scapegoating, judgment, ability questioned, took credit for target's work
19 Labeled, stigmatized (mentally ill, insubordinate, troublemaker, problem employee)
20 Subject to close supervision, micro-managing, surveillance
21 Inconsistent treatment (different standards for different employees, makes–breaks promises, fails to provide standards—criticizes after the fact, charming then harsh/callous)
22 Hints target should quit job, moved/transferred against target's will
23 Insulting messages, telephone calls, "flame" emails

Emergence of Interest in Workplace Bullying

International Interest

Heinz Leymann (1990), a German physician working in Sweden, began studying adult bullying in the early 1980s and is considered a pioneer in the field. His work with children bullied at school engendered an awareness of similar experiences of his adult patients. Leymann adopted the term "mobbing" from ethologist's descriptions of animal behavior in which a group of smaller animals attacked a single larger animal (Lorenz, 1991, cited in Leymann, 1996). Leymann's work drew other Scandinavian researchers who initiated studies of workplace aggression, bullying, and mobbing (e.g., Björkqvist, Osterman, & Hjelt-Back, 1994; Einarsen, 1999).

A decade later the topic surfaced in the UK. In 1990, a freelance journalist named Andrea Adams (Adams and Crawford, 1992) brought the issue to public attention in Britain through a series of BBC radio broadcasts; she labeled the phenomenon "bullying." As a result of Adams' work and public concern, interest in and the study of bullying intensified in the UK (e.g., Hoel & Cooper, 2000; Rayner, 1997). Although Scandinavia and the UK continues to lead thought in this area, bullying and mobbing research now includes scholars and professionals in Australia, New Zealand, South Africa, the European Union, and Japan, among others (Zapf, Einarsen, Hoel, & Vartia, 2003).

United States' Interest

In the United States the history of adult bullying research has been less straightforward. A U.S. psychiatrist named Carroll Brodsky (1976) conducted one of the first studies of workplace harassment and subsequently published *The Harassed Worker*. Despite the groundbreaking nature of his work, the book stirred little interest at the time. Brodsky's research was revived in the early 1990s when interest surged in Britain, and although out-of-print the work is still often cited. Around this same time, the study of human aggression expanded to include aggression at work (Spector, 1975), research that was centrally concerned with perpetrators.

In the early 1980s nursing professor Helen Cox (1991) began studying verbal abuse in medical settings when it appeared to be driving away gifted nursing students. Around the same time rare but highly visible occurrences of workplace murder sparked a flood of research that extended into the next two decades (e.g., Allen & Lucerno, 1996; Baron & Neuman, 1998; Chen & Spector, 1992; Neuman & Baron, 1997). Over time academic interest widened to include the study of antecedents to violence, such as perceived injustice, incivility, and mistreatment (e.g., Andersson & Pearson, 1999; Keashly, 1998; Price Spratlen, 1995). In the late 1990s research with a distinctly target-focused agenda emerged which addressed the issue of employee emotional abuse (i.e., workplace bullying) (Keashly, 1998). Around the same time Gary and Ruth Namie (2000) published a self-help book on the subject and established the Workplace Bullying Institute (WBI) to help targets. Interest in U.S. workplace bullying began to flourish in the early 2000s and continues to grow at an exponential rate.

Naming of the Phenomenon

The terms used to describe persistent primarily psychological employee abuse vary from author to author, discipline to discipline, and country to country. Especially in the United States the array of terms is daunting, even for those of us who study the subject. U.S. researchers use labels such as *employee emotional abuse* (Keashly, 1998), *generalized workplace abuse* (Rospenda, Richman, Wislar, & Flaherty, 2000), *mistreatment* (Meares, Oetzel, Derkacs, & Ginossar, 2004), and *perceived victimization* (Aquino & Bradfield, 2000)—to name only a few. The involved disciplines are as far ranging as the terminology and include, but are not limited to, management (Neuman & Baron, 2003), psychology (Keashly & Neuman, 2005), sociology, (Hodson et al., 2006), anthropology (Davenport, Schwartz, & Elliott, 2002), and organizational communication (Tracy, Lutgen-Sandvik, & Alberts, 2006). Conversely, international research chiefly emerged in psychology and management and with few exceptions labels the phenomenon *bullying* or *mobbing*—terms that are for all intents and purposes synonymous.

Workplace Bullying as a Distinct Phenomenon

Workplace bullying is a distinct communicative phenomenon that is identified by its characteristic features. These features differentiate bullying from one-time aggressive or discriminatory acts. We catalogue these in what follows.

- *Repetition.* Bullying is recurring and frequent. "Hammering" and "chipping away" are laced throughout target stories and represent abuse that occurs on a nearly daily basis in one form or another (Leymann & Gustafsson, 1996; Tracy et al., 2006). Repetition differentiates the phenomenon from infrequent negative interactions (Rayner, Hoel, & Cooper, 2002).
- *Duration.* The long-term nature of bullying is a prominent feature giving bullying its corrosive character. Researchers usually adopt the minimum of six months articulated by Leymann (1990), but targets typically report bullying lasts much longer (Lutgen-Sandvik et al., 2007; Namie, 2003a).
- *Escalation.* Bullying intensifies over time if left unchecked (Leymann, 1990; Lutgen-Sandvik, 2003). During early phases targets may have difficulty encoding their experience aside from describing feelings of unease or heightened discomfort (Adams & Crawford, 1992; Lutgen-Sandvik, 2008). In later stages they lack the language to label the experience *bullying* but are unmistakably aware of being under attack (Einarsen et al., 2003).
- *Harm.* Bullying is exceedingly destructive and is associated with targets' impaired physical, mental, and occupational health; deterioration of personal relationships outside work; and economic jeopardy. Witnessing coworkers also report increased stress and intent to leave (Lutgen-Sandvik, et al., 2007; Vartia, 2001).

- *Attributed intent.* Targets and witnesses typically believe bullies' actions are purposeful—that perpetrators know exactly what they are doing and even work at it. Although researchers generally omit intent in definitions (discussed in Rayner et al., 2002), persons on the receiving end are *convinced* that bullying is intentional and find it impossible to believe that such egregious acts are inadvertent (Lutgen-Sandvik, 2006; Namie & Namie, 2000).
- *Hostile work environment.* Bullying constitutes and is constituted by hostile work environments (Liefooghe & MacKenzie-Davey, 2001; Salin, 2003) that are marked by pervasive fear and dread of workgroup members. Bullying is both an outcome of and a recursive resource for hostile work environments (Lutgen-Sandvik & McDermott, 2008).
- *Power disparity.* Bullying at work is marked by a difference in power between actors and targets (Einarsen et al., 2003) that exists prior to the onset of bullying (e.g., abusive supervision) or arises as a result of ongoing harassment (e.g., peer-to-peer abuse) (Keashly & Nowell, 2003).
- *Communication patterning.* Bullying is typically a constellation of verbal and nonverbal acts that constitute a discernable, recurring pattern to targets and witnesses (Keashly, 1998). Targets believe their experiences cannot be understood outside this contextual patterning, which makes bullying difficult to describe straightforwardly (Tracy et al., 2006).
- *Distorted communication networks.* Communication networks are typically blocked or stifled in bullying environments. Open day-to-day communication is risky and in some cases even forbidden and punished (Lutgen-Sandvik, 2006; Rayner et al., 2002). The situations "that scare a bully most are the possibility of more than one person getting together to complain and [thus,] ... their behavior becoming public" (Crawford, 2001, p. 26).

As becomes apparent, bullying is more than simply a list of negative communication behaviors. It is a complex pattern of negative interactions exacerbated by distinctive descriptive features.

Explanations for Workplace Bullying

The complexity of this communicative phenomenon is rivaled only by the multiplicity of explanations for it. As key researchers note, to fully understand the phenomenon one must "take a broad range of potential causes of bullying into account, which may lie with the organization, the perpetrator (bully), the social psychology of the work group, and also the victim" (Zapf & Einarsen, 2003, p. 166). Global economic environments as well as social and cultural tradition also contribute to bullying (Lutgen-Sandvik &

McDermott, 2008). We first review an explanatory classification for bullying and then present antecedents categorically (i.e., individual, organizational, social).

Etiological Explanations

Etiological explanations for bullying origins usually include dispute-
related bullying (Einarsen, 1999) and three types of predatory-bullying:
authoritative-, displaced-, and discriminatory (Lutgen-Sandvik, 2005).
Another etiological explanation is organizational-bullying that identifies
organizations and organizational systems as the causative forces behind
abuse (Liefooghe & MacKenzie-Davey, 2001).

- *Dispute-related bullying* begins with interpersonal disagreements that
  build into extremely escalated, entrenched conflicts (Einarsen, 1999).
  Actors may begin to objectify their opponents and "the total destruction of the opponent is seen as the ultimate goal" (Einarsen et al.,
  2003, p. 19).
- *Authoritative-bullying* is the abuse of power granted through organizational position and is the most commonly reported (Hoel, Cooper,
  & Faragher, 2001; Namie, 2003b, 2007; Rayner, 1997). In workgroups of authoritative actors serial bullying usually occurs, in which
  many workers are bullied, usually one after the other.
- *Displaced-bullying* or scapegoating is aggressing "against someone
  other than the source of strong provocation because aggressing
  against the source of such provocation is too dangerous" (Neuman &
  Baron, 2003, p. 197). It occurs when increased frustration or stress
  caused by workplace factors result in employees taking frustrations
  out on others.
- *Discriminatory-bullying* is simply abusing someone out of prejudice,
  usually workers who differ from or refuse to accept the norms of the
  rest of the workgroup (Rayner et al., 2002) or "belong to a certain outsider group" (Einarsen et al., 2003, p. 19).
- *Organizational-bullying* indicts organizational practices that are
  oppressive, exploitive, and over-controlling as seeding abuse
  (Liefooghe & MacKenzie-Davey, 2001) (e.g., corporate downsizing,
  outsourcing jobs, forcing uncompensated overtime work, closing
  entire plants to relocate for low-cost labor).

Individual Antecedents

Most researchers conclude that there is probably no such thing as a "victim" personality and it is equally unlikely that there is a "bully" personality (Rayner et al., 2002; Zapf & Einarsen, 2003). However, researchers

have attempted to parse out the individual factors that might increase the likelihood of bullying or being bullied (Coyne, Seigne, & Randall, 2000; Zapf & Einarsen, 2003). We review this literature while counseling caution on the reliance on any simplistic, individual explanations for the phenomenon.

Targets

There appears to be no sex bias in being targeted. Men and women are equally likely to report being bullied at work (Namie, 2007; Rayner, 1997; Zapf et al., 2003). However, organizational position and certain traits or behaviors are linked to being targeted. Organizational position is inversely associated with being targeted. The higher the organizational position, the lower the incidence of bullying; low-status workers are simply more vulnerable (Hodson et al., 2006).

Certain traits, behaviors, or markers are associated with increased risk, but the inconsistency of associated markers fails to convey a reliable picture of targets. For example, appearing too weak, anxious, submissive, unassertive, or conflict-aversive is claimed to provoke aggression in others (Coyne et al., 2000). Conversely, communicating aggressively, rejecting less-ethical group norms, and overachieving are also suggested as antecedents to being targeted (Adams & Crawford, 1992). On one hand, targets are characterized as "literal minded, ... somewhat unsophisticated ... over-achiever[s]" (Brodsky, 1976, p.89) who lack social, communication skills, have low self-esteem, and are suspicious of others (Coyne et al., 2000). On the other hand, research identifies employees who are particularly talented, conscientious, and well-liked by others as persons likely to be targeted (Coyne, Chong, Seigne, & Randall, 2003; Lutgen-Sandvik, 2006; Namie, 2003a). Plainly, there is no clear marker-cluster that categorizes targets.

Perpetrators

Men are more often reported as bullies in most studies, but research findings are somewhat mixed. Some find that bullies seem to be male more often (Hoel & Cooper, 2000; Zapf et al., 2003) and others suggest the opposite (Namie, 2003a). There does appear to be a relationship between position and bullying others—supervisors or upper-managers are identified as abusers in 60–80% of cases (e.g., Hoel & Cooper, 2000; Lutgen-Sandvik et al., 2007; Namie, 2003a; Rayner, 1997). In a nationally representative survey (Namie, 2007), 72% of reported bullies were managers, some of whom had the sponsorship and support of executives, managerial peers, or human resources.

Workplace violence researchers have invested considerable effort in identifying precursors of potentially violent organizational actors. The traits and behaviors associated with such aggression likely play a part in bullying. These include lack of self control, self-reflection, empathy, and perspective-taking (Douglas & Martinko, 2001); personal volatility; history or tendency toward depression; Theory X beliefs; Type A personalities; negative affectivity; and unstable, unrealistic high self-esteem (Neuman & Baron, 1998; Tepper, 2000; Zapf & Einarsen, 2003). For example, inflated views of self that are "unstable or heavily dependent on external validation" (Zapf & Einarsen, 2003, p. 168) are particularly vulnerable to being interrogated, contradicted, or censured.

Other alleged markers include lack of social or communicative adeptness (Einarsen, Raknes, & Mattheisen, 1994), growing up around domestic violence, or being a victim of child abuse (Randall, 2001). Alcohol and drug abuse and aggressive behavior in one's personal life may also be predictors of workplace bullying (Douglas & Martinko, 2001). Whatever the constellations of markers bullies act in ways identified as pathological, power-addicted, and controlling (Namie & Namie, 2000; Tracy et al., 2006). Bullies are perceived as being good at "managing up" and ingratiating themselves with higher-level persons. As with targets, however, there is little research directly linking any specific personality type to perpetrators of workplace bullying (Rayner et al., 2002).

Organizational Antecedents

When workplaces are chaotic, unpredictable, and marked by high levels of job insecurity, role-conflict or strain, workers are far more likely to report being bullied (Hodson et al., 2006; Lawrence, 2001). In chaotic environments actors may see their activities as maintaining control in situations where the actor has insufficient work control or high levels of work conflict (Einarsen et al., 1994). The physical environment can also exacerbate aggressive acts. Lack of space or privacy, physically uncomfortable equipment and accommodations, and electronic surveillance may increase the risk of bullying (Barling, 1996).

Pressures to increase productivity while decreasing production costs (reduced workforce) can create "boiler room" environments that place "enormous stress on managers and employees and ... [trigger] abusive behaviors in managers" (Bassman, 1992, p. 137). Managers and workers may use bullying instrumentally to deal with these chaotic, demanding situations. Some claim that bullying occurs due to "inadequate transformation of leadership and power in reaction to [global economic] shifts" (Vandekerckhove & Commers, 2003, p. 41). Economic pressures drive expectations for boosted profitability, but such expectations often occur within structural, procedural, and leadership vacuums.

Generally speaking, two management styles are associated with harassment and bullying: coercive/authoritarian (Hoel & Salin, 2003) and laisse-faire (Di Martino, Hoel, & Cooper, 2003). The former may use bullying to "motivate" workers; the latter typically fails to intervene when workers report being abused. Unfortunately, when most employers are notified about bullying incidents they either do nothing or worsen the situation by fostering retaliation against the complainant (Keashy, 2001; Namie, 2007).

Some organizational cultures have an adversarial and aggressive approach to working and interpersonal relationships that encourages aggressive communication (Hoel & Cooper, 2000). These climates and professional cultures may reward bullying with promotions, access to leadership, and most importantly, the granting of invariant personal credibility or voice. Bullying seems more prevalent in work cultures that accept aggression as an aspect of doing business (e.g., law enforcement, corrections, legal firms, etc.) (Hoel & Salin, 2003). Wright and Smye (1998) describe three types of culture and associated forms of abuse: *win/lose* or forcing competition among members, *blaming* or making people fearful of stepping out of line, and *sacrificing* everything in workers' lives for their work.

Salin's (2003) overview of the enabling, motivating, and precipitating structures and processes that contribute to bullying is informative. Enabling factors explain why bullying might be rewarded: "perceived power imbalance" (p. 1218), "low perceived costs" (p. 1220), and "dissatisfaction and frustration" (pp. 1221–1222). Motivating factors are reasons for why it might flourish: "high internal competition and a politicized climate" (p. 1223) and "reward system and expected benefits" for the perpetrator (p. 1224). Precipitating factors are triggers for its occurrence: "restructuring, downsizing, ... other crises [, and organizational changes]" (p. 1225).

Societal/Cultural Antecedents

Beyond economic globalization and the pressure this creates, other social and cultural belief systems influence employee abuse. Lutgen-Sandvik and McDermott (2008) argue that meaning systems contributing to workplace bullying include the ideological link between work and religion, philosophies of individualism and meritocracy, a reverence for hierarchical power, profit as an ultimate goal, and Theory X notions of workers as lazy and in need of goading.

Related cultural ideologies that might stimulate adult bullying are those that praise power, profit, and position (Du Gay, 1996); devalue human and stakeholder interests (Deetz, 1992); and stigmatize victims or disadvantaged persons (Lutgen-Sandvik, 2008; Ryan, 1976). An important but often unrecognized effect of these value systems is to whom such values confer voice. Bullied workers (victims) in subordinate positions (low position-power) are rarely believed (Keashly, 2001), especially if they have been bullied by a highly productive (profit) or politically astute (position-power) aggressor.

Considerable evidence points to national culture as a key factor in bullying prevalence. Scandinavia has far lower bullying rates than the United States and Britain (Hoel & Cooper, 2000; Lutgen-Sandvik et al., 2007)—arguably due to low-power distance and feminine/egalitarian norms (Hofstede, 1980). Since bullying is a power-down phenomenon, less power and status differences between people in different positions likely results in less bullying. In feminine and egalitarian cultures with high concern for the quality of interpersonal relations one might also expect persons to communicate more respectfully.

Consequences: Actors and Organizations

Given the range of antecedents, it becomes clear that bullying is a complex phenomenon. As important as its antecedents, however, are its consequences for organizations and their members. Although targets suffer the greatest degree of damage, witnessing coworkers are also impaired (Lutgen-Sandvik et al., 2007). What is more, when workers are bullied, there is a deterioration or disabling of the organization (Keashly & Jagatic, 2003).

Targets

Empirical and anecdotal evidence indicate that bullying affects all aspects of targets' lives. Their self-esteem (Price Spratlen, 1995), physical and emotional health (Duffy, Ganster, & Pagon, 2002; Rospenda, 2002), and cognitive functioning (Brodsky, 1976) are at risk or damaged. Targets report higher levels of anxiety, depression (Namie, 2003a), alcohol abuse (Richman, Rospenda, Flaherty, & Freels, 2001), and suicidal ideation (Leymann, 1990) than do non-bullied workers. Longitudinal research suggests that perceptions of workplace injustice (no doubt experienced by targets) are associated with chronic stress, high blood pressure, and increased risk of coronary heart disease (De Vogli, Ferrie, Chandola, Kivimäki, & Marmot, 2007).

Targets of long-term workplace abuse also experience symptoms of post-traumatic stress disorder (PTSD). Namie's (2003a) research found that a third of women and a quarter of men experienced the key symptoms of PTSD: hypervigilance, thought intrusions, avoidance-disassociation. This corresponds with Leymann's (1996) earlier work. Some targets are so damaged that they cannot reintegrate into the workforce or can do so only after intensive rehabilitation therapy (Leymann & Gustafsson, 1996). Being abused at work also impairs relationships outside of work. Although this issue has yet to receive widespread attention, anecdotal evidence suggests disastrous effects on family functioning, relationships, and communication (Jennifer, Cowie, & Anaiadou, 2003; Rayner et al., 2002; Tracy et al., 2006).

Coworkers

Witnesses of bullying, those considered *secondary* targets, are "employees who themselves were not violated but whose perceptions, fears and expectations are changed as a result of being vicariously exposed to violence" (Barling, 1996, p. 35). These workers report increased levels of "destabilizing forces at work, excessive workloads, role ambiguity and work relationship conflict" (Jennifer et al., 2003, p. 495). Non-bullied witnesses report elevated negativity and stress and, in contrast, decreased work satisfaction when compared to non-exposed workers (Lutgen-Sandvik et al., 2007).

Organizations

The central consequences to organizations include lost productivity, decreased worker commitment and satisfaction, increased operating costs, loss of positive public relations, and, over time, impoverished workforces. Supervisory abuse reduces organizational citizenship behaviors—discretionary acts that promote organizational effectiveness (Zellars, Tepper, & Duffy, 2002). Not surprisingly, facing persistent harassment and humiliation increases absenteeism. Indeed, an EEOC officer explained that one of the key indicators her office used to identify if problems existed in a workgroup was employee use of sick leave (P. Kendall, personal communication 9/27/2007).

Presenteeism can also be a problem in hostile work environments. This usually means "slack productivity from ailing workers" (Cascio, 2006, p. 245), but can occur when bullied workers fear missing work because of what might transpire in their absence when they are not there to defend themselves (e.g., rumors, work destruction, key task removal). These workers may be present but are usually not producing at their peak potential as enormous levels of energy are necessary to cope with, defend against, and make sense of persistent harassment and humiliation (Lutgen-Sandvik, 2006).

Organizations most likely also face increased premiums for workers' compensation (Brodsky, 1976) and medical insurance (Bassman, 1992). Law suits associated with bullying (e.g., wrongful or constructive discharge), although rare, are exceedingly costly both in legal fees and staff hours (Rayner et al., 2002). Quite commonly, organizations also suffer loss of positive public images (Bassman, 1992) and find it increasingly difficult to recruit staff, especially when word spreads within a specialized group of employees about an employee-abusive organization (Lutgen-Sandvik & McDermott, 2008).

Workplace bullying simply drives away good employees, both targets and witnesses (Lutgen-Sandvik, 2006; Rayner et al., 2002). Turnover and associated recruiting, hiring, and training new employees are directly linked to increased operating expenses. Over time these organizations can end up with impoverished workforces as a direct result of worker-exit waves. The first exodus wave includes those with high occupational capital (e.g., skills, technical knowledge, experience). A second wave leaves when hope of change is lost, and the third wave includes new employees who enter and then leave shortly afterward once they recognize the negative dynamics. Unfortunately, employee exodus usually leaves behind a less talented, less confident cadre of workers with fewer occupational options and fewer organizationally valued assets (Lutgen-Sandvik, 2005).

Prevention and Intervention: Constructive Ways of Organizing

Given the destruction wrought by bullying, it is important to examine approaches to prevention and intervention. No single response is likely to resolve workplace bullying, especially if aggressive interactions have become sedimented and widespread harm has occurred. We present those with the most potential for positive organizing in what follows.

Individual Responses

Individual responses suggest that accountability for bullying resides in the targeted individual, which simply is not the case. What is more, individual efforts to stop bullying are usually less than successful (Keashly, 2001; Lutgen-Sandvik, Alberts, & Tracy, 2008). Nonetheless, those targeted are keen to know what they can do to stop abuse. We discuss a number of potential approaches targets may take, including how coworkers can help in these situations.

Being able to name abuse "workplace bullying" is an important first step to understanding what is occurring and what to do about it (Namie, 2006). Information about bullying (e.g., research articles, books) coupled with being able to name bullying as a distinct phenomenon also bolsters employee claims to upper-management and human resources (HR) (Lutgen-Sandvik, 2006). Certainly, confronting actors is a possibility. Rayner et al. (2002) claim that if done early before abuse is entrenched speaking with bullies can effectively alter negative communication patterns. Such an approach can be risky, however; many targets report that abuse escalates after such conversations (Lutgen-Sandvik, 2006).

Targeted workers may also decide to file formal or informal complaints to unions, EEOC, the bully's boss, or attorneys (Macintosh, 2006). When making reports to organizational authorities, detailed documentation (e.g., dates, times, events) can be useful since authorities typically need formal evidence of wrongdoing (Lutgen-Sandvik, 2006). Targeted workers may also consider filing lawsuits against employers. Although there is no legal protection against bullying in the United States some workers find grounds for sexual harassment, racial discrimination, constructive discharge, or wrongful termination cases (Davenport et al., 2002).

Ensuring self-care and social support is especially important. This may mean taking time off, trying not to take the experience personally, and spending time with trusted others (Namie & Namie, 2000). Gaining peer support is easier if other organizational members understand bullying and know that it is occurring. Informally educating peers can be done by distributing articles and talking about bullying in a manner that protects vulnerable persons (Macintosh, 2006). As is often the case when individual tactics fail, workers commonly choose to quit or transfer. In fact, when asked what others facing bullying should do, targets' most frequent recommendation is leaving the organization (Lutgen-Sandvik, 2006; Zapf & Gross, 2001). Although leaving does not change organizational dynamics, we believe this response is empowering and positive—analogous to domestic violence victims leaving their perpetrators.

Coworkers can be very helpful for supporting targets' stories and breaking the bullying cycle (Macintosh, 2006); concerted voice simply increases believability (Lutgen-Sandvik, 2006). Collective voice also reduces some of the risk of being labeled troublemakers, mentally ill, or problem-employees. Non-targeted workgroup members may not be as stigmatized, since they lack the victim label. But even with collective resistance, there is the risk of being pejoratively branded when speaking out against abuse and oppression (Lutgen-Sandvik, 2006).

What Stops Bullying—A Reality Check

In this section, we discussed several options for individual action. However, the WBI-Zogby Survey (Namie, 2007) sheds light on two important aspects of targets' efficacy in dealing with bullying. The respondents who either experienced or witnessed bullying tell us what bullied targets did: 40% took no action, 37% informally reported to the organization (e.g., bully's boss or HR), 19% filed formal internal or external complaints, and 3% filed individual or joined class-action lawsuits. When we describe bullying as a silent epidemic (Namie & Namie, 2004), it is due to the relatively low rate of formal action taken by targets—usually out of fear that things will get worse.

We began this section reproving targets' practical responsibility to stop the bullying. The WBI-Zobgy Survey (Namie, 2007) supports this claim. Of those targeted for which the bullying had stopped, 40% quit their jobs, 24% were involuntarily terminated, and 13% changed jobs in their current organizations. Bullies were negatively sanctioned in 23% of cases;

however, this is likely an inflated artifact of questionnaire wording that used the term "harasser" to identify the bully. Indeed harassers who commit illegal acts are more likely to be terminated and negatively sanctioned. As such, we move on to more fruitful organizational responses.

Organizational Responses

Bullying is clearly an organizational not an individual problem. Executive decisions collectively create and sustain working environments. Employers unilaterally establish work conditions except when constrained by the rare collective bargaining agreements (only 7.5% of the U.S. private sector is unionized). Solving the problem is not only an organization-wide responsibility but successful efforts require the total commitment of top-level organizational leadership, involvement of middle- management, and engagement of employees (Tehrani, 2001). Short-term approaches such as identifying lone perpetrators while ignoring the factors that enable or motivate byllying often fails to produce meaningful, lasting change. The following outlines organizational responses for more constructive ways of organizing.

Top-level Commitment

We cannot overstate the importance of top-level commitment to dignity for all workers. The communication behavior of persons perceived as representatives of the organization and all that their communication implies will set the tone for other organizational members' interactions. "Employees will quickly become cynical when ... exhort[ed] ... to behave in a way that bears little relationship to the action behaviors of the managers they observe in their daily life" (Tehrani, 2001, p. 136).

In the Namies' work with organizations when top managers do commit to stopping bullying some of the reasons include a CEO's desire to leave a personal legacy, the begrudging severance of a long-term friendship between sponsor and bully, response to patient/client endangerment complaints by ethical practitioners, and a newfound intolerance of emotional tirades by a partner in a professional practice. Surprisingly, the commitment is rarely based on financial or employee-protection reasons despite considerable evidence that workplace bullying costs organizations dearly.

Member Engagement

Although top-level commitment is crucial, a solely top-down approach is unlikely to fundamentally change a communication climate. Members at all levels and functional areas need to be involved and engaged in assessing the current communication climate, determining areas for improvement, and implementing changes. One effective approach to spearhead the effort is creating a cross-level, cross-functional team (or a number of them depending on organizational size) to work collaboratively with external researchers or experts (for an outstanding example, see Keashly & Neuman, 2005, and Keashly & Neuman, Chapter 16 this volume). Together teams identify problems and outline potential solutions.

An important group to include are middle managers who "have the greatest opportunity to demonstrate that a culture that respects the dignity of individual employees is possible" (Tehrani, 2001, p. 137). If middle managers are entrenched in an aggressive, autocratic style of supervision, they may be highly suspicious of changes that appear to strip them of power. Upper management must provide adequate training and encouragement to assist middle managers in the shift from their current style to a style that is conducive to creating a dignity-based climate. A core element of such training is interpersonal communication skills—an area that is often most challenging during the transition. In what follows, we outline the core elements of an organizational approach.

Organization-Wide Assessment and Planning

Chances are, organizations are not aware of the extent to which workers may be bullied because the phenomenon is woefully under-reported (Lutgen-Sandvik et al., 2007; Namie, 2007). Assessments identify the presence (or absence) of bullying and identify the types of bullying (if present) in each workgroup so that action plans can be tailored, as one-size-fits-all approaches rarely succeed (Tehrani, 2001). Assessment usually includes anonymous surveys followed by worker interviews or focus groups to flesh out the quantitative findings. Academics are extremely useful for developing assessment measures, conducting confidential interviews, and analyzing resultant data. From the assessment cross-functional teams can develop action plans relative to the presenting dynamics.

Implementation and Follow-up Evaluation

Based on the action plan, organizations then move to implementation of solutions. At the very least respectful communication climates should include creating equitable reward systems, valuing diversity in people and ways of working, and promoting employee-level control over tasks (Tehrani, 2001). The range of intervention and prevention efforts is potentially unlimited. We address some possibilities in the concluding portion of this section. Based on the success criteria developed during the assessment and plan-development phases, organizations will want to evaluate the results measured against outlined objectives and hoped-for benefits. If interventions fail to achieve desired ends, teams should return to earlier problem-solving steps (i.e., clarify problems) or choose another course of action.

Certainly as important as any other aspect of creating respectful climates is rewarding desirable behavior and doing so publicly. Organizational members will in most cases do what is rewarded, especially if rewards are meaningful. As Noreen Tehrani (2001) explains:

> The importance of recognition cannot be overestimated in the achievement of excellence. Organisations that use reward as an incentive ... [are] particularly successful .... Recognition is particularly important to achieve changes in culture ... [and] does not have to be financial to be effective, indeed a financial reward can be counterproductive. A number of organisations used the presentation of certificates or medals ... as an effective sign of recognition .... Recognition can also be achieved in the appraisal process where appropriate objectives are set to assess the levels of respect shown to colleagues and teams. (pp. 148, 151)

Organizations will also want to consciously shift reward systems away from any type of direct or indirect championing of aggressive communication—even ignoring such behavior in hopes that it will go away (see Pearson, 1998).

Unfortunately, an aspect of developing a feedback system also includes a system of negative sanctions for those who fail to treat others with respect. If and when abuse occurs, failure to intervene will doom efforts to build climates marked by dignity (De Vogli et al., 2007). At times, firm management and negative sanctions (including employment termination) will be required to communicate to the entire workforce that bullying will not be tolerated (Crawford, 2001). This is typically one of the most difficult tasks upper-managers face when trying to create respectful workplaces because it involves confrontation—interactions that are rarely pleasant.

Prevention and Intervention Efforts

When an organization fully implements and sustains an anti-bullying initiative, it restores its focus on mission, a focus often lacking in employee-abusive workplaces. In what follows we provide elements that could comprise an anti-bullying initiative. We give particular attention to policy issues, ideas grounded in the Namies' extensive work with organizations seeking to redress the issue. Additionally, we review other approaches proposed in bullying research.

Anti-bullying Policies

Organizations may wish to create an explicit anti-bullying policy. A stand-alone policy communicates the seriousness of the problem and the depth of leadership's commitment to its correction and prevention. Anti-bullying provisions could also supplement existing anti-harassment or violence prevention policies since bullying is a different (albeit legal) form of harassment and a sub-lethal, non-physical form of violence.

Policies should precisely declare the unacceptability of bullying but avoid communicating or expecting "zero tolerance". At first multiple offenses may need to be allowed (although not ignored) because changing the climate requires relearning by everyone. Most organizational members will abandon abusive tactics when the consequences for harming others outweigh the personal rewards. Operant learning principles apply—using consequences to reform behavior. With multiple confirmed violations, however, the penalties should grow increasingly severe. Constraint of unacceptable conduct should be the organization's goal. In some cases upper-management will have to terminate the employment of intractable, repeat offenders who are unwilling or unable to change.

Policies should define bullying; "a definition is crucial as it enables all staff ... to understand what the organization terms 'workplace bullying'" (Richards & Daley, 2003, p. 250). Most policies also list omnibus categories and a limited set of examples. For instance, organizations might summarize the breadth of misbehavior encoded in the Negative Acts Questionnaire (Einarsen & Hoel, 2001) with the following categories: verbal abuse; threatening, intimidating, or humiliating communication and behavior; and work obstruction that undermines legitimate organizational interests. As with assessment teams, including a representative stakeholder group to collaboratively write both the policy and enforcement procedures is imperative. Internal groups—non-supervisory staff, unions, supervisors, senior management, governing boards, legal counsel, and human resources—should be a part of the development process.

Enforcement of policies even when executives are confirmed violators is the employer's chance to show a genuine desire to change the culture and climate of aggression. Procedures must be designed to be fair and credible to employees, especially those who have been bullied. Unenforced policies promote employee cynicism. Informal employee communication networks will swiftly transmit news of disingenuous investigations of alleged policy violations. Trained peer fact-finders, practical listeners, or external investigators can be effective at overcoming employee doubts.

Policies should include methods for handling informal complaints as a first stage of policy invocation. When employers provide an opportunity to speak in confidence and without fear of reprisal many potential formal complaints are precluded. There is power in providing for individual voice and an opportunity "just to be heard." Formal action may follow but only if the individual chooses. Confidential ombudspersons or practical listeners can provide this informal service.

The formal complaint process should be relatively quick to optimize value for participants, witnesses, and the organization. Witnesses and involved parties should be informed of the decision—complaint was upheld or not upheld. In current human resources investigations for the sake of the offender's confidentiality, affected coworkers and even complainants never learn outcomes. Cynicism and distrust become employees' perceptions by default because they are "left in the dark." To have the new anti-bullying policy transform the culture, participants in the fact-finding procedures need to be informed of results in a way that is respectful to all involved.

For policies to be effective they "need to be backed by designated groups who are responsible for the sensitive dissemination and maintenance of the policy" (Crawford, 2001, p. 25). Upon creation and implementation of the new policy and enforcement procedures employees at all levels need to be made aware of its goals and provisions. Mandatory education as practiced by many employers for anti-discrimination and sexual harassment conveys the organization's commitment to stopping bullying. Ideally, handouts, brochures, flyers, and posters mounted permanently in prominent places accompany training. Training should also be repeated at designated intervals (e.g., annually).

External Investigators

When workers report bullying organizations might bring in external investigators to assist in investigation and policy implementation. External experts are warranted in cases where organizational members have little experience or expertise in dealing with bullying, where alleged perpetrators hold senior management positions, and when the authority of an external person may be helpful during or dealing with the aftermath of the investigation (Merchant & Hoel, 2003). Investigations can be fairly conducted by impartial, outside professionals who specialize in workplace bullying and aggression interventions. These experts can also teach upper-managers how to more effectively deal with similar situations should they arise in the future.

Training

In addition to policy training, organizations will want to provide ongoing, organization-wide training on both bullying and respectful communication (Keashly & Neuman, 2005). As an element of hands-on training, some organizations have "bullying drills ... similar to fire drills" to prepare them with appropriate responses in the event that bullying occurs (Macintosh, 2006, p. 675). Training must include human resources or employee assistance program professionals and focus on recognizing bullying and protecting reporting workers from harm. Managers in particular need to recognize the warning signs of bullying and respond swiftly to complaints, so they can intervene early when intervention is most effective (Rayner et al., 2002). Furthermore, managers should be encouraged to develop a more compassionate, caring management style that includes developing and constructively using emotional intelligence skills.

Restorative Interventions

Organizations may want to provide support for bullied individuals and affected work teams. Coworker witnesses are often vicariously affected by seeing the suffering of a peer and being helpless to make it stop (Vartia, 2001). Developing target and witness-oriented support is an important aspect of dealing with bullying. Organizations might provide confidential support for targets by persons other than those whose first loyalty is to the employer (e.g., HR, employee assistance programs or EAPs). (Workers should understand that the primary loyalties of HR and EAPs are typically to the employing organization rather than the suffering employee.) A good example of such confidential support is the *practical listeners* (Rains, 2001) program implemented by the UK's postal service. In this program trained volunteer peer staff members provide social support, validate targets' experiences, listen nonjudgmentally, suggest possible choices of action, help handling formal procedures, and maintain confidentiality. On a smaller scale, organizations can establish an ombudsperson with explicit training in bullying.

Pre-employment Screening

Pre-employment screening might be another adopted element of an antibullying effort (Bulatao & VanderBos, 1996). Unless organizations use proven psychological testing and professionals to administer and evaluate test results, however, such testing strategies alone may fail to "screen-out" undesirable workers (Babiak & Hare, 2006). Interviewing techniques such as behavioral interviewing can also help discriminate among candidates. Referencing checking beyond persons the candidates supply is also a promising strategy.

Multi-rater Evaluation Systems

Multi-rater systems such as 360° evaluations can provide a more comprehensive picture of individual behavior (Tehrani, 2001). These can also reduce the possibility of aggressive workers receiving positive evaluations since it is not unusual for managers who supervise bullies to fear them and thus fail to honestly evaluate their performance (Pearson, 1998). What is more, multi-rater systems can include confidential staff evaluation of supervisors—a communicative channel that has the added benefit of identifying supervisory bullying (Lutgen-Sandvik & McDermott, 2008).

Societal-Level Responses

Although cultural norms are the slowest to change, such norms have a profound impact on human communication behavior. We examine two societal-level responses to bullying.

Statutory Protection

As noted, discounting of the problem can be partially explained by lack of statutory protection against bullying. Nearly all organizations produce enforceable anti-discrimination policies to ensure legal compliance. However, only one-fifth of bullying incidents meet the legal criteria for a potential discrimination violation (Namie, 2007). That is, bullying is four times more frequent than illegal discrimination and harassment, but employers can ignore it with little risk of liability because U.S. statutes provide no legal protection against being bullied at work. Thus, organizations may have little impetus to intervene in these situations.

Moreover, courts are typically reluctant to pass judgments that limit commerce (i.e., find in favor of plaintiff employees) (Yamada, 2000). For this reason between 2003 and 2007 advocacy groups pressed legislators in 15 U.S. states to introduce some version of anti-bullying workplace legislation written and disseminated by the Workplace Bullying Institute's Legislative Campaign (Namie, 2006; Yamada, 2000). Currently no state has yet passed a law, although internationally there are good models for such statutory protection. For example, two Canadian provinces have addressed bullying (psychological harassment) in different ways. Quebec implemented an anti-bullying law in June 2004, and Saskatchewan revised the Health and Safety Code in October 2007 to prohibit bullying of employees by codifying bullying as an occupational health hazard. Ireland also prohibits bullying through workplace health and safety codes, and worker protections exist in Scandinavia.

Public Health Campaigns

Longitudinal medical research provides convincing proof that bullying and injustice at work are detrimental to worker health (Elovainio et al., 2006). As such, public health campaigns are an important societal-level response to the risks bullying poses. In this respect, organizational and health communication scholars could join expertise. Indeed, a key challenge facing health and organization communication academics is how to mobilize the power of mass communication to empower organizations to adopt healthy behaviors, to direct policy makers' attention to important health communication issues, and to frame those issues for public debate and resolution.

Conclusion

In this chapter we have reviewed the issue of workplace bullying: its causes, consequences, and potential corrections. The human and institutional losses associated with bullying are inexcusable since it is completely preventable. Despite certain capital-labor ideologies that dehumanize workers and posit that increased pressure increases productivity, there is no evidence that bullying nets any substantive gains for organizations. Quite the contrary—workplace bullying is counter to the best interests of organizations and their stakeholders. There is considerable evidence that bullying affects millions of U.S. workers. As such, it deserves concerted attention by researchers, practitioners, and public policy makers.

References

Adams, A., & Crawford, N. (1992). *Bullying at work: How to confront and overcome it.* London: Virago Press.

Allen, R. E., & Lucerno, M. A. (1996). Beyond resentment: Exploring organizationally targeted insider murder. *Journal of Management Inquiry, 5*(2), 86–103.

Andersson, L. M., & Pearson, C. (1999). Tit for tat? The spiraling effect of incivility in the workplace. *Academy of Management Review, 24*(3), 454–471.

Aquino, K., & Bradfield, M. (2000). Perceived victimization in the workplace: The role of situational factors and victim characteristics. *Organization Science, 11*(5), 525–537.

Babiak, P., & Hare, R. D. (2006). *Snakes in suits: When psychopaths go to work.* New York: HarperCollins.

Barling, J. (1996). The prediction, experience and consequences of workplace violence. In G. R. VanderBos & E. Q. Bulatoao (Eds.), *Violence on the job* (pp. 29–50). Washington, DC: American Psychological Association.

Baron, R. A., & Neuman, J. H. (1998). Workplace aggression – the iceberg beneath the tip of workplace violence: Evidence on its forms, frequency and targets. *Public Administration Quarterly, 21*(4), 446–464.

Bassman, E. S. (1992). *Abuse in the workplace: Management remedies and bottom line impact.* Westport, CT: Quorum Books.

Björkqvist, K., Osterman, K., & Hjelt-Back, M. (1994). Aggression among university employees. *Aggressive Behavior, 20*(2), 173–184.

Brodsky, C. (1976). *The harassed worker.* Lexington, MA: D.C. Health and Company.

Bulatao, E. Q., & VanderBos, G. R. (1996). *Violence on the job: Identifying risks and developing solutions.* Washington, DC: American Psychological Association.

Cascio, W. F. (2006). The economic impact of employee behaviors on organizational performance. In E. E. Lawler & J. O'Toole (Eds.), *America at work: Choices and challenges* (pp. 241–256). New York: Palgrave McMillan.

Chen, P. Y., & Spector, P. E. (1992). Relationships of work stressors with aggression, withdrawal, theft and substance use: An exploratory study. *Journal of Occupational and Organizational Psychology, 65*(3), 177–184.

Cox, H. (1991). Verbal abuse nation wide, part II: Impact and modifications. *Nursing Management, 22,* 66–67.

Coyne, I., Chong, P., Seigne, E., & Randall, P. (2003). Self and peer nominations of bullying: An analysis of incident rates, individual differences, and perceptions of working environment. *European Journal of Work and Organizational Psychology, 12*(3), 209–228.

Coyne, I., Seigne, E., & Randall, P. (2000). Predicting workplace victim status from personality. *European Journal of Work and Organizational Psychology, 9*(3), 335–349.

Crawford, N. (2001). Organisational responses to workplace bullying. In N. Tehrani (Ed.), *Building a culture of respect: Managing bullying at work* (pp. 21–31). London: Taylor & Francis.

Davenport, N., Schwartz, R. D., & Elliott, G. P. (2002). *Mobbing: Emotional abuse in the American workplace* (2nd ed.). Ames, IA: Civil Society Publishing.

De Vogli, R., Ferrie, J. E., Chandola, T., Kivimäki, M., & Marmot, M. G. (2007). Unfairness and health: Evidence from the Whitehall II Study. *Journal of Epidemiology and Community Health, 61*(3), 513–518.

Deetz, S. A. (1992). *Democracy in an age of corporate colonization.* Albany, NY: SUNY.

Di Martino, V., Hoel, H., & Cooper, C. L. (2003). *Preventing violence and harassment in the workplace.* Dublin: European Foundation for the Improvement of Living and Working Conditions.

Douglas, S. C., & Martinko, M. J. (2001). Exploring the role of individual differences in the prediction of workplace aggression. *Journal of Applied Psychology, 86*(4), 547–559.

du Gay, P. (1996). *Consumption and identity at work.* London: Sage.

Duffy, M. K., Ganster, D. C., & Pagon, M. (2002). Social undermining in the workplace. *Academy of Management Journal, 45*(2), 331–351.

Einarsen, S. (1999). The nature and causes of bullying at work. *International Journal of Manpower, 20*(1/2), 16–27.

Einarsen, S., & Hoel, H. (2001, May). *The Negative Acts Questionnaire: Development, validation and revision of a measure of bullying at work.* Paper presented at the 10th European Congress on Work and Organisational Psychology, Prague.

Einarsen, S., Hoel, H., Zapf, D., & Cooper, C. L. (2003). The concept of bullying at work. In S. Einarsen, H. Hoel, D. Zapf & C. L. Cooper (Eds.), *Bullying and emotional abuse in the workplace: International perspectives in research and practice* (pp. 3–30). London: Taylor & Francis.

Einarsen, S., Raknes, B. I., & Mattheisen, S. B. (1994). Bullying and harassment at work and their relationships to work environment quality: An exploratory study. *The European Work and Organizational Psychologist, 4*(4), 381–401.

Elovainio, M., Kivimäki, M., Puttonen, S., Lindholm, H., Pohjonen, T., & Sinervo, T. (2006). Organisational injustice and impaired cardiovascular regulation among female employees *Occupational and Environmental Medicine, 63*(2)41–144.

Hodson, R., Roscigno, V. J., & Lopez, S. H. (2006). Chaos and the abuse of power: Workplace bullying in organizational and interactional context. *Work and Occupations, 33*(4), 382–416.

Hoel, H., & Cooper, C. L. (2000). *Destructive conflict and bullying at work.* Manchester: University of Manchester Institute of Science and Technology (UMIST).

Hoel, H., Cooper, C. L., & Faragher, B. (2001). The experience of bullying in Great Britain: The impact of organizational status. *European Journal of Work and Organizational Psychology, 10*(4), 443–465.

Hoel, H., & Salin, D. (2003). Organisational antecedents of workplace bullying. In S. Einarsen, H. Hoel, D. Zapf & C. L. Cooper (Eds.), *Bullying and emotional abuse in the workplace: International perspectives in research and practice* (pp. 203–218). London: Taylor & Francis.

Hofstede, G. H. (1980). *Culture's consequences: International differences in work-related values.* Newbury Park, CA: Sage.

Jennifer, D., Cowie, H., & Anaiadou, K. (2003). Perceptions and experience of workplace bullying in five different working populations. *Aggressive Behavior, 29*(4), 489–496.

Keashly, L. (1998). Emotional abuse in the workplace: Conceptual and empirical issues. *Journal of Emotional Abuse, 1*(1), 85–117.

Keashly, L. (2001). Interpersonal and systemic aspects of emotional abuse at work: The target's perspective. *Violence and Victims, 16*(3), 233–268.

Keashly, L., & Jagatic, K. (2003). By any other name: American perspectives on workplace bullying. In S. Einarsen, H. Hoel, D. Zapf & C. L. Cooper (Eds.), *Bullying and emotional abuse in the workplace: International perspectives in research and practice* (pp. 31–91). London: Taylor & Francis.

Keashly, L., & Neuman, J. H. (2005). Bullying in the workplace: Its impact and management. *Employee Rights and Employment Policy Journal, 8*(3), 335–373.

Keashly, L., & Nowell, B. L. (2003). Conflict, conflict resolution and bullying. In S. Einarsen, H. Hoel, D. Zapf & C. L. Cooper (Eds.), *Bullying and emotional abuse in the workplace: International perspectives in research and practice* (pp. 339–358). London: Taylor & Francis.

Lawrence, C. (2001). Social psychology of bullying in the workplace. In N. Tehrani (Ed.), *Building a culture of respect: Managing bullying at work* (pp. 61–76). London: Taylor & Francis.

Leymann, H. (1990). Mobbing and psychological terror at workplaces. *Violence and Victims, 5*(1), 119–126.

Leymann, H. (1996). The content and development of mobbing at work. *European Journal of Work and Organizational Psychology, 5*(2), 165–184.

Leymann, H., & Gustafsson, A. (1996). Mobbing at work and the development of post-traumatic stress disorders. *European Journal of Work and Organizational Psychology, 5*(3), 251–275.

Liefooghe, A. P. D., & MacKenzie-Davey, K. (2001). Accounts of workplace bullying: The role of the organization. *European Journal of Work and Organizational Psychology, 10*(4), 375–392.

Lutgen-Sandvik, P. (2003). The communicative cycle of employee emotional abuse: Generation and regeneration of workplace mistreatment. *Management Communication Quarterly, 16*(4), 471–501.

Lutgen-Sandvik, P. (2005). *Water smoothing stones: Subordinate resistance to workplace bullying,* Doctoral dissertation. Tempe, AZ: Arizona State University.

Lutgen-Sandvik, P. (2006). Take this job and ... : Quitting and other forms of resistance to workplace bullying. *Communication Monographs, 73*(4), 406–433.

Lutgen-Sandvik, P. (2008). Intensive remedial identity work: Responses to workplace bullying trauma and stigma. *Organization, 15*(1), 97–119.

Lutgen-Sandvik, P., Alberts, J. K., & Tracy, S. J. (2008, February 15–19). *The communicative nature of workplace bullying and responses to bullying.* Paper presented at the Western States Communication Association Annual Convention, Denver/Boulder, CO.

Lutgen-Sandvik, P., & McDermott, V. (2008). The constitution of employee-abusive organizations: A communication flows theory. *Communication Theory, 18*(2), 304–333.

Lutgen-Sandvik, P., Tracy, S. J., & Alberts, J. K. (2007). Burned by bullying in the American workplace: Prevalence, perception, degree, and impact. *Journal of Management Studies, 44*(6), 837–862.

Macintosh, J. (2006). Tackling workplace bullying. *Issues in Mental Health Nursing, 27*(6), 665–679.

Meares, M. M., Oetzel, J. G., Derkacs, D., & Ginossar, T. (2004). Employee mistreatment and muted voices in the culturally diverse workforce. *Journal of Applied Communication Research, 32*(1), 4–27.

Merchant, V., & Hoel, H. (2003). Investigating complaints of bullying. In S. Einarsen, H. Hoel, D. Zapf & C. L. Cooper (Eds.), *Bullying and emotional abuse in the workplace: International perspectives in research and practice* (pp. 259–269). London: Taylor & Francis.

Namie, G. (2003a). The WBI 2003 report on abusive workplaces. Retrieved 10/19/03, 2003, from www.bullyinginstitute.organization.

Namie, G. (2003b). Workplace bullying: Escalated incivility. *Ivey Business Journal, 68*(2), 1–6.

Namie, G. (2006). Bully Busters: Guide to citizen lobbying. Bellingham, WA: The Workplace Bullying Institute.

Namie, G. (2007). The Workplace Bullying Institute 2007 U.S. Workplace Bullying Survey. Retrieved September 16, 2007, from http://bullyinginstitute.org/wbi-zogby2.html.

Namie, G., & Namie, R. (2000). *The bully at work: What you can do to stop the hurt and reclaim your dignity on the job.* Naperville, IL: Sourcebooks.

Namie, G., & Namie, R. (2004). Workplace bullying: How to address America's silent epidemic. *Employee Rights and Employment Policy Journal, 8*(2), 315–333.

Neuman, J. H., & Baron, R. A. (1997). Aggression in the workplace. In R. A. Giacalone & J. Greenberg (Eds.), *Antisocial behavior in organizations* (pp. 37–67). Thousand Oaks, CA: Sage.

Neuman, J. H., & Baron, R. A. (1998). Workplace violence and workplace aggression: Evidence concerning specific forms, potential causes, and preferred targets. *Journal of Management, 24*(3), 391–411.

Neuman, J. H., & Baron, R. A. (2003). Social antecedents of bullying: A social interactionist perspective. In S. Einarsen, H. Hoel, D. Zapf & C. L. Cooper (Eds.), *Bullying and emotional abuse in the workplace: International perspectives in research and practice* (pp. 185–202). London: Taylor & Francis.

Pearson, C. M. (1998). Organizations as targets and triggers of aggression and violence: Framing rational explanations for dramatic organizational deviance. *Research in the Sociology of Organizations, 15*(1), 197–223.

Price Spratlen, L. (1995). Interpersonal conflict which includes mistreatment in a university workplace. *Violence and Victims, 10*(4), 285–297.

Rains, S. (2001). Don't suffer in silence: Building an effective response to bullying at work. In N. Tehrani (Ed.), *Building a culture of respect: Managing bullying at work* (pp. 155–164). London: Taylor & Francis.

Randall, P. (2001). *Bullying in adulthood: Assessing the bullies and their victims.* New York: Brunner-Routledge.

Rayner, C. (1997). The incidence of workplace bullying. *Journal of Community and Applied Social Psychology, 7*(1), 199–208.

Rayner, C., Hoel, H., & Cooper, C. L. (2002). *Workplace bullying: What we know, who is to blame, and what can we do?* London: Taylor & Francis.

Richards, J., & Daley, H. (2003). Bullying policy: Development, implementation and monitoring. In S. Einarsen, H. Hoel, D. Zapf & C. L. Cooper (Eds.), *Bullying and emotional abuse in the workplace: International perspectives in research and practice* (pp. 247–269). London: Taylor & Francis.

Richman, J. A., Rospenda, K. M., Flaherty, J. A., & Freels, S. (2001). Workplace harassment, active coping, and alcohol-related outcomes. *Journal of Substance Abuse, 13*(3), 347–366.

Rospenda, K. M. (2002). Workplace harassment, service utilization, and drinking outcomes. *Journal of Occupational Health Psychology, 7*(2), 141–155.

Rospenda, K. M., Richman, J. A., Wislar, J. S., & Flaherty, J. A. (2000). Chronicity of sexual harassment and generalized workplace abuse: Effects on drinking outcomes. *Addiction, 95*(12), 1805–1820.

Ryan, W. (1976). *Blaming the victim.* New York: Vantage Books.

Salin, D. (2003). Ways of explaining workplace bullying: A review of enabling, motivating and precipitating structures and processes in the work environment. *Human Relations, 56*(10), 1213–1232.

Spector, P. E. (1975). Relationships of organizational frustrations with reported behavioral reactions of employees. *Journal of Applied Psychology, 60*(5), 635–637.

Tehrani, N. (2001). A total quality approach to building a culture of respect. In N. Tehrani (Ed.), *Building a culture of respect: Managing bullying at work* (pp. 135–154). London: Taylor & Francis.

Tepper, B. J. (2000). Consequences of abusive supervision. *Academy of Management Journal, 43*(2), 178–190.

Tracy, S. J., Lutgen-Sandvik, P., & Alberts, J. K. (2006). Nightmares, demons and slaves: Exploring the painful metaphors of workplace bullying. *Management Communication Quarterly, 20*(2), 148–185.

Vandekerckhove, W., & Commers, M. S. R. (2003). Downward workplace bobbing: A sign of the Times? *Journal of Business Ethics, 45*(1), 41–50.

Vartia, M. (2001). Consequences of workplace bullying with respect to the well-being of its targets and the observers of bullying. *Scandinavian Journal of Work Environment and Health, 27*(1), 63–69.

Wolf, T. M., Randall, H. M., Von Almen, K., & Tynes, L. L. (1991). Perceived mistreatment and attitude change by graduating medical students: A retrospective study. *Medical Education, 25*(2), 184–190.

Wright, L., & Smye, M. (1998). *Corporate abuse.* New York: Simon and Schuster.

Yamada, D. (2000). The phenomenon of "workplace bullying" and the need for status-blind hostile work environment protection. *Georgetown Law Journal, 88*(3), 475–536.

Zapf, D., & Einarsen, S. (2003). Individual antecedents of bullying. In S. Einarsen, H. Hoel, D. Zapf & C. L. Cooper (Eds.), *Bullying and emotional abuse in the workplace: International perspectives in research and practice* (pp. 165–184). London: Taylor & Francis.

Zapf, D., Einarsen, S., Hoel, H., & Vartia, M. (2003). Empirical findings on bullying in the workplace. In S. Einarsen, H. Hoel, D. Zapf & C. L. Cooper (Eds.), *Bullying and emotional abuse in the workplace: International perspectives in research and practice* (pp. 103–126). London: Taylor & Francis.

Zapf, D., & Gross, C. (2001). Conflict escalation and coping with workplace bullying: A replication and extension. *European Journal of Work and Organizational Psychology, 10*(4), 497–522.

Zellars, K. L., Tepper, B. J., & Duffy, M. K. (2002). Abusive supervision and subordinates' organizational citizenship behavior. *Journal of Applied Psychology, 87*(6), 1068–1076.

Chapter 3

Workplace Incivility and Organizational Trust

Matthew J. Gill and Beverly Davenport Sypher

Over the past few decades, U.S. organizations have consistently moved toward models that have created market-like, distant, and transactional relationships and further away from values that help steward employee well-being (Cappelli, 1999). Indeed, it appears that organizations have taken great pains to limit their obligations to members and to focus on factors thought to increase productivity and market shares. Not surprisingly, there are a number of negative consequences associated with employee neglect including high turnover, low commitment and loyalty, and questionable levels of efficiency, not to mention decreased morale, alienated employees, and competitive and uncooperative workers engaged in uncivil and destructive communication practices. According to Pfeffer (Chapter 17 this volume) and others, the adoption of more communal forms of organizing characterized by civil discourse and high levels of employee and organizational trust could reverse such downward spirals and enhance organizational potential.

By most accounts, incivility and antisocial behavior in the workplace are on the rise (Andersson & Pearson, 1999; Pearson, Andersson, & Porath, 2000) with a pervasive sense of individualism and disgruntled entitlement that makes building community and encouraging democracy difficult (Arnett & Arneson, 1999; Bellah, Madsen, Sullivan, Swidler, & Tipton, 1985; Carter, 1998; Forni, 2002; Sypher, 2004). Despite considerable press on high-profile incidents of workplace violence (e.g., Allen & Lucerno, 1996), incivility is far more widespread and insidious, and many more employees are targets of disturbing and destructive verbal aggression. Reports suggest that nearly three-fourths of employees have experienced or witnessed incivility at work (Cortina, Magley, Williams, & Langhout, 2001). The prevalence of incivility is attributed to longer work weeks, constant change, increased technology, escalating demands, less sleep, expressed psychological disorders including depression and anger, work-home tensions, and the mental and physical problems associated with sustained stress (Sypher, 2004). Factors associated with low organizational trust exacerbate incivility: perceived incompetence; lack of openness, honesty, and concern for employees; unreliable managers who fail to follow through, and lack of identification or connectedness to one's place of employment (Shockley-Zalabak, Ellis, & Cesaria, 2000). Authors in this volume and elsewhere argue that civility and trust are the foundations upon which community, democracy, and leadership are built; both are necessary to create highly effective organizations that also protect employees' dignity and well-being.

This chapter highlights findings from a long-term study of an IT organization that expressed on-going collective concerns about trust. In an effort to more fully understand why disgruntled employees so often attributed their concerns to lack of trust, we looked closely at the communication choices employees were using and experiencing, paying particular attention to the issue of incivility. In this chapter, we review findings from this four-year study to examine the interrelationship of civility and trust and explain how each might be enhanced to foster more meaningful relationships and positive experiences at work. The goal of this chapter is to recast incivility as an overarching term for destructive communication and to point out that the less intense forms appear to have stronger negative effects on organizational trust than the more intense forms often considered most dangerous and harmful. A discussion of the various forms of incivility, followed by a review and conceptualization of organizational trust, help frame the argument that unprincipled communicative choices, as situated and context-dependent as they are, occur far too frequently and prevent the type of community building called for in this volume.

In addressing the destructive nature of incivility, especially its capacity to erode organizational members' trust in leaders, coworkers, and organizations, we organize this chapter around definitions of civility and incivility and then move to a discussion of the relationships between trust and distrust. In each section we outline the contributing factors to, and the associated consequences of, these phenomena. Following these definitional distinctions, we examine the interrelationship of incivility and trust at both the individual and organizational levels; we close the chapter with considerations for how organizations might increase the kind of civil discourse that increases trust.

Civility and Incivility

Civility is the act of showing regard, respect, and responsibility for the social demands of the situation. It is in effect being person-centered and other-oriented in ways that protect one's own and others' "positive face." It is the ethic upon which Habermas defines competent communication and entails a "social responsibility and moral imperative that reminds us of our obligations to one another" (Sypher, 2004, p. 258). Civility norms remind us how to address others if we are to "accomplish the task of co-constituting meaning between persons in a postmodern age of virtue, confusion, and contention" (Arnett & Arneson, 1999, p. 1). It is more than just manners, rules of etiquette, or a set of standards for public argument; civility is "the sum of the many sacrifices we are called to make for the sake of living together" (Carter, 1998, p. 11), knowing full well that a gesture of sacrifice and civility may differ from one context or culture to another.

A situated notion of civility suggests there might be considerable debate about specific forms of communication that are considered civil. Some might even argue that manners as a basis of civility impose a class distinction and threaten a hegemony that undermines and excludes those from different social classes or cultures. We argue, however, that civility is much more than manners or rules of social comportment. Civility demands that one speaks in ways that are respectful, responsible, restrained, and principled and avoid that which is offensive, rude, demeaning, and threatening. Although specific forms may vary across cultures, we argue that the appreciation of human dignity, human rights, and social justice is the foundation of civility or *civitas*, that which is good for the community. Although the specific discursive inventions may vary, the goals and intentions of civility demand that employee-face needs are understood and protected in situationally appropriate ways. Such face-saving means that employees' public self-image is protected, and they protect the self-image of others. This does not mean that people must be overly nice or unnecessarily gratuitous, or that conversations must be free from debate or disagreement. It does mean that people are listened to, held responsible for their actions, restrained from doing or saying anything they want, and given the choice to participate or be silent.

Communication behaviors that demean, demoralize, and degrade others define incivility. When incivility ensues, it threatens democracy, community, and the sense of trust that is necessary for both. We submit that incivility varies in both intensity and intention and take issue with the definition of incivility as only "low intensity deviant behavior with ambiguous intent to harm the target, in violation of workplace norms for mutual respect" (Andersson & Pearson, 1999, p. 457). Uncivil behaviors, they add, are characteristically rude and discourteous and display a lack of regard for others. While we agree with the latter, we argue that incivility is not necessarily or even often *subtle* or *ambiguous*—it is often fairly clear when people are rude and disrespectful. Neither is it always or even often *unintentional* and *low* in intensity. Unlike the argument made by Cortina and colleagues (2001) that incivility is a "milder" form of psychological mistreatment, the findings reported by Gill (2007) and reviewed in this chapter suggest that less intense forms of incivility are not particularly *mild*. In fact, less intense forms of incivility were more strongly related to low levels of both interpersonal and organizational trust and thus potentially more destructive over time than more intense but less frequent incidents of bullying and harassment. Thus, we disagree that even lower levels of incivility are necessarily "milder" in terms of harm done over time. Perhaps people who speak softly and use polite speech to undermine and manipulate for self-gain can be just as destructive, if not more so, than those who yell, scream, throw things, threaten, and use profanity.

In our work, the low-level workplace aggression described by Baron and Neuman (1996) was more strongly related to low levels of organizational trust than were more intense forms of verbal aggression. Although incivility can take a variety of forms, from the less intense behaviors of interrupting and ignoring others to the more intense forms of threats, intimidation, and verbal aggression, we argue that it is not always or even often subtle, and the intent to harm is not always absent. Quite often incivility is an overt attempt to disarm, distance, disrespect, or silence another in ways that privilege one's own views, position, and possibilities. Moreover, the incivility that is considered less intense is ubiquitous, more often goes unchecked, and is rarely constrained by policy. Over time it leads to withdrawal, anger, low self-esteem, lethargy, and low levels of trust that are immensely problematic and destructive to individuals and organizations. Any form of incivility is potentially destructive, and we worry that defining it as "low-intense," "subtle," and "ambiguous" renders it less problematic and potentially less deserving of our attention.

Consequences of Incivility

All forms of incivility have the potential to seriously influence work, workers, and the workplace in exceedingly destructive ways. Less intense incivility, especially when it is a pervasive feature of organizational life, may be more harmful than intense, intentional, and more aggressive forms of workplace interaction. Sypher (2004) argued that:

> Repeated instances of disregard, exclusion, interrupted talk and insults are no less troublesome and no less likely to escalate and lead to feelings of isolation, anxiety and lowered self esteem than more intense and intentional forms of name calling, profanity, put downs and other more verbally aggressive displays considered deviant, unjust, and harassing. (p. 260)

The effects of continuous exposure to low-intensity, uncivil communication can build over time and create a great deal of harm and distress for those targeted (Baron & Neuman, 1996).

Incivility can be frustrating, anger-producing, and consequently harmful to the well-being of the one repeatedly interrupted, questioned, disregarded, and accused of being wrong. It is clearly harmful to the relationships necessary for cooperative behavior. Exposure to persistent incivility is associated with a number of individual problems including health issues such as stress, depression, anxiety, insomnia, poor eating habits, increased smoking and drinking, and psychological issues such as low self-esteem, withdrawal, and depression (Cortina et al., 2001; Sypher, 2004). In this same vein, incivility also negatively affects organizational outcomes. It can decrease job involvement, job satisfaction, and organizational commitment, and increase absenteeism, tardiness, turnover, and time spent worrying, all of which results in decreased productivity and increased costs to organizations (Cortina et al., 2001; Pearson et al., 2000). Incivility also damages or destroys the trust necessary for building communities, relationships, and organizations (Gill, 2007); thus an understanding of trust helps us better understand civility and the lack thereof.

Organizational Trust and Distrust

Trust in organizations is members' faith in or reliance on the integrity, strength, ability, and surety of organizations and their leaders. It connotes confidence and belief in the uprightness of organizational actions and actors. When trust is present, members rely on and place their confidence in employing organizations, supervisors, and coworkers. Trust, therefore, is not

> *cordial hypocrisy*: the strong tendency of people in organizations, because of loyalty or fear, to pretend that there is trust when there is not, being polite in the name of harmony when cynicism and distrust are active poisons, eating away at the very existence of the organization. (Solomon & Flores, 2001, p. 4)

Rather, *authentic trust* is social and relational; trust is developed, maintained, and changed through interaction. "It is something we make, we create, we build, we maintain, we sustain with our promises, out commitments, our emotions, and our sense of our own integrity" (Solomon & Flores, p. 5). It is then something we create and maintain communicatively, through honesty, openness, concern for others, and follow through (Shockley-Zalabak et al., 2000).

Trust has been identified as a fundamental element and an unavoidable part of social interaction (Gambetta, 1988), often considered an important and desirable resource for social systems (Cook, 2001; Fukuyama, 1995; Hardin, 2002; Kramer & Cook, 2004a; Kramer & Tyler, 1996; Putnam, 1993, 1995, 2000; Sztompka, 1999). Trust is an important and fundamental component of the organizing process, sensemaking, and the construction of reality for organizational members. It only comes into being through social interaction, however, and the characteristics of these interactions are constantly shifting due to personal differences, situational requirements and constraints, and the historical nature of relationships (Heimer, 2001).

Most scholars agree that our day-to-day trust decisions are made without much cognitive processing. Messick and Kramer (2001) call this "swift trust," the propensity to make quick, unevaluated, yet lasting, decisions to trust. As Putnam (2000) argued, "If we don't have to balance every exchange instantly, we can get a lot more accomplished" (p. 21). In organizational settings trust can help reduce transaction costs, socialize others and facilitate appropriate forms of address (Kramer & Cook, 2004a). Trust enables us to manage uncertainty, reduce vulnerability and accept risk, but this makes trust highly exploitable and potentially costly when diminished (Gambetta, 1988). Because social life is risky and people are vulnerable, there is always the "possibility of exit, betrayal, and defection" (Gambetta, pp. 218–219) that can jeopardize relationships, threaten organizational functioning, and make trust such an important organizational resource.

In effect, trust is both an antecedent and consequence of communication choices. Deutsch (1958) found that individuals were more likely to trust each other if they communicated freely before making a decision. Trust is a language-based phenomenon that "results from acts of interpretation" (Shockley-Zalabak et al., 2000, p. 8). Earlier studies focused on trust as a static variable to be manipulated. For example, the timing and perceived adequacy of feedback (Folger & Konovsky, 1989; Konovsky & Cropanzano, 1991; Muchinsky, 1977; O'Reilly & Roberts, 1974; Sapienza & Korsgaard, 1996) and perceived accuracy, explanations for decisions, and openness (Ellis & Shockley-Zalabak, 1999) were found to correlate strongly with trust in supervisors. More recent approaches focus on the dynamic and relational factors that develop, maintain, and damage trust.

Trust becomes more important when social bonds exist and attributes of trustworthiness are affected by relational issues rather than instrumental ones (Tyler & Degoey, 1996). It is influenced by the actions of authorities, and respect, perceived standing with authorities, and benevolent intentions—prime determinants of trustworthy attributions. Therefore, trust is enhanced when employees respect their supervisors and believe they are attempting to do good, not just that they get the job done.

Mayer et al. (1995) argued that the nature and bases of trust for organizationally-based relationships may be different from other relationships. Kramer (1999) suggested six bases of trust in organizational settings: dispositional, history-based, third-party conduit, category-based, role-based, and rule-based. Dispositional trust is the tendency to trust without others earning that trust—what Deutsch (1958) called a *pathology of trust.*

History-based trust stems from the willingness to believe in others based on a past relationship, a form of trust that is fostered or damaged depending upon cumulative experiences (Boon & Holmes, 1991; Deutsch 1958). Third-parties act as trust conduits when influential colleagues provide information (possibly skewed and biased) about others based on their personal experiences or gossip (Burt & Knez, 1995). This is a sort of balance theory notion of trust. You trust someone who is trusted by someone you trust. Category-based trust suggests we are more likely to trust those who share membership in a common group because we tend to ascribe positive characteristics to persons similar to ourselves (Brewer, 1981). Rule-based trust is based on the "shared understandings regarding the system of rules regarding appropriate behavior" (Kramer, 1999, p. 579), a form of trust typically sustained by organizational socialization (March & Olsen, 1989).

There appear, then, two general types of trust—those stemming from social interaction (history-based, third-party conduits) and those stemming from organizational culture (category-, role-, and rule-based trust). These bases of trust provide important insights into its antecedents and consequences for organizations and highlight the importance of relational history, information gathered from third parties, perceived in-group status, and socially constructed norms and rules in determining trust among coworkers.

Consequences of Decreased Trust

Trust violations at work have been found to decrease current levels of trust, reduce trust to zero, or potentially create distrust (Lewicki & Bunker, 1996). It is important to note here that distrust is not necessarily the opposite of trust. Both are cognitive and emotional processes in which actors are suspicious of motives, doubt the veracity of claims, and lack confidence in organizations or their members. Scholars are generally of two opinions regarding the relationship between trust and distrust. Some believe they are opposing ends of one continuum, a continuum across which people move back and forth (Barnes, 1983; Bigley & Pearce, 1998; Kramer, 1999; Lewicki, McAllister, & Bies, 1998). Others argue that distrust and trust are unique constructs (Keyton & Smith, 2003; Tomlinson & Lewicki, 2003), and we can have varying degrees of trust and varying degrees of distrust.

Lower levels of trust are linked to a variety of negative consequences including lost productivity, inefficiency, reduced profits, damaged social identities, diminished effectiveness, lower levels of satisfaction, and unhealthy organizations and personal lives (Bies & Tripp, 1996; Ellis & Shockley-Zalabak, 1999; Kramer & Cook, 2004b; Shockley-Zalabak et al., 2000). In fact, Helliwell and Huang (2005) found that when respondents increased their trust in management by one point on a ten-point scale, the resulting job satisfaction increase was equivalent to receiving a 36% pay increase. Moreover, a decrease of one point reduced job satisfaction equal to receiving a 36% pay decrease.

High levels of distrust exacerbate all of these negative outcomes. Workers are more than dissatisfied and suspicious; they get cynical, angry, withdraw, retaliate, and often explode when trust is violated. They potentially lose confidence in their supervisors, their coworkers, and themselves, and they develop a sense of futility, take legal action, and act in other ways that negatively affect their own and the organization's quality of life.

Bies and Tripp (1996) suggest two types of trust violations—ones that harm the civic order or ones that harm social identity. Harm to the civic order occurs when there are rule violations, honor violations, or abusive authority "judged to violate a fundamental trust between the employee and the organization and its management" (Bies & Tripp, p. 248). Rule violations are those actions perceived to violate rules and regulations (e.g., changing the rules after the fact or a breach of a formal contract). Honor violations are actions that are inconsistent with the dominant ethical code or organizational norms (e.g., shirking job responsibilities, breaking promises, lying, stealing ideas or credit, and revealing secrets). Abusive authority or abuses of power result from abuses of position for personal gain (e.g., the intolerable boss, the corrupt boss, the toxic boss). These actions violate explicit or implicit trust between organizational members and the organization or management. Harm to social identity occurs when people believe they are victims of interpersonal attacks that "had the effect of impugning or undermining their social identity or reputation" (Bies & Tripp, p. 251). In effect, face-threatening acts violate trust. These attacks included such acts as public criticism, insults, and wrongful or unfair accusations or uncivil acts that demean, degrade, or demoralize. Thus, incivility violates an implicit trust about the sanctity of one's dignity and respect.

In summary, trust is a dynamic, fragile but exceedingly important organizational resource. The context in which trust occurs is an important consideration because the various constraints and expectations of the workplace alter the manner in which trust develops, and is maintained, valued, and violated. Trust is the foundation upon which relationships are developed and connectedness to others and workplaces are built. Because it helps reduce uncertainty, buffer risk, and manage vulnerability, there are also potentially large negative and harmful interpersonal and organizational outcomes associated with violations of trust.

The Impact of Incivility on Trust

Ongoing incivility is likely a contributing factor to eroded and damaged organizational trust because it cripples organizational members' ability to communicate, discuss, and dialogue in ways that build communal organizations. Moreover, there is evidence that the increase of incivility coincides with a decrease in trust. For example, in a recent survey over half (52%) of the respondents said they did not trust their organization's management and did not believe the information they received (Katcher, 2002). In an ALF-CIO study (2001), almost two-thirds of the employees reported little or no trust in their employers. Incivility may provide an explanation for these low levels of trust.

In a study of a hightech, fastpaced, IT organization, we examined subtle and intense forms of incivility and their effect on organizational and interpersonal trust (Gill, 2007). The subtle forms of incivility were drawn from Cortina et al.'s (2001) measure of incivility, and the intense forms came from the high end of Sypher's (2004) intensity continuum (see Table 3.1 for descriptions of the uncivil acts examined). In particular, the relationships and interpersonal trust between supervisors and direct reports were revealing.

Impact of Incivility on Trust

Interpersonal-Level Trust

Focusing on the interpersonal relationship between employees and their immediate supervisors, our findings revealed a strong negative correlation between trust with one's supervisor and incivility. That is, the more uncivil employees considered their supervisors to be, the less trust they reported having in their supervisors. More importantly, we found (as argued earlier in this chapter) that subtle forms of incivility appeared to be more harmful to the relationships employees had with their supervisors than more intense forms. This finding is consistent with Sypher's (2004) concern

Table 3.1 Low- and High-intensity Incivility Acts

Subtle- or Low-intensity
Paid little attention to statements or showed little interest in subordinate's opinions
Made demeaning or derogatory remarks about subordinate
Addressed subordinate in unprofessional terms
Doubted subordinate's judgment on a matter over which he or she has responsibility
Put subordinate down or was condescending
Ignored or excluded subordinate from professional camaraderie
Made unwanted attempts to draw subordinate into a discussion of personal matters

High-intensity
Threatened subordinate
Yelled at subordinate
Swore or used profanity offensively toward subordinate
Physically assaulted subordinate

about the potential cumulative effect of disrespectful actions and behaviors. Excluding, ignoring, or demeaning an employee appears potentially more damaging in terms of trust than yelling, threatening, or being verbally or physically aggressive. Perhaps the subtle forms happen more often, go unchecked longer, are tolerated more, and consequently have a more negative cumulative effect than the stronger or more intense outbursts that may happen very infrequently.

Yelling, swearing inappropriately, threatening, and verbally abusing or harassing behaviors had weaker associations with lower trust levels. In fact, the predictive ability of subtle incivility for interpersonal trust was found to be very high (a B value of −0.698 with an absolute value of the beta coefficient of 0.642). The lack of predictive power for the more intense forms of incivility on trust was surprising but understandable after examining the degree and scope of incivility reported. Since subtle forms of incivility have such a negative effect on trust, one might assume that more intense forms of incivility would have an even stronger negative effect. However, these data did not paint such a picture.

The most intense form of incivility included in this study, physical violence, was the act least correlated with trust and its dimensions. One potential explanation for intense incivility's lack of predictive power is that when the intense forms of incivility occur they are affecting a different construct than trust. Perhaps the more intense forms of incivility are affecting distrust more strongly than trust. Such an explanation would support the conceptualization that trust and distrust are two related, but different concepts (Keyton & Smith, 2003; Tomlinson & Lewicki, 2003). Even though this study was not designed to examine whether trust and distrust are separate constructs, this hypothesized distinction between the two gains footing in this study's findings and presents a possible explanation for the different effect of intense and subtle incivility on trust.

As Tomlinson and Lewicki (2003) argued, trust is not necessarily the opposite of distrust. The two constructs may represent two different continua. As such, intense incivility then could actually increase *distrust* rather than lowering trust. For example, employees might not trust a supervisor as much if he or she is subtly uncivil, but they might actually distrust those who are intensely uncivil and abusive. The intense incivility scale developed for this study then might provide the operational definitions for Bies and Tripp's (1996) list of trust violations and clarify the relationship between trust and distrust. This is an area we would like to explore further.

Another finding from the Gill (2007) study is worth noting here. Both the cognitive and affective dimensions of trust (McAllister, 1995) were damaged by incivility, but it was the cognitive dimension that was damaged more by both low-level and intense incivility. Past research on incivility and interpersonal communication more generally suggests that high levels of interpersonal insensitivity reduce degrees of liking, and Gill's findings substantiate this. Incivility predicted low levels of affect-based trust. This suggests when supervisors are disrespectful, even in subtle ways, their employees do not see them as open, supportive, caring, or trusted bosses. However, we found that uncivil supervisors even more strongly damaged the cognitive dimensions of trust. Uncivil bosses were considered less competent, professional, dedicated, and reliable. So not only do these findings suggest employees like uncivil supervisors less than civil supervisors (and co-workers), they also suggest that employees question the managerial competency of uncivil supervisors more than civil supervisors. Indeed, position or legitimate power does not excuse incivility or impede employees from doubting another's competence or ability. Incivility appears not only to affect significantly the emotional attachments people have with others, it affects even more strongly people's perceptions of the offenders' professional competence which might potentially thwart their aspirations for upward mobility (at least in the same workplace). Perhaps we may have less patience and tolerance for "brutal bosses" (Hornstein, 1996) and greater acknowledgement of the harm that even their subtle incivilities can do to the organization and employees.

Another explanation for why incivility is more strongly related to cognitive rather than affective bases of trust could be the trend to more transactional and market-like relationships in American workplaces that some argue have left workers less emotionally attached to their coworkers and supervisors (Pfeffer, Chapter 17 this volume). As a result, employees may be hurt less emotionally by incivility from their supervisors because they are not emotionally invested in the relationship to begin with. Transactional organizational relationships have led workers to base more decisions, particularly where to work and for how long, on compensation rather than the type of organization, the meaningfulness of the work, and the treatment of employees. People may be more concerned with the ability to advance and earn more money than with more existential aspects such as meaningful work and satisfying relationships. Also since high levels of incivility were shown to result in lower levels of cognitive-based trust, people may be more concerned with a supervisor's ability to lead them or do their job well (especially in a competitive, fast paced, changing, high-tech company) than with their ability or willingness to develop an emotional connection to employees. However, the display of incivility jeopardizes both. Since judgments of competence are at stake, uncivil supervisors potentially damage their own career opportunities while also damaging their employees' quality of work life.

Overall, the data collected in the Gill (2007) study support the notion that incivility is a significant predictor of interpersonal and organizational trust. The data demonstrate that acts of less intense forms of incivility were more damaging to interpersonal trust than acts of intense incivility. In short, these findings position incivility at the center of focus in explanations of trust (and potentially distrust). The two are related in important ways on an interpersonal level, and what happens at the interpersonal level, especially between employees and their supervisors, is a strong predictor of organizational-level understandings and outcomes.

Organizational-level Trust

While interpersonal trust is based on relationships between organizational members, organizational trust refers to the level of trust employees have in their organizations. This trust, however, is fostered through interaction between co-workers, supervisors, and organizational leadership. Shockley-Zalabak and colleagues (2000) developed a multidimensional, five-factor model of trust that includes competence, openness and honesty, concern for employees, reliability, and identification.

Competence is leadership effectiveness and the degree to which the organization can survive in the marketplace. Openness and honesty are associated with organizational trust (Gabarro, 1987); the more open and honest organizational leaders are, the more likely organizational members will trust the organization (Ellis & Shockley-Zalabak, 1999). Concern for employees is a third dimension of trust, and the degree to which the organization is considered reliable (e.g. consistent and dependable) is the fourth dimension of the trust scale. The fifth dimension is identification, the degree to which organizational members are connected to the organization's goals, values, norms, and beliefs. These five dimensions are embedded in Zalabak-Shockley et al.'s (2000) measure of organizational trust examined in the Gill (2007) study.

In addition to asking about interpersonal civility (i.e., supervisors), we asked about perceived incivility at the organizational level. Only a handful of the employees in this study had observed intense organizational incivility (less than 2%), but considerably more reported observing less intense incivility (42.5%) across the organization. Both levels of organizational incivility were higher than interpersonal incivility (.3% and 11.7% respectively), but lower than previous studies. Rayner (1997), for example, reported that more than 70% of employees experienced incivility. In Cortina et al.'s (2001) study, 71% of judicial system employees reported experiencing incivility from their supervisors or coworkers within the last five years. At the same time, the employees in our study reported a level of trust above the midpoint (X = 3.31) and significantly higher than the international normative data (X = 2.70) presented by Shockley-Zalabak et al. (2000). Therefore, although the organization did not indicate what one might consider a high level of trust, it did have a rather high level of trust compared to the average of organizations making up the organizational trust normative database.

The comparatively low level of workplace incivility and high level of organizational trust was somewhat surprising given that the organization expressed concerns about trust *and* had many of the antecedents associated with incivility. At the time of the study the organization had undergone a great deal of change over the last five to seven years. Moreover, it functions in a high stress, high-velocity environment, and in interviews workers pointed to multiple instances of disrespect and disregard. In a number of unsolicited e-mails during the course of the study, employees described a laundry list of actions that led us to believe we would find low trust and high incivility, but such was not the case.

One potential explanation is that the nature of the work at this organization has prepared the employees to deal with many of the things expected to cause incivility. For example, in an IT organization, change is both expected and embraced. There are constant changes to computer hardware and software, and the entire IT industry is one of constant change, growth, and turnover. Therefore, IT workers may be better suited to deal with organizational change than the average worker. It may very well be that incivility is not a result of the nature of work but is rather dependent upon the type and composition of relationships employees have at work. If employees have strong, positive relationships at work, then incivility should be low and trust high. Organizations must nurture those types of relationships, however, something not likely to happen as long as Americans continue to view work relationships as transactional and market-like in nature.

Similar to the findings on the interpersonal level, subtle forms of incivility had much stronger associations with organizational trust than did intense forms. This was also true for each dimension of the organizational trust scale. Once again these findings support the notion that the less intense behaviors that occur more often (versus more severe but less frequent forms of organizational mistreatment) have a stronger impact on trust. However, at the organizational level, trust was not as strongly correlated with incivility as was interpersonal trust. Although every scale was significantly correlated with both subtle and intense incivility, none of the correlations were strong. Most values did not exceed the 0.400 level, but when taken together, the overall organizational trust measure correlated with incivility a bit stronger ($r = 0.532$).

There was a difference in terms of how the various dimensions of organizational trust correlated with incivility, however. At the interpersonal level, incivility was a stronger predictor of cognitive-based aspects of trust. At the organizational level, incivility demonstrated stronger correlations with what would be considered affect-based trust subscales. Incivility was most strongly correlated with *openness and honesty* and *concern for employees*. One potential explanation for this contradictory finding between levels is differing targets of respondent answers. On the interpersonal level, respondents answered questions regarding a very specific and important organizational relationship (e.g., with supervisor). On the organizational level, respondents answered questions about a generalized group of others. Perhaps when people are emotionally invested in relationships, they are willing to explain away incivility in order to develop or maintain the emotional and professional connections with others who have direct importance and control over their work lives. In this way, the data may support the "love is blind" hypothesis that argues prior trust would soften the blow of betrayal and that people are, therefore, granted the benefit of the doubt because of an accumulated history of otherwise benign and positive experiences (Robinson, Dirks, & Ozcelik, 2001). Or, this result may be due to a "love is forgiveness" hypothesis. Even though people recognize incivility for what it is, they tolerate it because they have little choice or because they want to maintain a level of decorum with bosses and coworkers. This is a fruitful question for future research.

Even though intense incivility proved to be a stronger predictor of organizational than interpersonal trust, its effect was always less than that of subtle incivility. One potential explanation is that intense incivility just did not occur enough to affect perceptions of trust. Although it had the stronger effect when present, it just was not present enough to make it more important to the prediction model than subtle incivility, which was far more common. In summary, we found that both interpersonal and organizational trust were negatively related to incivility and subtle incivility was a stronger predictor of organizational trust than intense incivility. The strong relationships between civility and trust prompts the question: How do we promote civility, and in turn build interpersonal and organizational trust that enhances the quality of worklife and work?

Promoting Civility

The path to increasing civility and trust is necessarily based on communicative choices, strategies, and avoidances we examine in this section. In what follows, we review choices that protect our own and others' face, position requests in ways that downplay imposition, privilege inclusive pronouns, employ politeness, use euphemisms when appropriate rather than distasteful or uncomfortable terms, control conversations with cooperative rather than disruptive interruptions, listen and show restraint in talk time, and show restraint in temper, desire, power, and ego. The answer is also a function of education, modeling, and values promotion.

This section focuses primarily on linguistic strategies that could be used to decrease the potential for incivility including insults and rude, disrespectful, offensive, exclusionary behavior. These acts have been shown to be more harmful over time perhaps because they are often tolerated, overlooked, and habituated and because they more strongly predict low levels of trust. However, these strategies are also offered as ways to prevent, manage, or perhaps blunt the bullying and harassment that demand the legal, structural, and policy-oriented strategies addressed in other chapters in this volume.

We first turn to civil communicative choices that are informed by a variety of research traditions including discourse and conversational analysis and interpersonal competence. The field of communication has long been informed by the now classic work of Irving Goffman (1955; 1981) and his suggestion that face management is a common conversational want and need that compels people to act in ways that preserve their own and others' public self images. One way then to promote civility is to avoid "negative face" (Brown & Levinson, 1987), the face-threatening acts that compromise the desire for autonomy, and threaten "positive face," the desire and need to be viewed positively by and connected to others. Attempts to dismiss the face needs of others often disallow positive face or "face saving." Understanding the need for positive face helps to explain why uncivil supervisors are considered less trustworthy and communicatively competent.

McGlone and Batchelor (2003) offer a specific face-management strategy that could promote civility: uncomfortable and distasteful topics might be spoken about euphemistically because referring to them directly, especially at work, threatens interactants' positive face. Such topics as sex and bathroom behaviors are those topics that often make people uncomfortable and ones in which euphemisms are not only less offensive but also more polite. They are, however, topics around which a good deal of profanity and insults have been created. Although fairly commonplace and not always offensive, such topics can make people feel uncomfortable and when their use is tolerated and even encouraged, the floodgates are opened for more inappropriate profanity and insults. Referring to a distasteful topic is a threat to positive face that could indicate a "blithe disregard" for others' sensibilities but also, "the communicator's face is threatened by the shadow his own utterance casts on his public self " (McGlone & Batchelor, p. 260). They used the discussion of urination and its linguistic manifestations to make the point. No doubt it is a common human act but one that coworkers would just as soon not discuss or hear discussed in expletives or common phrases.

Euphemism (eu + pheme), they add, has face value because its Greek roots translates to pleasant speaking, a way to protect the positive face of the speaker and those addressed. Speaking euphemistically is a way to avoid embarrassing and making others uncomfortable, as well as avoiding being crude or discourteous. Although there clearly are situations in which people negotiate the appropriateness of euphemisms and "pleasant speaking," this communicative tactic does suggest a level of manners and professionalism regarding civility at work. People simply do not speak publicly at work the way they do at home, in the gym, in the privacy of an office, or at other places where negotiated understandings of acceptable talk are necessarily different.

Another way to navigate threats to one's own and other's face is by making both direct and indirect requests in ways that downplay imposition. Rather than giving blatant commands or making demands of coworkers or subordinates, managers preserve civility and even gain credibility by asking employees to take on a task by recognizing its potential as an imposition. Such recognition helps to protect positive public self-images of the persons making the request (i.e., speakers reveal their ability and willingness to think in terms of the other) and saves the face of those to whom the request is directed. We disagree with McGlone's and Batchelor's (2003) suggestion that impositions should be downplayed, but we agree that face-saving is more likely when requests are accompanied with preconditions for compliance. For example, "Are you able to take on this assignment?" or "Would you be willing to be a part of this task force?" Simply giving orders and making demands is threatening, demeaning, face threatening, and in effect, uncivil.

There are a variety of other linguistic choices that could encourage civility in the workplace. Using inclusive pronouns, avoiding overuse of first person pronouns, and avoiding second person pronouns (e.g., "What are *you* going to do?" vs. "What are *we* going to do?") also make for a more unified collective. Gibb's (1961) typology of defensive communication suggests that questions of "how" are less likely to produce defensiveness than questions of "why." Additionally, using the pronoun "you" is more likely to produce defensiveness than "we." He, among others, admonishes us to take the "I" out of talk and make "we" the norm. Such choices reveal micro-inequities that, intentional or not, privilege oneself over others. In effect, certain types of requests are less likely to produce defensive responses, and inclusive pronouns can promote civility.

Micro-affirmations can also promote civility. One of the most underutilized and under-appreciated management strategies is saying "thank you." Reaffirming people's contributions, self worth, good judgment, and sensibilities is one of the best ways to build self-esteem and create a culture of respect for others. Thank you is a universal politeness strategy that mitigates face threats, engenders trust, helps develop meaningful relationships, and encourages commitment to the work, the organization, and to one another (Brown & Levinson, 1987).

Cooperative interruptions are yet another conversational strategy that can engender respect, reaffirm inclusion, value others' contributions, and reduce competition. Although interruptions and topic shifts are typically seen as disruptive, rude, or self-serving attempts to take control and abuse power, *cooperative* interruptions are much less likely to be competitive and most often show agreement, support, and enthusiasm for others' contributions and voice (Zhao & Gantz, 2003). In effect then, interruptions, used in situationally-appropriate and negotiated ways, are a form of turn-taking that encourage identification, affirmation, and convey listening—one of the single best ways to empower large numbers of people (Voehl, 1995). Not only is listening reaffirming to those addressed, it also generates benefits for the listener. Better listeners are promoted more often and found at higher levels in the organization more often than those with less developed listening abilities (Sypher, Bostrom, & Seibert, 1989). Listening can also be a significant predictor of upward mobility (Sypher & Zorn, 1986). Indeed one must listen to lead, as it enhances the credibility or "positive face" of the listener and enhances the self image of those listened to.

This is hardly an exhaustive list of ways to promote civility. Self deprecation, humor, smiles, remembering others' concerns and needs, offering support and comfort, modeling what is expected and needed in others, showing restraint, and tempering emotional outbursts are also important. Apologies go a long way in restoring dignity, promoting harmony, preserving one's dignity, and, thus, promoting civility and trust. The enactment of civility and development and preservation of trust are complex and calibrated sets of face-saving and face-protecting strategies and competencies, but they are also as simple as managing micro-inequities through the use of inclusive pronouns and modeling micro-affirmations through cooperative interruptions and expressions of gratitude. Although we should not ignore Brown and Levinson's (1987) universal politeness strategies and Goffman's (1955) explanation of face-work, we also should be mindful of the complex nature of situated meanings and negotiated understandings of what is reaffirming, appropriate, and possible. All of this is to say that civility can and must be promoted. It is first and foremost constituted through communicative choices, linguistic avoidances, and ever-mindful attempts at restraint, respect, and responsibility to others and the collective.

Conclusion

The content, tone, and form of communication have serious consequences for organizations and organizational life. When civility prevails, possibilities present themselves and potential increases. When incivility is the norm, we harm ourselves, those with whom we work, and the organizations that employ us. We also likely take that pain to our homes and negatively affect our partners and families. Indeed incivility is insidious. Moreover, managing damaged relationships and the work lost because of them takes time away from tasks and potentially damages productivity. Investments in civility increase "opportunity costs" by shaping meaningful work lives and organizations; trust and community are the dividends of

such investments. Repeated instances of disregard and disrespect are lia-
bilities that will bankrupt the person and the collective. If left unchecked,
incivility can create a hostile, unpleasant, and mean workplace that makes
cooperation and consideration impossible and workdays unbearable. It
makes both people and organizations literally sick and can become habituated and intensified with little understanding of what has happened.
Even if there is no intent to harm, damage is done. Even if unpleasantries
are ambiguous, people will fill in their own meanings and question their
own competencies. In an age where human capital remains our greatest
asset, we cannot afford such a downward spiral. It is bad for the individual, the workplace, and society.

Our goals should be to resist incivility and thwart or at least contain others' tendencies for the same. To create organizations as communities, we
must help employees in need, celebrate accomplishments, forgive mistakes, express gratitude, learn face-work, become better listeners, and
avoid what makes people uncomfortable and that which is distasteful. We
must be mindful and control our impulses, reign in our egos, back away
from individualism and self-promotion, recognize others' needs and tal-
ents, find ways to introduce performance opportunities, and invest in the
opportunity costs that enhance commitment and loyalty. Other important
considerations are to promote long-term employment, ease work-family
tensions, cultivate trust through honesty and reliability, and champion
practices and policies that encourage community and enable human
possibilities.

References

AFL-CIO. (2001). *Workers rights in America: What employees think about their jobs and employers.* Washington, DC: AFL-CIO.
Allen, R. E., & Lucerno, M. A. (1996). Beyond resentment: Exploring organiza-
tionally targeted insider murder. *Journal of Management Inquiry, 5*(2), 86–103.
Andersson, L. M., & Pearson, C. (1999). Tit for tat? The spiraling effect of incivil-
ity in the workplace. *Academy of Management Review, 24*(3), 454–471.
Arnett, R. C., & Arneson, P. (1999). *Dialogic civility in a cynical age: Community,
hope, and interpersonal relationships.* Albany, NY: State University of New
York Press.
Barnes, L. B. (1983). Managing the paradox of organizational trust. *Harvard Busi-
ness Review, 61*(3), 107–116.
Baron, R. A., & Neuman, J. H. (1996). Workplace violence and workplace aggres-
sion: Evidence on their relative frequency and potential causes. *Aggressive
Behavior, 22*(1), 161–173.
Bellah, R. N., Madsen, R., Sullivan, W. M., Swidler, A., & Tipton, S. M. (1985).
Habits of the heart: Individualism and commitment in American life. Berkeley,
CA: University of California Press.
Bies, R. J., & Tripp, T. M. (1996). Beyond distrust: Getting even and the need for

revenge. In R. M. Kramer & T. Tyler (Eds.), *Trust in organizations* (pp. 246–260). Thousand Oaks, CA: Sage.

Bigley, G. A., & Pearce, J. L. (1998). Straining for shared meaning in organizational science: Problems of trust and distrust. *Academy of Management Review, 23*(2), 405–421.

Boon, S. D., & Holmes, J. G. (1991). The dynamics of interpersonal trust: Resolving uncertainty in the face of risk. In R. A. Hinde & J. Groebel (Eds.), *Cooperation and prosocial behavior* (pp. 167–182). New York: Cambridge University Press.

Brewer, M. B. (1981). Ethnocentrism and its role in interpersonal trust. In M. B. Brewer & B. E. Collins (Eds.), *Scientific inquiry and the social sciences* (pp. 345–359). New York: Josey-Bass.

Brown, P., & Levinson, S. C. (1987). *Politeness: Some universals in language usage.* Cambridge: Cambridge University Press.

Burt, R. S., & Knez, M. (1995). Kinds of third party effects on trust. *Rationality and Society, 7*(1), 255–292.

Cappelli, P. (1999). *The new deal at work: Managing the market-driven workforce.* Boston: Harvard Business School Press.

Carter, S. L. (1998). *Civility: Manners, moral, and the etiquette of democracy.* New York: Basic Books.

Cook, K. S. (Ed.). (2001). *Trust in society.* New York: Russell Sage Foundation.

Cortina, L. M., Magley, V. J., Williams, J. H., & Langhout, R. D. (2001). Incivility in the workplace: Incidence and impact. *Journal of Occupational Health Psychology, 6*(1), 64–80.

Deutsch, M. (1958). Trust and suspicion. *Journal of Conflict Resolution, 2*(1), 265–279.

Ellis, K., & Shockley-Zalabak, P. (1999, November). *Communicating with management: Relating trust to job satisfaction and organizational effectiveness.* Paper presented at the National Communication Association Annual Convention, Chicago.

Folger, R., & Konovsky, M. A. (1989). Effects of procedural and distributive justice on reactions to pay raise decisions. *Academy of Management Journal, 32*(1), 115–130.

Forni, P. M. (2002). *Choosing civility: The twenty-five rules of considerate conduct.* New York: St. Martin's Press.

Fukuyama, F. (1995). *Trust: The social virtues and the creation of prosperity.* New York: Free Press.

Gabarro, J. (1987). *The dynamics of taking charge.* Boston: Harvard Business School Press.

Gambetta, D. (1988). Can we trust trust? In D. Gambetta (Ed.), *Trust: Making and breaking cooperative relationships* (pp. 212–235). Cambridge, MA: Blackwell.

Gibb, J. R. (1961). Defensive communication. *Journal of Communication, 11*(3), 141–148.

Gill, M. J. (2007). The relative predictability of incivility on interpersonal and organizational trust. Doctoral dissertation. West Lafayette, IN: Purdue University.

Goffman, E. (1955). On face-work: An analysis of ritual elements in social interaction. *Psychiatry, 18*(2), 213–231.

Goffman, E. (1981). *Forms of talk*. Philadelphia: University of Pennsylvania Press.

Hardin, R. (Ed.). (2002). *Trust and trustworthiness*. New York: Russell Sage Foundation.

Heimer, C. A. (2001). Solving the problem of trust. In K. S. Cook (Ed.), *Trust in society* (pp. 40–88). New York: Russell Sage Foundation.

Helliwell, J. F., & Huang, H. (2005). *How's the job?: Well-being and social capital in the workplace*. Paper presented at the Canadian Economics Association Annual Meeting, Hamilton, Ontario.

Hornstein, H. A. (1996). *Brutal bosses and their prey: How to identify and overcome abuse in the workplace*. New York: Riverhead Books.

Katcher, B. (2002). *How to improve employee trust in management*. Retrieved September, 2006, from www.hr.com.

Keyton, J., & Smith, F. L. (2003, June). *A comparative empirical analysis of theoretical formulations of distrust*. Paper presented at the International Association for Conflict Management, Melbourne, Australia.

Konovsky, M. A., & Cropanzano, R. (1991). Perceived fairness of employee drug testing as a predictor of employee attitudes and job performance. *Journal of Applied Psychology, 76*(5), 698–707.

Kramer, R. M. (1999). Trust and distrust in organizations: Emerging perspectives, enduring questions. *Annual Review of Psychology, 50*(1), 569–598.

Kramer, R. M., & Cook, K. S. (2004a). Trust and distrust in organizations: Dilemmas and approaches. In R. M. Kramer & K. S. Cook (Eds.), *Trust and distrust in organizations: Dilemmas and approaches* (pp. 1–18). New York: Russell Sage Foundation.

Kramer, R. M., & Cook, K. S. (Eds.). (2004b). *Trust and distrust in organizations: Dilemmas and approaches*. New York: Russell Sage Foundation.

Kramer, R. M., & Tyler, T. R. (Eds.). (1996). *Trust in organizations: Frontiers of theory and research*. Thousand Oaks, CA: Sage.

Lewicki, R. J., & Bunker, B. B. (1996). Developing and maintaining trust in work relationships. In R. M. Kramer & T. R. Tyler (Eds.), *Trust in organizations: Frontiers of theory and research* (pp. 114–139). Thousand Oaks, CA: Sage.

Lewicki, R. J., McAllister, D. J., & Bies, R. J. (1998). Trust and distrust: New relationships and realities. *Academy of Management Review, 23*(3), 438–458.

March, J. G., & Olsen, J. P. (1989). *Rediscovering institutions: The organizational basis of politics*. New York: Free Press.

Mayer, R. C., Davis, J. H., & Schoorman, R. D. (1995). An integrative model of organizational trust. *The Academy of Management Review, 20*(5), 709–734.

McAllister, D. J. (1995). Affect- and cognition-based trust as foundations for interpersonal cooperation in organizations. *The Academy of Management Journal, 38*(1), 24–59.

McGlone, M. S., & Batchelor, J. A. (2003). Looking out for number one: Euphemism and face. *Journal of Communication, 53*(2), 251–265.

Messick, D. M., & Kramer, R. M. (2001). Trust as a form of shallow morality. In K. S. Cook (Ed.), *Trust in society* (pp. 89–118). New York: Russell Sage Foundation.

Muchinsky, P. M. (1977). An intraorganizational analysis of the Roberts and O'Reilly organizational communication questionnaire. *Journal of Applied Psychology, 62*(1), 184–188.

O'Reilly, C. A., III, & Roberts, K. H. (1974). Information filtration in organizations: Three experiments. *Organizational Behavior and Human Performance, 11*(2), 253–265.

Pearson, C. M., Andersson, L. M., & Porath, C. L. (2000). Assessing and attacking workplace incivility. *Organizational Dynamics, 20*(1), 123–137.

Putnam, R. D. (1993). *Making democracy work: Civic traditions in modern Italy.* Princeton, NJ: Princeton University Press.

Putnam, R. D. (1995). Bowling alone: America's declining social capital. *Journal of Democracy, 6*(1), 65–78.

Putnam, R. D. (2000). *Bowling alone: The collapse and revival of American community.* New York: Simon & Schuster.

Rayner, C. (1997). The incidence of workplace bullying. *Journal of Community and Applied Social Psychology, 7*(2), 199–208.

Robinson, S. L., Dirks, K. T., & Ozcelik, H. (2001). Untangling the knot of trust and betrayal. In R. M. Kramer, & K. S. Cook (Eds.), *Trust and distrust in organizations: Dilemmas and approaches* (pp. 327–341). New York: Russell Sage Foundation.

Sapienza, H. J., & Korsgaard, M. A. (1996). Managing investor relations: The impact of procedural justice in establishing and sustaining investor support. *Academy of Management Journal, 39*(4), 544–574.

Shockley-Zalabak, P., Ellis, K., & Cesaria, R. (2000). *Measuring organizational trust: A diagnostic survey and international indicator.* San Francisco: International Association of Business Communicators.

Solomon, R. C., & Flores, F. (2001). *Building trust: In business, politics, relationships, and life.* New York: Oxford University Press.

Sypher, B. D. (2004). Reclaiming civil discourse in the workplace. *Southern Communication Journal, 69*(2), 257–269.

Sypher, B. D., Bostrom, R. N., & Seibert, J. H. (1989). Listening, communication abilities and success at work. *Journal of Business Communication, 26*(2), 293–305.

Sypher, B. D., & Zorn, T. E. (1986). Communication abilities and upward mobility: A longitudinal investigation. *Human Communication Research, 12*(3), 420–431.

Sztompka, P. (1999). *Trust: A sociological theory.* New York: Cambridge University Press.

Tomlinson, E. C., & Lewicki, R. J. (2003). Managing interpersonal trust and distrust. In G. Burgess & H. Burgess (Eds.), *Beyond intractability* (pp. 123–148). Boulder, CO: Conflict Research Consortium.

Tyler, T. R., & Degoey, P. (1996). Trust in organizational authorities: The influence of motive attributions on willingness to accept decisions. In T. R. Tyler (Ed.), *Trust in organizations: Frontiers of theory and research* (pp. 331–356). Thousand Oaks, CA: Sage.

Voehl, F. (1995). *Deming the way we knew him.* Coral Springs, FL: Strategy Associates Inc.

Zhao, X., & Gantz, W. (2003). Disruptive and cooperative interruptions in prime-time television fiction: The role of gender, status, and topic. *Journal of Communication, 53*(2), 347–363.

Part II

Cultural and Organizational Pressures

Chapter 4

Managing Burnout and Moving Toward Employee Engagement

Reinvigorating the Study of Stress at Work

Sarah J. Tracy

My alarm blared, but I yearned to stay tucked under the covers. The idea of going to work seemed overwhelming. I was tired of dealing with everyone else's whines and needs. It was just too much—too much work, too many conflicting responsibilities, too high of expectations. All of it was dragging on me, pushing me into a puddle of cynicism. Whereas I used to greet my work with energy, aspiration and passion, the job had slowly but surely eaten away at my confidence, enthusiasm and sense of control. What used to feel meaningful now felt like a chore. I coped by going on automatic pilot, and turned my coworkers and clients into faceless, nameless others—trying to disable them from sapping the little energy I had left. I felt depleted, bored, disengaged and exhausted.

I was burned out.

Those who can identify with this anecdote viscerally understand the feelings that accompany organizational burnout. However, like all aspects of identity, burnout and stress are not just internal feelings. They are constructed, caused, shaped, and lived through communication. Communication scholars provide unique insights on these destructive dimensions of organizational life by elucidating the ways various organizational communication practices contribute to, buffer, and counteract burnout. Furthermore, communication is central for providing an environment wherein employees are engaged, passionate, and confidant—the opposite of those who are burned out.

My hope is that this critical literature review of stress and burnout can assist employees dealing with burnout, managers trying to prevent burnout, and academics who want to study burnout. Comprehensive literature reviews on stress and burnout can be found elsewhere (Cordes & Dougherty, 1993; Lee & Ashforth, 1996; Maslach, Schaufeli, & Leiter, 2001; Schaufeli & Enzmann, 1998). However, these reviews are dated, and gloss the contributions to stress and burnout theory developed by communication scholars. My goal here is to overview stress and burnout as a particular aspect of destructive organizational communication and, in doing so, reinvigorate the study of stress and burnout in the communication field. The essay overviews the primary processes of stress and burnout, the historical roots that contextualize current research trends, the primary causes and consequences of burnout, ways that burnout may be best addressed, and fruitful areas for future inquiry. Along the way, it discusses how we might alleviate alienation and exhaustion and construct organizational contexts that encourage resilience, purpose, and drive amongst employees.

Introduction

The language of stress and burnout are ubiquitous. More than 2500 books, journal articles and dissertations examined burnout between 1974 to 1990 alone (Maslach & Schaufeli, 1993). Some called stress the "Black Plague of the eighties" (Cooper & Cartwright, 1994, p. 456). And while the study of these issues has flagged in recent years, a perusal of self-help books and magazines indicates that the popular imagination is still very concerned about stress and burnout. But what does this mean? Where did these terms even come from?

The Emergence of Stress and Burnout

Much of the stress research was developed during World War II in order to test and select soldiers who would be the most "stress fit" (Newton, 1995). Early stress researchers focused on instincts, the fight-or-flight response, and individuals' physiological reactions to certain stressors. Today's primary organizational stressors—which include the pressure of meeting others' demands, intense competition, the drive to make more money, and feelings of being deprived of things that are rightly deserved (Farber, 2000)—are quite different and more varied than those faced by soldiers. However, the early research set the stage for later work, focusing on the fitness and coping abilities of individual employees.

The term "stress" was coined by Hans Selye ([1956] 1976) and was developed from studies in the health field. Selye advanced the theory that stress has three stages: (1) alarm reaction, (2) resistance, and (3) exhaustion. Perhaps the most widely received definition of stress views stress as the difference between worker satisfaction—as represented by individual need fulfillment—and the realities of the work situation as experienced by the individual (Kahn, Wolfe, Quinn, Snoek, & Rosenthal, 1964).

The term "stress" has often been used interchangeably with "burnout" probably because the terms share similar histories and definitions. "Burnout" was coined by Freudenberger (1974) after he noted the stress responses exhibited by employees in halfway houses and free clinics.

Burnout is typically conceived of as a general "wearing out" from the pressures of work, which is almost the same as stress's "exhaustion." If there is any distinction between the two terms, it is that stress is occasionally used as an umbrella phenomenon, with burnout being conceived as a reaction to stressors that cannot be managed (Cordes & Dougherty, 1993; Ray, 1983). Burnout manifests in feelings of alienation, cynicism, ineffectiveness, and emotional exhaustion (Maslach et al., 2001).

Burnout research emerged as a grass-roots approach derived from individuals' experiences—rather than being a "top-down" scholarly theory (Maslach et al., 2001). The early research was characterized by a strong applied orientation and the focused qualitative study of interpersonal relationships. In the 1980s, the research became much more empirical with a focus on testing and assessing burnout (most using the Maslach Burnout Inventory or MBI) developed by Maslach and Jackson (1981). The MBI (see Maslach, Jackson, & Leiter, 1996 for its latest version) conceptualizes burnout as a three-dimensional concept characterized as (1) emotional exhaustion (2) depersonalization or a negative shift in responses to others, particularly clients, and (3) a decreased sense of personal accomplishment. In the 1990s, burnout research extended to other (non-human service) occupations, and structural equation modeling was used to single out various contributors to burnout. However, we still do not have a measure to know at what point stress and burnout become debilitating. Research is moving toward such with an eight-phase model of burnout (Golembiewski, Boudreau, Sun, & Luo, 1998), but more development is needed before we are able to compare and contrast levels of burnout across various populations.

Pictures and Places of Stress and Burnout

What does burnout look like and where can it be found? Emotional exhaustion is the most widely reported and thoroughly analyzed component of burnout (Maslach et al., 2001). Exhaustion prompts dedicated employees to distance themselves emotionally and cognitively from their job and clients. When employees detach, they have a tendency to become cynical, depersonalized, and callous. They begin treating humans as objects, use more jargon, and infuse (formerly personalized) service with bureaucratization (Lee & Ashforth, 1996). They become alienated from clients, as well as from one's own emotions and identity (Hochschild, 1983).

To the employee, depersonalization feels like a defense mechanism. Indeed, communication research suggests that work demands can seem more manageable and that employees can feel more comfortable when they perceive their clients in a depersonalized manner. From this standpoint, depersonalization should not be equated with stress (Hullett,

McMillan, & Rogan, 2000), but rather seen as a result or sequential component of it. Furthermore, it is important to look beyond individual defense mechanisms for causing depersonalization. Professional socialization is at least partly responsible for employees' tendency to become callous and aloof; depersonalizing is often treated as an acceptable and professional response to clients (Cordes & Dougherty, 1993).

Although much research has found a sequential progression from emotional exhaustion to depersonalization, the subsequent link to personal accomplishment or inefficacy is less developed (Maslach et al., 2001). However, being exhausted and depersonalized is likely to interfere with material effectiveness as well as one's subjective feeling of accomplishment.

It is significant that the term burnout was coined through research in social service and health organizations. Some have suggested that "burnout" should only be applied to caregivers, and that we should use other terms to refer to the wearing out of all other workers. Pines, Aronson, and Kafry (1981) suggest the concept of "tedium" to assess workers' experience of physical, emotional, and mental exhaustion. Tedium (emotional and physical depletion) results from prolonged chronic pressure while burnout is considered a more specific emotional pressure. Still another measure simplifies the MBI to two factors rather than three. The job demands-resources (JD-R) model of burnout suggests that job demands and (lack of) job resources result in exhaustion and disengagement, respectively (Demerouti, Bakker, Nachreiner, & Schaufeli, 2001).

In order to better generalize the concept of burnout for non-service related professions, Maslach and her colleagues revised their original burnout inventory and created three versions of the measure (Maslach et al., 1996). One is designed for those working in human services and health care and another is targeted toward educators. In both these versions, the three components studied include the original components of emotional exhaustion, depersonalization, and reduced personal accomplishment. A third version is designed for employees who do not work as closely with people, and is slightly different, measuring exhaustion, cynicism (or a distant attitude), and reduced professional efficacy.

Despite the expansion of the burnout concept, a scan of the literature shows that most burnout studies are focused on employees who work closely with clients, such as nurses, healthcare providers, teachers, and other helping professionals (Cordes & Dougherty, 1993; Lee & Ashforth, 1996). The emotional exhaustion of employees is connected to their *frequency* and *intensity* of interpersonal contact with others. Social workers, teachers, and nurses have frequent, intense contact with clients, and they report high levels of burnout. Moderate levels of burnout are found in professions with high frequency of interpersonal contact, but low intensity (such as receptionists and salespeople), or high intensity but low frequency interpersonal contact (such as paramedics, public defenders, or police detectives). Meanwhile, professionals who experience low frequency and low intensity interpersonal contact with others experience less emotional exhaustion as is the case with laboratory technicians or oil rig workers (Cordes & Dougherty, 1993). Boundary-spanning positions (e.g., public relations practitioners) and supervisors also have higher burnout because they must represent and juggle multiple interests (Tracy, 2000).

Costs and Scope of the Problem

The U.S. Bureau of Labor Statistics identifies stress as costing U.S. employers an estimated $10,000 per worker per year (reviewed by Neuman, 2004). The National Institute for Occupational Safety and Health (NIOSH) estimates that 40% of the U.S. workforce is affected by stress, making it the number one cause of worker disability (Wojcik, 2001). Research consistently finds stress and burnout to cause absenteeism, lowered job performance, reduced commitment, increased health insurance claims, and lost productivity, costing up to 150 billion a year; moreover, nearly 80% of employees report that work is the primary source of their stress (DeFrank & Ivancevich, 1998).

Insurance premiums have skyrocketed as employers must replace staff who have suffered heart-attacks, coronary heart disease, depression, mental breakdowns, and other health disorders associated with stress and burnout (Cooper & Cartwright, 1994). Compounded with the financial effects, stress and burnout are associated with increases in organizational conflict and aggression (Neuman, 2004). Burnout tends to be contagious, spreading throughout the organization and spilling over into people's home life. In short, stress and burnout are costly in terms of morale, productivity, mental and physical health, and personal well-being.

Key Processes of Stress and Burnout

A scan of the stress and burnout literature shows it to be replete with box-and-arrow models that identify discrete causes, intermediaries, and consequences. By virtue of the existing literature, the following review is organized around similar dimensions: (a) stressors, or organizational factors that cause psychological discomfort; (b) individual factors that make some employees more prone to burnout; (c) resources and buffering processes that moderate, disrupt, or counteract burnout and stress; and (d) consequences. Most research has attempted to pinpoint specific variables of burnout, and existing models suggest that stress and burnout proceed in a linear, causative fashion—although some studies have also shown reversed causation (Zapf, Dormann, & Frese, 1996). As I will return to in the conclusion, the topic area is ripe for thick descriptions that detail how various individual and contextual factors are communicatively constructed, and theories that explain how the variables interact as a dynamic fluid process.

Stressors or Organizational Factors

A good place to begin looking for the causes of stress and burnout is the organization itself. Primary organizational factors of burnout include role stress, work overload, surveillance, and other contextual factors such as prestige, work–life stress, lack of power, and change.

Role Stress

Role conflict and role ambiguity, often combined under the umbrella term of role stress, have consistently and strongly been shown to be precursors to burnout. Role conflict occurs when employees face conflicting demands or incongruent messages, and by complying with one they cannot effectively comply with others (Katz & Kahn, 1966). Role ambiguity occurs when employees lack adequate guidance and are bewildered as to how to effectively perform in the job.

The early role stress research focused on contradictory demands within a single workplace; however, research also suggests that role stress becomes salient when employees face contradictory or paradoxical roles in society. For instance, Gaines and Jermier (1983) found that the contradictory mandate of police officers—to enforce rules they did not create and from which they may not benefit—leads to tension, strain, and emotional exhaustion. When "enforcement" is a primary part of a job (e.g., IRS agents, correctional officers, police officers, meter maids), "success" on the job can feel elusive, if not paradoxical (Tracy, 2005). Added to this, many of these employees face the double-whammy of doing "dirty work" which is accorded low prestige and public misunderstanding (Tracy & Scott, 2006).

One's position in the organizational network can lead to role stress. Research suggests that employees or managers who must juggle a variety of priorities or clients, and hold "boundary-spanning" or "linking" roles within the organization, can be more susceptible to burnout. Ray (1991) hypothesized the "combination of doing their job plus the information and relationship processing demands on linkers may make them more vulnerable to burnout" (p. 97). Albrecht, Irey, and Mundy (1982) similarly discovered that linkers report more burnout than other group members due to their location at the "crossroads of information" and their need to process more information from more sources. Furthermore, such employees must manage multiple identifications, which can be stressful and alienating (Tracy, 2000).

Workload

Another factor that figures into the concept of burnout is workload, or the amount of work that must be accomplished. Both quantitative overload ("too much" work) and qualitative overload (work that is "too difficult") have been linked to a variety of physiological, psychological, and behavioral strain symptoms among workers (Miller, Ellis, Zook, & Lyles, 1990). Employees who feel they do not have the skills or experience to do the work will burn out, and this is exacerbated if workers perceive severe consequences for not handling the demand. At the same time, we should not assume that a certain amount of work automatically leads to burnout. Perceived workload is highly subjective and depends on an employee's capacity and access to various resources. Material resources as well as social support, information, and feedback help to moderate the stressor of workload (Demerouti et al., 2001).

Surveillance

Organizational surveillance and monitoring imply mistrust, and can create increased burnout and tension. A study of 110 administrative worksites found that monitoring invades worker privacy, increases stress, reduces quality, and hinders productivity (Nussbaum & duRivage, 1986). Electronic monitoring adversely affects employee perceptions of their working conditions and is related to increased levels of job boredom, tension, anxiety, depression, anger, and fatigue.

Power and Control Factors

When employees feel powerless in the face of organizational politics, they are more likely to experience burnout and stress. Organizational politics, considered to be behavior that is strategically designed to maximize self-interests, is linked to higher levels of anxiety and tension among employees (Cropanzano, Howes, Grandey, & Toth, 1997). Ostracism, isolation, feeling "out of the know," and lack of decision-making power are also associated with burnout and stress (Tracy, 2005). Given the feelings of powerlessness and confusion associated with organizational change, it is of little surprise that downsizing and mergers, as well as the mere anticipation of change, lead to burnout (Ashford, 1988).

Individual Factors

The ability to manage stress and burnout differs amongst employees depending on a number of factors such as workload capacity, predispositions, coping skills, cognitive differences, and ability to differentiate between empathic concern and emotional contagion. Furthermore, research has attempted to link burnout with various demographic markers.

Workload Capacity

As noted, workload and role stress can lead to burnout, but depending on employees' capacity for stress and for amount and type of work, their burnout will differ. In fact, burnout may actually serve organizations in that the employees who stick around are also the ones who can deal with the workload. A study of teachers and burnout found that teachers are *not* very stressed or burned out, and this may be because teachers have good coping skills and those without these skills have self-selected out of the profession (Ray, 1991). Likewise, research with employees at a psychiatric hospital found that a heavy workload is not necessarily bad (Miller et al., 1990). Although workload can lead to burnout, it is often also linked to increased perceptions of personal accomplishment. To the extent that workload is not exhausting, it can stimulate increased satisfaction with work. Burnout becomes a concern only when the amount of work is perceived as unmanageable.

Coping Skills and Predispositions

Burnout, therefore, depends on the personal coping skills and predisposition of employees; it is an individually subjective response that results from an interaction between social conditions and personal characteristics. A Type-A personality—which is characterized by a chronic sense of time urgency, a hard-driving and competitive orientation, a strong distaste for idleness, and chronic impatience—would react quite differently to work stress than a Type-B personality—which is more contemplative, and less concerned with desires to succeed, time deadlines, or participation in numerous activities (Smeltzer, 1987). Burnout candidates tend to be idealistic and/or self-motivating achievers and also tend to seek unattainable goals (King, 1986). Indeed, when employees hold high or unmet personal expectations for the job and for themselves, they are likely to report higher levels of burnout (Cordes & Dougherty, 1993).

Employees who have little tolerance for bureaucracy, change, or powerlessness also tend to experience more burnout. Connor and Douglas (2005) argue that employees' orientation or predisposition toward bureaucracy and structure affect their level of stress. People who have little openness to change or have an external locus of control (attribute events to chance or external others) rather than internal locus of control (attributions to one's own ability) are also more prone to burnout (Maslach et al., 2001). Consequently, it is not sufficient to simply relate burnout to organizational stressors. Individual personality and behavioral style must also be taken into consideration.

Cognitive Dissonance

Another individual dimension of burnout is how much a person feels his or her self-concept differs from the type of work they are doing. Discrepancies between the actual self-state (the self-concept) and the ideal self-states (representations of an individual's beliefs about others' hopes and expectations) result in dejection-related emotions, such as disappointment, dissatisfaction, and sadness. Various theories have suggested that individuals are motivated to match their self-concept to contextual messages (Festinger, 1957; Higgins, 1987). Performing one identity, and believing oneself to inhabit another, is an uncomfortable psychological state and may lead to burnout (Ray, 1983).

Empathic Concern Versus Emotional Contagion

Among the most substantial contributions to the burnout literature from the communication discipline is the "empathic communication model of burnout" developed by Kathy Miller and her colleagues in the late 1980s and extended and verified in a number of subsequent studies (Miller, Birkholt, Scott, & Stage, 1995). This model conceptualizes empathy as a two-pronged concept, consisting of (a) *emotional contagion*, in which the caregiver experiences emotional responses parallel to the client's emotion and (b) *empathic concern*, which is a concern about the welfare of the other without feeling parallel emotions of the other. In a study of caregivers and administrative supporters at a psychiatric hospital, researchers found that (a) emotional detachment is important in therapeutic relationships, (b) a caregiver's sense of worth in a job is based largely on his or her ability to communicate empathically, and (c) emotional exhaustion has a negative impact on occupational commitment (Miller, Stiff, & Ellis, 1988). Although empathic concern and emotional detachment lead to increased satisfaction, when employees move to the polar extremes of emotional contagion (complete emotional involvement) or complete depersonalization, they are more likely to burn out.

Demographic Variables

Myriad demographic variables, including gender, age, education, and marital status have been correlated with burnout. Of all the demographic factors, age is the one that is most consistently related to burnout. Younger employees experience more stress than those in their 30s or 40s (Maslach et al., 2001). This is likely because younger employees are more idealistic, hold higher expectations for themselves and their jobs (Cordes & Dougherty, 1993), and report experiencing higher levels of verbal and physical abuse at work than older workers (Lutgen-Sandvik, 2007; Schat, Frone, & Kelloway, 2006).

Sex differences have been inconsistent except that men tend to be more cynical than women. In terms of marital status, the research is mixed. While some studies have found that single and divorced individuals report higher levels of burnout (Maslach et al., 2001), other studies have found that married individuals can be more burned out, especially when they hold jobs that are misunderstood and denigrated (Tracy & Scott, 2006). As is typical in much of the burnout research, we have very little qualitative explanation as to *why* the studies on the effect of marriage on burnout are inconsistent. The interaction picture is largely missing.

Consequences of Burnout and Stress

As noted, burnout can be "productive" insomuch that it acts as a mechanism causing people to self-select out of some professions and into others (Ray, 1983). Despite this burnout "benefit," the bulk of the literature suggests that burnout has high costs for both individual employees and the organization in terms of employee health, productivity, morale, and quality of interpersonal relationships (Cordes & Dougherty, 1993; Maslach et al., 2001).

As long as 300 years ago, the relationship between type of job and type of disease was proposed by Bernardo Ramazzini in Italy, and doctors were encouraged to ask patients about their job so that health problems might be better understood (Rosen & Parr, 1959). Burnout is linked to health problems such as increased blood pressure, ulcers, depression, coronary heart disease, increased drinking, fatigue, insomnia, headaches, and gastrointestinal disturbances (Cordes & Dougherty, 1993; Maslach et al., 2001). Burnout also results in psychological discomforts such as tension, displeasure, frustration, confusion, and anxiety (Miller, Zook, & Ellis, 1989; Starnaman & Miller, 1992). Employees report a range of mental health issues, including helplessness, depression, and irritability (Cordes & Dougherty, 1993; Maslach et al., 2001). In addition, when care-givers see themselves treating patients in a "depersonalized" manner, they feel less personal accomplishment and more emotional exhaustion (Miller et al., 1990).

Burnout also harms the organization. Stress-related outcomes cost organizations billions each year (Neuman, 2004). These costs come in the form of low employee performance and high turnover (Albrecht et al., 1982; Miller et al., 1990; Starnaman & Miller, 1992). In addition, organizational stress may seriously impair employees' abilities to process information and may constrict their decision-making capabilities, thus reducing employee communicative effectiveness during critical times (Pincus & Acharya, 1988). One of the most important outcomes of burnout is a decrease in commitment, which is thought to lead to increases in absenteeism and turnover (Eisenberg, Monge, & Miller, 1983). As Maslach (1982) pointedly noted, "a psychiatric nurse becomes a carpenter or a counselor turns to farming. They swear they will never return to their original occupation with its crush of people and emotional demands" (p. 81). There is compelling evidence that the final step in the burnout process is the desertion of the stressful occupation (Miller et al., 1988).

Furthermore, the effects of burnout spill over into private sectors. Employees who experience stress and burnout report lower quality relationships with friends, family, and coworkers (Cordes & Dougherty, 1993; Maslach et al., 2001). Burned-out correctional officers, for instance, have trouble "taking off the uniform" and the domineering attitude that accompanies it. One officer's wife said that her husband acted like a jerk for an hour or so after he came home from work (Tracy, 2005). Burnout also harms employees' private lives and relationships because it is linked to increased alcohol use and higher levels of depression (Cordes & Dougherty, 1993).

Interventions, Resources, and Remedies

In light of the overwhelmingly negative personal, organizational, and familial effects of burnout, research points to a number of protective factors—interventions, resources, and remedies—that can buffer, ameliorate, or counteract stress at work. Protective factors have received less attention than the causes and consequences of burnout. Nevertheless, attending to these factors are vital insomuch as they counteract and problematize the linear cause-effect results of stress (Demerouti et al., 2001).

In order to contextualize the work that has been done on stress/burnout interventions, it is important to remember that most organizational research and training have treated these issues as *individual* pathologies rather than organizational, structural dilemmas (Newton, 1995). Employees are trained to identify and tackle their stressors using tactics such as biofeedback, meditation, and relaxation techniques. And when workers are considered to be too stressed out to do their work effectively, they are often referred to stigmatized employee assistance programs (EAPs). These individualistic stress interventions may assist with personal coping, but they oftentimes miss the *working patterns* that contribute to and define stress (Tracy, 2007). Furthermore, while they may assist employees with the exhaustion dimension of burnout, individual techniques have little effect on changing employees' feelings of cynicism or efficacy (Maslach et al., 2001) or the organizational dynamics contributing to stress/burnout.

Although the overall focus of interventions has been at the individual level, communication scholars have been leaders in focusing on some of the interactional and structural processes that can counteract and buffer burnout. These include social support from group members, positive supervisor-subordinate relationships, participation in decision-making, network integration, toxin management, and other structural approaches.

Social Support

Supportive interactions, or those in which "coworkers are able to vent feelings, clarify perceptions and mutually define the work environment," (Ray, 1983, p. 188) are vital for reducing organizational ambiguity (a precursor to burnout). Close interaction with coworkers can assist individuals in making sense of their work, especially when employees have a lot of client contact (Miller et al., 1989). Moreover:

> Supportive communication helps people when the process functions to decrease the anxiety and stress caused by the experience of the unknown .... The significance of supportive communication that reduces one's perceptions of uncertainty is that it helps the receiver in developing a sense of perceived control over stressful circumstances. (Albrecht & Adelman, 1987, p. 24)

In addition to reducing organizational uncertainty, feedback from group members can help workers monitor perceptions of themselves and their job and reconcile cognitive discrepancies (Ray, 1983). In terms of controlling burnout, it is important for the work group to support colleagues' personal goals, protect colleagues from the boss, help each other, not be disorganized or pressuring, and be close-knit (Smeltzer, 1987).

Social support can come in several different forms (Albrecht & Adelman, 1987), and each form counteracts stress and burnout in its own way (Ellis & Miller, 1994). *Instrumental support* (an exchange of time, resources, or labor) helps prevent emotional exhaustion and depersonalization, and as such, may enhance the care and treatment of clients. *Informational support* (related to role definition, general information about the job, are skills training) is related to increased retention. *Emotional support* (empathy, caring, acceptance, and assurance) is directly related to retention, commitment, and all dimensions of burnout.

Research also outlines how various *sources* of social support differ—for example, support from the organization, the workgroup, a single coworker confidante, supervisors, or friends and family. The research suggests that no single source of social support is categorically "best." Some studies demonstrate that strong cohesion with the work group is more important than a strong sense of identity with the entire organization for preventing burnout (Smeltzer, 1987). However, the organization's role toward support is also significant, and affects the efficacy of social support. For example, caregivers feel more accomplished when employees believe their organization values supportive communication with patients (Hullett et al., 2000). Other studies have identified support from individuals, rather than that from work groups or the larger organization, to be most important in terms of alleviating burnout. In a study of educational organizations, Ray (1991) argued that support groups may actually be a stressor and speculated that a single confidante may be most effective for controlling burnout.

Positive superior–subordinate relationships also alleviate burnout. Some research suggests that it is this relationship, more so than relationships with peers, that is the most influential factor for increasing occupational commitment (Starnaman & Miller, 1992) and reducing burnout (Miller et al., 1989). Supportive supervisors are neither too directive nor too delegative, and facilitate employees' sense of influence and control.

Similar to the research on *form* of social support (instrumental, informational, or emotional), different support *sources* distinctively affect the various dimensions of burnout. For example, support from coworkers (vs. family) increased employees' feelings of personal accomplishment, but was also related to higher levels of emotional exhaustion (Leiter, 1988). Support from friends and family was better for alleviating emotional exhaustion. Overall, it seems that support from various sources can be helpful for counteracting stress and burnout. However, most of these quantitative self-report studies do little to flesh out what this support looks like, or *how* or *why* the different sources are helpful or harmful.

Participation in Decision-Making

Another key communicative remedy to burnout is active participation in decision-making. When employees feel they have no voice in formulating the policies that affect their job, they feel powerless and less accomplished (Tracy, 2005). The more participation afforded employees, the more likely they will feel satisfied and confidant in understanding their work role and expectations of the job (Miller et al., 1990; Schuler & Jackson, 1986). Participation in decision-making is especially important for administrative employees who must juggle multiple and fragmented responsibilities (Miller et al., 1989).

Network Integration

Connected to participation and social support is network integration. Employees who are isolated from each other and from supportive supervisors face risks of burnout, while those who are closely integrated into a communication network are often more satisfied (Albrecht et al., 1982; Ray & Miller, 1991). This research suggests that managers and administrators should design organizational structures and practices so that employees can regularly interact with one another—especially those like social workers or correctional officers who consistently work with troubled or mentally disturbed clients. Especially when it is outside the gaze of superiors or clients, network integration with like-minded peers allows employees to co-construct preferred identities and sidestep the contagion that threatens employees who work with stigmatized populations (Tracy, 2005).

Toxin Management

Emotions like depression, stress, and burnout are contagious. To guard against the rampant spread of negativity, managers are beginning to realize the importance of infusing excitement and gratitude into the workplace, and employing effective "toxin handlers" (Frost, 2004). Toxin handlers are the managers, secretaries, or intermediaries who address, eliminate, and assuage the conflicts, stressors, problems, abuse, and hurt feelings that are all too common in organizations. Toxin handlers recognize how pain strips others of self-confidence and effectiveness, and therefore they step in, reframe anxiety-producing situations, and help people get back to work. Tasks of the toxin handler include listening, holding space for healing, buffering pain, extricating others from painful situations, and helping others transform painful situations.

Other Structural Interventions

Recent research has begun examining several other structural issues that can help counteract burnout. Development of non-maligned workplace-wellness programs (in contrast to traditional EAPs that are often denigrated) are associated with improvement in employee physical and mental health, reductions in absenteeism, and multi-million dollar savings to organizations in accident and sickness benefits (Cooper & Cartwright, 1994). Research also touts the importance of examining the match of employee and organizations (Maslach & Leiter, 1997). This research suggests that employees may be better able to deal with the causes of burnout (e.g., overload) when they are valued, feel rewarded, or are doing something that aligns with their ethical goals.

Although a number of issues may help buffer and counteract burnout, interventions are not uniformly positive. Briner and Reynolds (1999) outline the costs, benefits, and limitations of organizational-level stress interventions. They warn researchers and practitioners from becoming "cock-eyed optimists" who make grand recommendations based on unproven, overly-simplified solutions. A fruitful area of future research is an empirical evaluation of burnout interventions, preferably through longitudinal studies that employ both qualitative and quantitative components.

Research Trends and Future Directions

After reviewing the literature on workplace burnout and stress, it might be easy to assume that its level of interest in the communication field has, well, burned out. Communication scholars turned their attention to the topic with a flurry of studies in the 1980s, and interest thrived through the mid-1990s. But, slowly, the journal articles have trickled. This is unfortunate because the practical need to better understand and deal with stress and burnout continues. Furthermore, as we move toward the end of the twenty-first century's first decade, many structural changes in work and society make it clear that we still have much to address.

Hot Topics for Future Research Engagement

The focus of much organizational research has been on negative states or problems. However, researchers are beginning to realize that it is at least as important to understand why it is that employees *flourish* in organizations. Leading this charge are researchers at The Center of Positive Organizational Scholarship (http://www.bus.umich.edu/Positive/ Center-for-POS/) and The Compassion Lab (www.compassionlab.com). Positive organizational scholarship is focused on analyzing the positive energetic connections among employees, the idea being that by specifically analyzing positive issues such as energy, compassion, and engagement at work, scholars can create theories and practical suggestions that can move beyond merely *preventing* negative behaviors to helping *construct* positive ones. One of the most promising directions for future burnout research, spurred by positive organizational scholarship, is the focus on workplace *engagement* as the antipathy of burnout (Maslach et al., 2001). Engagement is characterized by energy, involvement, and efficacy. Research is beginning to explore employee vigor, activation, pleasure, dedication, willingness to invest effort, the ability to resist fatigue, and total immersion in one's work (Maslach et al.). Similarly, a focus on organizational "health" is emerging as a proactive way of addressing occupational stress and burnout (Cooper & Cartwright, 1994). Communication scholars are especially well prepared to understand how issues of health and emotional states of engagement are constructed and constrained through communication, interaction, organizational policies, and larger societal structures.

Employee-Organization Match

Another emerging line of burnout research has emerged in the realization that it is important to examine individual and organizational factors *in tandem*. Although much of the work in the 1980s and 90s focused on single variables of burnout and discriminating which variables led to "how" much of a specific burnout dimension, researchers are now beginning to examine the larger context. This includes investigating societal trends, such as changes in the psychological contract (Rousseau, 1995) and even work-life issues that affect burnout (Lawrence, 2006). Furthermore, I see a hopeful space for future communication research in terms of examining how the employee and environment intersect.

Maslach and Leiter (1997) have proposed six areas of worklife that may be especially susceptible to mismatches between employee expectations/ capabilities and the organizational environment. These include workload, control/authority, reward, community (positive connection with others in the workplace), fairness (confirmation of respect and self-worth), and values (ethics). These mismatches do not just summarize research findings but provide a more complex conceptual framework for re-imagining burnout research in terms of relationships and interaction. Unfortunately, this framework has yet to make its way into communication research.

Culture and Ethnicity

A third area of promising research is that of comparing and contrasting stress and burnout internationally. Burnout has been studied around the globe, with equivalent terms in other languages, and the Maslach Burnout Inventory has been translated into many languages (Maslach et al., 2001). Studies show a lower level of burnout in European countries than in North American countries, but this may be because North Americans are more willing to admit cynicism or respond extremely to the MBI self-report measures. In order to better understand the reported differences, it would be useful to conduct more qualitative research to explain and expand the survey data. Furthermore, we know very little about how stress and burnout vary across ethnicity. It would be valuable to examine cultural differences, not only in terms of how different ethnicities and cultures score on traditional burnout measures, but how burnout fundamentally manifests differently across culture and ethnicity.

Work-life Effects

A fourth area of recent research—the effects of work–life balance on burnout—recognizes that we must move beyond the container metaphor of organizations for understanding stress. Work-life conflict generally afflicts women more so than men, since women usually manage more labor in the home and typically lack influential social support at work (Geller & Hobfoll, 1994). Women rarely have the same level of social support in traditional patriarchal workplaces, as they are often barred from certain powerful networks (e.g., the "old boys' club"). Low levels of household assistance have also exacerbated work-life conflict. Women work a second shift (Hochschild & Machung, 1989), spending at least twice as much time on housework and childcare as men, even when women work full-time and earn 50% or more of a family's income (Alberts & Trethewey, 2007). On its face, this data would suggest that women face increased risks of being burned out. However, several self-report studies of burnout and household help report a counterintuitive finding—that women's experience of tedium and job stress are actually *more extreme* when they report receiving *more* household assistance from their partners (Geller & Hobfoll, 1994). Future qualitative research could fruitfully unpack the reasons behind this counterintuitive finding, in particular, and work–life balance issues and organizational stress, in general. It may be that women who receive higher levels of household help feel less "womanly," or that the help may be "high hassle support" accompanied by negative feelings of having to "nag."

Similarly, we do not know the reasons behind the mixed findings regarding the effect of having families and experiencing burnout (Maslach et al., 2001). Some research suggests that married individuals and people with children report less burnout simply because they are older, and therefore, more mature and less idealistic. Or, it could be that families lend support or a balance to work. However, families can also provide another burden, another arena to manage, and some studies have found that married individuals are more burned out.

Methodological Considerations: Moving from Boxes and Arrows to Narratives

When we consider how the concept of burnout originally emerged, it is ironic that the research is so dominated by quantitative self-report studies, structural equation modeling, and cross-sectional correlational designs. The study of burnout is traced to Freudenberger (1974) who collected direct accounts of employees who experienced emotional exhaustion, and Maslach (1976) who conducted interviews with human service workers. Despite these qualitative beginnings, an extensive review of burnout literature (Cordes & Dougherty, 1993) found that only research by Maslach and Pines (1977; Pines & Maslach, 1980) used case studies and only five studies were longitudinal. Another notable qualitative study is by Cherniss (1995) who conducted a set of case-study interviews as a 12-year follow-up. Observational reports are needed but missing (Handy, 1988), and experimental research could assist in testing the burnout models and potential interventions (Briner & Reynolds, 1999). Although organizations have begun to institute burnout trainings, there is little empirical data that clearly indicate their success. Program evaluation is another important area for future exploration.

After reviewing the available research, it becomes overwhelmingly clear that we need theories that explain the *relationships* between individual variables and the effects of various interventions. It is simply not good enough to unproblematically rely on box-and-arrow diagrams that linearly connect individual causes, organizational factors, buffering variables, and consequences. We need to know the types of interactions, feelings, and communication that *construct* the boxes, as well as the recursive nature of the relationships among boxes. We need to have thick descriptions of those little arrows. In other words, we need to better understand what happens *in between* the boxes. Communication scholars can very competently attend to this need.

In closing, I would specifically encourage communication researchers to consider a narrative approach to the study of burnout. As we know from narrative theory, stories do not just represent individuals' life experiences, they fundamentally construct plot lines for different identities (Lawler, 2002). Comparing and contrasting narratives from burned-out employees and those who are engaged and resilient would be fascinating. What are the different turning points in the stories? Who are the main actors? What metaphors are used?

Furthermore, it would be interesting to study the effects of telling and writing narratives of burnout and stress as a type of intervention technique. People better handle their emotions and illnesses associated with trauma when they are able to disclose them, whether that is verbally or in writing. "Confronting deeply personal issues has been found to promote physical health, subjective well-being, and ... adaptive behaviors" (Pennebaker, 1997, p. 162). Past communication research of workplace bullying bolsters the therapeutic nature of writing, talking, and drawing negative workplace emotions (Tracy, Lutgen-Sandvik, & Alberts, 2006), but such an approach has not been investigated in terms of assisting with stress and burnout.

The current literature provides an excellent overview of the causes, consequences, and buffering variables of burnout. However, there is still much work to be done in understanding how and why these factors work together as a process and how interaction and communication can construct burnout, or conversely, engagement. Narratives are integral to providing a window into how employees make sense of and respond to their work, their identities, the world, and their relationships (Lawler, 2002). Narratives are not just representations of "real" life, but are fundamentally productive of interpretations and reactions, some which are healthy, engaged, and resilient, and some that lead to alienation, cynicism, and burnout. Communication scholars have much to offer in terms of telling this—as of yet—untold story of burnout and stress.

References

Alberts, J. K., & Trethewey, A. (2007). Love, honor and thank. *Greater Good, 4* (Summer), 20–22.

Albrecht, T. L., & Adelman, M. B. (1987). *Communicating social support.* Newbury Park, CA: Sage.

Albrecht, T. L., Irey, K. V., & Mundy, A. K. (1982). Integration in a communication network as a mediator of stress. *Social Work, 27*(2), 229–234.

Ashford, S. J. (1988). Individual strategies for coping with stress during organizational transitions. *The Journal of Applied Behavioral Science, 24*(1), 19–36.

Briner, R. B., & Reynolds, S. (1999). The costs, benefits, and limitations of organizational stress interventions. *Journal of Organizational Behavior, 20*(5), 647–664.

Cherniss, C. (1995). *Beyond burnout.* New York: Routledge.

Conner, D. S., & Douglas, S. C. (2005). Organizationally-induced work stress: The role of employee bureaucratic orientation. *Personnel Review, 34*(2), 210–224.

Cooper, C. L., & Cartwright, S. (1994). Healthy mind; healthy organization: A proactive approach to occupational stress. *Human Relations, 47*(3), 455–471.

Cordes, C. L., & Dougherty, T. W. (1993). A review and integration of research on job burnout. *The Academy of Management Review, 18*(4), 621–655.

Cropanzano, R., Howes, J. C., Grandey, A. A., & Toth, P. (1997). The relationship of organizational politics and support to work behaviors, attitudes, and stress. *Journal of Organizational Behavior, 18*(2), 159–180.

DeFrank, R. S., & Ivancevich, J. M. (1998). Stress on the job: An executive update. *Academy of Management Executive, 12*(1), 55–66.

Demerouti, E., Bakker, A. B., Nachreiner, F., & Schaufeli, W. B. (2001). The job demands-resources model of burnout. *Journal of Applied Psychology, 86*(3), 499–512.

Eisenberg, E. M., Monge, P. R., & Miller, K. I. (1983). Involvement in communication networks as a predictor of organizational commitment. *Human Communication Research, 10*(2), 179–201.

Ellis, B. H., & Miller, K. I. (1994). Supportive communication among nurses: Effects on commitment, burnout, and retention. *Health Communication, 6*(1), 77–96.

Farber, B. A. (2000). Understanding and treating burnout in a changing culture. *JCLP/In Session: Psychotherapy in Practice, 56*(4), 589–594.

Festinger, L. (1957). *A theory of cognitive dissonance.* Stanford, CA: Stanford University Press.

Freudenberger, J. J. (1974). Staff burn-out. *Journal of Social Issues, 30*(2), 159–165.

Frost, P. J. (2004). Handling toxic emotions: New challenges for leaders and their organizations. *Organizational Dynamics, 33*(1), 111–127.

Gaines, J., & Jermier, J. H. (1983). Emotional exhaustion in a high stress organization. *Academy of Management Review, 26*(4), 567–586.

Geller, P. A., & Hobfoll, S. E. (1994). Gender differences in job stress, tedium, and social support in the workplace. *Journal of Social and Personal Relationships, 11*(4), 555–572.

Golembiewski, R. T., Boudreau, R. A., Sun, B. C., & Luo, H. (1998). Estimates of burnout in public agencies: Worldwide how many employees have which degrees of burnout, and with what consequences? *Public Administration Review, 58*(1), 59–65.

Handy, J. A. (1988). Theoretical and methodological problems within occupational stress and burnout research. *Human Relations, 41*(3), 351–369.

Higgins, E. T. (1987). Self-discrepancy: A theory relating self and affect. *Psychological Review, 94*(3), 319–340.

Hochschild, A. R. (1983). *The managed heart: Commercialization of human feeling.* Berkeley, CA: University of California Press.

Hochschild, A. R., & Machung, A. (1989). *The second shift: Working parents and the revolution at home.* New York: Viking.

Hullett, C. R., McMillan, J. J., & Rogan, R. G. (2000). Caregivers' predispositions and perceived organizational expectations for the provision of social support to nursing home residents. *Health Communication, 12*(2), 277–299.

Kahn, R. L., Wolfe, D. M., Quinn, R. P., Snoek, J. D., & Rosenthal, R. A. (1964). *Organizational stress: Studies in role conflict and ambiguity.* New York: John Wiley & Sons.

Katz, D., & Kahn, R. L. (1966). *The social psychology of organizations.* New York: John Wiley & Sons.

King, S. S. (1986). The relationship between stress and communication in the organizational context. *Central States Speech Journal, 37*(1), 27–35.

Lawler, S. (2002). Narrative in social research. In T. May (Ed.), *Qualitative Research in Action* (pp. 242–258). London: Sage.

Lawrence, S. A. (2006) An integrative model of perceived available support, work-family conflict and support mobilization. *Journal of Management and Organization, 12*, 160–178.

Lee, R., & Ashforth, B. E. (1996). A meta-analytic examination of the correlates of the three dimensions of job burnout. *Journal of Applied Psychology, 81*(1), 123–133.

Leiter, M. P. (1988). Burnout as a function of communication patterns. *Group and Organization Management, 13*(1), 111–128.

Lutgen-Sandvik, P. (2007). "But words will never hurt me": Abuse and bullying at work: a comparison between two worker samples. *Ohio Communication Journal 45*(1), 81–105.

Maslach, C. (1976). Burned-out. *Human Behavior, 5*(9), 16–22.

Maslach, C. (1982). *Burnout: The cost of caring.* Englewood Cliffs, NJ: Prentice-Hall.

Maslach, C., & Jackson, S. E. (1981). The measurement of experienced burnout. *Journal of Organizational Behavior, 2*(2), 99–113.

Maslach, C., Jackson, S. E., & Leiter, M. P. (1996). *Maslach burnout inventory manual* (3rd ed.). Palo Alto, CA: Consulting Psychologists Press.

Maslach, C., & Leiter, M. P. (1997). *The truth about burnout.* San Francisco: Jossey-Bass.

Maslach, C., & Pines, A. M. (1977). The burn-out syndrome in the day care setting. *Child Care Quarterly, 6*(1), 100–113.

Maslach, C., & Schaufeli, W. B. (1993). Historical and conceptual development of burnout. In W. Schaufeli, C. Maslach, & T. Marek (Eds.), *Professional burnout: Recent developments in theory and research* (pp. 309–330). Washington, DC: Taylor & Francis.

Maslach, C., Schaufeli, W. B., & Leiter, M. P. (2001). Job burnout. *Annual Review of Psychology, 52*(3), 397–422.

Miller, K. I., Birkholt, M., Scott, C., & Stage, C. (1995). Empathy and burnout in human service work: An extension of a communication model. *Communication Research, 22*(1), 123–147.

Miller, K. I., Ellis, B. H., Zook, E. G., & Lyles, J. S. (1990). An integrated model of communication, stress, and burnout in the workplace. *Communication Research, 17*(2), 300–326.

Miller, K. I., Stiff, J. B., & Ellis, B. H. (1988). Communication and empathy as precursors to burnout among human service workers. *Communication Monographs, 55*(2), 250–265.

Miller, K. I., Zook, E. G., & Ellis, B. H. (1989). Occupational differences in the influence of communication on stress and burnout in the workplace. *Management Communication Quarterly, 3*(2), 166–190.

Neuman, J. H. (2004). Injustice, stress, and aggression in organizations. In R. W. Griffin & A. M. O'Leary-Kelly (Eds.), *The dark side of organizational behavior* (pp. 62–102). San Francisco: Jossey-Bass.

Newton, T. J. (1995). *'Managing' stress: Emotion and power at work.* London: Sage.

Nussbaum, K., & duRivage, V. (1986). Computer monitoring: Mismanagement by remote control. *Business and Society Review, 86*(56), 16–20.

Pennebaker, J. W. (1997). Writing about emotional experiences as a therapeutic process. *Psychological Science, 8*(2), 162–166.

Pincus, J. D., & Acharya, L. (1988). Employee communication strategies for organizational crises. *Employee Responsibilities and Rights Journal, 1*(2), 181–199.

Pines, A. M., Aronson, E., & Kafry, D. (1981). *Burnout: From tedium to personal growth.* New York: The Free Press.

Pines, A. M., & Maslach, C. (1980). Combating staff-burn-out in a day care center: A case study. *Child Care Quarterly, 9*(1), 5–16.

Ray, E. B. (1983). Job burnout from a communication perspective. *Communication yearbook, 7,* 738–855.

Ray, E. B. (1991). The relationship among communication network roles, job stress, and burnout in educational organizations. *Communication Quarterly, 39*(1), 91–102.

Ray, E. B., & Miller, K. I. (1991). The influence of communication structure and social support on job stress and burnout. *Management Communication Quarterly, 4*(4), 506–527.

Rosen, G., & Parr, L. W. (1959). History of public health. *Science, 129*(2), 236–238.

Rousseau, D. (1995). *Psychological contracts in organizations. Understanding written and unwritten agreements.* Thousand Oaks, CA: Sage.

Schat, A. C. H., Frone, M., R., & Kelloway, E. K. (2006). Prevalence of workplace aggression in the U.S. workforce: Findings from a national study. In E. K. Kelloway, J. Barling, & J. J. Hurrell (Eds.), *Handbook of workplace violence* (pp. 47–89). Thousand Oaks, CA: Sage.

Schaufeli, W. B., & Enzmann, D. (1998). *The burnout companion to study and practice: A critical analysis*. Philadelphia: Taylor & Francis.

Schuler, R. S., & Jackson, S. E. (1986). Managing stress through PHRM practices: An uncertainity interpretation. *Research in Personnel and Human Resource Management, 4*, 183–224.

Selye, H. ([1956] 1976). *The stress of life* (2nd ed.). New York: McGraw-Hill.

Smeltzer, L. R. (1987). The relationship of communication to work stress. *The Journal of Business Communication, 24*(1), 47–58.

Starnaman, S. M., & Miller, K. I. (1992). A test of a causal model of communication and burnout in the teaching profession. *Communication Education, 41*(1), 40–53.

Tracy, S. J. (2000, November). *Identification and burnout in boundary-role-spanning positions: A literature review and survey study of public relations and advertising practitioners*. Paper presented at the National Communication Association Annual Conference, Seattle, WA.

Tracy, S. J. (2005). Locking up emotion: Moving beyond dissonance for understanding emotion labor discomfort. *Communication Monographs, 72*(2), 261–283.

Tracy, S. J. (2007). Power, paradox, social support, and prestige: A critical approach to addressing correctional officer burnout. In S. Fineman (Ed.), *Contours of emotion in organizations: Critical perspectives* (pp. 27–43). Oxford: Blackwell.

Tracy, S. J., Lutgen-Sandvik, P., & Alberts, J. K. (2006). Nightmares, demons and slaves: Exploring the painful metaphors of workplace bullying. *Management Communication Quarterly, 20*(2), 148–185.

Tracy, S. J., & Scott, C. (2006). Sexuality, masculinity and taint management among firefighters and correctional officers: Getting down and dirty with "America's heroes" and the "scum of law enforcement." *Management Communication Quarterly, 20*(1), 6–38.

Wojcik, J. (2001). Cutting costs of stress. *Business Insurance, 35*(15), 22.

Zapf, D., Dormann, C., & Frese, M. (1996). Longitudinal studies in organizational stress research: A review of the literature with reference to methodological issues. *Journal of Occupational Health Psychology, 1*(2), 145–169.

Chapter 5

Excessive Careerism and Destructive Life Stresses

The Role of Entrepreneurialism in Colonizing Identities

Stacey M. B. Wieland, Janell C. Bauer, and Stanley Deetz

Discussions on the street, in mass media, and scholarly publications suggest an overworked America with predicable costs to communities, families, social lives, and individuals' health. The issue of work–life balance seems to be everywhere. The increased home-care responsibilities and tax burdens from an aging population and the need to repay loans in a debt-ridden society are likely to increase these pressures. Clearly individuals have made, and will continue to make, choices about how to live their lives and how to engage work. These choices have consequences for the definition of and ability to achieve healthy lives, healthy societies, and general well-being.

In this chapter we consider the ways contemporary work organizations shape these choices and contribute to this social situation. Our analysis will inevitably be partial. Given the complexity of contemporary societies, probably nothing can be said about contemporary work–life that is simultaneously coherent and true. People have radically different relations to work; they work for different reasons. Ethnicity, class, and gender each produce different normative structures, opportunities, and expectations. Accounts of work–life are often narrative "mash-ups" pulling together tales and future visions from many genres.

We pull together one account by showing how a particular work–life orientation called careerism is developed and sustained in individuals' choices. Our choice may seem very limited—we are only looking at a life narrative developed most often in a particular class of professional white males. Careerism, however, is socially developed in such ways that others are drawn into the narrative, and the narrative often serves as a normative ideal to which other lives are compared and evaluated. In many ways it becomes a defining conception of work today.

We develop the notion of careerism as a particular example of corporate colonization, the domination of instrumental, particularly economic, values in social life. Although individuals enact careerism, it is more than a personal choice; it is a produced social configuration with wide-ranging consequences. We begin by showing how corporate colonization occurs by shaping the meanings of personal identity and quality of life. We argue that corporation colonization today operates through careerism by linking personal identity with a consumption-based quality of life that both sustains and is sustained by consumer society. We follow this discussion by showing how entrepreneurial culture, the predominant belief in the individual's ability to actively and profitably control his or her own situation, has been appropriated in an age of corporate colonization such that it facilitates both extreme careerism and consumerism. As should be clear from the start, corporate colonization is not necessarily bad. It has also had civilizing effects and has often worked against traditional authority-based relations and prejudices. Following the themes of this book, we, however, will explore the destructive implications of careerism as it is manifest in the entrepreneurial age for communities, organizations, families, and individuals.

Corporate Colonization Develops through Careerism and Consumerism

The concept of corporate colonization draws attention to the ways workplace organizations have usurped the meaning-giving functions of other types of institutions such as religion, family, and community (Deetz, 1992). In different historical periods these institutions have dominated meaning, and personal identities may have been more firmly located within them. In an age of corporate colonization, however, corporations (i.e., profit-driven entities) shape decision-making processes and ways of life more powerfully than in the past. In such an environment, human actors often derive personal identity from the workplace and work processes.

Conceptually, colonization of this sort might be represented in the following way. Imagine three spheres of life—private (home), public (community, government), and workplace. These most often coexist in tension-marked relationships, each having its own logic and demands. Colonization occurs when one of the spheres begins to encroach on the others, replacing the logic and demands of those spheres with its own. In corporate colonization, a particular form of workplace relations comes to dominate all three spheres. For example in cases of corporate colonization of the public sphere, work organizations have increased power in legislative and policy-making processes; economic decision processes might gradually replace political processes. We are especially interested in the encroachment of the workplace into the private space—the colonization of the personal. The private space includes our feelings and emotions, senses of value, personal relations, and child-rearing practices.

In corporate colonization instrumental reasoning becomes the primary form of reasoning. Ends are stressed over means, resulting in people, things, and processes being assessed in terms of their rational, measurable impacts on the world. Substantive values, such as living a meaningful life and participating in one's community, become understood and evaluated through the logic of values such as profit and productivity. They are increasingly assessed in terms of their instrumental worth rather than as something inherently worthwhile.

Careerism Links Identity to Production

Historically, the Western world has had a complex relationship with work that has generated continuously evolving social and personal meanings of work. In pre-industrial societies work was largely viewed as a means to an end; thus, people worked only enough to accomplish the necessary outcomes. Personal identity emerged from multiple social relationships between family and community and work. Today, we experience a different relationship with work. A set of events and methods of reasoning have enabled the colonization of identity. It is to these processes that we now turn. We argue that work has moved from being one way of establishing identity among many, to being the primary locus of identity. We begin by looking at the progression of the Protestant Work Ethic.

The rise of Protestantism and Calvinism dramatically changed the dominant conception of work, as working became imbued with religious value. According to the Protestant work ethic, work was respected as a primary means to honor God and to contribute to the community. Protestant teachings infused work not only with meaning for individual accomplishment and value, but also with moral goodness. Edgell (2006) explained the impact of Protestantism on work: "In effect it meant a reversal of the traditional attitude of doing no more than is necessary, to one in which the creation of wealth via unrelenting hard work became the main object in life" (p. 15). Through this connection between religion and work, a person's ability to produce through paid labor gained footing as one of the most powerful influences on identity. With the rise of the industrial revolution, non-religious institutions such as government and business corporations quickly embraced the value and morality of hard work associated with the Protestant work ethic but strayed from the religious commitment to asceticism (Edgell).

This partial adoption of the Protestant work ethic, adhering to a commitment to work without a commitment to saving earnings, created space for a rise in the value of work for profit and the subsequent obsession with the production of material goods. Weber (1976) noted that work became focused on making a profit, not making a product. The momentum of economic growth during the industrial revolution and the validation of moral value in work placed organized paid labor at the center of economic success and moral obligation. Edgell (2006, p. 26) explained that, "during the establishment of this revolutionary type of society, a dominant conception of work emerged that prioritized work that was capitalist, industrial, patriarchal, and modern over other types of work, such as unpaid housework which did not conform to this model." Following the industrial revolution, organizational life rapidly expanded, creating a close connection between work and success. Success was progressively more defined through production, creating a dramatic emphasis on paid work. Consequently, identity, which was previously multi-faceted and influenced by various elements of life experience, became increasingly and inextricably linked to production.

Work thus transitioned from occupying a marginal, typically functional, space in life to influencing nearly all realms of life including the personal, social, and familial. Most aspects of life began to function around business interests as individual success and identity were increasingly linked to organizational (i.e., economic) success. Persons in managerial, professional, and highly technical fields especially came to be identified by their work. For many, the concept of work as a *part* of life transformed into "career" and corporate advancement as *central* to life. That is, work shifted from what employees "do" to who employees "are." As du Gay (1996, p. 9) aptly notes, "As a fundamental human category, work is represented not only as livelihood, but also as a stable, consistent source of self-identity."

With organizational life and economic advancement occupying center stage, corporations took advantage of their prime position to focus on maximizing the commitment and efficiency of workers. Management strategy during the beginning of the twentieth century emphasized the creation of meaning through organizational work. Organizational strategy focused on aligning the values of workers with the values of the organization (e.g., Cheney, 1983; Maneerat, Hale, & Singhal, 2005). In this way, workers could feel they were contributing to their own goals by contributing to the organization, and, thus, organizational success would lead to personal satisfaction.

As identity became linked to production, colonization occurred. The instrumental values of productivity and efficiency became dominant, leaving little room for employees to identify with other values or aspects of life such as family, spirituality, or community. Through the transformation of organizational members' relationships to work, identity has become deeply bound to career advancement and professional success. The colonization of identity is manifest through careerism, as one's career becomes valued above all other life experiences. Values not tied to paid work become subordinated, and life becomes structured to accommodate career. The more this colonization of identity occurs the more the corporation becomes the dominant institution in society. The corporation maintains this dominant position through the rise of consumption, which binds people more tightly to their paid work.

Consumerism Links Quality of Life to Consumption

The American Dream, rooted in the Protestant work ethic, promises prosperity through hard work and meritocracy. The primary logic is, "If I work hard, I will prosper." Calvinistic associations between external markers of wealth and internal goodness add a secondary logic to this which is, "I must prosper; therefore, I must work hard." And nothing so "proves" the extent of prosperity as the accumulation of wealth markers (i.e., consumables). The Protestant work ethic, which revered hard work and asceticism, has been colonized by corporate values, creating a work-to-spend ethic where spending wages to support the economy and the capitalist system is the morally right thing to do. Work-to-spend has become the dominant normalized view of work within visible sectors of the workforce. In 1990, the average American owned and consumed more than twice as much as he or she did in 1948 and worked one month more per year in 1987 than they did in 1969 (Schor, 1991).

But why are Americans consuming more? Although many would argue that it is not money that matters but the attainment of the good life, the good life has become defined by purchasing or owning things—cars, houses, vacations, or children's college educations. This perception of lifestyle quality has been normalized through business and business-lobbied government interests that encourage workers to spend in support of the production model. Du Gay (1996, pp. 76–77) argues,

> As 'consumers', people are encouraged to shape their lives by the use of their purchasing power and to make sense of their existence by exercising their freedom to choose in a market in which 'one simultaneously purchases products and services, and assembles, manages and markets oneself.'

What is more, consuming not only communicates an enviable social position, but also can be framed as providing for voice or social action. For example, popular women's magazines claim, "Do good while you shop," and "Look good while doing good," and link AIDS prevention and awareness of global warming to buying products.[1] Ruskin and Schor (2005) connect the ubiquitousness of overt commercial messages in schools, and cultural institutions and the more subtle proliferation of product placement, with the creation of a "more materialistic populace" (para. 21).

The value placed on consumption as a central reward or measure of success begins very young. Schor (2005) claimed that the true pervasiveness of the consumption lifestyle was fueled by commercial advertising. Her research illustrates the negative social impact of raising children who are constantly bombarded by commercial marketing. In an early work (Schor, 1991), she asserted that the need to earn money in order to buy things was becoming a compulsion in young people working full-time jobs while still in school full-time. As students worked their way through college and business schools to gain the degrees necessary to compete and 'succeed' in corporate America, they also accumulated debt that tied them to the need for a big paycheck—even before the first day of their careers. According to Ruskin and Schor (2005),

> In 2003, the annual UCLA survey of incoming college freshmen found that the number of students who said it was a very important or essential life goal to "develop a meaningful philosophy of life" fell to an all-time low of 39%, while succeeding financially has increased to a 13-year high, at 74%. (para. 21)

Once out of school these young urban professionals sought lucrative, yet demanding careers. They worked 60- to 100-hour weeks. "Work consumed their lives. And if they weren't working, they were networking" (Schor, 1991, p. 18). Little suggests that this pattern is waning. Rather, the extreme focus on work continues to be fed by commercial and political messages that persuade Americans that happiness and success (as well as nationalism and patriotism) can be found and secured through the ability to earn and spend.

The result is that the majority of professional workers are striving to achieve the kind of high-level career success that only 1% of professionals will actually achieve, despite complete devotion to career advancement (Elsass & Ralston, 1989). It follows that workers will strive harder and harder, devoting more and more time to achieve a largely elusive and unattainable goal. Through consumerism and careerism, there is only one path to "get ahead" and one definition of success. Success can only be realized through a hyper-vigilant focus on career achievement as recognized and measured through increased monetary reward. Here instrumental values dominate our conception of "the good life" and our view of valuable social contributions. With an increasing amount of time spent at work, less time is available to spend with family or in the community. Sadly, many lack the time to enjoy the material goods they work so hard to secure. In response to the ever-increasing focus on consumption, fueled by increasing corporate power, alternative organizations such as the *Center for a New American Dream* ("New American Dream,") strive to reclaim a space for responsible consumption and a better balance between work and life.

In summary, the modern vision of career success leaves workers driven to devote more and more energy and resources to work. We assert that this has led to a social system that predominantly supports paid organizational careers and marginalizes other types of work and social sources for identity construction. This careerism is manifest in workers' willingness and desire to center their lives around work; their primary value system focuses on the ability to achieve the monetary success enabling them to stand out in a consumer society. Colonization develops through a mutually reinforcing relationship of careerism and consumerism. As identity becomes understood as based primarily in production, quality of life simultaneously becomes understood as based primarily in consumption.

This history makes fairly clear how careerism developed in conjunction with consumption and why corporate leaders might use company resources to perpetuate it. Its sustaining power seems less clear. As women and others with different values entered the workplace, careerism was more costly to them than were other social configurations. With the middle-class layoffs and restructurings of the 1980s and 1990s, why did companies' disloyalty to employees and disregard of the prevailing social contract fail to engender disidentification with work and the work organization? In many senses it did. Careerism-as-organization-man was seen as a mistake, but rather than disappearing, careerism became reconfigured in a more powerful way.

Careerism in an Entrepreneurial Age

As we have argued, careerism and consumption together facilitate the domination of instrumental values. Careerism positions subjects primarily as producers; consumer society positions subjects primarily as consumers. Such a configuration does not extend to all workers and is sustained in the face of contravening forces. In this section we will show how entrepreneurial culture is leveraged to strengthen this colonized production and consumption mentality. We discuss the one-sided lives that persist even as organizations and organizational leaders lose legitimacy and the ability to socialize and control workers.

To develop this argument we first explain what we mean by entrepreneurialism and the corresponding entrepreneurial identity. Second, we argue that entrepreneurialism has been brought into play in a way that furthers corporate colonization, even though entrepreneurialism could have displaced and resisted it. We explore the ways that careerism and consumer society draw upon entrepreneurial culture and, in so doing, become woven together as primary means by which the entrepreneurial worker gains worth. In our discussion, we delineate the difference between active and passive careerists and argue that the position of the active careerist has become normalized within entrepreneurial culture, leading to escalating expectations for all subjects as careerists. We take this normalization as strong evidence that entrepreneurialism has been leveraged for corporate colonization rather than to further open democratic communication.

By entrepreneurial culture, we mean an economic and social shift that favors enterprise. This shift can be seen most clearly in organizational life, as the preferred organization type becomes that of the privately-owned company in a free-market economy. In an entrepreneurial age, this preference extends beyond traditional for-profit arenas to shape various types of organizations such as educational, governmental, and cultural organizations. As Keat (1991, p. 3) explained, in an entrepreneurial age "'the commercial enterprise' takes on a paradigmatic status, the preferred model for any form of institutional organization and provision of goods and services." The commercial enterprise is favored because the culture of enterprise values organizational competition, claiming that competition breeds excellence. In this entrepreneurial context, several structural changes in organizations occur, including shifts away from bureaucracy toward flatter, more flexible structures.

These structural changes have vast implications for organizational members, and the value of enterprise extends beyond organizations to also shape individual ways of living. At the core of entrepreneurial culture is the importance of individual choice—responsibility and accountability become essential values (Heelas & Morris, 1992). Because of this focus on the autonomy and responsibility of the individual, the entrepreneurial self becomes self-reflexive and self-motivated, consciously directing its life project. As such, the entrepreneurial self presumably takes control of its fate, assuming primary responsibility for its success. Rose (1992) described the entrepreneurial self in what follows:

> The enterprising self will make a venture of its life, project itself a future and seek to shape itself in order to become that which it wishes to be. The enterprising self is thus a calculating self, a self that calculates *about* itself and that works *upon* itself in order to better itself. (p. 146, emphasis in original)

The entrepreneurial self then is an autonomous, reflexive entity that steers its life, pursuing the qualities cherished by the entrepreneurial logic: "initiative, self-reliance, risk-taking and the ability to accept responsibility for oneself and one's actions" (du Gay, 1996, p. 23). Thus, entrepreneurial selves are constantly and consciously involved in sustaining and developing their worth.

The Colonization of the Entrepreneurial Self

Where the entrepreneurial self could seek to better itself in a variety of ways, position in the workplace and the marketplace narrowly defines the entrepreneur's worth (Rose, 1992). As the entrepreneur's worth becomes tied to production and consumption, entrepreneurial culture and the entrepreneurial self become leveraged in the process of corporate colonization.

Entrepreneurs as Workers and Consumers

The first major measure of one's worthiness in the entrepreneurial age comes through one's paid work. As Rose (1992, p. 154) explained,

> Economic success, career progress and personal development intersect in this new expertise of autonomous subjectivity: Work has become an essential element in the path to self-realization, and the strivings of the autonomous self have become essential allies in the path to economic success.

The entrepreneur clings to work as a way of working on the project of self. Increased responsibility at work and the development of performance management systems facilitate this interpretation of worthiness (du Gay, 1996). Performance reviews, for example, are opportunities for the enterprising self to work directly on its project of the self and also moments in which others shape that self (Rose, 1992). As Rose noted, "enterprise forges a link between the ways we are governed by others and the ways we should govern ourselves" (p. 142). The workplace is one site at which this association becomes apparent, as enterprising selves tune in to the ways they can enhance their self project within this arena. Individuals are seen as having the ability to shape their success within the world of work and thus are given the responsibility to successfully manage their project of the self by successfully managing their careers.

The second measure of one's worthiness comes from the marketplace. Through consumption, subjects are able to establish and amplify their worth. Rose (1992, p. 155) explained, "Consumers are constituted as actors seeking to maximize their 'quality of life' by assembling a 'life-style' through acts of choice in a world of goods." Purchasing products and services positively shapes entrepreneurial selves and guides projects of the self. The entrepreneurial value of competition comes into play here as the social context shapes consumption choices.

In short, in entrepreneurial culture individuals purportedly have both the ability and responsibility to shape their social status and producing and consuming have become two primary ways that individuals do so. The emphasis on producing and consuming as ways of developing the self has obvious connections to our discussion of careerism and consumerism as manifestations of colonization. The entrepreneurial self becomes instrumentalized as its worth becomes tied primarily to production and consumption.

Entrepreneurialism Reconsidered

The question we want to raise at this point is whether the entrepreneurial self, by definition, must attain its worth through production or consumption or whether it has merely been pointed in that direction by corporate colonization. Although seeing entrepreneurial culture and entrepreneurial identity as manifestations of corporate colonization is tempting, we argue that entrepreneurial culture, in and of itself, does not necessarily correspond with corporate colonization. Instead, entrepreneurial culture appears to be more of a mechanism that corporate colonization *leverages*. Rather than being inherently tied up with the instrumentalism that comes in colonization, we argue that entrepreneurialism stands outside of it. As such, entrepreneurialism could also lead to greater diversity and a plurality of voices, aspects of a more democratic communication situation.

Keat (1991) pursued this line of thinking extensively, initially by distinguishing between two possible meanings of enterprise. First, enterprise is the extension of the free market economy such that institutions throughout society move to this more entrepreneurial model. Second, enterprise is increasing individual responsibility and choice. These two meanings of enterprise most commonly become equated with one another or understood as mutually dependent. Keat argued that if we question the idea that there exists a relationship between the two conceptualizations of enterprise, this questioning might lead to more democratic outcomes.

The recent shift to calling students "consumers" illustrates Keat's (1991) point. One way to interpret the equation of students with consumers is to see this as paving "the way for a more complete assimilation of educational institutions to commercial enterprises, ... [and transforming education] into a purchasable commodity, with all the obvious implications of justice and equality" (Keat, p. 12). This perspective merges the two meanings of enterprise. As the two meanings become indistinguishable, consumer society leverages enterprise to further the act of colonization, as education becomes instrumentalized toward economic ends.

There is, however, a second way to interpret students-as-consumers. Keat's (1991) second interpretation would view the practice as indicating the importance of institutional responsiveness to students. Such an interpretation implies "instead, the need to make educational institutions more responsive and accessible to those who enter them ('consumer-friendly'...) and to reduce the non-accountable authority of teachers and administrators" (Keat, p. 12). From this perspective, the language of enterprise might lead to institutions that responsively listen to the student-consumer voices. This second interpretation of enterprise, in contrast with the first, has the potential to lead to a more democratic society.

Keat (1991, p. 13) clarified the importance of distinguishing between and untangling the two possible interpretations of enterprise:

> The political function of this implied identity [as consumer] can, at least in principle, be quite easily reversed, so that the appeal to

consumer sovereignty is taken to support, not the extension of the free market, but a shift towards more democratic forms of control over institutions that had previously been insufficiently responsive to those whom they supposedly served. ... There is the fundamental need to ensure that the various characteristics of the enterprising self are understood in such a way that it will seem 'natural' to associate them exclusively or primarily with the conduct of commercial enterprises in a free economy: to prevent, in other words, the two main senses of the term 'enterprise' being pried apart.

Typically, the two meanings of enterprise are conflated rather than treated separately, which supports the dominant interpretation of enterprise as advancing a free market economy. This dominant interpretation suggests that "enterprise" has been colonized in support of instrumental rationality.

Entrepreneurial Careerism

We are specifically interested in exploring how careerism leverages entrepreneurialism in such a way that furthers colonization. Significant shifts in the character of paid work facilitate the efforts of colonization. Previously, workers entered an organization at the beginning of their careers and expected to follow a linear career path through that organization until retirement (Buzzanell & Goldzwig, 1991). In contrast, the new social contract does not revolve around the values of trust and loyalty nor the expectation of a long-term relationship (Buzzanell, 2000; Sennett, 1998). Instead, workers can expect to work in a variety of jobs at an assortment of organizations throughout the course of their careers. As such, they must take responsibility for their career trajectory.

The combination of having responsibility for one's career and enduring a great deal of uncertainty about that career creates a context in which production becomes the primary means of reducing uncertainty and creating a "successful" project of the self. Fournier (1998) describes this entrepreneurial version of careerism:

> The new career model knows no boundary; it extends its logic to all domains. All life experiences (leisure, social relationships...) are to be harnessed and translated into career opportunities; and movement is no longer constrained to the confines of one organization, occupation or profession. The new career ostensibly breaks through all conventional barriers to open up "a world of opportunities." (p. 59)

Given the uncertainty around and simultaneous responsibility for one's career, instrumentalism pervades through all parts of life in this entrepreneurial context.

Deetz's (1998) discussion of strategized self-subordination suggests how the instrumentalization of the self occurs. Strategized self-subordination occurs as members actively subordinate themselves to corporate structures and practices in order to obtain money, security, meaning, or identity, even beyond what the organizational expects or demands of them. When employees subordinate themselves for material and symbolic gains, they consent to a very narrow set of instrumental values embodied by the corporation. These processes can be seen most clearly in self-employment, when companies out-source a business function. The same person who in a prior time might be an employee of the company now works as a self-employed contractor, an "entrepreneur." Self-employed individuals typically work longer hours, which put more pressure on families, than is the case when they are employees. The company benefits in this contrived relation and others (i.e., the self-employed entrepreneurs) assume the costs.

In the entrepreneurial context, the costs are especially high for those who pursue "extreme jobs" (Hewlett & Luce, 2006). These jobs are typically unpredictable, fast-paced, span beyond regular work hours, require the worker to be available around-the-clock, and include a broad scope of responsibility. One such worker reported putting in over 120 hours a week; another worked six or seven days a week from various locations; many were never home—over half of these high-earning individuals worked more than 50 hours a week. These extreme jobs are not an anomaly. Hewlett and Luce (p. 51) claim, "our data reveals an enormous increase in work pressure for high-caliber professionals across ages, genders, sectors, and continents."

Similarly, Connell and Wood's (2005) research highlights the extent to which Australian businessmen go for career success. These men reported working extremely long hours, constantly traveling, and managing their bodies in various ways (similar to Hewlett & Luce, 2006). Many leveraged the entrepreneurial perspective and "bought in" to self-help products and services to shape themselves into the successful careerist. One respondent, Bruce, indicated that he saw a personal trainer and a naturopath. He stated, "It's all about managing your own body and being smart" (Connell & Wood, 2005, p. 355). For much of society this perspective of careers is not viewed as extreme but as "normal." Those studied clearly believed that workers must constantly improve themselves and either take action to move up or opt-out of the business environment.

Those who do take the extreme path to attain career advancement and success are most often proud and rewarded. "Extreme workers wear their commitments like badges of honor" (Connell & Wood, 2005, pp. 51-52), and well over half report loving their jobs. These workers, committed to their career at all costs, are not viewed in a negative light as "workaholics" or lonely individuals without family. Rather, "today's overachieving professionals are recast as road warriors and masters of the universe"

(Hewlett & Luce, 2006, p. 50). These careerists energetically pursue this life(work)style because they receive exceptional rewards in career advancement and subsequent power. As such, they are rarely troubled by the non-economic costs of such a lifestyle.

Active and Passive Careerists

These examples illustrate how the entrepreneurial approach to self and career places workers in the position of *choosing*—even *fighting* for—this work-focused life. They select this all-encompassing commitment to work as a way to ensure gainful employment, to achieve significant financial success, and to amass personal and professional power. We might usefully refer to those who aggressively pursue work as a means to establish their self-worth as *active careerists*. By this title we are referring to their active choice to privilege paid work over other life pursuits, in fact, to view paid work as *the* life pursuit.

Naming this subject position, *active careerist*, enables a contrast to its opposite, the *passive careerist*. The active careerist is the subject that vigorously grounds his or her entrepreneurial self in production, unabashedly pursuing advancement in the workplace and primarily seeking self-worth through his or her work. In contrast, the passive careerist is the subject who would not otherwise position work as the central element of their identity but is forced into this position within the context of the colonized entrepreneurial self, increased consumerism, and accumulated debt. Organizational structures and practices, including the aggressive competition posed by active careerists, make the discourse of careerism difficult to resist. Concern about career livelihood drives passive careerists to compete with their active careerist counterparts so that they are, at the least, perceived as wholly committed to their project of self via production.

Oftentimes organizations capitalize on the work habits of active careerists by using their commitment to face-time for setting standardized policies. For example, organizational authorities can consider simply being physically present as an indication of dedication, a sentiment suggested by this employee handbook excerpt: "Time spent on the job is an indication of commitment. Work more hours" (Hochschild, 1997, p. 19). In this context, the active careerist "sets the bar," defining the preferred subject position for all workers. Passive careerists are interpellated into that position and motivated to build a perception of themselves as active careerists, usually for material rewards or out of fear of losing their jobs. The following illustrates the associated tensions a working mother faces:

> Gradually, ... Gwen's workday has grown longer. She used to work a straight eight-hour day. Now it is regularly eight and a half to nine

hours, not counting the work that often spills over into life at home. Gwen is not happy about this. She feels Cassie's ten-hour day at Spotted Deer (the corporate day-care center) is too long, but at the same time she is not putting energy into curbing her expanding workday. (Hochschild, 1997, p. 12)

Many parents like Gwen work for companies with family-friendly policies and options for flex-time but feel they cannot actually take advantage of the formal policies without cost to their careers (Haley, Perry-Jenkins, & Armenia, 2001; Kirby & Krone, 2002). Alternate work–life-styles that emphasize balance between work and home are trivialized and "othered" because they do not fit with careerism or the work-to-spend value system. Although corporations stand to benefit from this drive for career success and excessive material consumption, the individual, family, and community pay the price. The cost is externalized, deflected from the employing organizations, into public and private spaces.

Active careerists excel in ways that further instrumental rationality, and those who want to pursue alternative ways of living and working become implicated by the actions of active careerists. The commitment, hours, and "heroics" of active careerists used to be considered abnormal and above-the-bar; however, through colonization these have become normalized. The extreme life/work relationship of the few has become the expected way of working for the many because organizational life richly rewards this orientation to work. Passive careerists are only able to continue in their careers by "passing" as active careerists. As such, careerism leverages the entrepreneurial values of individual responsibility and competition to further the economic ends of instrumental rationality, usually ends that fail to serve workers equitably. The self then becomes an instrumental means by which to achieve career success.

Our concern lies not with the existence of the active careerist position, but rather with the implications of this position in the competitive entrepreneurial context. The active careerist's understanding of self-worth as based in production and consumption comes to dominate other possible interpretations of self-worth, especially those that retain tensions between various self-interests. As the extreme is normalized, viewed as the acceptable norm, this normalization diminishes many other plausible ways of living and working in favor of one primary option. Through the promotion of the entrepreneurial self, the tenuous work contract, and escalating pressures to consume, workers accept, as given, narrowly defined conceptions for success and rigidly prescribed paths to achievement. Indeed, the active careerist has changed the landscape of work and the common conception of career success for all workers. The "ideal worker" has been transformed into an individual committed to personal career advancement and devotion to career success as a chief or sole aim. This commitment often comes at the expense of personal life, ethical beliefs, or any number of other equally important commitments.

Destructive Implications of Entrepreneurial Age Careerism

We have argued that careerism has leveraged the entrepreneurial self to further the domination of instrumental values over substantive values. In this section we consider the destructive implications of this process for communities, organizations, families, and individuals.

On a community level, a destructive aspect of this all-or-nothing view of entrepreneur as careerist is that it serves to normalize masculinity, closing off possibilities for alternative ways of being. The past traditional conception of the "organizational man" (Whyte, 1956), is of one who is unaffected by life outside work; who has a wife to attend to physical, emotional, and childcare needs so that these do not interfere with commitment to work; and who becomes reproduced in practice in the colonization of the entrepreneurial self. This masculine success-image has become normalized and even reified to the point that there are no unproblematic spaces for alternatives. Options (if at all) to work part-time, to leave work for family commitments, and to negotiate a different conception of successful work performance are marginalized and devalued to the point that many leave professional fields for self-employment or other alternative low-paying work. According to Hewlett and Luce (2006), only one-third of extreme workers are women. They speculated that women are less likely to tolerate the demands of extreme careerism because they are more aware of the "opportunity costs" including time away from children.

In this environment many of the tensions that would arise from work demands become invisible through the ways that professionals eliminate or silence competing demands from family or community, all in the name of freedom. For workers who are unable or unwilling to do this, work–life tensions become the problem of the individual. Workers retain responsibility for their career success or failure—they can either work harder to manage their lives and careers or they can "opt out" (Belkin, 2003; Whyte, 1956). A colonized notion of career makes opting out a viable option. Wieland (2006) explains:

> Without the overarching ideology that having a "successful" career is an all-or-nothing endeavor, the idea of opting out of one's career would not be a plausible or compelling approach to managing work–life tensions .... The discourse of opting out perpetuates the assumption that a committed worker is one whose primary (or only) focus is succeeding at work. (The discourse of Opting Out and the Discourse of Careerism Section, ¶ 5)

The choice of many women to opt out of this career fails to challenge the assumption that career is a totalizing aspect of identity.

In addition to increasing limited options for women, the normalized image of masculinity and professional work makes it more difficult for men to experience and acknowledge the intensity of work–life tensions. The conception of masculinity is so intertwined with career that it seems natural for men to *choose* to be committed to work, even to the extent that work crowds out space for all else. The fact that women are those who primarily opt out illustrates the embeddedness of masculinity and paid work. Further, successful women too must embody the masculine un-attached image of the active careerist. Only in light of women's attempts and failures to build successful careers and healthy homes does the narrowness of men's possibilities for relating work and life become clear (e.g., Newell, 1993).

At the organizational level, the colonized entrepreneur is destructive in that his or her presence can lead to negative organizational decision making. To the extent that career is the defining issue, business decisions become increasingly influenced by the perceived consequences of the decision on one's career. This may work against company health, leading to shifting of responsibilities and safe but bad choices. Further, with many active careerists in middle-management positions, their extreme entrepreneurial drive is applied and enforced on subordinates.

For example, Marra and Lindner (1992) found that the parental leaves which are most costly to organizations are those supervised by managers that demonstrate the least family-supportive attitudes. Other research supports this finding (Bond, Galinsky, & Swanberg, 1997) and suggests that job performance diminishes when work interferes with personal and family well-being by leading to a negative "spillover" from home to work. Many organizations now recognize the cost of work–life stress and have begun to develop more family-friendly policies (e.g., the value of flexible time). Despite this recognition, only a small percentage of companies take advantage of this knowledge.[2] Hochschild (1997) emphasized the prevalence of middle managers who do not support family-friendly policies; one manager in her study bluntly stated, "My policy on flextime is that there is no flextime" (p. 32).

Ciulla (2000) speculated that employees may have sensed that companies' family benefits actually conflict with job security. The actions and attitudes of active careerists diminish the available options for workers who would like more flexibility in defining their relationship between work and home. Ultimately the organization suffers the effects of passive careerists who attempt to pass as active careerists but are stressed, distracted, frequently absent, and more prone to turnover as a result of the lack of options for negotiating work and life. As Connell and Wood (2005, p. 354) claimed, "treating oneself as an entity to be managed is likely to mean limited loyalty to the corporation one currently works for." The manic careerism associated with entrepreneurialism leads to a more individualistic orientation, which is detrimental both to communities and organizations.

Costs are also externalized to families (and in turn, communities) as family and community become secondary to career success. The narratives collected by Hewlett and Luce (2006) effectively demonstrate this dynamic. For example, one man rearranged his grandmother's funeral to accommodate a meeting. Others gave up vacation time and neglected housework and duties of care (childcare and eldercare) in order to fulfill career demands. As studies emerged naming the negative consequences of locating childcare, missed work, and stress, organizations responded with assistance (Ciulla, 2000). Employers rationalized the cost of assistance by recognizing that employees would be more able to concentrate on their work and be more productive if they were not preoccupied by the stress of childcare (Galinsky, 2001). In addition to providing financial or referral assistance for childcare, the popularity of on- or near-site childcare is growing (Bond et al., 1997). This move repositions childcare from the domain of the family to the domain of the organization. Deetz (1992) suggests that such shifts may alter or eliminate the ways that children are educated about communal and home values.

In many cases childcare is taking place neither in the home nor in outside care—but is being neglected altogether. Schor (1991) identifies the impact of increased work demands on children, citing staggering statistics on the number of children left home alone. "A major problem is that children are increasingly left alone, to fend for themselves while their parents are at work" (Schor, p. 12). Hewlett (1991) connected the deficit in parenting to a variety of problems affecting American youth: poor performance in school, mental problems, drug and alcohol use, and teen suicide. Although it seems likely that these negative effects would alter the perpetuation of careerist values in future generations, we can actually see how the value system is colonized by instrumental values before people even enter the workforce. With parents working long hours (often identifying financial gain and career success as justification), the presence of diverse values and ways of living diminish in the younger generations. In fact, more and more teens substitute consumer goods for leisure, perpetuating the work-and-spend pattern of their parents (Ciulla, 2000). In this context, families and communities pay a high cost as energies and efforts are directed less and less in service of life world values associated with families and communities.

Finally, costs are also born by the individual. As Ciulla (2000) aptly noted, "we live under the shadow of the idea that time is money" (p. 172) and so for careerists, well-used time is time earning money. Indeed, research continues to underscore that workers are bending over backwards in pursuit of career often to their own detriment. Extreme careerists increasingly suffer from poor health, exhaustion, a lack of physical activity, unhealthy diets, and substance abuse as a result of overwork (Schor, 1991; Hewlett and Luce, 2006). "In 1997 the National Study of the Changing Workforce also found that employees with more demanding jobs and less supportive workplaces experience more stress and have poorer coping skills, worse moods, and less energy off the job—all of which jeopardize their personal and family well-being" (Galinsky, 2001, p. 172). In addition, workers and their spouses, partners, children, friends, and so forth are missing out on personal relationships. The stress of work is placing tremendous burdens on marriages (Schor, 1991). Although most people understand that time with family improves personal relationships, they still place work first. In what may even be a worse development, "as households and families are starved for time, they become progressively less appealing and both men and women begin to avoid the home" (Hochschild, 1997, p. 55).

Many workers (usually passive careerists) can articulate the stress and strain that work demands impose. "One-third of Americans say they always feel rushed; just over one-third say that their lives are out of control; two-thirds say they want more balance; and about 60% would like to simplify their lives" (Schor, 1998, p. 113). Despite the ability to articulate a desire for change, many feel trapped by the normalized dominance of work over life. The costs can be great for losing or leaving a job when the workplace acts as an "all-inclusive, self-regulating social system" (Ciulla, 2000, p. 133) and employees become increasingly dependent on work to fulfill social and personal needs that might otherwise have been filled outside of work. Job descriptions may even include attending "social" work functions such as breakfasts and cocktails to build community (and loyalty) at work. "The workplace is now the source of many people's social lives" (Hochschild, 1997, p. 54). With so much time at work and the consequent interpersonal bonds that develop, losing or leaving a job can also mean extended losses of social support and friendships.

A common symptom of these individual costs is burnout (see Tracy, Chapter 4 this volume). Burnout is costly on all of the levels—individual, familial, organizational, and communal—but its cause and solution is often simplistically understood as residing on the individual level (Newton, 1995). The lives of individuals who suffer from burnout are left in shambles, which also affects the communities, families, and organizations of which they are a part. As a result of burnout, organizations experience higher turnover rates, lost workdays, and employee dissatisfaction. Burnout is an indication of this social context in which self-worth and success are narrowly interpreted.

More Constructive Ways of Organizing in an Entrepreneurial Age

We are living in an age of corporate colonization in which individual and organizational choices tend to further careerism and consumerism. This context thrives within the entrepreneurial age, as the entrepreneurial self takes "heroic" measures to craft a positive self-project, defined primarily through one's involvement in work and the marketplace. A narrow conceptualization of the entrepreneurial self fuses a free-market orientation with a sense of individual autonomy, creates a competitive context that limits individual choices about work and life, and encourages the instrumentalization of self through paid work. This arrangement has destructive consequences for communities, organizations, families, and individuals.

Although not inherently wed to entrepreneurial culture, entrepreneurialism has been leveraged by corporate colonization. Entrepreneurial culture can partly account for the non-responsiveness of work organizations to the needs of their various members. Of course, there are potentials for organizing in more constructive ways and possibilities for change are always present. If the expectation of individual choice and responsibility were extricated from a free-market orientation, entrepreneurial culture might provide a context in which the consequences are clearer and the voices of various organizational stakeholders are taken seriously. In this context, organizations could respond to the needs of their employees and consumers because these stakeholders would be seen not merely as instrumental means to an economically productive end but rather as cohabitants of the life world. More constructive organizations would consider various logics—beyond simple economics—when making crucial organizational decisions. Logics of care, emotion, relationships, and communities would be brought into processes of decision-making. Organizations can expand decision making processes and organizational values to include a focus on sustainability and on a better work–life balance (Schor, 2005). In short, more constructive organizational contexts would make room for and acknowledge tensions between various values.

Managers and coworkers in more constructive organizations would acknowledge the varied needs of workers, recognizing that all employees have meaningful involvement in public and private spheres in addition to their involvement in the workplace. Life–work tensions would not be seen as problematic, but instead as evidence that one has varied allegiances. Constructive organizational policies and practices would recognize that employees have multiple commitments and interests rather than glossing over these conflicting demands. Solutions such as flextime, for example, acknowledge the conflicting demands between paid work and other parts of life because they enable individuals to adjust their work schedules to match their familial and communal responsibilities. Developing and encouraging alternatives to opting out—such as temporary leave or part-time schedules—for those pursuing careers while caring for children or elders might begin to challenge the all-or-nothing association of career. The hope is that more responsive organizations would enable diverse interpretations of "career" that leave room for individuals to pursue a variety of activities as part of their projects of self. Rather than a simple all-or-nothing orientation, opening up the meaning of careerism so that it takes varied forms will broaden the focus of self-projects to include not only one's role as employee and consumer, but also as partner, parent, relative, friend, neighbor, and citizen.

Notes

1 *Lucky* magazine, August, 2007; *InStyle* magazine, August, 2007; *Marie Claire* magazine, August, 2007.
2 Despite the fact that 88% of Fortune 500 manufacturing firms offer flexible time, only 3–5% of employees took advantage of it, according to a 1990 study of 188 Fortune 500 manufacturing firms (Hochschild, 1997, p. 27).

References

Belkin, L. (2003, October 26). The Opt-Out Revolution. *New York Times Magazine*, 42–47, 58, 85–86.
Bond, J. T., Galinsky, E., & Swanberg, J. E. (1997). *The 1997 national study of the changing workforce*. New York: Families and Work Institute.
Buzzanell, P. M. (2000). The promise and practice of the new career and social contract: Illusions exposed and suggestions for reform. In P. M. Buzzanell (Ed.), *Rethinking organizational and managerial communication from feminist perspectives* (pp. 209–235). Thousand Oaks, CA: Sage.
Buzzanell, P. M., & Goldzwig, S. R. (1991). Linear and nonlinear career models: Metaphors, paradigms and ideologies. *Management Communication Quarterly, 4*(4), 466–505.
Cheney, G. G. (1983). On the various and changing meanings of organizational membership: A field study of organizational identification. *Communication Monographs, 50*(3), 342–362.
Ciulla, J. B. (2000). *The working life: The promise and betrayal of modern work*. New York: Three Rivers Press.
Connell, R., & Wood, J. (2005). Globalization and business masculinities. *Men and Masculinities, 7*(4), 347–364.
Deetz, S. A. (1992). *Democracy in an age of corporate colonization*. Albany, NY: State University of New York Press.
Deetz, S. A. (1998). Discursive formations, strategized subordination and self-surveillance. In A. McKinley & K. Starkey (Eds.), *Foucault, Management and Organizational Theory* (pp. 151–172). London: Sage.
du Gay, P. (1996). *Consumption and identity at work*. London: Sage.
Edgell, S. (2006). *The sociology of work: Continuity and change in paid and unpaid work*. London: Sage.

Elsass, P. M., & Ralston, D. A. (1989). Individual responses to the stress of career plateauing. *Journal of Management, 15*(1), 35–47.

Fournier, V. (1998). Stories of development and exploitation: Militant voices in an enterprise culture. *Organization, 5*(1), 55–80.

Galinsky, E. J. (2001). Toward a new view of work and family life. In R. Hertz & N. Marshall (Eds.), *Working families: The transformation of the American home* (pp. 168–186). Berkeley: University of California Press.

Haley, H., Perry-Jenkins, M., & Armenia, A. (2001). Workplace policies and the psychological well-being of first-time parents. In R. Hertz & N. Marshall (Eds.), *Working families: The transformation of the American home* (pp. 227–250). Berkeley: University of California Press.

Heelas, P., & Morris, P. (1992). Enterprise culture: Its values and value. In P. Heelas & P. Morris (Eds.), *The values of enterprise culture: The moral debate* (pp. 5–24). London and New York: Routledge.

Hewlett, S. A. (1991). *When the bough breaks: The cost of neglecting our children*. New York: Basic Books.

Hewlett, S. A., & Luce, C. B. (2006). Extreme jobs: The dangerous allure of the 70-hour workweek. *Harvard Business Review, 85*(4), 136.

Hochschild, A. R. (1997). *The time bind: When work becomes home and home becomes work*. New York: Metropolitan Books.

Keat, R. (1991). Introduction, Starship Britain or universal enterprise? In R. Keat & N. Abercrombie (Eds.), *Enterprise culture* (pp. 1–17). London: Routledge.

Kirby, E. L., & Krone, K. J. (2002). "The policy exists but you can't really use it": Communication and the structuration of work-family policies. *Journal of Applied Communication Research, 30*(1), 50–77.

Maneerat, N., Hale, C., & Singhal, A. (2005). The communication glue that binds employees to an organization: A study of organizational identification in two Thai organizations. *Asian Journal of Communication, 15*(2), 188–214.

Marra, R., & Lindner, J. (1992). The true cost of parental leave: The parental leave cost model. In D. E. Friedman, E. Galinsky & V. Plowden (Eds.), *Parental leave and productivity: Current research* (pp. 119–128). New York: Families and Work Institute.

New American Dream. Retrieved April, 17, 2008, from http://www.newdream.org.

Newell, S. (1993). The superwoman syndrome: Gender differences in attitudes towards equal opportunities at work and towards domestic responsibilities at home. *Work, Employment & Society, 7*(2), 275–289.

Newton, T. (1995). *Managing stress: Emotion and power at work*. Thousand Oaks, CA: Sage.

Rose, N. (1992). Governing the enterprising self. In P. Heelas & P. Morris (Eds.), *The values of enterprise culture* (pp. 141–164). London: Routledge.

Ruskin, G., & Schor, J. B. (2005). Every nook and cranny: The dangerous spread of commercialized culture. *Multinational Monitor, 26(1/2)*. Retrieved May 1, 2008, from http://www.multinationalmonitor.org/mm2005/012005/ruskin.html.

Schor, J. B. (1991). *The overworked American: The unexpected decline of leisure*. New York: Basic Books.

Schor, J. B. (1998). *The overspent American: Upscaling, downshifting, and the new consumer*. New York: Basic Books.

Schor, J. B. (2005). Sustainable consumption and worktime reduction. *Journal of Industrial Ecology, 9*(1–2), 37–50.

Sennett, R. (1998). *The corrosion of character: The personal consequences of work in the new capitalism.* New York: W. H. Norton and Company.

Weber, M. (1976). *The Protestant ethic and the spirit of capitalism.* London: Allen and Unwin.

Whyte, W. H. (1956). *The organization man.* New York: Simon & Schuster.

Wieland, S. M. (2006). Discourses of careerism, separatism, and individualism: A work/life communication response to the opt-out revolution. *Electronic Journal of Communication, 16*(3 & 4).

Chapter 6

The Construction of Civility in Multicultural Organizations

Lorraine G. Kisselburgh and Mohan J. Dutta

Expanding work hours, work–life balance stresses, loss of community structures, economic uncertainties, and national security threats are bringing increased stresses to the lives of organizational members. Coupled with societal shifts toward informal cultures and discourse, one of the consequences of these stressors may be a growing trend toward uncivil behavior in the workplace—rudeness, hostility, harassment, desk rage, flaming, and even workplace bullying (Lutgen-Sandvik & McDermott, 2008; Lutgen-Sandvik, Tracy, & Alberts, 2007; Namie, 2003; O'Sullivan & Flanagin, 2003; Sypher, 2004). These behaviors vary in their intent and intensity, although even the less overt forms can be intimidating, discriminatory, harmful, controlling, and silencing. Many have called for a restoration of civility in the workplace (e.g., Forni, 2002; Gonthier, 2002; Pearson, Andersson, & Porath, 2000; Sypher, 2004).

Without a doubt, hostile and uncomfortable work environments have very real and material consequences—including stress, lost productivity, sick time, turnover, and burnout (Cortina, Magley, Williams, & Langhout, 2001; Sypher, 2004). Although few would encourage rude, obnoxious, and hostile behavior in the workplace, what are the implications of these calls for restoring civility? Specifically, what are the implications of re-introducing and enforcing particular social behavior norms when our organizations have become more diverse, multicultural, and global?

Global and Multicultural Organizations

In the past 15 years, the rapid growth of global economies has created a corollary change in organizational structures. Increasingly today, large (and even some small) corporations are transnational, sometimes multinational, multicultural, and global in both material and discursive ways. The cultural homogeneity that defined local and national organizations of the past is quickly being supplanted by cultural diversity and heterogeneity. Acknowledging this heterogeneity requires organizational communication scholars to revisit past research and its assumptions, and to explore new contexts and theoretical frameworks to understand organizational and communicative behaviors.

Within the context of destructive communication, globalization and the international flow of labor in transnational and multinational corporations creates more diverse organizational cultures and changes the discourse and norms. What is acceptable and unacceptable in organizational discourse and discursive practices is set against the backdrop of global geopolitics. Furthermore, global organizations find themselves in the midst of a *postcolonial predicament*, marked at the intersections of colonial histories in which colonizing powers defined the colonized, neocolonial logics of modern-day multinational corporations reinforcing these discourses, and international divisions of labor (Broadfoot & Munshi, 2007; Dutta, 2007, 2008; Shome & Hegde, 2002; Spivak, 1987). Postcolonialism engages with and contests colonialism's discourses, power structures, and social hierarchies (Gilbert & Tompkins, 1996). Organizational articulations of civility and incivility operate in postcolonial logics that are articulated in the realm of multinational organizations operating within Western-Eurocentric norms (Dutta, 2008).

In this chapter, we examine the process by which civility is constructed in organizational settings, the consequences such constructions may have for marginalizing voices in multicultural and global organizations, and alternative approaches that offer constructive solutions to this paradox. Specifically, we examine destructive communication from a broader macro-level perspective that attends to the politics of postcolonialism, articulating the structures and processes through which dominant constructions of civility serve hegemonic interests (Spivak, 1999). In doing so, we respond to the call issued by Broadfoot and Munshi (2007) for exploring postcolonial contexts of organizing.

While we acknowledge the real consequences of destructive communication and behaviors, we ask, What are the political and cultural consequences of dominant articulations of civility introduced by global corporations in postcolonial contexts? We contend that calls for civility, and attempts to define civility according to cultural norms, may be processes that are *paradoxically destructive* in multicultural environments.

To explore these questions, we begin by critically examining civility in organizational contexts and discussing issues of power, structural constraints, and the marginalization of voices that may ensue when organizations attempt to (re-)impose standards of civility on members. We move, then, to a larger macro-social perspective, taking a postcolonial lens to discuss the historical and cultural basis of the constructions of civility, and its modern counterpart. Drawing from literature on civil society, we use *Subaltern Studies* to examine the structures and normative values by which civility is constructed, discussing civility and the colonizing mission, civility and transnational hegemony with its links to neocolonialism (Dutta, 2008), and marginalized and silenced voices. Thus we draw parallels in the silencing of subaltern populations with the marginalization of voices in organizations, a potentially unintended consequence of imposing universal norms for civil behavior.

Finally, we offer a culture-centered approach as an alternative lens to the discussions of the issue. Through this approach we deconstruct the assumed notions of what constitutes civil behavior and the colonizing mission of the articulation of the term civility, and locate discussions of civility in the realm of colonial logics of dominant discourses that operate to silence the voices of subalterns. In doing so, we situate discussions of civility at the intersections of culture, structure, and agency, and emphasize dialogues that are imbued with the politics of post-coloniality.

The Construction of Civility or Civil Discourse

A large body of literature in organizational communication examines organizational effectiveness from the micro-level of the individual, including studies of communication competence (Jablin & Sias, 2001; Sypher & Zorn, 1986, 1988) and organizational assimilation and socialization (Jablin, 2001). This research focuses on individual-level competencies that can be refined to positively contribute to individual and organizational success. Within this framework, constructive communication contributes to individual satisfaction, workplace harmony, and organizational success. Civility in this context is a positive attribute; incivility in contrast is counterproductive to such goals.

Critical Lens

Taking a *critical approach* to organizations (Deetz & Mumby, 1990) we ask whether factors such as assimilation, socialization, and communication competence are in fact important for organizational success—or even for individual satisfaction and success—or whether the lens taken and the instruments chosen to measure such attributes only perpetuate perceptions we have about organizational success.

Power and Control

A critical approach questions the dominant voices and structures of power (Deetz, 2005; Deetz & Mumby, 1990), and asks whether civility is important for organizational success, or perhaps a call for conformity by those in positions of power. That is, organizational leaders may prefer and reward communicative behaviors that promote organizational conformity, assimilation, and workplace harmony. And in doing so, such rewarded individuals become successful and advance to positions of authority, and thus reinforce the cycle. Civility as a form of organizational discourse is itself a notion of conformity, defined as behavior that conforms to social norms of good citizens. Incivility, however—construed widely from a lack of respect to more threatening acts of bullying, aggression, and violence— is derived from the Latin *civis*, and implies the uncivilized, savage, barbaric, or even lack of "good breeding" (Oxford English Dictionary).

The very notion of what constitutes civil communication, however, is socially and culturally constructed, built upon mainstream notions of civility and on the access that privileged social actors have to the discursive space defining what constitutes civility and incivility. In other words, the notion of civility is constructed by privileged voices in privileged institutions or societies. Thus, what constitutes civil communication is fundamentally tied to the goals and objectives of dominant social actors within the discursive spaces, and to the value systems embodied by these dominant actors. Consequently, the normative ideal of civility is a white, middle-class, *corporatized* notion. In this sense, the notion of civility serves dominant social actors by valuing certain standards that count as effective forms and styles of communication. In doing so, the construction of civility marginalizes voices deemed uncivil, closes off the discursive space for such members, and minimizes opportunities for resistance.

In short, the imposition of civility can be viewed as a mechanism of control by those in power and a means of silencing those who fail to conform to mainstream values and definitions of civility. Civility is an attractive value to hold when organizational members have the position, authority, and resources that they need; its appeal wanes to an extent commensurate with one's deprivation. And, the closer one gets to the bottom of the system of reward and privilege, the less power one has to exercise meaningful incivility.

Voice and Participation

Also central to the critical perspective is the question of *voice*. Scholars in the past have cautioned against calls for politeness in organizational settings because it carries the risk of inhibiting participation and democratic goals (Lyotard, 1984; Schudson, 1997). Mumby and Stohl (1996) suggest the *problematic of voice* as a way to challenge the managerial-dominated discourse that has ruled organizational communication and business literature for so many years. This problematic challenges the dominant ways we interpret the structure, practices, and processes of organizations, and examines not only "who gets to speak," but also "who gets to speak for the members of another culture" (p. 55). In this framework, scholars can examine the perspectives of marginalized voices, groups, and forms of organizing.

The problematic of voice reminds us that although respect and civility are important to organizations, we need to ensure that discourse does not silence those who play important roles in balancing organizations. For example, incivility and holding diverse values can become a positive and constructive force in organizations. Ethical scandals like Enron's demonstrate the important role that whistleblowers and other radicals play in righting the wrongs when leaders begin to stray. Such voices can raise consciousness, balance power, nourish innovation, and call attention to harmful or unethical practices. Dissenting and sometimes uncivil voices of protest groups have also played important roles in our institutions and societies by raising awareness and consciousness of organizational inequities and discriminations, and thus helping us to modify discourse, practices, and structures that have enabled such inequities.

The *organizational fool* or corporate jester can also play roles that moderate narcissism, act as safety valves, or serve as important change agents. Kets deVries (1990) discusses the role of the organizational fool who uses dissent, humor, and questioning as tools to balance a leader's (or organization's) arrogance, pride, or just plain lack of sense. Similarly, Firth and Leigh (1998) describe the corporate fool as "doing the undoable, thinking the unthinkable, saying the unsayable, and driving your sensible organization mad with creative folly" (p. 1). In short, voices of dissent and jest can provide an important balance to organizations, foster dialogue, and enhance new ideas that nourish creativity and innovation (see Mumby, Chapter 15 this volume). Because multicultural organizations are more likely to be comprised of diverse individuals and diverse voices, it is important to be aware of and sensitive to practices that silence and marginalize voices outside the mainstream, to ensure full participation of their organizational members.

Structure and Agency

Through the critical perspective, organizational communication scholars examine not only voice and participation, but also the role of structure and agency in the construction of civility and the constraints in which civility is enacted. By emphasizing the individual's enactment of communicative processes within the organization, civility discourse shifts attention away from the broader structural inequities that plague organizations (Giddens, 1984). An emphasis on civil discourse shifts focus from the structural policies and practices within organizations that create and sustain unhealthy conditions of work. For example, the discussion of civil discourse in the context of *desk rage* draws attention away from the structural injustices in organizations such as long hours, excessive e-mail, and unrealistic deadlines. In identifying uncivil communication such as yelling, verbal abuse, and physical violence, civility discourse dislocates such practices from the broader structural contexts within which they are enacted. The emphasis is placed on the individual's communication style and the communicator is identified as deviant, without attending to the inequities that produce the conditions of incivility. In other words, an individual-level emphasis on civil discourse shifts attention away from the structural violence that can be perpetrated by organizations and minimizes opportunities for resistance to these structures.

Furthermore, the current literature on civil discourse does not engage the nature of communicative processes vis-à-vis organizational structures. The same communication phenomenon takes on different meanings on the basis of its locus within the organization's structure. For instance, a communicative situation where a manager *ignores* the communication of a temporary worker in the organization is very different from the communicative situation where the temporary worker ignores communication from the manager. In other words, the meanings, implications and outcomes of a communicative act differ vastly on the basis of who makes the utterance to whom and under what structural context. Likewise, structural constraints can be perceived differently based upon the standing of one's membership in a group. Central members in a group, organization, or society are more likely to view structure as *comfort* that ensures familiar standards of communication and interaction. In contrast, persons who have been marginalized or have experienced exclusion or discrimination are more likely to view structure as *stricture* that prevents them from full participation.

Therefore, organizational communication research on civil discourse must address structural questions such as: What are the implications for civility in the context of response to what is perceived as unfair organizational practices? What are the implications for civility in the face of organizational injustices such as the exploitation of labor? What are the implications for civility in the realm of what might be more violent structural inequities within the organization?

Post-colonial Lens (and Subaltern Studies)

We can reach a broader macro-level understanding of civility by examining the literature on civil societies. The term *civility* is derived from the Latin *civis* or citizen, and *civitas*, or city, recognizing that to be civil is to adhere to norms and standards of the community that promote civic harmony—treating people ethically and with respect in order to maintain social harmony and facilitate interaction in a community. Civility is based upon Aristotle's *civil society* as a framework for the goals of democratic voice and participation in societies. More recently in U.S. history, Papacharissi (2004,

p. 264) notes that a more "bourgeois interpretation" of civility emerged that associated good manners and morality with the principles of democracy (see also, Calhoun, 2000). The writings of the founders of U.S. democracy framed those interpretations and envisioned civility as a form of morality and a shaper of character and honor (Jacobs, 2002; Kesler, 1992). Thus, civility became equated with moral character in modern U.S. American constructions. Rudeness, for example, is considered to be a moral failing of individuals and an act that violates social norms (Westacott, 2006). But even these interpretations included an implication of social conformity that "could inhibit free expression" (Papacharissi, p. 264).

But the concept of civil society, vis-à-vis its values, outcomes, and feasibility, and particularly in terms of oppressed cultures, has been questioned. Civil society "serves the goals of the transnational elite and actively participates in the marginalization of the Third World participant" (Dutta-Bergman, 2005, p. 1). In postcolonial contexts, civility has been attached to the civilizing mission, which in turn, has offered the human face for the oppressive agendas of colonialism. The articulation of the *civil* is juxtaposed against the *uncivil*, as a dichotomy, has served to justify the colonizing agendas of Empires and suggested that the primitive colonies needed to be colonized (i.e., civilized) so that they could receive the enlightening mantras of the colonizers (Dutta, 2008).

For instance, historically the agendas of the East India Company to civilize the native masses in India served as the logic for the underlying economic interests of the Empire in colonizing India. Here, the show of an altruistic motive hid the deep-seated interests of the colonizer in exploiting the resources in the colonies. Similarly, in neocolonial contexts, the circulation of Western-centric standards of civility often serve to mark out the territories for appropriate employee communication in postcolonial contexts, defining the terrains of communication, and simultaneously serving the broader agendas of transnational hegemony. In contemporary global history, promises of bringing civility and civilization have been offered as arguments for U.S. military actions in Afghanistan and Iraq (Dutta, 2008). The paradox suggested by the postcolonial approach lies in the very juxtaposition of the promises of bringing civility through oppressive mechanisms such as war and occupation.

Furthermore, Beverly (1998) points out that civil society is a *modernist* construct that is:

> tied up with the normative sense of modernity and civic participation, which by virtue of its own requirements (literacy, nuclear family units, attention to formal politics and business news, property or a stable income source) *excludes signification sectors of the society* from full citizenship. (p. 120, emphasis added)

The dominant Western criteria for civil societies are used to construct marginalized cultures as *uncivilized* (Dutta-Bergman, 2005; Spivak, 1990, 1996, 1999). In that frame, civility became a social construction based upon Eurocentric values and capitalistic principles of what constitutes the core of a civil society. This construction was extended through the use of communication processes, discourses, and strategies that served to *mark* uncivil groups and to limit their participatory opportunities. The result, of course, was further marginalization of the individuals in such cultures, and an effective silencing of their voices.

The Subaltern in Organizations

Dutta-Bergman (2005) has proposed *Subaltern Studies* as an entry point for articulating communicative practices in marginalized groups and populations. The term *subaltern* is derived from the British military, denoting a subordinate officer of lower rank (Spivak, 1988). In postcolonial studies, the term came to refer to marginalized groups and lower classes outside the structures of political representation (see also, Guha & Spivak, 1988; Spivak, 1988; and *testimonio* literature, Brabeck, 2004; Gugelberger & Kearny, 1991). Guha (1988) extended the definition to include "the general attribute of subordination whether this is expressed in terms of class, caste, age, gender, and office or in any other way" (p. 1).

In critical terms, subaltern status is a state that renders a person without *agency* by virtue of his or her status and denotes individuals that are not just subordinated, but also silenced and marginalized (Spivak, 1988). Civility and civil society, then, become means of maintaining and reproducing those in power (Spivak, 1990, 2003) and silencing the voices of the subaltern. Beverly (1998) reminds us that the characteristic silence of the subaltern is observed primarily from the perspective of a dominant and elite value system. That is, the acquiescent, silenced voice is the individual *as represented* within a dominant society or structure.

The consequences, then, are that calls for civil behavior in these societies are in fact a call for the adoption and assimilation of citizens into behavior that was not necessarily normative for its society but was normative for the elite. This, of course, had the effect of further marginalizing those non-elite citizens and denying them opportunities to express their voice—and particularly to express resistance. Thus, civil society created *confines* for membership, and represented a paradox to the goal of democratic participation. Furthermore, calls for civil behavior historically were mobilized to justify colonizing Empires, providing an aesthetic for the *civilizing mission*, an alternative name for the colonial enterprise (Spivak, 1987).

Participatory discourse in global and multicultural organizations can become a problematic extension of this issue. When organizations move to democratize their environments, they must be sensitive to the possibility of promoting only dominant and mainstream values, even in the face of consensus among members. Privileging collaboration can serve to stifle voices of opposition and the input and perspectives those voices bring to the organization. Stohl and Cheney (2001) refer to this as a *paradox of homogeneity*, in which "the very unity that helps to maintain a democratic organization or give life to democratic practices may also be its limiting factor" (p. 389).

Issues of dominance in social structures, elitist norms, and silenced subaltern populations can be linked to culturally-sensitive understandings of organizations, particularly in terms of the perspectives of hegemony, voice, and marginalization. The literature on Subaltern Studies informs our understanding of marginalized voices in organizations in important ways regarding diversity. For example, Mellinger (2003) uses the concept of the subaltern in examining racial diversity discourse in organizations. Calling up Fraser's concept of *subaltern counterpublics*, Mellinger notes the presence of "parallel discursive arenas where members of subordinated social groups invent and circulate counter-discourses, which in turn permit them to formulate oppositional interpretations of their identities, interests, and needs" (Fraser, 1997, as cited in Mellinger, 2003, p. 146). In other work on social tolerance, Persell and colleagues (Persell, Green, & Gurevich, 2001) examined data from the General Social Survey during the years 1972 to 1994, and reported that as economic security increased, a vibrant civil society produced greater trust and increased espoused social tolerance. This connection between social tolerance and civil society, particularly as it affects the tolerance of marginalized groups such as racial and ethnic minorities and those with disabilities and alternative sexual orientations, has important implications for discourse about civility.

Similarly, Van Dijk and colleagues (Van Dijk, 1993, 1996, 1997; Van Dijk, Ting-Toomey, Smitherman, & Troutman, 1997) have discussed the political discourse used in elite Western cultures when describing *Others*, particularly pertaining to illegal aliens and racism. This work focuses on the construction of threats inherent in the discourse about *alien* cultures, with an underlying theme of threats to our "norms, values, principles, or religion ... to the economy and social structure; and ... to our standard of living and our wallets" (Van Dijk, 1997, pp. 61–62). In all of these discourses, "our own group, culture, and civilization are idealized and uncritically presented as the great example" (Van Dijk, p. 62). Thus, cultural differences *between* groups are exaggerated while differences *within* cultures are ignored. This focus on *Others* represents positive self-presentation strategies and "one of the most effective and insidious ways in which to marginalize and problematize Others" (Van Dijk, p. 62).

Although these works focus on macro-level societal spheres of discourse, they are applicable to organizational discourse and our examination of civility in organizations. In other words, when economic and organizational environments become more secure and stable, individuals are less threatened and more trusting and tolerant of social diversity. In contrast, when organizational environments are dynamic, unpredictable, and rapidly changing, individuals may attempt to silence dissenting and diverse voices in order to yield greater social harmony.

The Construction of Civility

The work on subalterns and political discourse is useful to organizational communication scholars in illuminating not how (in)civility is *expressed*, but how civility gets *constructed* in social and organizational institutions—as a threat to (elite) norms of behavior, particularly a threat to the standards of discourse that organizational structures promote. From this perspective, we see that constructions of civility create dichotomies between the civil and uncivil that are in conflict with the goals of diversity.

Civility in Organizations

From an organizational perspective, the emphasis on workplace civility assumes the inherent value and superiority of certain styles of communication. Civility discourse in the workplace demonstrates an inherent value system that privileges certain forms and styles of communication as civilized and moral, and simultaneously undermines other communicative processes in alternative spaces outside the realm of the dominant configurations. Communicative platforms and processes are inaccessible to and remain outside the realm of the subaltern. Furthermore, communication styles in mainstream civil societies create conditions of marginality by categorizing who is included and who is excluded from the discursive space. The silencing of subaltern groups in organizations occurs because of the very communicative choices of dominant actors in mainstream organizations. Our notions of what constitutes *civil* forms of communication are inherently tied to deeply-rooted ideological processes that value certain forms of communication as desirable and simultaneously label other communicative forms as undesirable. Privileging these dominant forms and styles of communication lies at the heart of the silencing and erasure of subaltern communities that exist outside mainstream civil societies.

Sypher (2004) discusses the relevance of civil communication that discourages various forms of antisocial behavior that "undermine democracy, mute voices, hurt feelings, damage self esteem, reduce worker involvement and productivity, and negatively influence individual and organizational health" (p. 258). In this context, it is important to examine what constitutes *social* and *antisocial* organizational communication styles. The very dichotomization of communication styles into social and antisocial poles values certain communication styles as configured by the dominant actors within social systems. Such distinctions in communication styles are deeply connected with social configurations of race, class, and gender, such that what defines *social* in organizational discourse is tied to the inherent values of privileged actors in powerful positions who define and drive the criteria for how civility is constructed. Furthermore, given the capitalist logic of global organizations operating under the demands of marketplace economics, the discourse of civility maintains hegemonic configurations by privileging the dominant communicative styles over other styles that offer opportunities for resistance.

Orbe (1995; 1998) made a similar contention in his examinations of the communication of African-American men. In an extension of muted group theory (Kramarae, 1981), which states that the dominant group in a culture controls avenues of expression, Orbe (1995) notes that the white European culture has dominated U.S. American culture so thoroughly that there is a cultural belief that all African-Americans communicate in a homogenous manner. Such constructions and misrepresentations ignore clear individual differences and illuminate the problem of voices that have been silenced and marginalized under dominant structures.

Value Systems

In the past, organizational communication scholars have examined the value systems of individuals within an organization and how organizational values are embedded in the interpersonal constructs of its members (Pacanowsky & O'Donnell-Trujillo, 1983). Recently, Sypher (2004) suggested that incivility may result from value systems that collide, expressed through contentious discourse. Specifically, she contrasts values that sanction an "in-your-face" workplace culture of "bounded discourse, confrontational listening, and rhetoric of silencing" with those that encourage "emotional restraint, emotional stewardship, and a 'disciplining of desires' ... [through] ... expressing respect and concern for others' views, ideas, and well-being" (p. 257). Her argument for encouraging workplace civility does not suggest the elimination of disagreement, but rather the reclamation of methods of argument that restore a sense of decency, decorum, and respect in organizational discourse. But if incivility results from differing value systems, how do organizations resolve incompatible values, particularly in the case of non-homogeneous global, multicultural, and multinational organizations? Diverse voices in workplace environments are "not primarily a problem of economic inequity and class exploitation ... but an issue of cultural valuation and recognition" (Mellinger, 2003, p. 17). Consistent with Dutta-Bergman (2005), this view claims that hegemonic discourse creates a dominance with a "disproportionate ability to shape the sociocultural understandings of society, especially those involving ... intergroup interactions" (Mellinger, p. 19).

The question remains. In a multicultural environment, whose standards do we adopt when determining civility in organizational structures? Furthermore, when articulating, what are the correct methods of argument, and who decides this correctness? Indeed, when we recognize that many global organizations span quite different cultures (e.g., United States, China, Eastern Europe, India), we realize the difficulty an organization might have in defining and implementing norms of civility. In Japan, for example, respectful behavior involves both face-saving individual communication (Fukada & Asato, 2004), as well as societal norms about how one displays respect to those in authority and to one's peers. Furthermore, the culturally acceptable signals of respect and civility in terms of eye contact and head height may differ. Direct eye contact is a sign of respect in the United States, whereas indirect eye contact conveys respect in South America. Head height is carefully attended to in Japanese social norms but not in United States settings. As such, when individuals in cultural minorities experience confusion about conflicting standards and subsequent isolation as a result of supposed uncivil acts, are we adopting a veiled form of marginalizing those whose standards of civility do not conform to Western views?

One might protest that these are less egregious forms of communicative behavior that differ significantly from overt acts of bullying and harassment. But, they can form the basis of nuanced communicative acts that are *tells* into cultural differences and, in doing so, marginalize one as *different* or *Other* in the context of organizational cultures. Even within homogeneous organizational cultures, there are variances in the values and contexts framing organizational discourse. For example, O'Sullivan and Flanagin (2003) studied flaming in online discussion groups and noted that the interpretation of whether a message was considered flaming often differed between and among interactants. Even profanity can vary in its meaning between interactants, from a tool of play or a point of emphasis to an intentionally malicious insult. Thus, the *context* of the setting and the shared understandings between the participants play important roles in what constitutes civility and incivility (O'Sullivan & Flanagin).

The point is, if we attempt to create normative definitions of civility, the very act of doing so is fraught with difficulties in multicultural organizations. And, if an organization insists on attempting to adopt such rules, a possible consequence can be the marginalization of voices—precisely the opposite, and an unintended, effect from the goal of inclusion that civility promotes. As the field of organizational communication expands its study to global and multicultural organizational forms, it is imperative that scholarship be cognizant of the cultural assumptions apparent in calls for civility. Given these issues, how do we reconcile the call for civil discourse in the workplace with critical approaches casting civility as a hegemonic tool of Western cultures that marginalizes (Dutta-Bergman, 2005)? More succinctly, how do we define civility in multicultural, multinational organizations with sensitivity to cultural differences? Do standards of civility and other forms of conformity become new mechanisms for the oppression and marginalization of populations that are not in power?

Universals

One possible consideration is whether we should attempt to define civility universals in the same way others have done for *politeness universals* (e.g., Brown & Levinson, 1987; Gu, 1990; Holtgraves & Yang, 1990). The premise is that across cultures there may be universal norms that define civil behavior upon which organizations can draw. Certainly violence and physically abusive behavior would generally be recognized as universally destructive and uncivil. Linguists have examined universal politeness theories from cross-cultural perspectives and demonstrated that politeness universals are generally language- and culture-specific and specifically ethnocentric to the (English) language and culture.

> Features of English which have been claimed to be due to universal principles of politeness are shown to be language-specific and culture-specific. Moreover, even with respect to English, they are shown to be due to aspects of culture much deeper than mere norms of politeness. … In particular, certain influential theories of speech acts (based largely on English) are shown to be ethnocentric. (Wierzbicka, 1985, p. 1)

Furthermore, when we traverse this road, we find another paradox: Universals come from space, geography, and locales and are in themselves *boundaried* in terms of norms, and these norms in turn tend to reflect and reinforce dominant norms, values, and voices. In postcolonial terms, they are situated within postcolonial politics. The paradox is that although we may call for creating platforms and spaces for the expression of more diverse voices, the very act of defining such a space creates a cycle in which the dominant voices are reinforced (see Dutta, 2007, 2008). The structures of such spaces and the rules invoked to define the participatory confines of the spaces are established within broader power structures that serve the interests of global transnational organizations.

Civil society is *culturally-bound*, there are not necessarily "universal ideals of humanity," and attempts to build global civil societies are value-laden attempts at "essentializing and procreating Western spaces elsewhere in the world" (Dutta-Bergman, 2005, p. 7). Thus, (re)erecting civil societies creates the possibility of oppressing and suppressing marginalized voices through global and multinational corporations. The act of creating consensus—whether in an organization or political sphere—is in and of itself an act of reproducing and reinforcing dominant discourses. Although this might be considered a *culture-sensitive* approach (Dutta, 2007), it is not a *culture-centered* approach (Dutta, 2008). In the culture-sensitive approach, the culture is labeled, its characteristics are extracted, and interventions are designed to target the culture. The culture becomes identified in terms of its absences, thus justifying the political economy of so-called interventions targeted toward addressing these absences.

Those studying cross-cultural communication are familiar with the term *cultural imperialism*, the practice in which the culture and language of one nation is imposed upon another (Tomlinson, 1991). The essence of cultural imperialism is that when powerful, elite, dominant institutions and cultures are introduced beyond their natural geographic borders, it is convenient and easy to assume that less-privileged cultures and institutions will welcome their introduction and eagerly adopt their mores. The emergence of scholarship on *glocal* organizations—global organizations enacted at local levels—recognizes that norms and behaviors of the situated organization are drawn from the local context, even when larger organizational goals are derived from the global context. New literature on communication in transnational organizations illustrates the tensions when organizational members are asked to perform one culture while at work and another when they are at home (Pal & Buzzanell, 2008).

Our core argument, then, is that (re)creating and defining normative behavior and expressions is an act that can create boundaries of acceptable membership, marginalizing members who are *different* from those norms. Although this may indeed establish clear boundaries for the exclusion and punishment of egregious behavior, a larger implication is that doing so can harm and marginalize a greater number of people who will be made aware that their behavior is *not quite normative*. If they are unable to find ways to adapt, the result will be silenced expression and behavior and the loss of what might be unique perspectives, innovative ideas, and challenging discourse. Particularly in today's organizational culture of innovation, creativity, and entrepreneurship, old mores of privileging behavior for the sake of harmonious relationships might be counterproductive to creating environments that foster, nurture, and value unique voices, perspective, ideas, and approaches. Thus, with the growth of globalization and rapidly changing entrepreneurial and innovative organizations, we must take care not to silence the very heart of that which we have created: diverse groups, global cultures, and a spirit of entrepreneurship and innovation that thrives upon unique perspectives and voices.

Constructive Ways to Approach Civil Discourse

The questions we have posed lead us to consider an alternative approach to civil discourse built from a culture-centered foundation. In addition to the critical perspectives of examining the power, voice, and structure in institutions, a culture-centered approach foregrounds marginalized voices within cultural contexts and calls for *reflexivity* in both theory and practice. It also acknowledges the multicultural values inherent in global and transnational organizations. In performing reflexivity, we include the practice and forms of *listening* that provide more space for both inclusion, as well as the opportunities for expression and resistance.

Culture-Centered Approach

The culture-centered approach examines the marginalizing communicative practices of mainstream civil society organizations and foregrounds the ways in which the dominant practices create conditions of marginality (Dutta-Bergman, 2005; Dutta-Bergman & Basnyat, 2006). Drawing from subaltern studies scholarship, this approach focuses on the erasures in the dominant discourses of mainstream organizations and brings forth the ways these narratives create conditions of marginality. The condition of subalternity is communicatively constituted through mainstream organizational discursive practices; deconstructing these practices is needed to understand how they silence and marginalize. As a deconstructive exercise, the culture-centered approach examines the "untold stories" and looks for what is "not there" in the discursive space—that which is marked by its absence.

Silences in the discursive space underscore the ways that dominant forces shape the structures of presence and absence, such that certain segments of the population are excluded. In doing so, the culture-centered approach studies the constitution of silencing, marginalizing communication at the intersections of structure, culture, and agency. It raises questions such as: What are the dominant structures that create and sustain the conditions for erasures of subaltern voices? What are the cultural contexts within which such voices are erased? How do calls for universal civility erase possibilities by setting the rules of the game, determining the standards, and establishing the criteria and the methods? Simultaneously, culture-centered deconstruction challenges how dominant social actors have traditionally constituted historical narratives and seeks to open opportunities for retelling alternative organizational narratives. Ultimately, by engaging in dialogue with subaltern voices, the culture-centered approach explores opportunities for bringing forth the ways that agency is enacted in subaltern contexts. The focus is on co-constructing alternative communicative interpretations and actions through opportunities of dialogue with the subaltern sectors of the population.

This approach to civil workplace discourse opens some key entry points for debate—entry points that suggest a need for questioning how organizational communication scholars currently theorize and examine workplace civility. The culture-centered lens illustrates that an emphasis on civility reflects an individualistic bias, marginalizes certain cultural communities by foregrounding and privileging dominant communities, and minimizes opportunities for resistance by narrowing the processes through which conflicts may be articulated and negotiated.

The notion of civility is built on the application of person-centered communication skills that recognize and adapt to others' autonomy and individuality (Sypher, 2004). Inherent in the this perspective is an individualistic notion of what constitutes the unit of communication within organizations; the universalistic logic assumes that tailoring the message to the others' individuality is perhaps the most meaningful way to communicate. Individual autonomy is centralized as is an emphasis on adapting to the individuality of other persons. The need to respond to other's individuality, however, is a reflection of the Eurocentric assumptions about individualistic communication in organizations that foregrounds the individual and his or her communicative needs. It simultaneously backgrounds collective processes through which communication is constituted and negotiated in other cultural contexts.

Thus, the discourse of civility privileges a Eurocentric framework of communication built upon the concept of the individual communicator as the locus of communication processes within organizations. There is a paradox in civility discourse, then, that locates person-centered communication skills as solutions to building social capital in workplaces: The emphasis on the individual and his or her needs is fundamentally in contradiction with the goals and necessities of the collective as constituted in the realm of social capital. Although we can argue that individual and community goals might be aligned in certain situations, questioning the emphasis placed on individual goals as the entry point of civil organizational discourse is nevertheless important.

In addition, categorizing communication as *uncivil* minimizes the opportunities for structural resistance and subsequent change. Subaltern groups challenge dominant structures and discursive processes within social systems, not only through the articulation of oppositional content, but also by fundamentally challenging the marginalization in dominant discursive spaces. For example, one of the ways that subaltern groups resist mainstream civil discourse is by *ignoring* dominant social actors' utterances—a strategy that both challenges exploitive, controlling practices and denies dominant social actors' communicatively constituted reality. Non-cooperation is a well-documented practice central to multiple subaltern movements. As such, categorizing ignoring as a form of incivility both serves to limit the resistive potential of the communicative act and to reinforce the dominant organizational structure.

Similarly, multiple subaltern movements have used *not listening* as a resistive strategy to deny dominant social actors' attempts at control.

Within organizations, not listening to a supervisor may be used as resistance that challenges the status quo. Once again, labeling this as *uncivil* minimizes its resistive potential. Nonetheless, the expression of *upward incivility*, or incivility originating from a subordinate and targeted towards one's superior (Sypher, 2004), has reciprocal, negative effects for those already marginalized. The very categorization of this as *uncivil* removes it from the realm of resistive capacities and locates it in deviant communicative practices associated with harmful effects.

In other words, resistance occurs through oppositional communication content that challenges the dominant discourses, but also through alternative communicative practices that rupture dominant constitutions of organizational discourse. In doing so, such ruptures create a discursive space for alternative communicative attempts that can challenge the structures constituting and constraining communication. We suggest that it is imperative to keep these discursive spaces open to provide opportunities for resistance. It is critical for organizational communication studies to explore possibilities for resisting the dominant discourses of civil society organizations rather than co-opting such possibilities by labeling them deviant.

Reflexivity

Although the expression of incivility is important, what we encourage here is a shift of perspective to an understanding of the *construction* of civility. In doing so, we become reflexive, deconstruct the assumptions and values in the dominant system, and examine the ways in which these values minimize, rather than maximize, participatory opportunities. Reflexivity in theorizing and practice explores the continuous interplays of power and control within which mainstream articulations of civility, democracy, and participation are situated (Dutta, 2008). Reflexivity in a culture-centered approach continuously deconstructs the foundations that are the basis for pronouncements about truth, normality, and deviance. A reflexive stance continually questions the languages of civility, the articulations of civility, the norms of civility, the actors who are privileged and silenced, and the tensions between erasures and participatory opportunities. Furthermore, rather than focus on expressions and their normative values, we instead focus on forms of *listening* as a specific form of respect. The act of listening and being open to multiple and diverse voices and forms of expression is the ultimate act of civility, that is, being sensitive and respectful of the diversity of human nature and human beings.

Conclusion

In this chapter we have provided a macro-level perspective on the discursive construction of civility in organizational contexts, especially in regard to the growing number of multicultural, transnational, and global organizations. In doing so, we have shifted the perspective from how (in)civility is *expressed* to the cultural assumptions that underlie the very *construction* of the notion of civility. We note that attempts to label or define acceptable civil and non-destructive organizational discourse or create normative forms of expression, particularly in multicultural and multinational organizations, must be approached with sensitivity to the wide array of cultural differences in global organizations. Our premise is that the perceived need to encourage appropriate forms of civil expression requires making assumptions about socially-normative behavior, assumptions that may not work in multicultural and global organizations. The unintended consequence of enacting such norms include silencing of voices and cultures that do not fit the norm; silencing these voices reduces their participatory opportunities in the organization. Thus the paradox of calls for civility in global organizational contexts is that such a call may mute diverse voices, reduce participation, and reinforce dominant values and norms that create problems for those who are not members of dominant groups. This may be particularly true for the member of a non-dominant culture in an organization dominated by Western-Eurocentric members and values.

In addition to a macro-social level perspective on destructive communication, our discussion demonstrates the utility of postcolonial and Subaltern Studies theories for examining issues in globalized organizational contexts. Such perspectives allow communication scholars to look beyond Western-Eurocentric articulations and explore alternative articulations by deconstructing the mainstream politics of organizing and opening up opportunities for co-constructing new discourses. With the increase in global organizations, coupled with the growing need to be sensitive to differences, scholars must be careful when promoting ideas that adhere to certain culturally-specific values, especially those favoring already-dominant groups. Indeed, we must proceed cautiously when establishing norms, values, and mores that may serve to marginalize those who are already disenfranchised. Particularly, we must recognize when demands for civility, and the imposition of civil standards, becomes a means of silencing voices inconsistent with dominant norms.

Further, as organizational communication scholars, we must do more than recognize and give voice to dissent, we need to construct models of organizing that embrace the dialectic of harmony and discord in all its fullness. Applying a culture-centered approach to civility discourse creates an opening for exploring the intersections of structure, culture, and agency in the realm of how civility is constructed within the workplace. By examining the absences and erasures in the dominant discourses of civility, this approach draws our attention to the ways in which the voices of marginalized groups are silenced within the mainstream spaces of organizations. The emphasis on marginalized voices creates openings for alternative conceptualizations of organizational discourse. Our focus is not to label civil discourse, but to question the process by which we attempt to impose norms of civil behavior. In globalized workforces this becomes problematic; thus, we need models that acknowledge such tensions and provide ideas for practical implementation.

References

Beverly, J. (1998). Theses on subalternity, representation, and politics. *Postcolonial Studies, 1*(3), 305–319.

Brabeck, K. (2004). Testimonio: Bridging feminist ethics with activist research to create new spaces of collectivity. In M. Brydon-Miller, A. McIntyre, & P. Maguire (Eds.), *Traveling companions: Feminism, teaching, and action research* (pp. 41–54). Westport, CT: Praeger.

Broadfoot, K. J., & Munshi, D. (2007). Diverse voices and alternative rationalities: Imagining forms of postcolonial organizational communication. *Management Communication Quarterly, 21*(2), 249–267.

Brown, P., & Levinson, S. C. (1987). *Politeness: Some universals in language usage.* Cambridge: Cambridge University Press.

Calhoun, C. (2000). The virtue of civility. *Philosophy and Public Affairs, 29*(3), 251–275.

Cortina, L. M., Magley, V. J., Williams, J. H., & Langhout, R. D. (2001). Incivility in the workplace: Incidence and impact. *Journal of Occupational Health Psychology, 6*(1), 64–80.

Deetz, S. A. (2005). Critical theory. In S. K. May & D. K. Mumby (Eds.), *Engaging organizational communication theory and research: Multiple perspectives* (pp. 85–112). Thousand Oaks, CA: Sage.

Deetz, S. A., & Mumby, D. K. (1990). Power, discourse, and the workplace: Reclaiming the critical tradition in communication studies in organizations. In J. Anderson (Ed.), *Communication yearbook 13* (pp. 18–47). Thousand Oaks, CA: Sage.

Dutta-Bergman, M. (2005). Civil society and public relations: Not so civil after all. *Journal of Public Relations Research, 17*(3), 267–289.

Dutta, M. J. (2007). Communicating about culture and health: Theorizing culture-centered and cultural sensitivity approaches. *Communication Theory, 17*(3), 304–328.

Dutta, M. J. (2008). *Communicating health: A culture-centered approach.* London: Polity Press.

Dutta-Bergman, M., & Basnyat, I. (2006). The radio communication project in Nepal: A culture-centered approach to participation. *Health Education and Behavior, 31*(5), 684–697.

Firth, D., & Leigh, A. (1998). *The corporate fool.* London: Capstone Publishing.

Forni, P. M. (2002). *Choosing civility.* New York: St. Martin's Press.

Fukada, A., & Asato, N. (2004). Universal politeness theory: Application to the use of Japanese honorifics. *Journal of Pragmatics, 36*(11), 1991–2002.

Giddens, A. (1984). *The constitution of society.* Berkeley, CA: University of California Press.

Gilbert, H., & Tompkins, J. (1996). *Post-colonial drama: Theory, practice, politics.* New York: Routledge.

Gonthier, G. (2002). *Rude awakenings: Overcoming the civility crisis in the workplace.* Chicago, IL: Dearborn Publishing.

Gu, Y. (1990). Politeness phenomena in Modern Chinese. *Journal of Pragmatics, 14*(22), 237–257.

Gugelberger, G., & Kearny, M. (1991). Voices for the voiceless: Testimonial literature in Latin America. *Latin American Perspectives, 18*(3), 3–14.

Guha, R. (1988). Preface. In R. Guha & G. Spivak (Eds.), *Selected subaltern studies.* Oxford: Oxford University Press.

Guha, R., & Spivak, G. C. (Eds.). (1988). *Selected subaltern studies.* Oxford: Oxford University Press.

Holtgraves, T., & Yang, J.-N. (1990). Politeness as universal: Cross-cultural perceptions of request strategies and inferences based on their use. *Journal of Personality and Social Psychology, 59*(6), 719–729.

Jablin, F. M. (2001). Organizational entry, assimilation, and disengagement/entry. In F. M. Jablin & L. L. Putnam (Eds.), *The new handbook of organizational communication: Advances in theory, research, and methods* (pp. 732–818). Thousand Oaks, CA: Sage.

Jablin, F. M., & Sias, P. M. (2001). Communication competence. In F. M. Jablin & L. L. Putnam (Eds.), *The new handbook of organizational communication: Advances in theory, research and methods* (pp. 819-864). Thousand Oaks, CA: Sage.

Jacobs, M. L. (2002). Civility in the workplace: It's a matter of character. Retrieved December 2, 2005, from http://www.cahs.colostate.edu/fyi/Newsletter/V4I2.pdf

Kesler, C. R. (1992). Civility and citizenship in the American founding. In E. C. Banfield (Ed.), *Civility and citizenship* (pp. 57–74). New York: Professors World Peace Academy.

Kets deVries, M. F. R. (1990). The organizational fool: Balancing a leader's hubris. *Human Relations, 43*(8), 751–770.

Kramarae, C. (1981). *Women and men speaking: Frameworks for analysis.* Rowley, MA: Newbury House.

Lutgen-Sandvik, P., & McDermott, V. (2008). The constitution of employee-abusive organizations: A communication flows theory. *Communication Theory, 18*(2), 304–333.

Lutgen-Sandvik, P., Tracy, S. J., & Alberts, J. K. (2007). Burned by bullying in the American workplace: Prevalence, perception, degree, and impact. *Journal of Management Studies, 44*(6), 837–862.

Lyotard, J. F. (1984). *The postmodern condition.* Minneapolis, MN: University of Minnesota Press.

Mellinger, G. (2003). Counting color: Ambivalence and contradiction in the American society of newspaper editors' discourse of diversity. *Journal of Communication Inquiry, 27*(2), 129–151.

Mumby, D. K., & Stohl, C. (1996). Disciplining organizational communication studies. *Management Communication Quarterly, 10*(1), 50–72.

Namie, G. (2003). Workplace bullying: Escalated incivility. *Ivey Business Journal, 68*(2), 1–6.

O'Sullivan, P. B., & Flanagin, A. J. (2003). Reconceptualizing "flaming" and other problematic messages. *New Media & Society, 5*(1), 69–94.

Orbe, M. (1995). African-American communication research: Toward a deeper understanding of interethnic communication. *Western Journal of Communication, 59*(1), 61–78.

Orbe, M. (1998). *Constructing co-cultural theory: An explication of culture, power, and communication.* Thousand Oaks, CA: Sage.

Oxford English Dictionary. (1989). "Incivility" (2nd ed.). Oxford: Oxford University Press.

Pacanowsky, M. E., & O'Donnell-Trujillo, N. (1983). Organizational communication as cultural performance. *Communication Monographs, 50*(2), 126–147.

Pal, M., & Buzzanell, P. M. (2008). The Indian call center experience: A case study in changing discourses of identity, identification, and career in a global context. *Journal of Business Communication, 45*(1), 31–60.

Papacharissi, Z. (2004). Democracy online: Civility, politeness, and the democratic potential of online political discussion groups. *New Media and Society, 6*(2), 259–283.

Pearson, C. M., Andersson, L. M., & Porath, C. L. (2000). Assessing and attacking workplace incivility. *Organizational Dynamics, 20*(1), 123–137.

Persell, C. H., Green, A., & Gurevich, L. (2001). Civil society, economic distress, and social tolerance. *Sociological Forum, 16*(2), 203–230.

Schudson, M. (1997). Why conversation is not the soul of democracy. *Critical Studies in Mass Communication, 14*(4), 1–13.

Shome, R., & Hegde, S. R. (2002). Postcolonial approaches to communication: Charting the terrain, engaging the intersections. *Communication Theory, 12*(3), 249–270.

Spivak, G. (1987). *In other worlds: Essays in cultural politics.* London: Methuen.

Spivak, G. (1988). Can the subaltern speak? In C. Nelson & L. Grossberg (Eds.), *Marxism and the interpretation of culture* (pp. 271–313). London: Macmillan.

Spivak, G. (1990). Questions of multi-culturalism. In S. Harasym (Ed.), *The postcolonial critic: Interviews, strategies, dialogues* (pp. 59–66). New York: Routledge.

Spivak, G. (1996). Bonding in difference: Interview with Alfred Arteaga. In D. Landry & G. MacLean (Eds.), *The Spivak reader: Selected works of Gayatri Chakravorty Spivak* (pp. 15–28). New York: Routledge.

Spivak, G. (1999). *A critique of postcolonial reason: Toward a history of the vanishing present.* Cambridge, MA: Harvard University Press.

Spivak, G. (2003). *Death of a discipline.* New York: Columbia University Press.

Stohl, C., & Cheney, G. (2001). Participatory processes/paradoxical practices: Communication and the dilemmas of organizational democracy. *Management Communication Quarterly, 14*(4), 349–407.

Sypher, B. D. (2004). Reclaiming civil discourse in the workplace. *Southern Communication Journal, 69*(2), 257–269.

Sypher, B. D., & Zorn, T. E. (1986). Communication abilities and upward mobility: A longitudinal investigation. *Human Communication Research, 12*(3), 420–431.

Sypher, B. D., & Zorn, T. E. (1988). Individual differences and construct system content in descriptions of liked and disliked coworkers. *International Journal of Personal Construct Psychology, 1*(1), 37–51.

Tomlinson, J. (1991). *Cultural imperialism: A critical introduction.* Baltimore, MD: The Johns Hopkins University Press.

Van Dijk, T. (1993). *Elite discourse and racism.* Beverly Hills, CA: Sage.

Van Dijk, T. (1996). Illegal aliens. *Discourse & Society, 7*(3), 291–292.

Van Dijk, T. (1997). Political discourse and racism: Describing others in Western parliaments. In S. Riggins (Ed.), *The language and politics of exclusion: Others in discourse* (pp. 31–65). Thousand Oaks, CA: Sage.

Van Dijk, T., Ting-Toomey, S., Smitherman, G., & Troutman, D. (1997). Discourse, ethnicity, culture and racism. In T. Van Dijk (Ed.), *Discourse as social interaction* (pp. 144–180). London: Sage.

Westacott, E. (2006). The rights and wrongs of rudeness. *The International Journal of Applied Philosophy, 20*(1), 1–22.

Wierzbicka, A. (1985). Different cultures, different languages, different speech acts: Polish vs. English. *Journal of Pragmatics, 9*(2), 145–178.

Part III

Difference and Discrimination

Chapter 7

Social Ostracism, Cliques, and Outcasts

Patricia M. Sias

Some time ago while carrying out a study of coworker relationships, I interviewed several people who worked in the same department of a large organization. Although I interviewed each individually, they all spoke unprompted about a particular woman in their workgroup—Sandy. According to the employees, Sandy was the "boss's pet," receiving raises, bonuses, and other perks not given to the other employees. To a person, these employees attributed Sandy's special status not to her competence, but to her ability to "kiss up" to the boss. They all said they disliked Sandy and avoided her whenever possible. One described that year's office Christmas party—a festive affair generally characterized by fun and good will. "At the party," he reported, "there was Sandy sitting at a table all by herself. No one wanted to sit by her." When invited to write a chapter on social outcasts and ostracism for this book, I immediately pictured Sandy sitting all alone at that holiday party—the embodiment of the workplace social outcast.

Why do some employees become outcasts and others "incasts" or important members of the social network? What are the consequences of being ostracized? And what can practitioners do to prevent the destructive processes of isolation and ostracism? These questions guide this chapter. First, I discuss the notion of informal organizational social networks and cliques. I then explore the various factors that influence one's social status at work. In the final section, I describe the consequences of social ostracism for both the target employee and the larger organization and provide suggestions designed for both intervention and prevention.

Workplace Social Networks

Organizations are not simply groups of people trying to coordinate their activities to accomplish goals. They are intricate social systems constituted through elaborate formal and informal social networks. An organization's formal network is typically illustrated in the organizational chart, which depicts the formal and sanctioned relationships among various employees at various hierarchical levels.

Informal networks defy such tidy illustration. Instead, they are complex, dynamic, and do not necessarily evolve along expected or formal lines. Employees, for example, form friendships with individuals from different and distant departments and with employees several hierarchical levels above or below their own (Bridge & Baxter, 1992). Moreover, as with any type of interpersonal relationship, workplace relationships change. And as relationships change, so does the social network they comprise. Such dynamism cannot be captured in a simple chart. Communication logs and network "maps" provide a glimpse of the social network at one moment in time but can be largely obsolete by the time they are created. In fact, researchers over the years have struggled to develop reliable ways to observe and "measure" social networks in ways that incorporate change and dynamism (Brass, 1995; Monge & Eisenberg, 1987). Although difficult to "measure," it is hard to deny the importance of social networks. As Kanter (1977) noted three decades ago, it is in the context of informal networks that members share important information and make important decisions. What Eisenberg and Goodall (2005) refer to as the "white spaces" of the organizational chart (i.e., informal social structures) are the center of the organizing process.

Scholars have explored workplace social networks from a variety of perspectives, conceptualizing social networks as networks of influence (Fulk, 1993), information exchange (Brass, 1995), support (Ray & Miller, 1990), and sensemaking (Weick, 1979). Although each approach focuses on a specific function or characteristic of social networks, they all share a communication-centered conceptualization—member interaction constitutes, reconstitutes, and transforms them.

The more people with whom an individual communicates, the more frequent that communication, and the more complex that communication, the more "connected" or "central" that employee is in the social network. Similarly, the fewer people with whom an individual communicates, the more infrequent and limited that interaction, the less connected and more isolated the employee (Brass, 1995). Thus, at a broad level, isolates and outcasts are organizational members who communicate infrequently, with very few people, and at a superficial level about a narrow, typically only work-related, range of topics. Workplace networks, then, are often comprised of various cliques, "narrow exclusive circle or group of persons; *especially*: one held together by common interests, views, or purposes" (Merriam-Webster Online Dictionary, 2007). Cliques, by definition, exclude certain people, specifically isolates and outcasts.

Before moving on, it is necessary to distinguish the terms isolate, outcast, and ostracism. Both isolate and outcast are defined in relation to a larger social grouping, such as a clique. They are not synonymous, however. An *isolate* is an individual who is separated from others by physical or social barriers (Free Dictionary, 2007b). In social network research, isolates are operationally defined as individuals with no or relatively few communication links with others (Monge & Contractor, 2001). In contrast, a social group actively rejects an *outcast* (Free Dictionary, 2007d). Thus, although both isolates and outcasts are separated from a larger social group or clique, an outcast's isolation is targeted and intentional, while an isolate may become separated without intention (e.g., simply going unnoticed or working in a remote location). Finally, *ostracism* refers to the "act of banishing or excluding," from a group (Free Dictionary, 2007c) and thus refers to the *process* by which outcast employees are "cast out" of a workplace clique. Ostracism can be both physical and social. Physical ostracism is placing the target in an isolated or solitary location; social ostracism is to "be ignored by others who are in one's presence" (Williams & Sommer, 1997, p. 693). In the following sections, I discuss various forms of isolation and ostracism and factors associated with the likelihood that an employee would be isolated or ostracized.

Isolation and Ostracism Processes

Employees isolate and ostracize their coworkers in a variety of ways. These processes vary in the extent to which they are *active* or *passive* and the extent to which they are *intentional* or *unintentional*. Active processes involve direct contact with the target employee. Passive processes, in contrast, are characterized by a lack of contact. Intentional processes involve the specific targeting of a particular employee for isolation or ostracism. Unintentional processes refer to situations in which employees isolate others without intent; the isolated employee simply goes unnoticed. Figure 7.1 depicts the processes along these two dimensions.

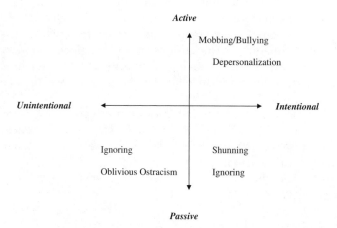

Figure 7.1 Dimensions of isolation and ostracism.

Ignoring someone can be intentional, but does not necessarily imply intent. Ignoring is defined as either "to be ignorant of or not acquainted with" or "to refuse to take notice of" (Free Dictionary, 2007a). For this reason, "ignoring" is included in both the intentional and unintentional quadrants of Figure 7.1 and is passive because it involves no direct confrontation or interaction with the target. Isolates can be ignored by going unnoticed for the reasons discussed above. The willful or intentional ignoring of another is related to the more intentional tactic of "shunning" discussed below.

Depersonalization and shunning are intentional ways of isolating an employee from a workplace clique. *Depersonalization* is an intentional and active tactic that refers to careful and deliberate editing of communication with the target employee such that employees communicate with the target only when necessary and only regarding work-related matters. Such communication effectively "depersonalizes" the target by acknowledging only the target's work-role and communicatively denying the employee as "whole person" (Sias, Heath, Perry, Silva, & Fix, 2004; Sias & Perry, 2004).

In contrast, *shunning* (e.g., silent treatment, deliberately excluding) is purposely cutting off all interaction with the target, for example, refusing to communicate with the isolated employee, encouraging other employees to cut off communication with the target, or both (Zimmerle, 2005). Although employees intentionally choose to shun target coworkers, this is passive ostracism in that it does not involve the active participation in interaction of any kind. Both of these ostracism tactics communicatively construct barriers between the outcast and the rest of the workgroup.

Thus, social ostracism can be active or passive and can be carried out for a variety of different motives (Sommer, Williams, Ciarocco, & Baumeister, 2001). Ostracism can be punitive and include acts of ignoring that are perceived or intended to be deliberate and aversive. The silent treatment and shunning are examples of this and usually are acts to punish targets for supposed social violations. Ostracism can also be oblivious and occur when actors simply have little or no regard for targets. Oblivious ostracism is not intentional; rather, actors merely deem the targets unworthy of their attention (Williams & Sommer, 1997).

Social ostracism can also be an indicator of more egregious workplace problems such as mobbing/workplace bullying. In fact, social ostracism is one of many negative acts associated with mobbing/bullying (Einarsen, 2000), although this phenomenon typically includes a complex constellation of "hostile and unethical communication" (Leymann, 1996, p. 168) marked by the characteristic feature of persistence (e.g., repetition, duration) (see Lutgen-Sandvik, Namie, & Namie, Chapter 2 this volume).

In sum, employees can be isolated or ostracized via a variety of processes that vary in the extent to which they are intentional and active. Ignoring is

Table 7.1 Causes and Consequences of Isolation and Ostracism

	Isolation	Ostracism
Personal Causal Factors	Dissimilarity: Sex Race and Ethnicity Physical Disability Sexual Orientation Target personality: Shyness Communication apprehension	Target personal characteristics: Sex Race and Ethnicity Physical Disability Sexual Orientation Aggressive Personality
Contextual Causal Factors	Lack of physical proximity Boundary-spanning position Communication technology	Organizational uncertainty Job insecurity Ineffective leadership, supervision Differential treatment Rigid norms/culture Whistleblowing

Consequences	For the target:
	Impaired information exchange
	Decrease in quality of task
	  performance
	Powerlessness
	Loneliness
	Stress
	
	For the organization:
	Impaired information sharing
	Impaired productivity
		For the target:
		Impaired information exchange
		Decrease in quality of task
		  performance
		Powerlessness
		Loneliness
		Stress
		
		For the organization:
		Impaired information sharing
		Impaired organizational productivity

the least intentional and most passive. Depersonalization and shunning are intentional efforts at ostracizing target employees; however, these tactics are passive in that they involve *not* communicating to the target either at all or about specific topics. In the following sections, I discuss factors that enhance the likelihood an employee will be isolated or ostracized at work. Table 7.1 summarizes both causes and consequences.

Factors Influencing Isolation

In general, all new employees are technically "isolates" the moment they join an organization. Their relationships with other employees are characterized by superficial communication regarding a narrow range of topics that are typically work-related (Kram & Isabella, 1985). As new employees, they are generally excluded from much informal conversation, especially discretionary and sensitive discussions and gossip (Sias & Cahill, 1998). A new employee's relationship with his or her supervisor is similarly narrow and limited. And, because the supervisor has a limited amount of time to divide among all employees, along with other managerial tasks, the new employee is often left alone after being given instructions and task assignments (Graen & Uhl-Bien, 1995).

As time goes on and the newcomer engages in conversation with coworkers and the supervisor, the employee's social status begins to take form. A number of factors are associated with the extent to which an employee is included in or isolated from the social network. These factors derive from the employee and from the workplace context.

Personal Factors

As noted earlier, cliques often form among people who share common interests, views, or purposes. Thus, perceived similarity is a primary developmental factor in employee relationships (Sias & Cahill, 1998). People tend to interact with others they perceive to be similar to themselves (Sherif, 1958; Turner & Oakes, 1986). Accordingly, isolates are often those who clique members find to be *dissimilar*.

Demographic dissimilarity is an especially important isolating factor, with members of gender and racial or ethnic minorities often left out of workplace social cliques. Demographic dissimilarity is cited by many as a primary contributor to the glass ceiling, with women and minorities finding it difficult to break through and move into the upper ranks of an organization, oftentimes because they are excluded from powerful informal friendship networks (Gray, Kurihara, Hommen, & Feldman, 2007; Kanter, 1977). Schneider and Northcraft (1999) describe the "dilemmas" of diversity in organizations, including the ways employees tend to organize their interactions along social identity lines. This segregation into homogeneous social networks creates a variety of "traps" and "fences" that prevent employees—and organizations—from developing and reaping the benefits of workplace diversity. Similarly, Graves and Elsass (2005) examined social exchanges among men and women in ongoing teams. They found that women reported lower levels of social exchanges, suggesting that women tend to be excluded from, or at least are less likely to participate in, informal networks than are men.

Moreover, those who do achieve promotion to upper management levels often find themselves isolated from the informal social networks at that level (Fisher, 2006; Ibarra, 1993). Networks at senior hierarchical levels are impacted by similarity, just as those at lower levels. If primarily high-ranking men comprise the informal network, women and minority employees find it difficult to break into such cliques. Ibarra (1995), for example, found that minority managers had fewer intimate network relationships than did majority managers. They also reportedly enjoyed less "access to career benefits" via social networks than did white majority managers. Thus, even when women and minority employees break through the glass ceiling and are promoted, isolation from social networks at that level makes them essentially "outsiders on the inside" (Gray et al., 2007, p. 149).

Personality traits can also contribute to an employee's isolation. Shy employees, for example, can effectively isolate themselves from the workgroup by avoiding communication, and therefore avoiding opportunities to develop relationships and actively participate in the social network (McDaniel, 2003). The related trait of communication apprehension (i.e., anxiety about communicating with others) is also linked to isolation. For example, Cole and McCroskey (2003) found that although supervisors suffering from communication anxiety do communicate with employees, their apparent discomfort with doing so makes them less likable to employees. Communication anxiety can inhibit the ability of supervisors to engage in effective interaction with employees and become active members of the network (Bartoo & Sias, 2004).

Contextual Factors

Networks are embedded in social contexts and, not surprisingly, many contextual elements are associated with an employee's role in the workplace social networks. Perhaps the most powerful of these is *physical proximity*. Workplace cliques tend to develop among employees who work in the same physical location, and informal relationships (e.g., friendships) are likely to develop among coworkers who work near one another (Hodson, 1996; Sias & Cahill, 1998). This is largely due to the fact that physical proximity affords opportunities for communication that physical distance denies.

Proximity highlights a problem associated with physical isolation at work. Employees who are physically isolated from others (e.g., working in an annex, at a satellite location, or perhaps telecommuting from home) enjoy fewer opportunities to interact informally with their coworkers and supervisor; this, in turn, contributes to increased social isolation. *Boundary spanners* (employees whose jobs require that they spend the bulk of their time away from work such as salespeople, recruiters, etc.) are particularly at risk of becoming isolated from the social network (Dubinsky, Yammarino, Jolson, & Spangler, 1995; Marshall, Michaels, & Mulki, 2007).

New communication *technologies* have also been linked to employee isolation (see Flanagin, Pearce, & Bondad-Brown, Chapter 11 this volume). Technologies such as e-mail and videoconferencing enable "virtual office" arrangements such as telecommuting. Although these arrangements provide many benefits to employees (e.g., flexibility, autonomy), according to recent studies, perceived isolation from office social networks is the most frequently reported complaint of virtual employees (Mann, Varey, & Button, 2000; Marshall et al., 2007; Pinsonneault & Boisvert, 2001). Telecommuters, for example, often describe feelings of isolation as a consequence of their distant and "virtual" employment status (Brake, 2006; Crandall & Gao, 2005).

As noted earlier, isolates and outcasts are not the same. Although outcasts may start out as isolates, their ostracism by other employees is intentional and targeted. In contrast to many isolates, the outcast is someone the other employees notice but intentionally exclude their from the clique. The following section details the reasons an employee might be ostracized or "cast out" from the social network.

Factors Influencing Ostracism

Ostracism involves noticing and intentionally targeting a particular employee to be "cast out" of the social clique or network. Like isolation, ostracism stems from both personal and contextual factors.

Personal Factors

Many *personal characteristics* have been linked to ostracism. Research suggests that lesbian, gay, bisexual and transgender (LGBT) employees are often likely targets of ostracism, and these individuals experience a great deal of anxiety regarding whether or not to "come out" at work (Day & Schoenrade, 1997; Embrick, Walther, & Wickens, 2007, see also Lewis, Chapter 9 this volume). Employees from ethnic and racial minorities are also more vulnerable to ostracism than are majority employees "because these workers already face a certain degree of isolation from majority groups" (Hodson, Roscigno, & Lopez, 2006, p. 386, see Allen, Chapter 8 this volume). For similar reasons, employees are often ostracized because of a physical disability (Zapf, 1999).

Although personality traits are linked to general isolation, scholars disagree on the extent to which *personality* is associated with the more active and intentional processes of ostracism. Zapf (1999), for example, found that individuals with deficient social skills, who actively avoid conflict, and who have pre-existing symptoms of anxiety, depression, and negative affect are more likely to be ostracized. Others note that "easy targets" for ostracism include employees who are shy, submissive, unassertive, introverted, and who have low levels of self-esteem (Aquino & Byron, 2002). On the other hand, highly aggressive employees can also be ostracized, since coworkers may fear the aggressor or fear being perceived as similar to the aggressor (Pearson, 1998).

Contextual Factors

The dynamics of ostracism are complex and involve more than simply an anxious person being targeted because of his or her personality or personal characteristics. Several studies indicate various elements of the organizational context that can enable and even encourage ostracism.

Rigid Norms or Cultures

In workplaces where there is little room for individuality or group norm interpretation, nonconforming employees are likely to be socially ostracized. Likewise, organizations with strong cultures, especially when those cultures are rigid and inflexible, will likely spawn social ostracism of those who do not "go along" (Brodsky, 1976). Certainly this was the case in the Enron disaster, a culture in which anyone who spoke against organizational leaders was shunned, shamed, and ostracized (McLean & Elkind, 2003). The social ostracism of whistleblowers may also be a consequence of rigid group norms and organizational cultures (Miceli & Near, 1992).

Leadership and Supervision

A particularly important element of the organizational context is leadership and supervision and many scholars point to failures of leadership and management at a broad level as a cause of ostracism. *Inattentive or neglectful leadership* allows ostracism to occur by ignoring the problem (Lutgen-Sandvik & McDermott, 2008). Supervisors who are "out of the loop" and distance themselves from the immediate work environment are likely to be unaware that any ostracism is occurring. The lack of attention, and of accountability, can encourage those who socially ostracize others to continue their harmful behavior.

Another important factor in ostracism and social status is the relationships the supervisor has with his or her various direct-report employees. My research suggests that supervisor–subordinate relationships in a workgroup are associated with the relationships among workgroup members. This body of work is grounded in Leader-Member Exchange (LMX) theory (Graen & Scandura, 1987), which posits that supervisors distribute resources (e.g., decision making influence, tasks, support, etc.) differentially among their various employees, and this *differential treatment* results in leader–member relationships that vary with respect to quality (Graen, Dansereau, & Minami, 1972). Such differential treatment can influence peer relationships and, in particular, lead to the ostracism of certain targeted employees (Sias, 1996; Sias & Jablin, 1995).

The primary influence on whether and how differential treatment leads to ostracism is the extent to which the coworkers perceive the differential treatment as fair. When employees perceive that their supervisor is treating a group member unfairly, the relationships among those employees became closer (Sias & Jablin, 1995). Specifically, when employees perceive that a coworker received unwarranted favoritism (like Sandy, mentioned in the introduction) from the supervisor, they turn to one another to make sense of the differential treatment and develop closer friendships with one another (Sias, 1996; Sias & Jablin). In contrast, they ostracize the recipient of the differential treatment (i.e., the "boss's pet") from the social network. As the story at the beginning of this chapter indicates, employees develop a strong dislike and distrust of the boss's pet (e.g., Sandy) and subsequently ostracize him or her from the workplace clique.

The opposite of the boss's pet is, of course, the "boss's victim." Again, coworkers evaluate the fairness of an employee being victimized by the boss and those perceptions impact the victim's social status. Victims, whom group members perceive to be receiving *unfair* negative treatment from the supervisor, tend to be viewed sympathetically and drawn into closer relationships with the other employees (Sias & Jablin, 1995). In contrast, when group members perceive that victims deserve unfavorable differential treatment (e.g., they have poor job performance, etc.), they tend to ostracize the victim from the social network in a manner similar to the boss's pet. However, the reason for ostracizing a victim is not just because he or she is disliked; ostracism can also occur because other employees want to avoid a negative "halo effect" and are concerned they may appear guilty by association (Lutgen-Sandvik, 2003; Sias & Jablin).

Consequences of Ostracism and Cliques

Being isolated or ostracized from a workgroup matters (see Table 7.1). By definition, outcast status means being left out of important informal communication networks and, therefore, being substantially uninformed relative to other workgroup members. Job performance depends largely on being informed; consequently, outcasts are disadvantaged with respect to their jobs and careers. Isolation and ostracism can also be painful and emotionally and physically draining (Leymann, 1990).

Performance Consequences

Ostracism impacts employee and organizational performance primarily via its impact on information exchange. Relatedly, such marginalization negatively affects an employee's power and influence in the workplace.

Information Exchange

One of the most serious consequences of being cast out of the workgroup clique is being uninformed. Many studies indicate important links between information and social network status. Brass and Burkhardt (1993) conceptualized communication networks as information distribution networks and found that others perceived individuals who played central roles in these social networks as powerful and influential in the organization. Conversely, those who were isolated from the social networks and held distant role in the network received significantly less information than other employees.

My research (Sias, 2005) indicates that there are strong links between an employee's relationships with peer coworkers and that employee's information experiences. Specifically, employees with close, intimate, and friendly peers and supervisor relationships are more likely to communicate frequently and to receive high quality information (i.e., accurate, timely, and useful information), than are employees who tended to be isolated from the workgroup.

Two important types of information shared informally, primarily via social networks, are rumors and gossip. Rumors are messages addressing topics of general uncertainty such as layoffs or downsizing. Gossip, on the other hand, refers to "informal and evaluative talk in an organization, usually among no more than a few individuals, about another member of that organization who is not present" (Kurland & Pelled, 2000, p. 429). Both types of information can be useful for employees. Receiving a "heads up" via the rumor mill or grapevine, for example, can help an individual prepare for potential organizational problems. In contrast, employees excluded from the grapevine will be caught by surprise and thus be slower to react and adjust to such events. Although gossip is often "trivial," it can also be useful information. And although gossip can, and often is, exchanged among acquaintances, it finds particular currency among the informal friendship network (Sias & Cahill, 1998).

Information exchange problems do not solely create problems for the uninformed employee, but also for the performance of the workgroup and larger organization. Organizational systems depend on effective information exchange to survive (Katz & Kahn, 1978). The willful withholding or misrepresentation of information between employees, especially those whose tasks are tightly linked or tightly coupled, harms those employees' performance, which damages the performance of the whole system (Weick, 1979).

Power and Influence

Many studies indicate relationships between an employee's participation in the workplace social network and that employee's power and influence in the organization. Much of this research suggests that power results from having access to privileged and often proprietary information. To the extent that "information is power," participation in workplace friendships can imbue employees with power by ensuring they have important, often discretionary or proprietary, information they need to make decisions and perform their jobs competently. The least powerful people in organizations tend to be uninformed employees who are marginalized from friendship networks and, consequently, "out of the loop" (Kanter, 1977).

Many scholars, for example, have examined associations between workplace friendship networks and power, particularly with respect to career advancement and decision-making (Brass & Burkhardt, 1993; Kanter, 1977; Lamertz & Aquino, 2004). Access to informal friendship networks enhances employees' ability to perform their jobs and to advance their careers. Lack of access to such networks is a primary reason women have trouble advancing to higher levels of management. At the same time, informal friendship networks (e.g., "old boys" networks) are a primary mechanism supporting the overwhelming majority of white males at the top of corporate hierarchies (Kanter).

Power does not derive from information exchange alone, however. Simply holding a position in friendship networks can provide employees with power via their *perceived* connections with others. Lamertz and Aquino (2004) examined links between an employee's position in organizational expressive networks (e.g., informal, friendship networks) and victimization, a phenomenon that can include social ostracism. Their results suggest that employees occupying central positions in the friendship network have access to referent and legitimate power. This access most likely reduces social ostracism via a variety of social dynamics including protection, patronage, and social influence.

Psychological and Physical Consequences

Given the above-noted threats and damage to the targets' performance, power, and self-esteem, it is no surprise that isolation and ostracism can have devastating effects on an employee's psychological and physical health. Research by organizational scholars, psychologists, and medical researchers identify a number of related harms reported by targets.

Threats to Belongingness

A primary complaint of isolated employees is *loneliness* resulting from feeling rejected by important others (Sommer et al., 2001). Researchers studying loneliness conceptualize it in relation to one's place in a social network. Weiss (1973), for example, argues that loneliness does not result from simply being alone, but is caused by "being without some definite needed relationship or set of relationships" (p. 17). More specific to the workplace context (versus, perhaps, the lack of a romantic relationship), research indicates that social-isolation loneliness results from "a lack of satisfying friendship relationships or a lack of access to social networks (Marshall et al., 2007).

Stress and Anxiety

Isolation and loneliness create *stress* and *anxiety* for isolated employees who may fear that being out of the loop will harm their task performance or result in being overlooked for occupational rewards such as promotions, bonuses, training, and social rewards such as high-quality relationships with their supervisor and coworkers (Kurland & Bailey, 1999; Sarbaugh-Thompson & Feldman, 1998). Anxiety and resultant stress are particularly elevated for ostracized employees. A number of studies consistently note that stress and anxiety are a primary consequence of ostracism because "these derive from threats to belongingness, esteem, meaningful existence, and control" (Sommer et al., 2001, p. 226). Particularly stressful are cases of social ostracism in which (a) the target feels unable to change the situation, or (b) targets do not understand why they are being ignored (Sommer, et al.).

Prevention and Intervention

Ostracism and isolation are clearly problematic for both the targets and organizations. Understanding the primary causes of these harmful processes suggests directions for more constructive ways of organizing. In particular, recognizing isolation and ostracism as fundamentally *communicative* in nature suggests a number of communication-centered practices that can both help organizational members and practitioners help prevent isolation and ostracism and effectively intervene at the times when such processes occur.

Leadership and Supervision

As noted above, ineffective leadership and supervision is linked to isolation and ostracism. Accordingly, preventing these damaging processes requires attention to leadership and supervision practices. Primary among these is ensuring that supervisors themselves are not isolated from the workgroup because such isolation ensures their ignorance of the isolation or ostracism of other employees. Supervisors, therefore, must be active participants in the social networks. This does not mean they must be "friends" with all their employees; previous research demonstrates the potential problems with such a dynamic (Bridge & Baxter, 1992; Sias & Jablin, 1995). It does mean, however, communicating *often* and with *all* employees. Frequently "checking in" with employees can help managers stay in touch with the nature of, and dynamic shifts in, the social network (e.g., who is talking to whom, who seems to be more or less informed, etc.).

Of particular concern are those employees who are physically isolated from the rest of the group, such as boundary spanners and telecommuters.

Supervisors must be diligent in keeping active and open lines of communication with these employees and enabling open lines of communication between them and others in the workgroup. Supervisors can accomplish this by scheduling regular activities (e.g., meeting or social functions) that require the employees to interact face-to-face. Research also suggests that assigning employees to work together on projects and tasks encourages the development of closer, friendlier relationships (Sias & Cahill, 1998). Employees in the same physical location as well as employees who are physically distant from one another can accomplish joint projects. Supervisors should similarly ensure the inclusion of other employees often excluded from workplace cliques such as women, members of ethnic and racial minority groups, and LGBT employees.

Supervisors must also understand how their relationships with employees impact the employees' relationships with one another. Although differential treatment is important and necessary (Sias & Jablin, 1995), it must be effectively managed. Supervisors should ensure that their treatment of employees is fair and equitable. Furthermore, supervisors must explain differential treatment to employees so that they avoid making faulty assumptions that can lead to the ostracism of the target of the differential treatment.

Organizational Practices and Conditions

A number of organizational factors enable, and even encourage, ostracism of employees. Accordingly, there are a number of organization-wide measures that can help prevent isolation and ostracism. For example, providing employees access to formal conflict resolution mechanisms such as employee grievance boards and neutral arbitrators or mediators can help prevent escalation of conflict (Resch & Schubinski, 1996). In addition, mechanisms such as employee sounding boards and suggestion boxes can provide a voice to employees who may be vulnerable to isolation or ostracism.

At a broad level, managers should examine their current production and other work processes to ensure that they are clear and well-organized, rather than chaotic. Keeping employees informed about issues such as job security, potential financial concerns of the company, and the like, can help reduce feelings of uncertainty and insecurity that have been linked to social ostracism. Finally, organizations should provide assistance to employees suffering the psychological and physical consequences of isolation and ostracism. Employee assistance programs (EAPS), for example, might provide counseling services or guidance toward effective counseling services to help employees recover from their victimization.

Conclusion

Informal social networks and cliques are both powerful and complex. Inclusion in and exclusion from such groups is of consequence for employees and the larger organization in which the social network is embedded. Isolation and ostracism can damage both the target's and the organization's performance. Moreover, the psychological harm to the targeted employee can be extensive and difficult to overcome. In this chapter, I highlighted the characteristics, and the primary causes and consequences of workplace isolation and ostracism. Understanding that these issues are fundamentally communicative highlights a number of communication-centered strategies which practitioners can use to prevent isolation and ostracism and, in the unfortunate event such processes occur, effectively intervene.

References

Aquino, K., & Byron, K. (2002). Dominating interpersonal behavior and perceived victimization in groups: Evidence for curvilinear relationship. *Journal of Management, 28*(1), 69–87.

Bartoo, H., & Sias, P. M. (2004). When enough is too much: The impact of communication apprehension on employee information experiences. *Communication Quarterly, 52*(1), 15–26.

Brake, T. (2006). Leading global virtual teams. *Industrial and Commercial Training, 38*(2), 116–121.

Brass, D. J. (1995). A social network perspective on human resources management. *Research in Personnel and Human Resources Management, 13*(1), 39–79.

Brass, D. J., & Burkhardt, M. E. (1993). Potential power and power use: An investigation of structure and behavior. *Academy of Management Journal, 36*(4), 441–471.

Bridge, K., & Baxter, L. A. (1992). Blended relationships: Friends as work associates. *Western Journal of Communication, 56*(2), 200–225.

Brodsky, C. (1976). *The harassed worker.* Lexington, MA: D.C. Health and Company.

Cole, J. G., & McCroskey, J. C. (2003). The association of perceived communication apprehension, shyness, and verbal aggression with perceptions of source credibility and affect in organizational and interpersonal contexts. *Communication Quarterly, 51*(1), 101–110.

Crandall, W., & Gao, L. (2005). An update on telecommuting: Review and prospects for emerging issues. *S.A.M. Advanced Management Journal, 70*(1), 30–38.

Day, N. E., & Schoenrade, P. (1997). Staying in the closet versus coming out: Relationships between communication about sexual orientation and work attitudes. *Personnel Psychology, 50*(1) 147–163.

Dubinsky, A. J., Yammarino, F. J., Jolson, M. A., & Spangler, W. D. (1995). Transformational leadership: An initial investigation in sales management. *Journal of Personal Selling & Sales Management, 15*(1), 17–32.

Einarsen, S. (2000). Harassment and bullying at work: A review of the Scandinavian approach. *Aggression and Violent Behavior: A Review Journal, 5*(4), 371–401.

Eisenberg, E. M., & Goodall, H. L., Jr. (2005). *Organizational communication: Balancing creativity and constraint* (4th ed.). Boston: Bedford-St. Martins.

Embrick, D. G., Walther, C. S., & Wickens, C. M. (2007). Working class masculinity: Keeping gay men and lesbians out of the workplace. *Sex Roles, 56*(6), 757–766.

Fisher, M. (2006). Wall Street women: Navigating gendered networks in the new economy. In M. Fisher & G. Downey (Eds.), *Frontiers of capital: Ethnographic reflections on the new economy* (pp. 209–236). Durham, NC: Duke University Press.

Free Dictionary. (2007a). "Ignoring." Retrieved November 26, 2007, from http://www.theFree Dictionary.com/isolate.

Free Dictionary. (2007b). "Isolate." Retrieved November 26, 2007, from http://www.theFree Dictionary.com/isolate.

Free Dictionary. (2007c). "Ostracism." Retrieved November 26, 2007, from http://www.theFree Dictionary.com/isolate.

Free Dictionary. (2007d). "Outcast." Retrieved November 26, 2007, from http://www.theFree Dictionary.com/isolate.

Fulk, J. (1993). Social construction of communication technology. *Academy of Management Journal, 36*(5), 921–950.

Graen, G. B., Dansereau, F., & Minami, T. (1972). Dysfunctional leadership styles. *Organizational Behavior and Human Performance, 7*(2), 216–236.

Graen, G. B., & Scandura, T. (1987). Toward a psychology of dyadic organizing. In B. S. L. L. Cummings (Ed.), *Research in organizational behavior* (Vol. 9, pp. 175–208). Greenwich, CT: JAI.

Graen, G. B., & Uhl-Bien, M. (1995). Development of Leader-Member Exchange Theory of leadership over 25 years: Applying a multi-level multi-domain perspective. *Leadership Quarterly, 6*(2), 219–247.

Graves, L. M., & Elsass, P. M. (2005). Sex and sex dissimilarity effects in ongoing teams: Some surprising findings. *Human Relations, 58*(2), 191–221.

Gray, J., Kurihara, T., Hommen, L., & Feldman, J. (2007). Networks of exclusion: Job segmentation and social networks in the knowledge economy. *Equal Opportunities International, 26*(2), 144–160.

Hodson, R. (1996). Dignity in the workplace under participative management: Alienation and freedom revisited. *American Sociological Review, 61*(6), 719–738.

Hodson, R., Roscigno, V. J., & Lopez, S. H. (2006). Chaos and the abuse of power: Workplace bullying in organizational and interactional context. *Work and Occupations, 33*(4), 382–416.

Ibarra, H. (1993). Network centrality, power, and innovation involvement: Determinants of technical and administrative roles. *Academy of Management Journal, 36*(4), 471–502.

Ibarra, H. (1995). Race, opportunity, and diversity of social circles in managerial networks. *Academy of Management Journal, 38*(6), 673–703.

Kanter, R. M. (1977). *Men and women of the corporation*. New York: Basic Books.

Katz, D., & Kahn, R. L. (1978). *The social psychology of organizations* (2nd ed.). New York: John Wiley & Sons.

Kram, K. E., & Isabella, L. A. (1985). Mentoring alternatives: The role of peer relationships in career development. *Academy of Management Journal, 28*(1), 110–132.

Kurland, N. B., & Bailey, D. E. (1999). Telework: The advantages and challenges of working here, there, anywhere, and anytime. *Organizational Dynamics, 28*(1), 53–68.

Kurland, N. B., & Pelled, L. H. (2000). Passing the word: Toward a model of gossip and power in the workplace. *The Academy of Management Review, 25*(2), 428–439.

Lamertz, K., & Aquino, K. (2004). Social power, social status and perceptual similarity of workplace victimization: A social network analysis of stratification. *Human Relations, 57*(6), 795–822.

Leymann, H. (1990). Mobbing and psychological terror at workplaces. *Violence and Victims, 5*(1), 119–126.

Leymann, H. (1996). The content and development of mobbing at work. *European Journal of Work and Organizational Psychology, 5*(2), 165–184.

Lutgen-Sandvik, P. (2003). The communicative cycle of employee emotional abuse: Generation and regeneration of workplace mistreatment. *Management Communication Quarterly, 16*(4), 471–501.

Lutgen-Sandvik, P., & McDermott, V. (2008). The constitution of employee-abusive organizations: A communication flows theory. *Communication Theory, 18*(2), 304–333.

Mann, S., Varey, R., & Button, W. (2000). An exploration of the emotional impact of tele-working via computer-mediated communication. *Journal of Managerial Psychology, 15*(6), 668–690.

Marshall, G. W., Michaels, C. E., & Mulki, J. P. (2007). Workplace isolation: Exploring the construct and its measurement. *Psychology & Marketing, 24*(2), 195–233.

McDaniel, P. A. (2003). *Shrinking Violets and Caspar Milquetoasts: Shyness, power, and intimacy in the United States, 1950 to 1995.* New York: New York University Press.

McLean, B., & Elkind, P. (2003). *The smartest guys in the room: The amazing rise and scandalous fall of Enron.* New York: Penguin Group.

Merriam-Webster Online Dictionary. (2007). "Clique." Retrieved November 26, 2007, from http://www.merriam-webster.com/dictionary/clique.

Miceli, M. P., & Near, J. P. (1992). *Blowing the whistle: The organizational and legal implications for companies and employees New York: Lexington.* New York: Lexington.

Monge, P. R., & Contractor, N. (2001). Emergence of communication networks. In F. M. Jablin & L. L. Putnam (Eds.), *The new handbook of organizational communication: Advances in theory, research and methods* (pp. 440–502). Thousand Oaks, CA: Sage.

Monge, P. R., & Eisenberg, E. M. (1987). Emergent communication networks. In F. M. Jablin, L. L. Putnam, K. H. Roberts & L. W. Porter (Eds.), *Handbook of organizational communication: An interdisciplinary perspective* (pp. 304–342). Newbury Park, CA: Sage.

Pearson, C. M. (1998). Organizations as targets and triggers of aggression and violence: Framing rational explanations for dramatic organizational deviance. *Research in the Sociology of Organizations, 15*(2), 197–223.

Pinsonneault, A., & Boisvert, M. (Eds.). (2001). *The impacts of telecommuting on organizations and individuals: A review of the literature.* Hershey, PA: Idea Group.

Ray, E. B., & Miller, K. I. (1990). Communication in health care organizations. In E. B. Ray & L. Donohew (Eds.), *Communication and health: Systems and applications* (pp. 92–107). Hillsdale, NJ: Lawrence Erlbaum.

Resch, M., & Schubinski, M. (1996). Mobbing – Prevention and management in organizations. *European Journal of Work and Organizational Psychology, 5*(3), 295–307.

Sarbaugh-Thompson, M., & Feldman, M. S. (1998). Electronic mail and organizational communication: Does saying "hi" really matter? *Organization Science, 9*(1), 30–42.

Schneider, S. K., & Northcraft, G. B. (1999). Three social dilemmas of workforce diversity in organizations: A social identity perspective. *Human Relations, 52*(11), 1445–1467.

Sherif, M. (1958). Superordinate goals in the reduction of intergroup conflicts. *American Journal of Sociology, 63*(4), 349–356.

Sias, P. M. (1996). Constructing perceptions of differential treatment: An analysis of coworker discourse. *Communication Monographs, 63*(2), 171–187.

Sias, P. M. (2005). Workplace relationship quality and employee information experiences. *Communication Studies, 56*(3), 375–396.

Sias, P. M., & Cahill, D. J. (1998). From coworkers to friends: The development of peer friendships in the workplace. *Western Journal of Communication, 62*(3), 273–299.

Sias, P. M., Heath, R. G., Perry, T., Silva, D., & Fix, B. (2004). Narratives of workplace friendship deterioration. *Journal of Social and Personal Relationships, 21*(3), 321–340.

Sias, P. M., & Jablin, F. M. (1995). Differential superior-subordinate relations: Perceptions of fairness, and coworker communication. *Human Communication Research, 22*(1), 5–38.

Sias, P. M., & Perry, T. (2004). Disengaging from workplace relationships: A research note. *Human Communication Research, 30*(4), 589–602.

Sommer, K. L., Williams, K. D., Ciarocco, N. J., & Baumeister, R. F. (2001). When silenced speaks louder than words: Explorations into the intrapsychic and interpersonal consequences of social ostracism. *Basic and Applied Social Psychology, 23*(2), 225–243.

Turner, J. C., & Oakes, P. J. (1986). The significance of the social identity concept for social psychology with reference to individualism, interactionism, and social influence. *British Journal of Social Psychology, 25*(2), 237–252.

Weick, K. E. (1979). *Social Psychology of Organizing* (2nd ed.). New York: McGraw Hill.

Weiss, R. S. (1973). *The loneliness of social isolation.* Cambridge, MA: MIT Press.

Williams, K. D., & Sommer, K. L. (1997). Social ostracism by coworkers: Does rejection lead to loafing or compensation? *Personality and Social Psychology Bulletin, 23*(7), 693–706.

Zapf, D. (1999). Organisational, work group related and personal causes of mobbing/bullying at work. *International Journal of Manpower, 20*(1/2), 70–85.

Zimmerle, H. (2005). Common sense v. the EEOC: Coworker ostracism and shunning as retaliation under Title VII. *Journal of Corporation Law, 30*(5), 627–646.

Chapter 8

Racial Harassment in the Workplace

Brenda J. Allen

Former clerk gets $44,000 racial bias settlement with Los Gatos clinic:
Supervisor used offensive code words
Corrections officer's suit alleges racial harassment
Racial slurs alleged in suit; CdA Paving tolerated harassing behavior,
lawsuit claims
Firm's owner used racial remarks: Newark animal-waste processor
shut down
Target Corp. To Pay $775,000 for Racial Harassment
Sara Lee settles race-harassment case
Nooses, Symbols of Race Hatred, at Center of Workplace Lawsuits

As these recent headlines imply, race-based conflict continues to occur in
the workplace, despite significant progress toward racial equality in the
United States. Large corporations such as Coca Cola, Eastman
Kodak, Texaco, FedEx, and Sara Lee Foods have faced class action lawsuits due to formal complaints of racial discrimination, resulting in payouts of billions of dollars. In 2006, the U.S. Equal Employment
Opportunity Commission (EEOC, 2006b) received over 27,000 charges
of racial discrimination, maintaining the longstanding record of race as the
most-alleged claim filed with the agency. During that year, the EEOC
resolved 25,992 race charges, and recovered $61.4 million in monetary
benefits for charging parties and other aggrieved individuals (not counting
litigation payouts).

These formal charges reflect only the tip of the iceberg, as research and
anecdotal data suggest that countless other racially-charged incidents in
the workplace go unreported (see, e.g., Haefner, & Ramsay 2007).
Employees may remain silent about their concerns due to fear of retaliation, apprehension about losing their job, a sense of futility, perceived or
actual lack of structures for filing complaints, and worries that others will
think they are hypersensitive. The problem is so serious that the EEOC
launched an outreach, education, and enforcement campaign known as
"E-RACE" (Eradicating Racism and Colorism from Employment) "to

advance the statutory right to a workplace free of race and color discrimination" (EEOC, 2007, para. 1). E-RACE focuses on new and emerging race and color issues in the 21st century workplace.

This chapter explores destructive workplace communication by focusing on racial harassment. First, I discuss the importance of the workplace as a critical context for addressing racial discrimination and harassment. Second, I offer a brief historical overview of race and racism because we need to understand these constructs in order to develop strategies for combating them and for creating social justice. Third, I summarize Title VII of the Civil Rights Act of 1964, which concentrates on race and color discrimination in the workplace. I also present examples of racial harassment cases filed with the EEOC and highlight communicative aspects of those cases. Fourth, I discuss consequences of racial harassment at work and provide ideas for organizing in more constructive ways around this issue. I conclude with implications for research and practice. My primary goal is to illuminate the potential of communication to both perpetuate and counteract racial harassment in the workplace.

The Critical Context of Work

The workplace comprises a critical context for addressing racial discrimination. After all, the workplace is not only where most of us spend the bulk of our waking hours, it also is "the single most significant site of regular interaction among adult citizens of different racial and ethnic identities" (Estlund, 2000, p. 21). At work, people increasingly must interact with racially different others, due to rising percentages of racial minorities and decreasing numbers of white persons in the United States. According to a report by the U.S. Department of Labor (DOL, 1999), by 2050, the U.S. population will increase by 50%, and minority groups will make up nearly half of the population.

The workplace is also a political site where members "enact, reinforce, or challenge various power relations endemic to society at large" (Allen, 2004, p. 82). For instance, many organizations are implementing programs to manage or value racial diversity. These programs are based on a belief, and research supporting this belief, that diverse workforces can improve profits, increase creativity, and deflect lawsuits (Richard, 2000). Thus, organizations often require employees to engage in diversity training and other related activities. Furthermore, although persons of color continue to disproportionately occupy lower levels of organizational hierarchies (due mainly to the legacy of racism), many of them have attained or are seeking roles of authority that whites traditionally have filled. Minority employees' efforts to advance often are supported by initiatives such as affirmative action programs and laws that offer recourse to perceived racial discrimination.

This situation can aggravate ongoing racial power dynamics, resulting for example, in backlash by some white workers who fear that affirmative action or diversity programs will hinder their own employment opportunities, or tendencies among some persons of color to pull "the race card" whenever they perceive conflict. In addition, although many whites view racism as a thing of the past, often invoking colorblindness, many persons of color believe that racism is still alive and well (Allen, 2007; Pierce, 2003). As a result, the workplace can become a breeding ground for racial strife. However, the workplace also is a promising setting for racial harmony. Through proactive, persistent, and informed efforts, organizations can help employees to value racial differences, counteract racism, and facilitate anti-racism.

An important common denominator in workplace scenarios of racial strife and racial harmony is communication. As employees use communication to produce, interpret, and share meaning with one another, they usually rely (consciously and non-consciously) on dominant societal discourses about race. For example, they often enact and enforce formal and informal policies based on racial stereotypes and attributions and Eurocentric norms during both personnel procedures (e.g., recruiting, hiring, evaluating, and promoting employees) and day-to-day interactions (Allen, 2004). The headlines at the beginning of the chapter implicate various aspects of communication and racial harassment, including language ("slurs," "offensive code words"), interaction ("racial remarks"), and symbols (nooses). They also demonstrate the potential for communication to effect positive change. Thus, communication serves both oppressive and liberatory roles in the quest for racial equality and harmony, in society in general, and the workplace in particular.

What is Race?

Race is an enduring construct conceptualized in the eighteenth century as a fixed, physical aspect of identity based primarily on skin color. During that time, European scholars (e.g., French naturalist George-Louis Leclerc, botanist Carl Linnaeus, German physical anthropologist Friedrich Blumenbach) developed an arbitrary hierarchical classification of human races. Describing this typology in 1795, Blumenbach proclaimed, "I have allotted the first place to the Caucasian ... which makes me esteem it the primeval one" (Orbe & Harris, 2001, p. 27). This typology generated a white supremacist ideology or belief system that helped to rationalize, legitimize, and maintain the idea that the white race was (and is) superior to others. In the United States, this ideology helped to justify oppression of native people and the institution of slavery, as well as mistreatment of various non-white immigrant groups. White supremacy attained its fullest ideological and institutional development in the southern United States between the 1890s and the 1950s.

Across that time span, the United States developed differing designations of racial categories. For instance, the first census (in 1790) distinguished white persons from black slaves; the 1900 form asked census takers to designate individuals as white, black, Chinese, Japanese, or Indian (American Indian). At one point, Jewish identity was listed as a racial category. Currently, the Office of Management and Budget (OMB), which is responsible for the census, cites five racial categories: American Indian or Alaska Native, Asian, Black or African American, Native Hawaiian or Other Pacific Islander, and White, and one ethnicity category, Hispanic or Latino. These categories relate race primarily with physical characteristics like skin color and hair texture and base ethnicity on cultural phenomena such as place of origin, language, and traditions.

The OMB maintains, however, that all of these categories are "sociopolitical constructs ... and should not be interpreted as being genetic, biological, or anthropological in nature" (U.S. Census Bureau, 2000, p. 15-3). Their definition designates race as *a social construction*, similar to the current stance of numerous disciplines (Omi & Winant, 1994; Orbe & Harris, 2001; Smedley & Smedley, 2005). Regarding racial categories, sociologist Howard Winant (2005, p. 1988) explains, "Although they refer to corporeal characteristics like skin color, hair texture, and eye shape, these categories acquired their significance for sociohistorical reasons, not because they have any 'natural' importance." As such, race is an artificial social construction that dominant groups have used to reinforce and perpetuate a racial hierarchy based on white supremacist ideology. As in other settings, this ideology facilitates racism and racial harassment in the workplace.

What is Racism?

Similar to race, racism as a social construction has undergone varying connotations and denotations. Although varying types of racism exist around the world, the most prevalent and pernicious form has historically been European racism against non-European peoples (Cashmore, 2003). Early versions of this brand of racism referred to "any theory or belief that a person's inherited physical characteristics, such as skin color, hair texture or facial features, determine human intellectual capacity and personality traits" (Cashmore, p. 352). This ideology assumes genetic differences between population groups, a related hierarchy of race categories, and a sense that the presumed superior race deserves privileged treatment while the presumed inferior races deserve mistreatment.

History of Racism in the United States

This type of racism was especially evident in the United States in the 1880s, when southern states and municipalities developed "Jim Crow" statutes to legalize segregation between blacks and whites. In 1896, the Supreme Court ruled in the *Plessy* v. *Ferguson* case that separate facilities for whites and blacks were constitutional. This landmark ruling precipitated discriminatory laws that segregated almost all public contexts and designated separate, generally inferior, institutions for blacks. By World War I, places of employment also were segregated. Throughout this timeframe, laws, policies, and practices targeted various racial groups in order to reinforce white supremacist ideology. Government legislation often was based on preference of white to non-white people, and skin color prevailed as a determinant. For instance, the Naturalization Law of 1790 reserved citizenship only for "free white immigrants."

After World War II, groups of citizens (people of color and whites) began a civil rights movement to challenge Jim Crow. Activism against this belief system included lawsuits, boycotts, marches, and sit-ins. These efforts led to historic governmental interventions, such as the 1954 Brown v. Board of Education case, in which the U.S. Supreme Court ruled unanimously against state-mandated segregation in pubic schools. Legislation such as the Civil Rights Act of 1964, the Voting Rights Act of 1965, and the Fair Housing Act of 1968 ended the legal sanctions of Jim Crow Laws. Most important to this chapter, the Civil Rights Act sought to eliminate racial segregation and discrimination in the workplace. Title VII of the Civil Rights Act prohibits "employment discrimination based on race, color, religion, sex, national origin, or protected activity" (EEOC, 2006a, Section 15, pp. 15–16).

Due to the Civil Rights movement and ensuing legal victories in the 1950s and 1960s, the United States began to make progress in racial matters. Blatant acts of racism declined as interracial marriages and interracial contact in public settings such as schools and the workplace increased. Plus, equal opportunity in employment improved. However, despite these and other gains, significant gaps still persist between whites and persons of color in terms of socioeconomic status and related aspects of life (Oliver & Shapiro, 1997). In essence, "racial inequality remains a robust feature of American life by nearly any commonly accepted measure of well-being" (Moran, 2006, p. 900).

Recent research projects repeatedly demonstrate racially discriminatory responses to persons of color that signify the tenacity of white supremacist ideology (Deitch et al., 2003). In several studies where researchers kept all variables constant except race, participants tended to prefer persons whom they perceived to be white to those whom they assumed were persons of color (Moran, 2005). A study in California found that temporary agencies selected white applicants three to one over African-American applicants (Bussey & Trasvina, 2003). Another project in Chicago and Boston reported that resumes of persons with "white-sounding" names (e.g., Emily, Brendan) were 50% more likely to elicit interview invitations than were the exact same resumes, only with "black sounding" names (e.g., Lakisha, Jamal) (Bertrand & Mullainathan, 2004).

Due to changes such as rising numbers of interracial marriages and families, immigration, and racial-ethnic minorities in the workforce, the issue of race discrimination at work has become more multi-dimensional and complex than in earlier times. For example, the EEOC has received a growing number of race and color discrimination charges related to multiple or intersecting categories (e.g., religion, age, disability, gender, and national origin) (EEOC, 2006a). Moreover, although conscious, blatant, violent acts of racism appear to have decreased, a resurgence of racially symbolic acts, such as hanging a noose in a person of color's workspace, seems to be occurring. That is, racism has become more covert, politicized, and strategic.

Racism's Connotations and Denotations

This synopsis embeds a history of changing connotations and denotations of racism that have important implications for workplace interactions. Early notions of racism depicted a *racial animus* model of explicit, overt, often violent acts that white individuals or groups perpetuated against people of color, especially blacks, to assert white superiority and black inferiority. This version of racism helped to inculcate *internalized racism*, a belief in white supremacy among persons of color that can lead to self-fulfilling prophecy as well as intra-racial discrimination. Initial civil rights reform efforts concentrated on the racial animus model and tended to target actions of individuals.

The Civil Rights movement also helped to implicate insidious, systemic racial issues that became known as *institutional racism*. In the late 1960s, black nationalist Stokely Carmichael coined this term to refer to collective patterns and practices that help to entrench racial inequality. Institutional (i.e., structural) racism draws attention to

> the endemic character of racial injustice and inequality. As a social structure, racism is understood to be a product of the systematic allocation of resources, privileges, and rights differentially by race: It is distributed across the whole range of social institutions both historically and in the present, and it does not require intention or agency to be perpetuated. (Winant, 2005, p. 1988)

To elaborate, "Institutional racism results from the social caste system that sustained, and was sustained by, slavery and racial segregation. Although the laws that enforced this caste system are no longer in place, its basic structure still stands to this day" (Head, 2007, p. 2).

Therefore, the history of white supremacist ideology and racial hierarchy influences and maintains institutional patterns and practices that reproduce inequalities. Institutions engage in this type of racism through overt behaviors, such as specifically excluding people of color, or in covert ways, such as adopting policies that are not specifically designed to bar people of color but can, nonetheless, result in exclusion. For instance, a policy of "seniority rules," which tends to apply to jobs that white persons historically have held, makes it difficult for more recently appointed persons of color to advance or to retain their jobs because of this "last in, first out" policy. Another example of institutional racism is the prevalence of standardized academic tests or criteria unrelated to job requirements or success that typically measure the cultural and educational norms of middle-class white males. Furthermore, informal corporate policies and procedures that interfere with minority hiring and promotion can lead to racist employment patterns. Indeed, the recurring class action lawsuits cited earlier imply an institutional bias perspective.

Conscious and Unconscious Racism

Subtle versions of racism encompass a complex, multifaceted, interlocking system that pervades many levels and contexts of society, involving individuals as well as institutions. As Moran (2006, p. 911) observes, "Both individual cognition and social structures remain tainted by the legacy of racism." Thus, racism emerges from individuals' behaviors, as well as from institutional or corporate policies. Both can be conscious or unconscious. For instance, individuals who realize that they may face sanctions may consciously veil discriminatory behaviors, or they may unconsciously enact biases based on how they have been socialized about race. On the other hand, perpetrators may genuinely be oblivious to the racist nature of their behaviors, and they will protest that they are not racist. Yet, "even people who are strongly motivated not to be racist are subject to automatic cognitive activation of stereotypes that can unconsciously influence behavior" (Deitch et al., 2003, p. 1317).

Psychological research, particularly studies using the Implicit Association Test (IAT),[1] provides convincing proof of the unconscious impact of living in the United States, "where we are surrounded every day by cultural messages linking white with good" (Gladwell, 2005, p. 85). Regardless of conscious beliefs, over 80% of persons taking the IAT had pro-white associations—even "people who explicitly disavow prejudice" (Greenwald & Banaji, 1995, p. 4). Such beliefs can have profound consequences: A study of physicians found a positive relationship between physicians' pro-white implicit bias and their likelihood of treating white patients and not treating black patients with acute coronary syndromes (Green et al., 2007). On the other hand, when persons were exposed to social texts about admired blacks (e.g., articles or films of Martin Luther King, Nelson Mandela, Denzel Washington) such exposure "significantly weakened automatic pro-white attitudes" (Dasgupta & Greenwald, 2001, p. 800).

The historical view of racism—blatant acts of individuals who believe explicitly in white superiority—allows many persons to deem racism as a thing of the past that occasionally rears its ugly head through atrocious behaviors of dysfunctional individuals. The before-mentioned IAT research refutes this notion. Indeed, an African-American participant in a qualitative study about physicians explained, "We have as a society figured out ways to systematically deny that racism exists. And that structure is in the medical institutions that train us. There is no way to have a discussion about it because it has been decided that it doesn't exist" (Nunez-Smith et al., 2007, p. 49).

Most people connote the label "racist" with someone who is forthrightly prejudiced against people of color and who believes unequivocally that whites are superior. Blatant expressions of racism are less socially acceptable today, and, as such, few persons will state such sentiments publicly (Deitch et al., 2003). Rather, some persons are enacting newer, covert forms of racism, including "modern racism" (McConahay, 1986), "aversive racism" (Dovidio & Gaertner, 2000), and "ambivalent racism" (Deitch et al.).

These forms of racism encompass less conscious and more subtle forms of racial prejudice than in earlier times. They basically refer to attitudes of white people who disdain racism, profess egalitarian values toward race, and characterize themselves as non-prejudiced. However, these persons also harbor negative attitudes towards persons of color. Although they will tend not to engage in direct acts of racial prejudice such as uttering racial slurs, they may indirectly enact racial biases in a way that maintains their sense of being non-racist. And, they will protect that image by rationalizing behaviors that others might construe as racist. For instance, an employer might invoke the premise that homogenous workgroups will work more harmoniously than racially mixed groups to justify hiring only white sales representatives (Brief, Dietz, Cohen, Pugh, & Vaslow, 2000).

These types of contemporary racism may help to explain persistent racial disparities in society as well as findings of research such as the project on "white sounding" versus "black sounding" names. In fact, research concludes that modern racist views can predict discriminatory behavior (Deitch et al., 2003). Thus, it is important to distinguish personal/individual racism (and its variations) from institutional/structural racism, while also recognizing potential threats and promises of both.

Title VII of the Civil Rights Act of 1964

The perspective of "multi-racisms" also reveals important complexities of racism and racial discrimination in the workplace. Notably, Title VII of the Civil Rights Act of 1964 acknowledged and allowed for most of these complexities by implicating individuals and institutions, by invoking past and present notions of race, and by encompassing conscious and unconscious behaviors. Consequently, Title VII offers a viable framework for understanding racism and racial discrimination in contemporary workplaces. In addition, examples of Title VII cases illustrate or indicate ways that communication processes facilitate racial harassment in the workplace. Therefore, this section details elements of Title VII regarding race discrimination.

Race and Color

Title VII "prohibits employer actions that discriminate, by motivation or impact, against persons because of race." Interestingly, Title VII does not define "race," although the EEOC Compliance Manual refers to the OMB's categories of race and ethnicity and its perspective that these are socio-political constructs (EEOC, 2006a). Race discrimination, as distinct from many other forms of discrimination, operates on a group basis; it works on perceived attributes and deficiencies of groups, not individualized characteristics. Discrimination occurs when groups are denied opportunities or rewards for reasons unrelated to their capabilities, industry, and general merit. They are judged solely on their membership in an identifiable racial group.

In addition to race discrimination, Title VII prohibits employment discrimination because of "color" as a separate item. Although the Compliance Manual does not define "color," it explains that "the courts and the [EEO] Commission read 'color' to have its commonly understood meaning—pigmentation, complexion, or skin shade or tone" (EEOC, 2006a, p. 15–16). The manual elaborates that color discrimination applies to acts "based on the lightness, darkness, or other color characteristics of an individual" (pp. 15–16). All of the issues related to racial discrimination apply equally to color discrimination. Title VII prohibits race and color discrimination "in every aspect of employment, including recruitment, hiring, promotion, wages, benefits, work assignments, performance evaluations, training, transfer, leave, discipline, layoffs, discharge, and any other term, condition, or privilege of employment" (pp. 15–16).

Intention, Liability, and Protected Class

Title VII prohibits intentional discrimination (based on the racial animus model), as well as job policies that appear to be neutral, yet disproportionately affect persons of a certain race or color, that are unrelated to the job and the needs of the business. Moreover, Title VII allows for liability of *any* parties in the workplace, not just those in positions of power, including supervisors, coworkers, and non-employees such as customers or business partners over whom employers have authority. Title VII's prohibitions apply to members of *all* racial or multi-racial groups. Prohibitions also apply to issues such as ancestry, physical characteristics, race-linked illness, reverse discrimination, and so forth.

Generally, race and color discrimination comprises three categories: (a) evaluating employment decisions; (b) equal access to jobs (recruiting, hiring and promotion, diversity, and affirmative action); and (c) equal opportunity for job success (racial harassment, racial bias in other employment terms and conditions, and retaliation). The following discussion centers on the third category, particularly racial harassment, because it is most germane to this chapter.

Hostile Environments and Racial Harassment

Title VII defines racial harassment as "unwelcome conduct that unreasonably interferes with an individual's work performance or creates an intimidating, hostile, or offensive work environment" (pp. 15–35). A hostile environment encompasses various types of conduct, including "offensive jokes, slurs, epithets or name-calling, physical assaults or threats, intimidation, ridicule or mockery, insults or put-downs, offensive objects or pictures, and interference with work performance" (15–35).

These types of conduct implicate various elements of communication, including nonverbal cues (e.g., use of voice, gestures), semantics, symbols, style, speech acts (e.g., assertions or threats), and so forth (Cashmore, 2003). These and other aspects of communication are evident in the following examples of allegations of racial harassment in the workplace[2]— uses of communication to enact various connotations of racism and thus reinforce and recreate the ideology of white supremacy.

In some workplaces, employees used symbols historically associated with racial violence, such as nooses, swastikas, and KKK garb, graffiti, and symbols. In addition, employees sometimes made remarks related to violence. One employee commented that it should not be against the law to shoot Mexican men, women, and children or to shoot African Americans and Chinese people. This employee also allegedly stated, "If I had my way I'd gas them [referring to black employees] like Hitler did the Jews."

Some cases also replicate racist beliefs that people of color are subhuman. In one worksite, someone posted a picture of a gorilla with an African-American employee's name written on it, while in another office, someone pasted a picture of an ape over an African-American's child's photograph. In yet another case, white postal workers threw bananas and made racist comments to 17 black postal workers who worked in a metal enclosure.

Reported acts of hostility include physical assault. An African-American male employed as a used-vehicle salesman said that his white manager grabbed him by the collar and dragged him through the dealership. He also reported that his manager berated him in front of coworkers and customers. Employees often report uses of racial slurs and epithets, such as calling an employee the "N" word. In one case, several employees, including supervisors, routinely used egregious ethnic slurs for African Americans, Hispanics, and Asians. In another situation, a middle-management Japanese American's white employer frequently used anti-Japanese slurs and racist slogans.

Racial harassment also emphasized dominant belief systems about language usage and race. An Asian employee said his supervisor ridiculed him for how he pronounced a word. In another lawsuit, the plaintiffs contended that the facility's managers prohibited Haitian workers from speaking in their native Creole even though they allowed other non-English speaking groups (of European descent) to converse in their native languages.

Some alleged behaviors referred to racial stereotypes and caricatures. A technician of Chinese and Italian ancestry was subjected to repeated racial and sexual harassment including mimicking martial arts movements and mockingly calling him "Bruce Lee." In another workplace, coworkers pulled their eyes back with their fingers to mock Asian appearance.

Internalized racism, which occurs when members of racial minority groups consciously or unconsciously accept tenets of white supremacist ideology, seems to function through harassment related to skin color based on an ascending order of dark to light (i.e., white) pigmentation. Members of racial groups that comprise a range of skin hues often socialize one another to value light skin over dark, thereby indoctrinating one another to white superiority. Thus, color bias is primarily an intra-racial phenomenon, and cases usually involve remarks based on skin color (Findley, Garrott, & Wheatley, 2004). A lighter-skinned black woman reported that her supervisor, a darker-skinned black female, made statements such as "you need some sun"; and "why don't you go back to where you belong?"'(p. 33). In another case, "a dark-skinned black waiter alleged that his light-skinned black supervisor ... called him a 'tar baby,' 'black monkey,' and 'jig-a-boo,' and directed him to bleach his skin" (p. 36).

Another example of intra-racial harassment involved a group of white employees who reported a hostile work environment due to their white coworkers' harassing behaviors towards some of their black coworkers. A final example of intra-racial harassment implied the "model minority" stereotype. In this case, a Korean supervisor with stereotypical beliefs about the superiority of Korean workers held the Korean plaintiff to higher standards than other employees, required him to work harder for longer hours, and subjected him to verbal and physical abuse when he did not meet those expectations.

Silencing Dissent: Minimizing, Stigmatizing, and Retaliating

Power plays often ensue when employees attempt to voice their concerns about perceived racial harassment. In many cases, supervisors minimize or ignore complaints and concerns. Employees who feel victimized report that when they inform their supervisors of incidents, the supervisors take no steps to resolve or prevent the hostile conditions. Sometimes supervisors dismiss employees' concerns, asserting that alleged perpetrators "were just joking." For instance, coworkers of an African-American employee "joked" that they were going to burn a cross in that person's yard, and they thought the person should laugh about their "joke" (Eng, 2007). In San Francisco, a swastika was placed near the desks of Asian-American and African-American inspectors in the newly integrated fire department. Officials explained that someone had presented the swastika to the battalion chief as a "joke" gift, several years earlier, and that it was unclear why or how it ended up at the work stations of the minority employees.

Persons of authority and coworkers often dismiss concerns by stigmatizing accusers and labeling them as hypersensitive or politically correct. Another stigmatizing reaction is simply to blame the victim (Wooten & James, 2004). Persons of authority also may retaliate by impeding promotion opportunities or even firing employees for speaking out against racial harassment on the job. In one case of retaliation, a Mexican American filed a lawsuit claiming that his coworkers called him names like "Taco Bob" and "Burrito Bob." Subsequently, the harassment increased, with the union local's blessing, because the claimant had violated their "no-ratting" policy by complaining to plant management. The employee said that someone wrote "Ratserio" and other epithets on the men's room wall in three-foot letters. In addition, the union local purchased 200 "No Rat" stickers for his coworkers to wear. In another case, the owner of a company attempted to force employees to withdraw their EEOC charges by making harassing telephone calls to one of the claimant's family members.

The preceding examples offer a glimpse of types of behaviors and attitudes that motivate employees to report feelings of racial harassment and stigmatizing responses to such reports. Employees who perceive that others are harassing them because of race often face a lose-lose dilemma: If they report the incident(s), others may retaliate by additional harassment; if they do not report, they may face additional harassment (Meares, Oetzel, Derkacs, & Ginossar, 2004). Due to contemporary ideas about racism based on traditional views of racial animus, they may not report perceived race discrimination for fear of being labeled hypersensitive (e.g., Nunez-Smith et al., 2007). In fact, research suggests that increased perceptions of racial discrimination are unrelated to increases in formal grievances (Ensher, Grant-Vallone, & Donaldson, 2001). As such, targeted workers may suffer in silence and endure a number of negative consequences.

Consequences of Racial Harassment

Actual and perceived racial harassment in the workplace can induce costly consequences for individuals, organizations, and society at large. People of color in workplaces where they routinely feel harassed report feelings of hopelessness and lowered organizational commitment and job satisfaction (Deitch et al., 2003). They also experience health problems, depression, and racial fatigue (i.e., feeling drained and weary due to permanent anxiety about racial strife at work) (Meares et al., 2004; Nunez-Smith et al., 2007; Pierce, 2003).

These workers can suffer from internalized racism, which can lead to self-fulfilling prophecy and feeling resigned to remain in lower levels of organizational hierarchies. Based on the stigma of racial prejudice and discrimination, they may segregate themselves and withdraw from their work duties, doing only the bare minimum. In workgroups, they may fail to contribute fully to accomplishing team goals. Indeed, for racially and ethnically-diverse workers, "perceived discrimination [can] have an effect on organizational commitment, job satisfaction, and organizational citizenship behavior" (Ensher et al., 2001, p. 53). In addition, some persons may lash out through physical violence against their perpetrators.

They also may feel shame. Beejey Enriquez, a Filipino worker who filed a complaint in the EEOC's San Francisco District Office, recounted how he was targeted for dismissal by his employer due to his race and ethnicity—despite his qualifications and special recognition by his company. He said, "Now I was just a checkbox to eliminate ... I was almost embarrassed to be who I was." He explained further, "I don't want anyone else to be ashamed of who they are, or who their parents and grandparents are" (EEOC, 2007).

White employees who are targets of racial discrimination from persons of color can experience similar consequences. In addition, if they witness other whites engaging in racial discrimination, they may experience various stressors of hostile work environments, including fear of retaliation and bystander guilt.

Organizations too can pay dearly for race and color discrimination through monetary costs (e.g., attorney fees, compensatory damages, punitive damages); negative public relations; reduced productivity; divided teams; low employee morale; decreased profit due to boycotts; higher turnover; and increased health care spending due to worker stress-related absences and illnesses (Meares et al., 2004). Hostile work environments also send negative signals about organizations to their current (and potential) workforce.

Finally, society at large endures incalculable costs associated with consequences of racial harassment in the workplace. If all members of the workforce do not feel empowered to reach their full potential, or to contribute to their greatest capacity, the United States will never meet its potential as a productive force in all areas of global and local commerce. Moreover, persistent racial strife at work reinforces and perpetuates racial disharmony and segregation across other contexts of society. To alleviate these and other costs, and to begin to reap benefits of multiracial, diverse workforces (see, Cox & Blake, 1991), organizations can strive to develop and maintain contexts that value racial differences. The discipline of communication can play a pivotal role in those efforts.

Communication Matters: Constructive Ways of Organizing

The preceding discussions about race, racism, and racial harassment illuminate a clear, though challenging, set of implications for research and practice that can move organizational communication in more constructive directions regarding race. Research on communication and racial harassment in the workplace must take a critical, discursive stance on how racialized power dynamics exist and occur through institutional practices and policies, as well as through individual communication processes. Research also should study recursive relationships between macro-level discourses about race and organizational micropractices, for instance by exploring ways that members of organizations reinforce or resist white supremacist ideology during everyday interactions (see, Ashcraft & Allen, 2003).

Research also must investigate varying connotations of racism, differing perspectives (between and among racial groups) about racism, and blatant-versus-subtle as well as conscious-versus-unconscious acts of racial harassment. We also should analyze diverse communicative experiences of members of all racial groups while acknowledging the salience of other intersecting identity categories (e.g., gender, age, class, sexuality, national origin, ability, religion, etc.). Two strands of scholarship provide preliminary starting points for such studies.

First, whiteness studies embody a relatively recent focus on the sociohistorical construction of whiteness and its implications. Whiteness studies extend scholarship about race and racism beyond foci on persons of color and oppressive aspects of race to encompass how race affects white persons. Scholars from various disciplines render "whiteness visible as a central aspect of racial inequality" (Pierce, 2003, p. 55). They contend that members of white power structures created race and a racial hierarchy to justify discrimination against persons who are not white. They believe that exposing systems of racial power will facilitate attaining equality in

American society. Advocates of whiteness studies strive to help white people understand their own racial identity, rather than view race as relevant only to persons of color.

For instance, sociologist Peggy McIntosh (1995) developed the concept of "white privilege" to illuminate ways that white persons routinely receive unearned advantages based solely on their race that persons of color do not receive. She hopes that edifying whites about their invisible privileges will motivate them toward anti-racist attitudes and behaviors. Communication scholars are among those engaged in this burgeoning area of study (e.g., Cooks, 2003; Mayer, 2005; Nakayama & Martin, 1999; Warren, 2001). Organizational communication researchers can refer to this work as they investigate whiteness in the workplace (see, Allen, 2007; Grimes, 2002).

Second, critical race theory (CRT) explicitly concentrates on key issues of institutional racism. CRT regards race as an ongoing site of struggle and asserts that racism is prevalent in U.S. culture. CRT scholarship seeks to eliminate racial oppression by unmasking everyday structures and practices that perpetuate race-based subordination. Thus, this perspective challenges dominant discourse about equal opportunity as well as "larger cultural discourse of liberal individualism" (Pierce, 2003, p. 68) by stressing the realities of race and racist structures that reinforce racial oppression (Hasian & Delgado, 1998; Matsuda, Lawrence, Delgado, & Crenshaw, 1983). CRT also advocates situating current racial dynamics in light of the history of race in the United States, and it disputes dominant perspectives on race of neutrality, objectivity, and color blindness. Along with whiteness studies, CRT shows strong promise for informing endeavors to eradicate racism in the workplace.

Although ridding the workplace of racism is admittedly a daunting proposition, many organizations are being proactive. Some of them require and provide diversity training for employees with race as the primary topic. Although diversity programs are not a cure-all, they can be effective:

> Diversity programs certainly cannot ameliorate the pervasive plight of racism in our society, but they can help make the workplace a less hostile, more accommodating, and healthier setting for all its members. Even where cooperation remains at the instrumental or superficial level, it has the proven potential to reduce stereotyping and bias, and to foster greater familiarity, greater empathy, and fairer judgments. The law has a limited capacity to prohibit, punish, or even detect the unconscious or well hidden biases and stereotypes that often infect judgments about and relations among individuals and groups. But the law can help—and has helped—to create social environments in which these destructive attitudes gradually wane. (Estlund, 2003, p. 83)

Based on projects about implicit bias such as the ones cited above, diversity training programs often include exercises to reveal participants' hidden prejudices (Babcock, 2006; Pendry, Driscoll, & Field, 2007). Trainers have begun to employ tools such as the Implicit Association Test and white privilege scales in hopes that participants will become more self-aware and thus receptive to diversity training. Although these approaches can be effective, they also can elicit a variety of responses from participants, including confusion, anger, sadness, and guilt (Pendry et al.). Thus, trainers must be prepared to deal with complex reactions from participants, or their efforts may backfire. Effective uses of the IAT in diversity training represents a promising area of research for organizational communication scholars.

Other diversity training strategies aimed at individuals include social identity exercises that invite participants to list and rank social groups to which they belong, and to discuss their lists with one another. This type of technique has proven effective in diversity training because it can increase the salience of coworkers' common social identity (e.g., as a member of a team or organizational unit), leading to improved cooperation in workgroups (Pendry et al., 2007). These and other diversity training techniques can sensitize individual members of organizations to racial issues, and provide strategies to enhance interracial interactions.

However, as this chapter implies, we cannot optimize the potential for transformation in the workplace if we do not also critique and change institutional practices, processes, norms, expectations, and policies (formal and informal). For starters, the EEOC encourages employers to clearly communicate to their employees that they will enforce policies on racial harassment, to adopt effective means for addressing complaints, and to train managers on how to recognize and respond immediately to racial harassment (EEOC, 2006b). The EEOC also enjoins employers to adopt "best practices" to reduce the likelihood of discrimination and to address impediments to equal employment opportunity (e.g., Thomas & Ely, 2001). Organizational communication scholars can conduct research and practice related to these issues.

We also need to explicitly name and frame racism as a persistent problem and to help organizational decision-makers understand and adapt to changing notions of racism and racial discrimination. Basically, we must help organizations to assess and address institutional and cultural issues while also enlightening and empowering individual employees.

A promising means for accomplishing these goals is the racial justice approach (Rogers, 2001). In contrast to diversity training programs, which tend to focus on individuals, the racial justice approach depicts racism as "a set of societal, cultural, and institutional beliefs and practices—regardless of intention—that subordinate and oppress one race for the benefit of another" (p. 12). This perspective advocates analyzing ways that organizational systems, along with individual attitudes and behaviors, perpetuate racism. Furthermore, the racial justice approach attends to differences in how persons of color and whites tend to experience race. It educates whites on privilege, new forms of racism, and alliance building, while helping persons of color to understand internalized racism and its impacts. Basically, "a racial justice approach requires an organizational transformation of power relations" (p. 13) that delves into racism and establishes "a basis for understanding systemic inequality and oppression based on other identities such as classism, sexism, heterosexism, and ableism" (p. 13).

Conclusion

In conclusion, I urge organizational communication scholars to consider whiteness studies, critical race theory, and the social justice approach as they develop and implement research and practice about racism and racial harassment in the workplace. I also invite them to identify other sources that might prove useful. Furthermore, I encourage all of us to engage these issues in our primary institutional setting—the academy (e.g., Artz, 1998). In particular, I endorse critical communication pedagogy as a framework for teaching students about issues raised in this chapter and this volume.

Critical communication pedagogy directly attends to assumptions about context, power, communication, and identity in educational settings and processes (e.g., Cooks, 2003; Fassett & Warren, 2007). This perspective advocates a dialogic, reflexive approach to teaching and learning where all actors collaborate with one another to critique educational practices and to generate ideas for social change while being mindful of the constitutive role of communication.

Although we might struggle to locate external organizations that might allow us (as researchers or consultants) to apply the social justice approach outlined above, most of us are empowered in our classrooms to create a learning context based on tenets of critical communication pedagogy (Ashcraft & Allen, 2009). In doing so, we can prepare students to enter the workplace with knowledge and skills to minimize racial harassment and other types of dysfunctional communication in the workplace. Moreover, we can incorporate our classroom experiences into our research and practice. Thus, we can help our discipline to make major headway towards eradicating racism in the workplace.

Notes

1 Available online: http://implicit.harvard.edu/implicit/.
2 Unless otherwise noted, these are taken from the EEOC Compliance Manual and the EEOC website.

References

Allen, B. J. (2004). *Difference matters: Communicating social identity*. Long Grove, IL: Waveland Press.

Allen, B. J. (2007). Theorizing communication and race. *Communication Monographs, 74*(2), 259–264.

Artz, L. (1998). African Americans and higher education: An exigence in need of applied communication. *Journal of Applied Communication Research, 26*(2), 210–231.

Ashcraft, K. L., & Allen, B. J. (2003). The racial foundation of organizational communication. *Communication Theory, 13*(1), 5–38.

Ashcraft, K. L., & Allen, B. J. (2009). Politics closer to home: Teaching and learning critical organization in our own work/place. *Management Learning, 40*(1), 11–30

Babcock, P. (2006). Detecting hidden bias. *HR Magazine, 51*. Retrieved 1–30–08 from http://www.shrm.org/hrmagazine/articles/0206/0206cover.asp.

Bertrand, M., & Mullainathan, S. (2004). Are Emily and Brendan more employable than Lakisha and Jamal? A field experiment on labor market discrimination *The American Economic Review, 94*(4), 991–1013.

Brief, A. P., Dietz, J., Cohen, R. R., Pugh, S. D., & Vaslow, J. B. (2000). Just doing business: Modern racism and obedience to authority as explanations for employment discrimination. *Organizational Behavior and Human Decision Processes, 81*(1), 72–97.

Bussey, J., & Trasvina, J. (2003). Racial preferences: The treatment of White and African-American job applicants by temporary job agencies in California. Retrieved August 17, 2007, from http://www.impactfund.organization.

Cashmore, E. (2003). *Encyclopedia of race and ethnic studies*. New York: Routledge.

Cooks, L. (2003). Pedagogy, performance, and positionality: Teaching about whiteness in interracial communication. *Communication Education, 52*(2), 245–257.

Cox, T. H., & Blake, S. (1991). Managing cultural diversity: Implications for organizational effectiveness. *Academy of Management Executive, 5*(3), 45–56.

Dasgupta, N., & Greenwald, A. G. (2001). On the malleability of automatic attitudes: Combating automatic prejudice with images of admired and disliked individuals. *Journal of Personality & Social Psychology, 81*(5), 800–814.

Deitch, E. A., Barsky, A., Butz, R. M., Chan, S., Brief, A. P., & Bradley, J. C. (2003). Subtle yet significant: The existence and impact of everyday racial discrimination in the workplace. *Human Relations, 56*(11), 1299–1324.

United States, Department of Labor (DOL) (1999). Futurework: Trends and challenges for work in the 21st century. *United States Department of Labor*. Retrieved August 19, 2007, from http://www.dol.gov/oasam/programs/history/herman/reports/futurework/report.htm.

Dovidio, J. F., & Gaertner, S. L. (2000). Aversive racism and selection decisions: 1989 and 1999. *Psycholgical Science, 11*(4), 315–319.

United States Equal Employment Opportunity Commission (EEOC) (2006a). Equal Employment Opportunity Commission Compliance Manual. *United States Equal Employment Opportunity Commission*. Retrieved July 15, 2006, from http://www.eeoc.gov/policy/docs/retal.html.

United States Equal Employment Opportunity Commission (EEOC) (2006b). Questions and answers about race and color discrimination in employment. *United States Equal Employment Opportunity Commission.* Retrieved August 17, 2007, from http://www.eeoc.gov/policy/docs/qanda_race_color.html.

United States Equal Employment Opportunity Commission (EEOC) (2007). EEOC takes new approach to fighting racism and colorism in the 21st century workplace. *United States Equal Employment Opportunity Commission.* Retrieved December 31, 2007, from http://eeoc.gov/press/2-28-07.

Eng, D. (2007). Success should breed willingness to lend a hand. *Television Week, 26*(10), 10–12.

Ensher, E. A., Grant-Vallone, E. J., & Donaldson, S. I. (2001). Effects of perceived discrimination on job satisfaction, organizational commitment, organizational citizenship behavior, and grievances. *Human Resource Development Quarterly, 12*(1), 53–72.

Estlund, C. L. (2000). Working together: The workplace, civil society, and the law. *Georgetown Law Journal, 89*(1), 1–91.

Estlund, C. L. (2003). *Working together: How workplace bonds strengthen a diverse democracy.* Oxford: Oxford University Press.

Fassett, D., & Warren, J. (2007). *Critical communication pedagogy.* Thousand Oaks, CA: Sage.

Findley, H., Garrott, S. C., & Wheatley, R. (2004). Color discrimination: Differentiate at your peril. *Journal of Individual Employment Rights, 11*(1), 31–38.

Gladwell, M. (2005). *Blink: The power of thinking without thinking.* New York: Little, Brown.

Green, A. R., Carney, D. R., Pallin, D. J., Ngo, L. H., Raymond, K. L., Lezzoni, L. I., et al. (2007). Implicit bias among physicians and its prediction of thrombolysis decisions for Black and White Patients. *Journal of General Internal Medicine, 22*(9), 1231–1238.

Greenwald, A. G., & Banaji, M. R. (1995). Implicit social cognition: attitudes, self-esteem, and stereotypes. *Psycholgical Review, 102*(1), 4–27.

Grimes, D. (2002). Challenging the status quo? Whiteness of the diversity management literature. *Management Communication Quarterly, 15*(3), 381–409.

Haefner, R., & Ramsey, N. (2007, 9/24). Discrimination on the American job. Retrieved August 17, 2007, from http://www.careerbuilder.com/JobSeeker/careerbytes/CBArticle.

Hasian, M., & Delgado, F. (1998). The trials and tribulations of racialized critical rhetorical theory: Understanding the rhetorical ambiguities of Proposition 187. *Communication Theory, 8*(3), 245–270.

Head, T. (2007). Institutional racism. Retrieved September 5, 2007, from http://civilliberty.about.com/od/raceequalopportunity/g/inst_racism.htm.

Matsuda, M. J., Lawrence, C. R., Delgado, R., & Crenshaw, K. W. (Eds.). (1983). *Words that wound: Critical race theory, assaultive speech, and the First Amendment.* San Francisco: Westview Press.

Mayer, V. (2005). Research beyond the pale: Whiteness in audience studies and media ethnography. *Communication Theory, 15*(1), 148–167.

McConahay, J. B. (1986). Modern racism, ambivalence, and the Modern Racism Scale. In J. F. Dovidio & S. L. Gaertner (Eds.), *Prejudice, discrimination, and racism* (pp. 91–125). Orlando, FL: Academic Press.

McIntosh, P. (1995). White privilege and male privilege: A personal account of coming to see correspondences through work in women's studies. In M. L. Anderson & P. H. Collins (Eds.), *Race, class, and gender: An anthology* (pp. 76–87). Belmont, CA: Wadsworth Publishing Company.

Meares, M. M., Oetzel, J. G., Derkacs, D., & Ginossar, T. (2004). Employee mistreatment and muted voices in the culturally diverse workforce. *Journal of Applied Communication Research, 32*(1), 4–27.

Moran, R. F. (2005). Whatever happened to racism? *St. John's Law Review, 79*(9), 899–927.

Nakayama, T., & Martin, J. (1999). *Whiteness: The communication of social identity*. Thousand Oaks, CA: Sage.

Nunez-Smith, M., Curry, L. A., Bigby, J., Berg, D., Krumholz, H. M., & Bradley, E. H. (2007). Impact of race on the professional lives of physicians of African descent. *Annals of Internal Medicine, 146*(1), 45–51.

Oliver, M. L., & Shapiro, T. M. (1997). *Black wealth, white wealth: A new perspective on racial inequality*. New York: Routledge.

Omi, M., & Winant, H. (1994). *Racial formation in the United States: From the 1960s to the 1980s*. New York: Routledge & Kegan Paul.

Orbe, M., & Harris, T. (2001). *Interracial communication: Theory into practice*. Belmont, CA: Wadsworth.

Pendry, L. F., Driscoll, D. M., & Field, S. C. (2007). Diversity training: Putting theory into practice. *Journal of Occupational and Organizational Psychology, 80*(1), 27–50.

Pierce, J. L. (2003). 'Racing for innocence': Whiteness, corporate culture, and the backlash against affirmative action. *Qualitative Sociology, 26*(1), 53–75.

Richard, O. C. (2000). Racial diversity, business strategy, and firm performance: A resource-based view. *The Academy of Management Journal, 43*(2), 164–177.

Rogers, D. (2001). Good for business but insufficient for social change. *Western Studies Center News* (Winter), 12–13.

Smedley, A., & Smedley, B. D. (2005). Race as biology is fiction, racism as a social problem is real: Anthropological and historical perspectives on the social construction of race. *American Psychologist, 60*(1), 16–26.

Thomas, D. A., & Ely, R. J. (2001). Cultural diversity at work: The effects of diversity perspectives on work group processes and outcomes. *Administrative Science Quarterly, 46*(2), 229–273.

U.S. Census Bureau. (2000). 2000 Census of Population, Public Law 94–171. Retrieved February 22, 2007, from http://quickfacts.census.gov/qfd/meta/long_68184.htm.

Warren, J. T. (2001). Doing whiteness: On the performative dimensions of race in the classroom. *Communication Education, 50*(1), 91–108.

Winant, H. (2005). Race and racism: Overview. In M. Horowitz (Ed.), *New dictionary of the history of ideas* (pp. 1987–1989). Detroit: Charles Scribner's Sons.

Wooten, L., & James, E. H. (2004). When firms fail to learn: The perpetuation of discrimination in the workplace. *Journal of Management Inquiry, 13*(1), 23–33.

Chapter 9

Destructive Organizational Communication and LGBT Workers' Experiences

Andrea P. Lewis

> Work is central to all of our lives. Our jobs enable us to support our families, utilize our talents, contribute to our communities, and fulfill our dreams. Like everyone else, GLBT Americans want our success to reflect our skills, motivation, and dedication. But this reasonable goal —to be judged on our merits—is not a reality for many GLBT people. That is because in 31 states, it is legal to fire someone because of their sexual orientation, and in 39 states, it is legal to fire someone because of their gender identity. (Solmonese, 2007, p.1)

The above excerpt, taken from a statement by the President of the Human Rights Campaign, America's largest civil rights organization, to the United States House of Representatives, indicates the continued political attention that lesbian, gay, bisexual and transgender (LGBT) employee issues receive. Although about 70% of the American public assumes homosexuals are covered under federal civil rights law, they are not (Mills, 2000). In 1994, the Employment Non-Discrimination Act (ENDA), which would ban workplace discrimination against employees based on gender and sexual orientation, was introduced to Congress and was defeated. In 1996 ENDA came within one vote of passing the U.S. Senate. Since 1996 including sexual orientation and gender identity as a protected class has come before the Congress numerous times but has continually been defeated. In the fall of 2007, the bill was again before Congress, and Congress heard testimony about the destructive nature of LGBT employee discrimination. Although there is no legislative decision yet, there is strong support for the inclusion of sexual orientation and gender discrimination in ENDA legislation.

The purpose of this chapter is to examine issues that LGBT persons encounter in organizations and the destructive potential for painful communication when these workers face social stigmatization (Goffman, 1963). The devastation of stigma and discrimination and the resulting discomfort experienced by LGBT workers are important forms of destructive organizational communication that deserve attention in their own right. The absence of legal protection, little public and scholarly knowledge or acknowledgment of LGBT discrimination, and the ensuing organizational and personal losses are focal points of this chapter. An underlying argument throughout this chapter is that much of LGBT employee mistreatment is caused by cultural ideologies and organizational environments that privilege heterosexuality. Specifically, the chapter examines LGBT discrimination and related legal struggles, explores processes of heteronormativity in organizational contexts, describes stigma of variant sexuality, and outlines some of the destructive outcomes linked to LGBT discrimination/stigma. The chapter concludes with suggestions for organizing in more constructive ways and potential avenues for future research.

LGBT Discrimination and Legal Struggles

According to a 2007 study by the Williams Institute on Sexual Orientation Law and Public Policy at UCLA, LGBT employees regularly face discrimination and inequity at work. Specifically, at least one in ten LGBT employees suffers discrimination—a similar percentage of heterosexual coworkers report witnessing discrimination against LGBT colleagues. Discrimination based on perceptions of one's sexuality is at least as likely as discrimination based on other minority statuses. In states where laws include sexual orientation and gender identity as a protected class, the number of sexual orientation discrimination complaints filed is similar to the number of complaints filed for sexual or racial discrimination (Bedgett, Lau, Sears, & Ho, 2007). Despite these statistics LGBT employees fail to receive the same legal protection as other minorities.

Discrimination against LGBT employees has a significant impact on the workplace environment. Victims may feel isolated from the organizational culture, and attacks on their personhood can compromise their happiness, security, and self-esteem. Additionally, the ongoing fear of having one's sexuality become the object of workplace harassment and possible job loss intensifies stress for LGBT employees. For example, when Jacquelyn Thomas' coworkers assumed she was gay, they confronted her and charged that AIDS exists because of people like her. When the homophobic comments continued and became more derogatory, she informed her employer that she was being harassed. After a brief investigation, her employer (a law firm) accused *her* of making a racial comment, removed her from the assignment on which she was working, and then fired her. Thomas had not disclosed her sexuality before the harassment but indicated that, had she been asked, she would have disclosed because "hiding one's sexual orientation takes work," but more importantly, "not coming out can take a terrible toll on a person's self-esteem and personal

186 Andrea P. Lewis

happiness" (Thomas, 2007, p. 1). In Thomas' case, the harassment by her coworkers was prompted by the *assumption* that she was a lesbian. When coworkers presume variant sexuality, it is particularly troubling because it reinforces traditional gender norms and subsequent harassment then underscores the high risks to non-conformers.

Statistics identifying workplace harassment due to variant sexuality (or the perception thereof) and real-life experiences such as Thomas', suggest that homophobia and LGBT discrimination are alive and well in organizations and that these forms of harassment are at least as prevalent as other forms of discrimination. Ironically, even with growing evidence, those who oppose inclusion of sexual orientation in ENDA legislation argue that such laws would afford "extra protection to a group that has not been disadvantaged" (Campaign, 2007, p. 1). This argument simply does not stand up in the face of Thomas' experience; perceptions of variant sexuality can result in hostile work environments and can, in many states, justify employment termination. Because many states do not include sexual orientation as a protected class, and federal laws such as ENDA fail to recognize variant sexuality, LGBT employees have little recourse against harassment and job loss. As such, LGBTs are indeed disadvantaged.

Even though U.S. legislative bodies are still trying to determine whether LGBT workers should be considered a protected class, a number of organizations are proactively implementing policies to extend benefits to LGBT employees. There is actually good reason for organizations to implement such policies since the U.S. workforce includes over 20 million LGBT employees, and this group had $641 billion in buying power in 2006 (Commercial Closet Association, 2007). Many organizations have begun to address issues of equality for this worker and consumer group. For example, 92.2% of Fortune 500 companies currently protect gay employees from discrimination, and 51% offer equivalent benefits to gay and lesbian employees (Human Rights Campaign Foundation, 2007). An inclusive workplace culture is important to organizations, if only for economic reasons. According to Hayward Bell, the Chief Diversity Officer at Raytheon, because over the next decade Raytheon is going to "need anywhere from 30,000 to 40,000 new employees we can't afford to turn our back on anyone in the talent pool" (Gunther, 2006, p. 94).

Offering benefits for LGBT families and instituting anti-discrimination policies are a positive beginning. However, benefits and policies can fall short in creating inclusive environments when organizations have homophobic cultures and when the policies are loosely defined or unenforced. In order to retain LGBT employees and attract a wide range of highly talented workers, organizations must work to foster an inclusive climate. The need to create safe environments and protection from discrimination for LGBT employees is perhaps best summed up by John Ferraro, Senior Vice

Chair for Ernst & Young LLP. "It was obvious that [LGBT people have] to make decisions every day on whom they could talk to and how much of themselves they could bring to work. I can't imagine coming to work every day and feeling afraid. It just felt wrong ... people are our top asset" (Human Rights Campaign Foundation, 2007, p. 7). Attitudes such as Ferraro's create environments where LGBT employees feel more valued and thus might be more productive.

Lack of Attention to LGBT Workers

Even though diversity has been a hot topic in much of the organizational literature, representation of the LGBT workplace experience in this body of work is sparse. A better understanding of LGBT employee experiences is needed because, like all aspects of identity, sexuality is negotiated in the workplace—it is discursively constituted, configured, and lived (Burrell & Hearn, 1989; Hearn, 1987). As such, communication scholars are well positioned to provide unique insights about destructive organizational practices and processes that lead to marginalizing LGBT employees. Furthermore, communication is instrumental in cultivating environments that are accepting (or stigmatizing), and LGBT issues can provide valuable information to organizations striving to combat various forms of discrimination. My hope is that this chapter will facilitate a discussion about better ways of organizing that will aid in fostering inclusive organizational cultures that value diversity.

Unlike other marginalized groups in the United States, LGBT employees can be fired for their sexual orientation or gender identity and are often the targets of various forms of harassment. To date, most research on diversity and discrimination in organizations has centered on gender, race, and ethnicity. Although there may be some common issues among these groups, LGBT employees are unique in that their experiences often revolve around social notions of sexual deviancy.

Unlike race and ethnicity, sexuality may be viewed by coworkers as a choice. The destructive outcomes of homophobia, and the discrimination spawned by this thinking, are two-fold. First, LGBT employees face marginalization for the presumed *choice* they have made while also enduring harassment, which may include efforts to "force" heterosexuality. For instance, after Jacquelyn Thomas indicated that she would be attending church for a holiday celebration, her coworker replied, "Well, you need to take a damn man to church with you" (Thomas, 2007, p. 1). This suggests that LGBT employees face issues that are unique and that differ from other marginalized groups. Second, the LGBT workforce is excluded from federal civil rights laws that protect other minority groups. As such, LGBT employees must either mask their sexuality or disclose their sexuality and risk losing their job.

Processes of Heteronormativity and Associated Stigma

In what follows, I examine two other issues unique to LGBT workers: widespread heteronormativity and the ability to mask stigma. In important ways, these factors may result in LGBT employees experiencing different types of discrimination than other minorities. Because the LGBT workforce is a unique population facing distinctive issues, conflating their experiences with other groups is problematic. Because cultural and social values strongly impact organizational values, I begin with the destructive nature of heteronormative environments for LGBT workers.

A Critique of Heteronormativity

Heteronormativity includes practices and institutions "that legitimize and privilege heterosexuality and heterosexual relationships as fundamental and 'natural' within society" (Cohen, 2005, p. 24). Deployed as a term to critique the normalizing of heterosexuality in society, Warner (1991) identified the pervasiveness of social policies and institutions reinforcing the idea that humans fall into two distinct and complementary categories: male and female. Warner also unmasked how the term "normal" is socially constructed around sexual and marital relations that occur between people of the opposite sex—relations in which each sex has certain "natural" roles. Privileging heterosexuality is highly problematic for those who do not fit within the strict binaries of masculinity and femininity. Questioning traditional notions of gender and sex that are defined by strident notions of male = masculine and female = feminine problematizes this normalization of (hetero)sexuality and challenges social notions that designate LGBT identities as "abnormal." Challenging heteronormativity ultimately provides a space for sections of a society, especially employing organizations, to create environments that embrace sexuality diversity.

Heteronormativity is ubiquitous and present in both explicit and implicit ways. For instance, failing to accept (as normal) relationships outside of the one-man-one-woman paradigm is explicit. Public debates often include this definition of marriage and link this definition to family values. As Cohen (2005) points out, though, heteronormativity is also present in implicit ways and is inseparable from other forms of oppression based on race, class, and sex. Evidence of implicit heteronormativity is the devaluation of mothers on welfare and the stigma assigned to sex workers who may be heterosexual but are not heteronormative; neither is considered "normal, moral, or worthy of state support" (Cohen, p. 26). Organizational environments are also effected by these heteronormative biases.

Heteronormativity in Organizations

Although the container metaphor for organizations is common (Fairhurst & Putnam, 2004), organizations typically mirror, at times in a transformed reflection, societal biases, beliefs, and behaviors. For example, overt evidence of heteronormativity in organizations is the fact that in 31 states, persons can still be fired for real (or perceived) variant sexuality. On the other hand, employees are not fired for being heterosexual—indeed, heterosexuality is an expectation and deviating from this expectation can have severe consequences. Likewise, although many organizations have implemented same-sex partner benefits, social systems, by and large, still privilege heterosexuality. For example, since the Federal Government does not recognize benefits for non-married partners as tax-exempt, associated costs are higher for LGBT employees (Reiter, 2007). That is, LGBT employees pay more for benefits packages than heterosexuals.

Disparity in costs is not the only consequence of inequitable benefit packages. For heterosexuals, participation in benefit systems is assumed upon gaining employment, whereas, access to benefits is not automatic for LGBT employees. The ramifications of not having access to company benefits, such as health insurance or retirement, are substantial. For example, in states that fail to acknowledge same-sex unions, state institutions such as universities and police departments are prohibited from disbursing retirement benefits to same-sex partners. In fact, many state retirement disbursement forms allow employees to donate retirement to virtually any entity (e.g., animal shelters, not for profit causes, etc.) but will not allow such disbursement to same-sex partners. Ultimately, in order to ensure partner compensation, many LGBT employees must have private retirement plans (to which the state will not contribute). Moreover, because benefit packages assume heterosexuality, LGBT employees must disclose sexuality in order to access benefits.

Privileging heterosexuality in benefit allocation is an important issue for LGBT employees, but the widespread, everyday, often unrecognized processes of heteronormativity also contribute to destructive organizational climates. Heteronormative processes are indicators of social meaning systems that denigrate variant sexuality. Indeed, implicit norms of heteronormativity are apparent in employees' everyday, taken-for-granted communication and behavior. These include displays of family photos, wedding rings, company invitations, and conversations (Deitch, Butz, & Brief, 2004; Herek, 1996). In interviewing "out" lesbian police officers, those who disclosed their sexual orientation, I found that even when organizational members attempted to be inclusive, the "other" status was often present (Lewis, 2006). For instance, when colleagues extended invitations to LGBT employees, they addressed the invitation to the LGBT employee and his or her "guest." Having a partner labeled as "guest" underrates the relational status of the employee and her or his partner. This failure is especially apparent when invitations to heterosexual workers are addressed to the employee and "family" or "spouse." Furthermore, even when LGBT employees do attend company-sponsored events, they often feel pressed to engage in behavior monitoring to avoid drawing attention to their sexual variance to avoid the associated stigma. Consequently, masking the nuances of variant sexuality keeps heterosexual colleagues in the dark, so to speak, regarding how to respectfully acknowledge and speak to LGBT differences.

Aside from social interactions at work, heterosexuality and the stigma associated with living outside it, is also apparent in various covert organizational processes. A unique paradox, or contradictory situation, emerges for employees who wish to make their work environments more inclusive. Often, LGBT employees want to make organizational life better for future generations and, thus, perform an activist role by reporting these destructive processes to management (Lewis, 2006). Similar to reporting workplace bullying or sexual harassment (Clair, 1993; Lutgen-Sandvik, 2006), doing so may increase reporting workers' difficulties, especially the likelihood of becoming targets of homophobic harassment. Likewise, destructive repercussions such as harassment and bullying may occur for heterosexual allies that support or actively voice the need to change heteronormative processes. For LGBT employees who mask their stigma through passing strategies, activism is not an option even though they may desire an accepting work culture. In what follows, I further examine the stigma generated by these situations.

Stigma and Variant Sexuality

Minorities often face discrimination that devalues their identity and negatively affects their ability to construct a rich and fulfilling sense of self. Goffman's (1963) germinal work is informative and suggests that a stigma is when specific characteristics of a person are used to question that person's humanity or to reduce that individual "in our minds from a whole and usual person to a tainted, discounted one" (p. 3). Like other minority positions such as race and gender, variant sexuality is stigmatizing because when one is suspected of deviating from the heterosexual standard, negative stereotypes and social devaluation taints both the person and the identity (Butler, 1990; Herbert, 1998; Walker, 2001). However, unlike other minority groups, LGBT status can sometimes be masked through passing strategies. Unlike stigma linked to visible signs of difference, what Goffman (1963, p. 4) calls the "discredited," variant sexuality constitutes certain workers as the "discreditable." That is, even though assumptions can be made about sexuality, sexual orientation is often "invisible" until disclosed.

Passing Inside the Organization: Strategies to Avoid Stigma

LGBT workers, like any other employee group, want to avoid being stigmatized. As such, they use a number of communicative strategies to create a sense of safety, the most common of which is passing. Passing is concealing *normal* information about oneself to "preserve, sustain, and encourage others' predisposed assumptions about one's identity" (Spradlin, 1998, p. 598). In this context, "normal" information exchanged by organizational members includes the ability to speak publicly about one's primary relationships, friends and activities, and events occurring outside of the organizational setting. For instance, normal information might include talking about having seen a current movie, attended a recent performance, or tried a new local restaurant. Such sharing means engaging in ordinary conversations and constitutes the ability to talk about non-work aspects of identity within the context of work.

LGBT employees pass as heterosexual by using specific tactics Spradlin (1998) labels distancing, dissociating, dodging, distracting, denying, and deceiving. These tactics mark her attempts to pass but are likely common strategies for many LGBTs attempting to pass. The following briefly outlines each of these. Distancing entails "removing oneself from informal conversational contexts so that the exchange of personal information is discouraged" (p. 599). It may include choosing not to participate in social contexts, such as departmental lunches and network opportunities, where personal information exchange often occurs.

Dissociating is when employees attempt "to separate oneself from gay or lesbian identification through behaviors that simultaneously uphold heterosexual associations and reject gay or lesbian association" (p. 600). These may include avoiding association with other gay or lesbian people, steering clear of local LGBT establishments, and only clandestinely supporting legislation such as ENDA. Like dissociating, dodging distances oneself from an LGBT identity and occurs when an employee redirects a conversation in an effort to hide personal information. Dodging often includes responding to questions with "yes" and "no" answers and then diverting attention away from oneself (Spradlin, 1998). When dodging LGBTs must be hypervigilant about the intricacies of conversations and quick-witted when responding to questions that may reveal too much, thus causing their sexuality to be suspect. For instance, an LGBT employee dodging might respond to the seemingly innocuous question, "Did you see *Hairspray* this weekend?" with "Yes, what did your family do this weekend?" If, on the other hand, the event referenced has an association with the LGBT community, the employee may feel obligated to lie—effectively dodging *and* dissociating.

Distracting is "the use of multiple or highlighted identity messages to produce confusion about one's gay identity" (Spradlin, 1998, p. 601). This can include participating in normal conversations but identifying only with those heterosexually-associated topics such as attending children's functions or revealing past heterosexual relationships (even those in the very distant past). As with the other strategies, distracting can be extremely stressful and requires LGBT employees to be constantly "on guard" due to the likelihood that these identifications will arise in future conversations.

Finally, denial and deceiving may result in questions of personal integrity (Lewis, 2006). Denial is consciously "withholding confirmation of a gay identity by refusing to grant the truth about one's primary relationship status" (Spradlin, 1998, p. 602) and can be particularly disturbing. A participant in my research acknowledged that using gender-neutral pronouns to mask her partner's sex negatively affected her own life: "It's like every time I make up something, or say *they*, or don't really talk about my partner, who she is to me, or whatever, every time I do that, I die" (Lewis, 2006, pp. 257–258). Deceiving is "intentionally constructing dishonest messages to indicate a heterosexual rather than a gay identity" (Spradlin, p. 603). The above example suggests the destructive potential of using deceit to pass as heterosexual, the metaphorical language of death underscores this. Such strategies are often ongoing and require employees to be particularly cautious about what they say, where they go, and with whom they are seen—even outside the workplace.

Vigilance Outside the Workplace

Passing strategies demonstrate the awkward and labor-intensive character of passing, the stress that it causes, and the destructive consequences to self-identity and personal relationships. Passing is not limited to workplace interactions though: It affects the ability for same-sex couples to attend work-sponsored events together, such as picnics and holiday parties, and also means continual monitoring of life outside of work. Passing is complicated further when LGBT employees, fearing the discovery of their sexuality, alter their personal lives for fear that a coworker may make assumptions if the LGBT couple is seen in public.

Encountering a coworker outside of the workplace is likely, and if coworkers see LGBT colleagues many times with his or her partner, questions of sexuality could arise. Consequently, those passing at work must also pass when not at work. As such, LGBT employees may feel they not only have to dissociate from LGBT life in workplace conversations, but, out of a fear of being "spotted," they must also dissociate from LGBT social life in general. This might be done by changing public spaces (such as attending a movie at a theatre that is a safe distance from work) or actually decreasing time spent in public with their partners. Fear of being spotted may also mean boycotting local gay establishments, gay events, the

LGBT section of local bookstores, fundraisers or support networks, and performances by LGBT social icons. Self-monitoring tactics increase as concerns increase regarding the possibility of encountering a colleague in everyday relational activities such as grocery shopping, going to the mall, or perhaps exercising at their local gym.

The Destructive Consequences of Heteronormativity and Masking Stigma

The underlying meanings inherent to stigmatizing any sexuality other than heterosexual bleed into organizations and the lives of their members. In what follows, I explore the destructive consequences for individuals, paying particular attention to passing as heterosexual. Beyond passing, however, numerous organizational systems and processes have destructive potential that are both overt and covert. These include benefit systems (or lack thereof), methods of employee orientation, discrimination and harassment, and impeded social networking.

Destructive Consequences Linked to Masking Stigma

It might be tempting to think that the ability to mask stigma would be empowering or desirable because it allows for the stigmatized identity to be backstage during interactions with coworkers. Certainly, passing has advantages because it could reduce the risk of discrimination, at least for those who have the ability to pass. However, not all LGBT persons can physically pass as heterosexual, and even for those who can, passing often compromises their personal life and relationships.

Spradlin (1998) notes that choosing to pass at work created specific tensions for her by preventing "authentic, healthy relationship development within the workplace, [eroding] self-esteem and integrity, [causing] excessive tension within [her] own primary relationship, and [... draining] professional and personal energy" (p. 603). In essence, passing has the potential to generate a destructive paradox. It can buffer LGBT workers from discrimination while hindering the development of healthy fulfilling workplace relationships and increasing stress in personal relationships. What is more, those who pass can suffer severe consequences if their secret is discovered, and they may also compromise levels of coworker trust (Lewis, 2006). Thus, passing may feel mandatory while coming out seems out of reach. The constant stress of discovery (and potential job loss) can simply be overwhelming. Indeed, the issues of coming out and the consequences of choosing to disclose or choosing to pass are the few well-research areas regarding this worker group (e.g., Burke, 1994; Day & Schoenrade, 1997; Spradlin, 1998).

Destructive Consequences in Heteronormative Organizations

Widespread processes of heteronormativity make disclosing variant sexuality particularly difficult. Beyond the destructiveness of sexual harassment and stress associated with potential job loss, LGBT employees must continually navigate spaces that allow for personal happiness without hindering professional development. Processes of heteronormativity complicate these spaces because they organize communication in ways that are detrimental to organizational goals by hindering the development of diverse workforces and reducing employee productivity and satisfaction. In fact, a brief visit to the Human Right's Campaign website reveals the destructive nature of homophobia and heteronormativity illustrated in the appalling stories of LGBT employee discrimination. Working environments organized around heteronormativity result in a number of destructive consequences for LGBT workers in the areas of partner benefit systems, employee orientation/training, harassment/discrimination, and social networks.

Benefit Systems

The destructive potential of working in organizations without domestic partner benefits (DPBs) is considerable. Without DPBs, LGBT employees are often unable to secure health insurance or retirement benefits for their partners and non-adopted children. When organizations do offer DPBs, LGBT employees are typically required to disclose their sexuality, prove cohabitation, and document relational tenure to qualify for such benefits. Although offering these benefits might be an attempt to create inclusive environments, the processes established by many organizations may actually harm the very individuals such benefits aim to help.

Orientation and Training

Heteronormativity also affects LGBT employees during organizational training seminars, particularly if organizations determine that spending training time or providing printed materials covering DPBs is inefficient because of the small number of employees who request such benefits. As such, human resource managers often simply announce that DPBs are available and encourage interested employees to contact Human Resources (Reiter, 2007). This lack of inclusion in the orientation process implies that variant sexuality is, at best, relegated to behind-closed-doors interactions, and at worst, offensive. In fact, LGBT employees are likely to assess the organizational culture's acceptance level by employment orientation content. Omitting DPBs information communicates an apathetic stance toward diversity and may discourage LGBT employees from sharing information.

Discrimination and Harassment

More overtly destructive consequences of being different in heteronormative work environments include being the object of discrimination or harassment. LGBT employees who disclose face the very real threat of being discriminated against at work, both formally and informally (Deitch et al., 2004). Formal discrimination includes refusing employment, restricting job duties, withholding promotion, denying rewards, or firing an individual due to sexual orientation. Proving sexual orientation discrimination, however, is expensive, stressful, time-consuming, and rarely successful (Lewis, 2006). As such, LGBT employees facing formal discrimination are more apt to quit than to fight or endure discrimination.

Informal discrimination includes verbal hostility, derogatory jokes and comments, sexual harassment, gossip, anonymous hate mail, violence, and so forth (Deitch et al., 2004). Additionally, some LGBT workers who choose and have the ability to pass may find themselves as unwilling participants in processes of harassment or discrimination. That is, the consequences of having their secret revealed may be so great that they can feel as if they also *must* participate in discriminatory processes to maintain secrecy. Thus, passing can be emotionally and personally destructive, but revealing one's sexuality can be equally destructive and result in discrimination, harassment, ridicule, ostracism, and even job loss (Day & Schoenrade, 1997).

Social Networks

Relationships with coworkers are especially important, particularly since people spend increasing amounts of time at work (see Sias, Chapter 7 this volume). If LGBT employees can and do choose to pass, they may avoid overt discrimination but also reduce their opportunities to build meaningful workplace relationships. LGBT employees most likely find it difficult to develop trust-based relationships if, in every interaction, they are preoccupied with deciphering peers' attitudes and monitoring what they say in order to avoid detection (Deitch et al., 2004). Given that social connections at work are organized around task, identity, and relationship goals, hiding one's sexuality seriously impedes the latter two of these. Furthermore, by avoiding social organizing at work, LGBT employees may lose networking communities vital to career advancement.

Organizational Consequences

Heteronormative norms also hinder organizational outcomes. Although the destructive consequences for organizations can be widespread, I explore three such consequences: reduced productivity, lost talent, and increased legal liability.

Reduced Productivity

Passing as heterosexual takes an enormous amount of energy and vigilance. Masking stigma affects the well-being of LGBT employees and increases negative job attitudes. Employees working to pass as heterosexual experience role ambiguity and conflict (Day & Schoenrade, 1997), and hiding variant sexuality reduces overall life satisfaction (Waldo, 1999). When LGBT employees spend much of their time hiding their sexuality, the time and energy they spend at work, as well as their commitment to the organization are negatively impacted. Furthermore, the continual stress of passing and fearing exposure to harassment contributes to job burnout and employee turnover (Deitch et al., 2004; Herek, 1996).

Lost Talent

Heteronormative work environments or the perception thereof reduce the pool of talented candidates who seek employment with organizations. My research with lesbian police officers suggests that many of these women applied to departments with reputations of inclusiveness, primarily because of the energy and stress involved in passing (Lewis, 2006). Furthermore, heteronormativity does not just affect those with variant sexuality. Other minorities may be hesitant about joining a homophobic organization because homophobia could indicate more endemic problems such as racism or strident masculinity—issues detrimental to their own minority status.

Increased Risk of Legal Liability

Finally, unbending heteronormativity increases the company's exposure to lawsuits. Even when organizations have sexual orientation and gender identity anti-harassment policies, they may not be immune to claims of discrimination from individuals seeking compensation. When organizations pay only "lip service" to anti-harassment policies but do not actively work to combat homophobia, the risk increases for LGBT employees to seek legal recourse. For organizations without such policies, LGBT employees may seek legal council to implement these policies (e.g., gain partner benefits). In either case, organizations lose valuable resources when they fail to create inclusive working environments.

Constructive Ways of Organizing Regarding LGBT Employees

In 2004 Deitch et al. noted that organizational research on LGBT workplace discrimination was sparse and, unfortunately, that is still the case.

Advocating sensitivity training might be a viable way of constructively organizing, but mandatory training on variant sexuality can just as readily have the unintended consequence of increased homophobia. Despite these issues, provision of DPBs and the subtle features of organizational climate can provide avenues for more constructive ways to organize.

Policies and Politics

Although findings are mixed and likely associated with the *application* of LGBT-friendly policies, some research suggests that these policies reduce sexual orientation discrimination (e.g., Button, 2001). Organizations can neutralize rigid heteronormativity by creating and implementing clear policies about discrimination, hostile work environments, and preferred company culture. As with workplace bullying (see Lutgen-Sandvik, Namie, & Namie, Chapter 2 this volume), policies without action will fail to foster inclusive environments. However, having a clearly written company policy on sexual orientation discrimination (either as a separate item or as part of broader nondiscrimination policies) reaffirms the organization's stance that discrimination is unacceptable. To be effective, policies must be distributed to all managers and employees, incorporated into employee orientation and management training programs, and reviewed and reintroduced periodically to ensure that the organizations commitment to an inclusive work environment is regularly affirmed.

LGBT-Supportive Climates

A recent study found that working for an organization perceived to be more gay-supportive was related to higher job satisfaction and lower job anxiety (Griffith & Hebl, 2002). This same study found a positive relationship between disclosing at work and job satisfaction. My research also suggests that disclosing sexuality can be positive. For instance, participating in conversations that include LGBT experiences can teach others how to respectfully communicate about variant sexuality. Through open communication with heterosexual coworkers, "out" lesbian police officers actually realized that their experiences were often excluded unintentionally because heterosexuals did not know how to talk about variant sexuality (i.e., proper language and fear of offending the LGBT employee) or thinking beyond heterosexual experience just did not occur to them (Lewis, 2006). Likewise, many of the lesbian officers indicated that they felt *more* accepted after disclosing their variant sexuality than they believed they would have had they remained silent (Lewis).

Benefits Packages and Training

Offering domestic partner benefits communicates organizations' acceptance and support for workers with variant sexuality. Organizations that offer DPBs are more likely to attract both LGBT workers *and* LGBT customers. Furthermore, offering DPBs and making them a visible component of benefits training seminars sends the message that the organization values diverse employees. When messages conveying acceptance are part of organizational discourse, they help to foster welcoming work environments. By offering DPBs organizations may also be, albeit indirectly, reducing homophobia and rigid heteronormativity.

Social Networks of Support

Creating social support networks for LGBT workers can increase job satisfaction and organizational commitment and decrease stress. These networks could foster inclusive environments and send messages of acceptance (rather than simply tolerance). There are many cost-effective ways companies could create these. For example, distributing handouts with contact information for community groups on parenting, family resources, and LGBT networks would be useful. Including such handouts in company displays would also increase visibility and communicate the organization's desire to embrace diversity.

Increasing Awareness

In order to fight the destructive side of heteronormativity, organizational managers would be wise to familiarize themselves with LGBT issues. For instance, sexual harassment toward LGBTs is often deployed differently and presents concerns distinct from (hetero)sexual harassment. Issues unique to LGBT sexual harassment include difficulty in reporting because targets must disclose their sexuality and fear being discounted because of their variant sexuality (Lewis, 2006). These issues, among others, make LGBT sexual harassment different from other forms of harassment. If organizational members are aware of these issues, they will be more successful in addressing and preventing them.

Recruiting and Marketing

Organizations can augment public visibility while also increasing their potential pool of talented applicants by actively recruiting workers at LGBT functions (e.g., pride festivals). Although organizational visibility alone will not solidify perceptions of sexual orientation acceptance, it can advance organizational goals of diversity. Additionally, the LGBT community may look favorably at creative marketing representing LGBT people and thus increase their consumer patronage of certain brand or organizational names. Top names such as Volvo™ and IKEA™ are noteworthy examples.

Organizational Functions

Creating inclusive environments also entails acknowledging the families of LGBT employees and using language that includes the employee and their partner or family. For instance, rather than addressing an invitation with "... and Guest" companies might consider using "... and family" or simply addressing the invitation to both individuals. Simple practices such as these underscore the organization's acceptance of difference and recognition of important people in LGBT workers' lives. This is important for two reasons; first, it works to increase feelings of safety and security in LGBT employees and second, it sends a clear message that discrimination rooted in variant sexuality will not be tolerated. Both of these are important to job productivity and workforce retention.

Indeed, organizations should take notice of the effects and repercussions their actions can have on LGBT employees. For instance, my campus recently purchased a block of comedy club tickets and encouraged faculty to promote these tickets to students. Unfortunately, the comedy routine was punctuated with homophobic and racist humor. Although an unexpected and unintended consequence, the university might have addressed the situation afterward by acknowledging the content and issuing a disclaimer of sorts. These incidences, if repeated and subsequently ignored by the organization, could increase discomfort for minorities and create organizational distrust.

Future Research

Although there is very little research on discrimination or bullying of LGBT workers, there is a considerable body of scholarship about disclosing variant sexuality in the workplace. The metaphor of *coming out* or *coming out of the closet* might be problematic, however, since it implies that this is an event rather than a process. Research following the lead of Kaufman and Johnson (2004) should account for *processes* of coming out and the unfolding nature of this life change—particularly in organizational, work-related contexts. My own research (Lewis, 2006) describes the processual nature of coming out in heteronormative organizations and notes the paradoxes of presumed heterosexuality. Future research on disclosure could explore the relationship between disclosure and self-esteem, types of disclosure, and the relationship between disclosure and key organizational issues (e.g., teambuilding, credibility, stress, burnout). This research should explicitly study how this process is unique in the workplace, since communication in organizations is unique from other settings (see Waldron, Chapter 1, this volume).

Research could also reposition variant sexuality as a product of larger systems of meaning, such as gender and sex. Doing so highlights the unique character of LGBT employees and recognizes inter-group differences. For instance, repositioning lesbianism as a byproduct of a constraining gender system places critical focus on the gender system rather than the lesbian body (Lewis, 2006). As such, lesbian bodies would represent fractures in the dominant gender structure and identify points for ideological reframing. Ultimately, this allows LGBT identities to be seen as organizational assets rather than organizational costs. In other words, how might we position LGBT identities in research to highlight the positive and constructive qualities they bring to organizations?

A final area for future exploration is the discursive and non-discursive interactions among LGBT employees who work together. My research underscores some dilemmas that might emerge between LGBT superiors and LGBT subordinates (Lewis, 2006). For instance, supervisors in my study assumed that their promotion sent an organizational message of LGBT acceptance and "open door policy" for other LGBTs. Subordinates, on the other hand, did not encode these promotions in the same way. Despite supervisors sharing their sexual orientation, subordinates continued to view supervisors as part of management and unapproachable. The managers, however, believed that sharing LGBT status would bridge occupational rank. Given this, investigations that explore LGBT workforces as well as different cultures within the workforce are warranted.

Conclusion

LGBT persons comprise a considerable portion of the U.S. workforce. This chapter identifies the destructive nature of heteronormative work environments and the consequences to these workers. LGBT employees may try to mask stigma through strategies of passing, but that too has significant destructive consequences for both the individual and organization. With the growing LGBT population, companies need to address processes of heteronormativity and discrimination against persons who do not fit into traditional notions of gender or who do not perform gender in traditional manners. Additionally, LGBT workers in supportive organizational climates might consider "teaching" others how to talk about the issues of variant sexuality in the workplace.

References

Bedgett, M. V. L., Lau, H., Sears, B., & Ho, D. (2007). *Bias in the workplace: Consistent evidence of sexual orientation and gender identity discrimination.* Los Angels, CA: The Williams Institute, VCLA School of Law.

Burke, M. E. (1994). Homosexuality as deviance: The case of the gay police officer. *British Journal of Criminology, 34*(2), 192–203.

Burrell, G., & Hearn, J. (1989). The sexuality of organization. In J. Hearn & D. L. Sheppard (Eds.), *The sexuality of organization* (pp. 1–28). London: Sage.

Butler, J. (1990). *Gender trouble: Feminism and the subversion of identity*. London and NY: Routledge.

Button, S. B. (2001). Organizational efforts to affirm sexual diversity: a cross-level examination. *Journal of Applied Psychology, 86*(1), 17–28.

Campaign, H. R. s. (2007). When homophobes bear false witness: The ENDA Edition. Retrieved September 26, 2007, from http://www.hrc.org/news/7611.htm.

Clair, R. P. (1993). The use of framing devices to sequester organizational narratives: Hegemony and harassment. *Communication Monographs, 60*(1), 113–136.

Cohen, C. J. (2005). Punks, bulldaggers, and welfare queen: The radical potential of queer politics? In E. P. Johnson & M. G. Henderson (Eds.), *Black queer studies* (pp. 21–51). Duke: Duke UP.

Commercial Closet Association. (2007). Best practices: Building GLBT awareness and inclusion in mass/business-to-business advertising. *HRC*. Retrieved September 6, 2007, from http://www.hrc.org/documents/Advertising-Best-Practices-Guidelines.pdf.

Day, N. E., & Schoenrade, P. (1997). Staying in the closet versus coming out: Relationships between communication about sexual orientation and work attitudes. *Personnel Psychology, 50*(2), 147–163.

Deitch, E. A., Butz, R. M., & Brief, A. P. (2004). Out of the closet and out of a job? The nature, import, and causes of sexual orientation discrimination in the workplace. In R. W. Griffin & A. M. O'Leary-Kelly (Eds.), *The dark side of organizational behavior* (pp. 187–234). San Francisco: Jossey-Bass.

Fairhurst, G. T., & Putnam, L. I. (2004). Organizations as discursive constructions. *Communication Theory, 14*(1), 5–26.

Goffman, E. (1963). *Stigma: Notes on the management of spoiled identity*. Englewood Cliffs, NJ: Prentice-Hall.

Griffith, K. H., & Hebl, M. R. (2002). The disclosure dilemma for gay men and lesbians: "Coming out" at work. *Journal of Applied Psychology, 87*(6), 1191–1199.

Gunther, M. (2006, December 2006). Queer Inc.: How corporate America fell in love with gays and lesbians. It's a movement. *Fortune, 154*(November), 94.

Hearn, J. (1987). *Sex at work*. Brighton: Wheatsheaf.

Herbert, M. S. (1998). *Camouflage isn't only for combat: Gender, sexuality, and women in the military*. NY: New York University Press.

Herek, G. M. (1996). Why tell if you're not asked? Self-disclosure, intergroup contact, and heterosexuals' attitudes toward lesbians and gay men. In G. M. Herek, J. B. Jobe, & R. M. Carney (Eds.), *Out in force: Sexual orientation and the military* (pp. 197–225). Chicago: University of Chicago.

Human Rights Campaign Foundation. (2007). The state of the workplace for gay, lesbian, bisexual and transgender Americans. *Human Rights Campaign; Washington, DC*. Retrieved January 20, 2007, from www.hrc.org/workplace.

Kaufman, J. M., & Johnson, C. (2004). Stigmatized individuals and the process of identity. *The Sociological Quarterly, 45*(4), 807–833.

Lewis, A. P. (2006). *Communicating lesbian identity: A critical analysis of popular culture representations and police officer narratives*. Unpublished manuscript, Tempe, AZ.

Lutgen-Sandvik, P. (2006). Take this job and ... : Quitting and other forms of resistance to workplace bullying. *Communication Monographs, 73*(4), 406–433.

Mills, K. I. (2000). GLBT employees make gains in workplaces nationwide. *Diversity Factor, 9*(1), 8–11.

Reiter, N. (2007). Work life balance: What DO you mean? The ethical ideology underpinning appropriate application. *Journal of Applied Behavioral Science, 43*(2), 273–294.

Solmonese, J. (2007). Testimony of HRC President Joe Solmonese before a house committee on the Employment Non-Discrimination Act. Retrieved August 5, 2007, from http://www.hrc.org/issues/workplace/7376.htm.

Spradlin, A. L. (1998). The price of "passing": A lesbian perspective on authenticity in organizations. *Management Communication Quarterly, 11*(4), 598–606.

Thomas, J. (2007). When coworkers decided I was gay. Retrieved September 27, 2007, http://www.hrc.org/issues/workplace/3859.htm.

Waldo, C. R. (1999). Working in a majority context: A structural model of heterosexism as minority stress in the workplace. *Journal of Counseling Psychology, 46*(2), 218–232.

Walker, L. (2001). *Looking like what you are: Sexual style, race, and lesbian identity.* New York: New York University Press.

Warner, M. (1991). Introduction: Fear of a queer planet. *Social Text, 9*(1), 3–17.

Chapter 10

Sexual Harassment as Destructive Organizational Process

Debbie S. Dougherty

Scholars have long argued that the process of organizing is a gendered process. Organizing is a means of "doing" gender (Mumby, 1998); however, organizing is also a means of resisting, rewriting, and reworking gender in society. Sexual harassment provides one illustration of the gendering of the workplace. Notably, men can be victims of sexual harassment (Waldo, Berdahl, & Fitzgerald, 1998), but most victims are women. Regardless of the gender of the victim, all sexual harassment sexualizes and feminizes (Berdahl, Magley, & Waldo, 1996). Although the actual act of sexual harassment is a gendered process, it is through public discourse about the meaning of sexual harassment that gender is most insidiously constructed (and reconstructed) as a destructive organizational communication process (Dougherty, 1999). That is, not only the harasser and target but all members of the organization constitute its meaning.

A discursive approach to understanding sexual harassment provides a particularly rich lens through which to view gendered processes because it "places communication at the core of sexual harassment" (Dougherty, 1999, p. 437). Consequently, a discursive framework pays particular attention to communication as a complex, socially constructed enactment of reality (Bingham, 1994). A discursive perspective discourages the understanding of sexual harassment as simply an interpersonal problem between two people. Instead, sexual harassment must be viewed as a social phenomenon that structures gender relations through communication. In this way we come to know who men and women should be, how they should behave, and how we define their "proper" roles in society (Grauerholz, 1994).

The goals of this chapter are to explore sexual harassment as a destructive process and open up the processes by which sexual harassment genders the workplace. To accomplish this I first define sexual harassment and provide a broader understanding of sexual harassment as a discursive process. Second, I illustrate the discursive processes of sexual harassment, specifically the ways in which sexual-harassment-prone organizational cultures develop, the ways organizational members use policies to create discursive openings, the perception that sexual harassment creates a dangerous environment for men, and the parallel perception that victims of sexual harassment are weak and problematic. Finally, I examine the consequences of sexual harassment and suggest some communication-centered ways in which sexual harassment can be better managed in the workplace.

Sexual Harassment Defined

According to the U.S. Equal Employment Opportunity Commission (EEOC, 2005), "unwelcome sexual advances, requests for sexual favors, and other verbal or physical conduct of a sexual nature constitute sexual harassment when this conduct explicitly or implicitly affects an individual's employment, unreasonably interferes with an individual's work performance, or creates an intimidating, hostile, or offensive work environment" (2005, Par. 2). Essentially, this definition represents two types of sexual harassment, quid pro quo and hostile environment. Quid pro quo sexual harassment literally translates as "something for something." This is the most recognized form of sexual harassment and occurs when a person in a hierarchically superior position makes employment or promotion contingent in exchange for sexual favors. Hostile environment occurs when the unwanted sexual attention is so prevalent or so severe that the workplace becomes destructive or damaging to the target of the unwanted behavior. The court system is increasingly recognizing a third type of sexual harassment called third-person sexual harassment. This occurs when the victim is not the person harassed but is negatively affected by the harassment. For example, when a person receives a promotion as a result of providing sexual favors to the boss, a qualified individual who was not promoted could claim third-person sexual harassment.

Interesting from a communication perspective, despite the clarity of this definition, men and women tend to define sexual harassment differently. For example, men and women tend to define different behaviors as sexual harassment, with women consistently viewing more behaviors as sexual harassment than do men (Garlick, 1994; Hemphill & Pfeiffer, 1986; Thacker & Gohmann, 1993; Williams, Brown, Lees-Haley, & Price, 1995). Similarly, women define sexual and physical behaviors as more offensive than men (Hemphill & Pfeiffer, 1986). These differences may be because sexual harassment functions differently for many men and women in the workplace. In one organization I found that men used sexual behavior to decrease stress, create camaraderie, and show care (Dougherty, 2001a). Most of the women did not view these sexual behaviors as functioning in any positive way and were consequently more likely to label the behaviors as sexual harassment. The marked differences between men and women's interpretations of sexual harassment have prompted communication scholars to shift away from researching sexual harassment as a legal issue to conceptualizing it as a discursive phenomenon. In other words, we now think about communication as central to understanding and managing sexual harassment.

Sexual Harassment as Discourse

So what does it mean when scholars claim that sexual harassment is a discursive process? Centrally, "a discursive focus places communication at the core of sexual harassment" (Dougherty, 1999, p. 437). Instead of viewing communication in simple terms such as reception or interpretation of messages, "a discursive framework understands communication as creating and shaping social reality rather than just being influenced by it" (Bingham, 1994, p. 9). Language as a constitutive force lies at the center of discourse (Wood, 1994). Words do not simply name what already exists; they shape the way we understand and talk about any given issue. Language shapes our reality. This constitutive function of discourse about sexual harassment can be seen in the language surrounding sexual harassment. Probably the cleanest example of sexual harassment as discourse lies in the very label "sexual harassment."

According to Julia Wood (1992), at one point in the fairly recent past there was no label or naming device available to describe or make sense of unwanted sexual attention in the workplace. Consequently, targets of these behaviors were unable to adequately describe the horror and humiliation of their experiences. In fact, prior to language to describe the experience, many people in organizations viewed predatory sexual behavior as normal and acceptable. Women who complained were viewed negatively. However, once the label "sexual harassment" was coined, women's concerns were legitimized. Moreover, the power of labeling this phenomenon marked predatory sexual behavior in the workplace as abnormal and unacceptable (Wood, 1994). Simply by creating the discourse of sexual harassment, women were able to problematize predatory sexual behavior at work.

The single most significant consequence in the shift toward a discursive understanding of sexual harassment is the increased complexity and fluidity involved in the process. No longer is sexual harassment simply about the harasser-target dyad. No longer is communication simply how organizational members communicate or respond to the harassment. Instead, scholars now tend to see sexual harassment as a socially complex phenomenon. The following section illustrates some of the complexity of sexual harassment as a discursive process.

Discursive Processes of Sexual Harassment

Over the past number of years, I have conducted numerous studies on sexual harassment in the workplace—in a large health care organization, a large governmental organization, and a university. Colleagues and I have also conducted studies on the sexual harassment of nurses by patients and with people from a range of occupations to understand the differences between flirting and sexual harassment. I draw from these various data sets to illustrate the processes discussed below. The following provides a sampling of ways that organizational members discursively construct the meaning of sexual harassment.

Sexual Harassment and Organizational Culture

The performance of gender is essentially a cultural phenomenon. Cultural rules and norms tell us who men and women ought to be and what is valued about them (Wood, 1994). This is also true in the workplace where organizational culture reveals underlying values and assumptions about gendered relations (Nadesan & Trethewey, 2000). Sexual harassment constitutes one such behavior, and, therefore, is best viewed as inextricably intertwined with organizational cultural (Dougherty & Smythe, 2004; Keyton, Ferguson, & Rhodes, 2001). Viewing sexual harassment from a cultural perspective means that the ways all members of an organization discursively construct sexual harassment is meaningful. Depending on the nature of the discourse, some organizational cultures come to support sexual harassment while others reject the behavior (Dougherty & Smythe, 2004).

So what are some of the discursive features of a sexual-harassment-prone organizational culture? The following illustrates a culture in which sexual harassment flourishes:

Anna: It was a wonderful place to work. They had just, they did so much for their employees. You know, they had ice cream every Wednesday in the summer; they had bagels and donuts every Tuesday and Thursdays. You know, they had huge parties all the time and, you know, just showered you with things.

Interviewer: Wow.

Anna: And um, just, almost made it a situation where it was too good to ever leave.

Interviewer: Oh wow.

Anna: Paid real well. You know, real flexible with hours. Good vacation.

Interviewer: Unhuh unhuh. Well tell me the flirting story.

Anna: Yeah they, it was just, it got to the point where all the upper management, they were all male.

Interviewer: Mmhm.

Anna: Maybe, I think at the time there was, I don't know 50, 60 managers. Maybe three were female. So it was very very male dominated.

Interviewer: Ok.

* * *

Anna: Um well, just 'cause the, the actions were more sexual harassment. But the flirting was just their everyday [behavior]. That's how they talked to you. That's how they did it.

Interviewer: So they just flirted constantly?

Anna: Constantly. It was constant. And if you ever gave them any attitude back—it was a sales organization. So it was competitive. It was commission based. And so every time, you know, you, you know if anyone talked back, or if anyone didn't like it, they were punished for it, and they didn't give them the good accounts, and they didn't do the ... And those girls, I mean everyone left.

Interviewer: Wow.

Anna: They have a huge turnover rate.

Although the interviewer and Anna were discussing flirting and not sexual harassment, the coercive nature of the flirting makes it clear that the behavior rises to the level of sexual harassment. The "girls" were punished if they protested the unwanted attention. Many of them left this organization that, ironically, made it "too good to ever leave." One key indicator that there was a culture of sexual harassment is the way the organizational environment was infused with unwanted sexual attention. It was "constant" and "everyday." Anna later revealed that there were at least 60 women from a single unit who were ultimately identified as targets of sexual harassment. The imbalance of formal power between the male and female workers likely exacerbated the cultural inclination toward unwanted sexual attention.

A second aspect of this conversation with Anna that reveals the cultural nature of sexual harassment is a bit more subtle. Because sexual harassment is so constant, it becomes normalized. Paradoxically, any behavior that is "normal" cannot possibly be sexual harassment. Anna's comments illustrate this. By acknowledging that the behavior could be viewed as sexual harassment but choosing to call it "flirting" because it happened everyday, Anna renamed this rather egregious behavior into a lesser offense. Indeed, by failing to properly label sexual harassment, targets inadvertently perpetuate the likelihood that it will continue to occur.

Although no single factor has been identified that characterizes a sexual-harassment-prone organization, one common thread seems to be the presence of a strong authoritarian management structure. Strong authoritarian management structures attempt to impose a single unified meaning system on workers, often with disastrous impacts on the workplace culture (Zak, 1994). Research suggests a significant relationship between sexual harassment and rigid authoritarian structures in military organizations (Firestone & Harris, 1999), healthcare organizations (Dougherty, 2001a), and blue collar work environments (Zak). Zak makes the most direct link between such management structures and harassment-prone cultures.

The primary disadvantage of an authoritarian style of management is the inflexibility in adapting to organizational change. Because authoritarian managers tend to have a singular, rigid, vision of the organization, they rarely provide a climate in which a new discourse community can develop. For example, AVTA, a vehicle maintenance unit of a larger organization, had no discursive structure for adapting to demographic diversification. As a result the "bully boys," those who saw themselves as the guardians of the old culture, began a systematic series of assaults on newcomers ranging from racial to sexual harassment (Zak, 1994). Although not all sexual-harassment-prone organizations have rigid authoritarian structures, inflexible authoritarianism can provide the conditions that nurture sexual harassment.

Predatory sexual behavior in sexual-harassment-prone organizations tends to be particularly intense, profuse, and strange. For example, the bully boys in Zak's (1994) study would simulate sexual intercourse with other men bending over an engine for repairs. One man claimed "I guess after you're humped 40 times, you're accepted as a mechanic" (p. 291). In another study a maintenance worker declared that he was "captain of the butt check team" and that a female worker could not leave the room until he "checked her butt" (Dougherty & Atkinson, 2006). In a yet unpublished study, the woman from the interview above told me that her African-American boss grabbed her butt and asked, "Have you ever made chocolate love?" It is important to understand that sexual harassment is not mundane, ordinary, or typical in any way. The behaviors are contextually inappropriate and even weird, lying far outside the scope of the relationship being breeched. This is particularly true in organizations that nurture this type of behavior, possibly because aggressive acts of sexual harassment have become normalized.

It is clear that organizational cultures can promote sexual harassment. In these contexts, sexual harassment is particularly peculiar and exaggerated. When told to an outsider, the behaviors seem unreal or even surreal. The fact that these predatory sexual behaviors become normalized and commonplace in these cultures should be of great concern to organizational leadership.

"Policies Don't Say What They Mean": The Discursive Reconstruction of Policy

A second process involves the informal discursive reconstruction of formal sexual harassment policies. Despite the widespread use of sexual harassment policies as a tool to control this destructive behavior, there is surprisingly little communication research directly confronting the effectiveness and discursive nature of these policies. Robin Clair's (1998) research examining the discursive implications of the sexual harassment policies in the Big 10 provides a noted exception. She argues that instead of stopping sexual harassment, these policies tend to reinforce gender relations by privatizing it—removing it from the public realm and reinforcing women's place in the "private" realm (e.g. homemakers). Furthermore, because privatizing sexual harassment precludes public identification of perpetrators, they are free to continue the behavior.

The intent of sexual harassment policies is to create organizational closure—that is, policies serve as the final word determining what counts as sexual harassment, what steps a target of sexual harassment should take, and what the organization's roles and responsibilities are if sexual harassment occurs. Despite the intent to create closure, my research suggests that organizational members tend to reinterpret policies to fit the members' perceptions of what sexual harassment ought to be. Consequently, they "reopen" the closed discourse. In the following excerpt, a mixed-gender group first read their organization's policy and then reinterpreted it:

Interviewer:	What is the intent of this policy?
Joy:	Intent to stop unwanted sexual harassment.
Mark:	[Interrupts] I didn't know there was a difference between desired sexual harassment and ...
Joy:	[Interrupts] There are some really strange people out there ...
Mark:	[Interrupts] Well, I understand that ...
Joy:	It's basically a tool or almost a weapon to stop it, if someone is doing something that you don't like or you see someone doing something that you don't like.
Mark:	I always thought it was more of a protection policy for folks who thought they were indeed being harassed if you will.
Interviewer:	So instead of stopping it, it protects them?
Mark:	Yeah, that's almost stated in your next question here. Who would it protect and as brought up yesterday you know everybody in the room is different and perceives things differently has a different background that they come from, and so they perceive other people's actions differently. And so what may be okay for me may not be okay for you, or

	whatever, and I guess it's in a sense, what I'm saying is, it's to protect you from any actions that I may perceive as actually acceptable, but you don't.
Interviewer:	Mmmhmm
Mark:	Not harassment where you're, that's a criminal defense and should be dealt with accordingly, but this is more for the unintended. It seems like this [policy] is directed toward the unintended, unintentional stuff that gets brought to light and run up the flagpole way more than it should.

* * *

Pedro:	I just see it as being a lot different. The intent of the policy, watching the [way the organization] works. The policy was to help show that they're doing something that was—that they're being proactive and taking care of things that have already gone on in the [organization]. This policy is created because of problems that already have happened. [The intent is to] create a paper trail of stuff that they [organizational leaders] can use later on to say, "Oh, we tried to perfect that." But being a person who's put some of that stuff [training] on, it was just, it's just covering their backsides or whatever.

Note that prior to this conversation, these individuals recently read their organization's sexual harassment policy. They talked about the policy the day before during same-sex groups and agreed to do so again in a mixed-sex context. All three people spoke about the intent of the sexual harassment policy, interpreting the intent of the policy differently. Joy's first statement indicated that the intent of the policy was to stop sexual harassment. Mark then disagreed with Joy and claimed that the intent of the policy was to protect organizational members from unwanted behavior by punishing the harasser. He seemed to believe that the policy was not designed to protect the victim as much as it was designed to punish the unwitting harasser whose unintended behavior was "run up the flagpole way more than it should." Pedro drew a darker interpretation from the policy. He argued that the intent of the policy was to protect the organization from law suits. This man interpreted the policy as a purely legal document created to protect the organization, rather than a policy to help the victim or sanction the harasser.

It is fascinating to me that these three rather different interpretations emerged as a result of reading the same documents. If I had not designed and executed the study, I might even question that these people had indeed read the same document. Each interpretation "opened" the meaning of the policy into new and unintended realms. Consequently, it appears that the document's central function was in negotiating what sexual harassment means, rather than stopping unwanted and illegal behavior in the organization. Policies then are an important starting place for organizations concerned with sexual harassment but should be considered only a place to begin rather than the final word.

Sexual Harassment Is "Dangerous for Men"

A third discursive process illustrates that discourse is never neutral—it is always political (Wood, 1994). Sexual harassment discourse often attempts to pit the needs of men against the needs of women. One of the more intriguing discursive constructions by organizational members is that sexual harassment creates a hostile work environment for men. For this hostile environment to exist, a number of discursive strategies are employed. First, workers are fragmented into absolute individuals. Everybody is very different. Second, this absolute fragmentation creates a constantly shifting, unstable, and "risky" environment in which men must work. Finally, this unstable environment makes even the most benign comments risky for men. One man in a study comparing flirting with sexual harassment describes this dangerous environment for men:

> But you know, just saying "Hi, boy you look good today," and other people within the situation, other women, they'd be very very jealous. They think that flirting is harassment. If you see somebody, you really don't know anymore what to say. If somebody really looks nice [you say] "God you really look nice. You've done something to cut your hair. You know, you look great." Then you have other people who all of a sudden say, "Hey, that, you're sexually harassing her." And it's a really a fine line what other people perceive is going on, [in] the other people's interpersonal relationships.

This man talks about gendered relationships as very uncertain, not necessarily because of the interpersonal relationship between the man and the woman, but because most women are "very very jealous" when a man complements another woman. These jealous women then charge the poor fellow with sexual harassment. Note the construction of gender. The man is just trying to be nice. The women are jealous, unreasonable, and nosey. These other women appear to be competing for male attention and are vindictive when attention is directed elsewhere. In some ways this type of argument can be compelling. In fact, I suspect that a number of readers agree with this man's assessment that sexual harassment charges create a hostile work environment for men. However, subsequent elements of his interview underscore the insidious character of this interpretation:

Interviewer: Do you know what he supposedly said to the client?

Steven: Yeah. [pause] he told her that uh, since she got the new boobs she looked really good.

Interviewer: [Laughs in disbelief].

Steven: And I thought to myself, "Why would you buy a new set of breasts and show 'em off and not want somebody to say something about 'em?"

Interviewer: Umhm [surprised disbelief]

Steven: And then when somebody says something about 'em, [they] get in trouble. A friend of mine. It's like, you're flirting ...

Interviewer: [Interrupting] Would you consider his behavior flirting?

Steven: Yes. I would. He had no power over her. And there was like, she's single. And he's trying to, you know, to my viewpoint, why would you go out and get a breast job and show 'em off if you don't want somebody to say something about 'em? And when you say something about 'em, [the woman] automatically becomes offended. And that's the dichotomy of where, that's just the epitome of where we are now, with the relationship between men and women. And corporation's involved and we're all so close and dynamically put together and everybody is so super-sensitive about anything anymore.

Steven sets very few limits on male behavior. Rather, he appears to believe that only managers in quid pro quo situations can sexually harass. Any other interpretation is "oversensitive" and irrational. What is more, during the interview this man even managed to find a way to comment on my breasts and other physical features—an exceedingly uncomfortable experience for me.

Many of those who make the "dangerous-for-men" argument are not sexual harassers and believe that some limits on male behavior are acceptable. In fact, many of the people who make this argument are women who work with men. However, their argument that women's irrational sensitivity turns men into victims of false accusations of sexual harassment makes it increasingly difficult to address uncontrolled sexual aggression by men. The following illustrates this problem. First, when asked, Joyce defines the line between flirting and sexual harassment in the following way:

Interviewer: How do you determine what the boundaries are?

Joyce: Um, I think between feeling good and feeling dirty.

Joyce is pretty clear. Flirting feels good. Sexual harassment feels dirty. However, she later explains that some women are oversensitive, creating a difficult environment for men who just want to be "nice":

Joyce: I, I think some women are, overdo it. They, I don't know
what it is about them that you can't even whistle at them or
you can't, like I said before, you know, you can't say anything nice to them without them filing some kind of grievance or something that this guy is saying something to
them. I mean, just stepping into an elevator and saying
'mmm you smell good.' That's not 'hey I want to go to bed
with you.' Maybe it is. It depends if she allows it I'm sure.
You know, I think [this type of comment] it's kind of feeling out people without using their hands.

                              * * *

Interviewer: Alright. Is there ever any room for someone flirting with
you, but you don't want them to be flirting with you?
Joyce: Oh, um, there are. I have experienced them not calling me
"Ma'am," but calling me "sweetie or honey," and they're
slime balls, but, you know, I don't ... . I think some guys
think they can get any girl, any woman, no matter what
they look like, and they're wanting really good looking
chicks and you wonder "God, what are you thinking
man?" But um, I don't think, I mean, I don't feel that it's
inappropriate, I just think that when they do it I do feel kind
of dirty.

One strategy I utilize when analyzing data is to look for inconsistencies
because they provide clues that a discursive shift has happened. I then
backtrack to identify when the shift occurred and how the shift functions.
The inconsistency for Joyce is in her use of the term "dirty." In the first
quote, she draws a clear line between flirting and sexual harassment with
feeling good on the flirting side and feeling dirty on the sexual harassment
side of the line. It appears that the major shift is in the way she discursively
constructs some women as overly sensitive. Once she constructed some
women in this way, she works diligently to be sure that she will not be
placed into that category. As a result, she avoids labeling certain behaviors
as sexual harassment, even when those behaviors meet her own criteria for
sexual harassment, "feeling dirty."

"I'm Too Tough to be A Victim": Discursively Avoiding the Label

Both scholarly work (Rapping, 1997) and popular books (Wolf, 1994)
make it quite clear that being labeled a victim is undesirable in contemporary society—especially when that victim label is a product of a woman-
targeted crime such as rape and sexual harassment. Second-wave feminists

recognize that this attitude disproportionately impacts women by silencing those who are hurt and privatizing crimes against women (Rapping). Unfortunately, some third-wave feminists have discursively constructed "victims" as mentally and physically weak (e.g. Wolf).

Like rape, being a target of sexual harassment is doubly victimizing. There is the behavior itself and then there is the stigmatization that occurs when others learn about the victimization. The workplace exacerbates this problem. A "good worker" is tough, aggressive, and task-oriented. The image of a victim of sexual harassment is the opposite of the "good worker." Victims are perceived as weak, passive, and emotional, and women workers justifiably fear this label. Because of the perception that victims of sex crimes are weak, many women doggedly avoid any association with that label. Women who have been sexually harassed tend to avoid using the label "sexual harassment" when describing their experiences—even when the experiences were physically aggressive. Those who have not yet been sexually harassed describe themselves as "too tough" to be sexually harassed. I focus on these women in this section.

Women who self-define as too tough to be sexually harassed discursively represent themselves as different from "most" women. Borrowing a term from media scholars, I label this tendency the third-person effect (Gunther & Storey, 2003). Essentially, the third-person effect leads people to believe that they are immune to influences that affect others. One of my favorite illustrations of the third-person effect and gender comes from a study by Street et al. (1995). When asked about psychological gender using the Bem sex role inventory, a majority of female college professors characterized most women as highly feminine. However, these same women typically rated themselves as highly masculine. In essence, they depicted themselves as unique from and superior to most other women. They did not seem to believe that they were influenced by gender in the same way that most other women were influenced. The fact that most other women made the same claim is tragically interesting.

My research on sexual harassment has found similar third-person tendencies. Most women with whom I have talked believe that they can not be victims because they are immune to the influence of predatory sexual behavior. For example, the number of women who claim that they would enact physical violence on anyone who sexually harassed them constantly surprises me:

Rosemary: I can't imagine like, somebody doing that cause *I'd proba-bly hit them*, like, "listen here!" But like, 'cause I also like, I think its how you let, 'cause some people let themselves, their personal bubble in closer to people, like to actually touch them and stuff like that, so I think there's different things there that I don't deal with 'cause people know that

	I have a huge personal bubble. Like I don't like, hug people. I don't do stuff like that just 'cause it makes me uncomfortable.
Interviewer:	Right.
Rosemary:	And so I think like, people that let people closer into their personal bubble, I think it's probably harder for them to fight somebody off. Like not physically fight somebody off but mentally like tell them, "Hey we're not, I'm not that kind of person."

* * *

Jennifer:	And I worked at the [bar], so I got to know everybody. And it was always friendly; it was always very, [slight pause] nobody made it very personal, like made derogatory remarks; it was always. And if you told them, "Hey that's enough; that's getting a little too far," they would stop; they would apologize. *Probably because they know I would slap them otherwise.*

Despite these claims, women rarely slap, hit, punch, kick, or otherwise enact violence toward perpetrators of sex-related crimes. Typically, these men (and most of them are men) are bigger, stronger, and socially and hierarchically more powerful than their women targets. Indeed, women who do enact violence in the workplace are likely to be arrested, fired, demoted, or otherwise shamed. Consequently, it is likely that such violent language functions less as a statement of fact, and more as a discursive enactment of the third-person effect. In other words, these women are claiming to be different from most women, and therefore, more organizationally competent.

Other scholars have identified similar bravado in women's responses to imagined versus real sexual harassment (Woodzicka & LaFrance, 2001). When confronted with a hypothetical case of harassment, most women (in one study) reported that they would confront a sexual harasser if they were ever targeted. Then the study design had these women attend a job interview in which they were sexually harassed by the interviewer. None of the women confronted the sexual harasser, despite strong feelings of discomfort (Woodzicka & LaFranse). Researchers examining workplace bullying find the same imagined-versus-real response dynamic (Rayner, 1997).

It appears that most women underestimate how frightening sexual harassment is when it happens. Consequently, they are unprepared for the intensity of the experience. Their planned response becomes inadequate to the situation, and the experience silences them. It is unlikely that most women would physically harm a harasser. However, by claiming that they would enact violence, these women discursively "protect" themselves from being perceived as potential victims of that behavior.

Consequences of Sexual Harassment

Organizational members often view sexual harassment as a minor irritant. My research participants repeatedly indicate that the real problem is not the harassment, but the inability of targets to deal with the behavior in appropriate ways. In reality, sexual harassment is almost always highly-aggressive behavior that not only is destructive for the organization, but also can destroy the lives of its victims. Women who are harassed can experience severe negative job-related and psychological outcomes (Schneider, Fitgerald, & Swan, 1997). These negative outcomes occur regardless of whether or not a person labels the behavior sexual harassment (Magley, Hulin, Fitzgerald, & DeNardo, 1999). Since my first published article on this topic in 1999, I have interviewed and talked to hundreds of people about sexual harassment. Counter to the victim stereotypes, these people are strong and courageous, and the stories they tell are heart-wrenching and frightening. Painfully, these people are trapped in an environment that discourages them from voicing their rage. In what follows, I discuss some of the consequences of sexual harassment including the fear it generates, the isolation targets feel, and the power of sexual harassment to obstruct women's career paths.

Fear

A woman sexual harassed at work reported the following:

> I mean, this guy scared the piss out of me, and I'm going to be on evenings. He's going to be there. What if he catches me down the hall where nobody's at? He's a large man. He could take me in a heartbeat.

A widespread consequence of sexual harassment is intense and enduring fear and dread. The woman quoted above fears for her physical safety. In fact, fear of physical violence is one of the factors that makes sexual harassment so distressing for women (Dougherty, 1999). Fear of sexual harassment at times includes the fear of sexual assault. Sexual harassment reminds women that men tend to be physically bigger and stronger, and renders the workplace a threatening, dangerous place.

Although many women discuss fear of physical violence after they have been sexually harassed, others express a more generalized fear that develops as a result of sexually harassing encounters. Their hearts race any time they think they may come into contact with the harasser. Many women fear losing their jobs. And, of course many women fear that others will see them as victims with all the negative associations (e.g., weak, ineffective). Imagine yourself going to work everyday, afraid that someone is going to hurt you. This is what some victims of sexual harassment face.

Isolation

A sense of community in the workplace is highly desired. For instance, it is striking how often people claim that the workplace is like their home and coworkers are like family (Miller, Considine, & Garner, 2007). When used to describe the workplace, the family metaphor is typically positively valenced; the metaphor usually ignores the fact that many families are abusive and dysfunctional. Feminist scholarship suggests that women find working *with* other people to be a particularly important source of pleasure and community—as it most likely also is for men. Sexual harassment shatters this sense of community, effectively isolating victims from their potential coworker "families."

This isolation results from a number of discursive constructions. First, managers and coworkers tend to trivialize women who complain about sexual harassment (Clair, 1994). This trivialization makes the women who complain appear abnormal and, therefore, someone to avoid (Dougherty, 1999). Second, women do not typically believe other women who claim they are sexually harassed. Ironically, women in one organization claimed that their greatest fear about sexual harassment was that others would not believe their claims if it happened (Dougherty, 2001b). These same women then reported believing that most women who claimed to be sexually harassed had fabricated the story. This failure to believe other women, in effect, recreated the conditions in which they would not be believed if sexually harassed.

Isolation from coworkers contributes to victims' stress, sadness, and loneliness. More importantly, those who are isolated from a community of workers are also more vulnerable to sexual harassment (Conrad & Taylor, 1994). They are ideal targets because the behavior is less likely to be observed by others. Thus, sexual harassment and isolation have a recursive relationship. Sexual harassment creates isolation, and isolation increases targets' susceptibility to sexual harassment.

The Glass Ceiling

The glass ceiling is "a barrier so subtle that it is transparent, yet so strong that it prevents women and minorities from moving up in the management hierarchy" (Morrison & Von Glinow, 1990, p. 200). A web of stereotypes and discrimination constitute this barrier, one that is difficult to penetrate and even more difficult to identify. Women and minorities reach a certain point in the organizational hierarchy and then hit this invisible barrier (Reuther & Fairhurst, 2000). Although there are a number of known causes for the glass ceiling, the ways in which sexual harassment contributes to the glass ceiling dynamic remains under-explored. I propose that sexual harassment can be an antecedent to the glass ceiling barrier.

Sexual harassment and the glass ceiling are related in several ways. First, sexual harassment makes victims appear weak and ineffectual; consequently, they are unlikely to be perceived as "management material." Second, victims tend to become isolated from their social networks, networks that are key to obtaining opportunities leading to professional advancement. Third, sexual harassment creates a great deal of physical stress for the victim. This stress likely decreases the productivity of the employee, again creating the illusion that victims are not management material. Finally, many victims of sexual harassment handle the experience by leaving the workplace altogether. Obviously these people will not be promoted. Although approximately 15% of sexual harassment targets are men (EEOC, 2005), the great majority are women. Consequently, the relationship between sexual harassment and the glass ceiling has a larger cumulative effect on women than on men. This impact is likely heightened for women of color whose experience with the glass ceiling is based on both race and gender.

Avenues for Correction

There are few known solutions for sexual harassment. Most sexual harassment remediation is a product of the legal system and often occurs after sexual harassment has been ignored or even promoted in the organization. What, if any, effect this type of remediation has on sexual harassment in the workplace is unclear. Instead of exploring legal solutions to sexual harassment, I focus on communication-centered means for managing the problem. I believe that the solutions presented here could minimize the problem if implemented by managers who value their employees, truly believe that sexual harassment is a problem, and are willing to commit the time and effort necessary to addressing the issue. Organizational members or individuals teaching organizational communication can enact other solutions suggested here.

Sexual harassment is primarily a social and cultural phenomenon (Kreps, 1993). Although the damage occurs in the workplace, larger social institutions and cultural meaning systems engender sexual harassment and allow it to persist (Grauerholz, 1994). Consequently, exploring a number of actions representing a range of social and organizational processes is necessary. Although there is no "silver bullet" for eliminating sexual harassment, there are some ways we can minimize it.

Social Evolution

The primary reason why gendered crimes, such as rape and sexual harassment, persist is due to the ways we socialize boys and girls by negatively differentiating them. Children, but especially boys, are taught from an early age that they are "different" from and better than girls (Grauerholz, 1994). I particularly find the term "he's all boy" distasteful. When people say this about my son, who is five, they are commenting on his general level of activity, his occasional acts of aggression, and the volume at which he speaks. When my daughter was five, was active, committed occasional acts of aggression (hitting a playmate for example), and spoke loudly, she was never called "all boy." I also wonder what a "part boy" might look like. I try to imagine a person declaring about my son (during the times when he is quiet, kind, and focused) "he's part boy" or "a little bit girl." Similarly, being accused of "throwing like a girl" or even being called a girl represent the worst possible insult for boys as they develop.

Habitually differentiating boys and girls creates two primary problems. First, differentiation negates the fact that boys and girls also have similarities. Both are imaginative, dress up in their parents' shoes, and have a great capacity for care and love. Second, habitually differentiating can cause boys and girls to emphasize differences. Differences should not play a greater role in identify formation than do similarities, especially since sexual harassment and rape are acts rooted in gender differentiation. These acts are carefully, if non-consciously, designed to communicate to a victim, "You are not a man, and, therefore, you are worth less than I am." Reducing differentiation should decrease the propensity toward these types of crime.

Organizational Culture

As mentioned earlier, sexual harassment is a product and process of organizational cultures. To manage sexual harassment, managing the organization's culture is crucial. Recognizing the extent to which sexualized language is diffused within the workplace is the first thing members, especially managers, need to do. This, of course, means talking to a diverse array of organizational members and not just upper-management. Cultures that are not highly sexualized need to be protected. A constant low-level vigilance should be adequate. On the other hand, if sexualized language and behavior is diffused throughout the workplace, then intensive remediation is necessary. The following are applied suggestions based on the processes outlined above.

Cultures Resistant to Sexual Harassment

Given the nature of sexual-harassment-prone cultures, it is important to ask how cultures can develop to resist the enactment of these behaviors. Although a number of scholars have examined organizational cultures infused with sexual harassment, less is known about cultures that resist sexual harassment in the environment. One case study of such a culture does provide some insight. Dougherty and Smythe (2004) suggest that to effectively deter cultures of sexual harassment, men and women must be equally committed to treating each other with respect. For example, in an academic setting, when an outsider sexually harassed three members of the department, members responded by listening to the women's stories, supporting the women, and rejecting the outsider by ridiculing him. In such an organization, sexual harassment is unlikely to be tolerated. Although the outsider's behaviors were likely common in his own workplace, members of the academic unit viewed these behaviors as intolerable and crude.

Policy Management

There is no way to prevent the informal reconstruction or reinterpretation of organizational policy. Formal policies are an important step in managing unwanted behavior, but listening to how organizational members talk about the sexual harassment policy is also vital. By so doing, organizational change agents can identify members' misinterpretations as well as their underlying anxieties and concerns. For example, members of one organization I studied seemed to be concerned that the policy would hurt the organization's collegiality. They worried that it had already created an environment of mistrust. Knowing this concern, change agents might address the underlying worry by supporting and encouraging a collegial, comfortable environment.

Sexual Harassment Training

Sexual harassment training can be an effective tool in minimizing sexual harassment. In my opinion, organizations make two common mistakes when conducting training. First, they use hypothetical examples with "trained actors" acting out their parts. Many people have told me that they see this type of training as "stupid" and unrealistic. Instead, organizational trainers should utilize the many examples that can be pulled from real cases of sexual harassment to illustrate this behavior. Second, in many organizations only managers receive training. For example, I worked with one health care organization that had spent a huge sum of money on sexual harassment training for its managers. The managers were fairly astute at identifying and defining sexual harassment. The rest of the staff, however, had varying definitions, some having no resemblance to either the legal or the organizationally-sanctioned definitions. Unfortunately, sexual harassment was rampant in this organization, and people in non-management positions were most commonly the perpetrators.

Men as Agents of Change

Most men are not sexual harassers. They are caring and concerned citizens of the organization. Unfortunately, much research on sexual harassment treats men as the enemy—especially white, middle class, heterosexual men (Dougherty, 1999; Townsley & Geist, 2000). The combination of sexual harassment policies and the discursive villanization of men may well combine to create the perception that organizations are dangerous for men. As such,

> Instead of treating white men as the enemy, it would be far more productive to attempt to understand how they may be part of the solution to sexual harassment. While acknowledging that it is the dominant white male privilege that often encourages sexual harassment in organizations, it is also important to identify ways that white men can participate in preventing sexual harassment. Scholars and practitioners should start with the assumption that white men want to do what is right. They have a human capacity for love and care and should be given an opportunity to protect their colleagues. White men are privileged as organizational insiders and therefore have an opportunity to confront sexual harassers in unique ways. (Dougherty & Smythe, 2004, p. 314)

Although these conclusions are drawn from a study looking at the reactions of white men to a case of sexual harassment, this argument should be extended to all men. Some men from all races and social classes can and do sexually harass. However, most men find this behavior unacceptable and are, therefore, potentially valuable allies in stopping the behavior. Men of color who are in positions of power have an understanding of how language marginalizes. These men may serve as particularly valuable allies in the movement to stop sexual harassment.

Victim Schema

The shock that sexual harassment could happen to them often prevents women from responding effectively. Because we associate being a victim with being weak and passive, women do not want to believe that they could be victims nor tell others that they have been victimized. Consistent with the third-person effect, women believe that *others* are victims, not themselves. As a result, when sexual harassment occurs, women have no real schemas for how to manage the behavior and respond effectively. After hundreds of formal and informal interviews with people, both for research and during private conversations, I have come to believe that the single most consistent predictor of sexual harassment is simply "bad luck." I have talked to women from all walks of life who have all been sexually harassed—rich, poor, white, black, old, young, U.S. American, Latin American, European, and Asian. None of them understood why they had been targeted. They were strong and assertive people—not the stereotyped "victim." Yet most remained silent when faced with the shock of being sexually harassed.

What these women lacked was realistic schemas or mental plans for how they would or could respond if sexually harassed. Because the experience was unexpected, these women were silenced by the behavior. Some of them had unrealistic schemas, such as violently attacking the perpetrator. This type of simplistic schema is not useful when faced with unwanted sexual attention at work. Instead, women must understand that sexual harassment could easily happen to them. Additionally, sexual harassment training can help women develop complex schemas for how to handle the behavior and manage their feelings if and when it occurs.

Conclusion

Sexual harassment is illustrative of the construction, reconstruction, and re(work)ing of gender in organizations. It tells women and some men that they are still on the margins of society, and that they may be gainfully employed but are still not equal. The processes provided here illustrate some ways that sexual harassment perpetuates inequality and gender anxiety in the workplace.

Some organizational cultures are prone to sexual harassment. These cultures are explicitly organized around socially-crafted gendered roles and sexual expectations. Policies, rather than providing the last word on sexual harassment, may create discursive openings where conflict over meaning occurs. Ironically, given the destructive outcomes of sexual harassment, many people interpret sexual harassment policies as creating a dangerous environment for men. Furthermore, victims tend to be villanized as creating problems by being passive and weak. These dynamics are simply illustrations of the many communicative processes that reconstruct sexual harassment, perpetuating it in the workplace.

Although researchers have been successful in delineating some of the communication processes involved in sexual harassment, there is much yet to learn. A discursive approach that places communication and meaning at the heart of the sexual harassment process creates new questions and opens opportunities for future research. For example, although we know that men and women tend to construct the meaning of sexual harassment differently, we still know little about how they construct these differences. What are some of the communication processes used to create these differences? What is the role of privilege and workplace expectations in these constructions? Furthermore, although it seems likely that sexual harassment enhances the glass ceiling effect, it is important to explore the interplay between sexual harassment and the glass ceiling more explicitly. Finally, although we have uncovered a great deal regarding sexual harassment in organizations, we know surprisingly little about how to effectively solve this problem. Most organizations use the legal model for managing the behavior. We do not know what impact the legal model has on sexual harassment. For example, it could drive sexual harassment underground into more political, manipulative forms. In other words, sexual harassment may become more subversive and, therefore, more difficult to recognize and remediate. Although I make some suggestions in this paper regarding communication-centered approaches to managing this issue, it is important to explore the efficacy of these solutions.

Despite the fact that very little research examines the effects of organizational responses to sexual harassment, I suggest a number of practical implications for both individuals who work for and organizational managers who care about the workplace environment. First, individuals can create a positive social evolution with their children by training boys and girls to see themselves as connected. This evolution would eliminate the need some men feel to differentiate between men and women through anti-social behaviors like rape and sexual harassment. However, being somewhat of a realist, I understand that many people are strongly tied to gender differences and my utopian world is unlikely to evolve. Consequently, I also provide more practical suggestions. For example, organizational change agents need to understand how policies are being interpreted and then address underlying concerns illustrated through those reinterpretations. Additionally, men should be included as part of the solution, and organizational communication scholars should teach students that being sexually harassed is possible and that they should have a complex schema for when it happens to them. Although these actions may not solve the problem, they may make sexual harassment more manageable—and, therefore, less destructive for organizational members.

References

Berdahl, J. L., Magley, V., & Waldo, C. R. (1996). The sexual harassment of men? Exploring the concept with theory and data. *Psychology of Women Quarterly, 20*(4), 527–547.

Bingham, S. G. (1994). Introduction: Framing sexual harassment—defining a discursive focus of study. In S. G. Bingham (Ed.), *Conceptualizing sexual harassment as discursive practice* (pp. 1–14). Westport, CT: Praeger.

Clair, R. P. (1993). The use of framing devices to sequester organizational narratives: Hegemony and harassment. *Communication Monographs, 60*(1), 113–136.

Clair, R. P. (1994). Hegemony and harassment: A discursive practice. In S. G. Bingham (Ed.), *Conceptualizing sexual harassment as discursive practice* (pp. 59–70). Westport, CT: Praeger.

Clair, R. P. (1998). *A world of possibilities*. Albany: State University of New York Press.

Conrad, C., & Taylor, B. (1994). The contest(s) of sexual harassment: Power, silences, and academe. In S. G. Bingham (Ed.), *Conceptualizing sexual harassment as discursive practice* (pp. 45–58). Westport, CT: Praeger.

Dougherty, D. S. (1999). Dialogue through standpoint: Understanding women's and men's standpoints of sexual harassment. *Management Communication Quarterly, 12*(3), 436–468.

Dougherty, D. S. (2001a). Sexual harassment as [dys]functional process: A feminist standpoint analysis. *Journal of Applied Communication Research, 29*(3), 372–402.

Dougherty, D. S. (2001b). Women's discursive construction of a sexual harassment paradox. *Qualitative Research Reports, 2*(1), 6–13.

Dougherty, D. S., & Atkinson, J. (2006). Competing ethical communities and a researcher's dilemma: The case of a sexual harasser. *Qualitative Inquiry, 12*(2), 292–315.

Dougherty, D. S., & Smythe, M. J. (2004). Sensemaking, organizational culture, and sexual harassment. *Journal of Applied Communication Research, 32*(4), 293–317.

EEOC. (2005). Sexual harassment charges EEOC & FEPAs combined: FY 1992- FY 2004. *United States Equal Employment Opportunity Commission.* Retrieved March 28, 2005, from http://www.eeoc.gov/stats/harass.html.

Firestone, J. M., & Harris, R. J. (1999). Changes in patterns of sexual harassment in the U.S. Military: A comparison of the 1988 and 1995 DoD surveys. *Armed Forces & Society: An Interdisciplinary Journal, 25*(4), 613–632.

Garlick, R. (1994). Male and Female Responses to Ambiguous Instructor Behaviors. *Sex Roles, 30*(1/2), 135–158.

Grauerholz, E. (1994). Gender socialization and communication: The inscription of sexual harassment in social life. In S. G. Bingham (Ed.), *Conceptualizing sexual harassment as discursive practice* (pp. 33–44). Westport, CT: Praeger.

Gunther, A. C., & Storey, J. D. (2003). The influence of presumed influence. *Journal of Communication, 53*(2), 199–215.

Hemphill, M. R., & Pfeiffer, A. L. (1986). Sexual spillover in the workplace: Testing the appropriateness of male-female interaction. *Women's Studies in Communication, 9*(1), 52–66.

Keyton, J., Ferguson, P., & Rhodes, S. C. (2001). Cultural indicators of sexual harassment. *Southern Communication Journal, 67*(1), 33–50.

Kreps, G. L. (1993). Promoting a sociocultural evolutionary approach to preventing sexual harassment: Metacommunication and cultural adaptation. In G. L. Kreps (Ed.), *Sexual Harassment: Communication implications* (pp. 310–318). Cresskill, NJ: Hampton Press.

Magley, V. J., Hulin, C. L., Fitzgerald, L. F., & DeNardo, M. (1999). Outcomes of self-labeling on sexual harassment. *Journal of Applied Psychology, 84*(3), 390–402.

Miller, K. I., Considine, J., & Garner, J. (2007). "Let me tell you about my job": Exploring the terrain of emotion in the workplace. *Management Communication Quarterly, 20*(3), 231–260.

Morrison, A. M., & Von Glinow, M. A. (1990). Women and minorities in management. *American Psychologist, 45*(2), 200–208.

Mumby, D. K. (1998). Organizing men: Power, discourse, and the social construction of masculinity(s) in the workplace. *Communication Theory, 8*(2), 164–183.

Nadesan, M. H., & Trethewey, A. (2000). Performing the enterprising subject: Gendered strategies for success (?). *Text and Performance Quarterly, 20*(2), 223–250.

Rapping, E. (1997). None of my best friends: The media's unfortunate 'victim/power' debate. In N. B. Maglin & D. Perry (Eds.), *Bad girls, good girls: Women, sex and power in the nineties* (pp. 265–274). New Brunswick, NJ: Rutgers University Press.

Rayner, C. (1997). The incidence of workplace bullying. *Journal of Community and Applied Social Psychology, 7*(1), 199–208.

Reuther, C., & Fairhurst, G. T. (2000). Chaos theory and the glass ceiling. In P. M. Buzzanell (Ed.), *Rethinking organizational and managerial communication from feminist perspectives* (pp. 236–256). Thousand Oaks, CA: Sage.

Schneider, K. T., Fitgerald, L. F., & Swan, S. (1997). Job-related and psychological effects of sexual harassment in the workplace: Empirical evidence from two organizations. *Journal of Applied Psychology, 82*(3), 401–415.

Street, S., Kromrey, J. D., & Kimmel, E. (1995). University faculty gender roles perceptions. *Sex Roles, 32*(4), 407–422.

Thacker, R. A., & Gohmann, S. F. (1993). Male/Female differences in perceptions and effects of hostile environment sexual harassment: "Reasonable" Assumptions? *Public Personnel Management, 22*(4), 461–472.

Townsley, N. C., & Geist, P. (2000). The discursive enactment of hegemony: Sexual harassment and academic organizing. *Western Journal of Communication, 64*(2), 190–217.

Waldo, C. R., Berdahl, J. L., & Fitzgerald, L. F. (1998). Are men sexually harassed? If so, by whom? *Law and Human Behavior, 22*(1), 59–79.

Williams, C. W., Brown, R. S., Lees-Haley, P. R., & Price, J. R. (1995). An attributional (causal dimensional) analysis of perceptions of sexual harassment. *Journal of Applied Social Psychology, 25*(13), 1169–1183.

Wolf, N. (1994). *Fire with fire: The new female power and how to use it.* New York: Fawcett Columbine.

Wood, J. T. (1992). Telling our stories: Narratives as a basis for theorizing sexual harassment. *Journal Applied Communication Research, 20*(3), 349–362.

Wood, J. T. (1994). Saying it makes it so: The discursive construction of sexual harassment. In S. G. Bingham (Ed.), *Conceptualizing sexual harassment as discursive practice* (pp. 17–30). Westport, CT: Praeger.

Woodzicka, J. A., & LaFrance, M. (2001). Real versus imagined gender harassment. *Journal of Social Issues, 57*(1), 15–30.

Zak, M. W. (1994). "Its like a prison in there": Organizational fragmentation in a demographically diversified workplace. *Journal of Business and Technical Communication, 8*(3), 281–298.

Part IV

Technology and Teams

Chapter 11

The Destructive Potential of Electronic Communication Technologies in Organizations

Andrew J. Flanagin, Katy Pearce, and
Beverly A. Bondad-Brown

In spite of some controversy about net effects (Brynjolfsson, 1993), electronic communication and information technologies (ECITs) provide organizations and their members with tremendous benefits. Compared to more traditional means, contemporary technologies can carry more information, faster, at a lower cost, to more people, while also offering enhanced information search, processing, and recombinant capabilities (Beniger, 1996; Fulk & DeSanctis, 1995). Furthermore, the use of advanced electronic technologies in organizations is widespread and commonplace due to the development of a dependable technical infrastructure, decreasing technology costs, and in many cases, the achievement of a critical mass of users where relevant (Gurbaxani, 1990; Markus, 1990). Indeed, contemporary technologies can be major factors in achieving substantial organizational benefits, across interpersonal (e.g., Compton, White, & DeWine, 1991; Walther, 1995), group (e.g., DeSanctis & Poole, 1997; Lipnack & Stamps, 1997), and organizational outcomes (e.g., Davidow & Malone, 1992; Nohria & Berkley, 1994).

Yet, technologies enable outcomes more than they determine them (see Barley, 1986; Markus & Robey, 1988), making it difficult to predict social or organizational effects from technological artifacts. Therefore, the use of electronic technologies in organizations is best viewed as a complex process where social outcomes result from a mix of environmental conditions, technical tools, organizational factors, and individual motivations, capabilities, and efforts. In some instances, benefits from technology use are obvious and well-documented. In other cases, however, technology use is accompanied by considerable deficits, which have not received as much direct attention to date.

Even simple examples of organizational technology use illustrate this complexity. For instance, carbon copying ("cc'ing") colleagues on emails to keep them appropriately informed may also contribute to information overload, which can contribute to stress (Farhoomand & Drury, 2002). "Cyberloafing" (i.e., abusing Internet privileges at work by performing non-work related tasks), which is often perceived as negative (Lim, 2002), can also serve as an important source of relaxation, thereby helping employees perform better in their work tasks. Moreover, the interpretation of destructive or beneficial outcomes of organizational technology use can vary by the perspective adopted. For instance, "whistle blowing," which can be enhanced by the anonymity potentially provided by e-mail and web technologies, can be used to call attention to illegal practices. Although this act can clearly yield positive outcomes for the organization, it may also be considered to be deceptive by some and, therefore, destructive.

This chapter considers how electronic technology use in organizations can contribute to destructive communication and outcomes. We propose that *destructive communication* consists of intentional or unintentional communication acts that are predominantly harmful to organizational members, groups within organizations, or organizations as a whole. Working from this definition, we examine the potentially destructive aspects of electronic technology use in organizations, by introducing five types of destructive activities. We elaborate on the various types of destructive communication behaviors within each category and, using an organizational case study, illustrate one example of how destructive communication acts may occur and discuss its consequences. We conclude by discussing processes for improving technology use within organizations and by offering suggestions on how to limit and prevent destructive communicative practices in the workplace.

Communication Technology Use and Destructive Organizational Activities

Organizational use of communication technology is widespread. Of the 77 million American workers who report using a computer on the job, 75% say they access the Internet or use e-mail (DOL, 2005). Many also report using instant messaging (IM) at work (AMA/ePolicy, 2006), with 90% of corporate users spending over 90 minutes a day actively using IM (AMA/ePolicy, 2004). Moreover, organizational members routinely use a wide range of technologies in their jobs. Communication technology common to organizations includes, but is not limited to, IM and other chat tools, electronic mail, Internet and web pages, video-conferencing tools, voicemail, mobile devices (i.e., cell phones and mobile Internet devices such as Treos, Centros, iPhones, and Blackberries), and personal data assistants. Our focus in this chapter is thus consistent with Culnan and Markus's (1987, p. 422) view of advanced communication and information technologies as "interactive, computer-mediated technologies that facilitate two-way interpersonal communication among several individuals" by means of "written text, recorded or synthesized voice messages, graphical representation of communicators or data, or moving images of the communicators or message content." Technology users are often geographically dispersed and may use these tools either synchronously or asynchronously.

In spite of their ubiquity and remarkable benefits, there exist substantial obstacles to effective and productive organizational technology use, as well as directly destructive outcomes from their utilization. In fact, the very features and uses of electronic technologies that result in tremendous cost-savings, efficiency gains, and other benefits can also yield destructive communication behaviors in organizations. To explore these potentially destructive outcomes, we propose several types of destructive communication activities facilitated by contemporary technologies.

Types of Destructive Communication Activities

We have identified five types of destructive activities found in organizational settings: counterproductive activities, nonproductive activities, inappropriate activities, deceptive and equivocal activities, and intrusive activities. Although neither mutually exclusive nor unique to technology use, these destructive communication activities have in common that they are all tied in meaningful and compelling ways to the organizational use of ECITs. Consequently, articulating these destructive activities serves both to increase awareness of this relatively understudied outcome of organizational technology use, and to suggest potential remedies to such destructive organizational activities.

Counterproductive Activities

Counterproductive uses of organizational technologies are those behaviors that conflict with organizations' goals and place employers at risk either legally or financially (Mastrangelo, Everton, & Jolton, 2006). Examples include such activities as chatting in a sexual manner with someone at work, creating CDs at work from downloaded music, and using the Internet while at work to visit money-making sites (Mastrangelo et al.). Although typically low-frequency, these activities can be harmful both to the individual (e.g., addiction to online gambling) and to the work team or organization as well (e.g., loss of productivity).

Counterproductive activities stemming from technology use also include behaviors that compromise organizations' data security. Violations of data security include a range of various "attacks" or successful misuses of computer systems (Gordon, Loeb, Lucyshyn, & Richardson, 2005). Network attacks are actions directed against computer systems to disrupt equipment operations, change processing control, or corrupt stored data (Wilson, 2005). Attackers include, among others, hackers, terrorists, and professional criminals with objectives such as political or financial gain, challenges to resource holders, or damaging organizations. The results of these attacks include information corruption and disclosure, and theft, and denial of service (Howard, 1997). Attacks can take many forms, including computer network, system, and information attacks, as well as the introduction of computer viruses and "malware." Computer network attacks usually involve malicious programming code that infects computers in order to exploit weaknesses of software, system configuration, or computer security practices. Such attacks can also occur when an attacker uses stolen information to enter a system. The result of a computer network attack is the disruption of integrity and authenticity of data.

Network attacks are relatively common. Howard's (1997) analysis of 4,299 security-related incidents between 1989 to 1995 concluded that a typical Internet domain was involved in about one security incident per year. Another study found that unauthorized use of computer systems occurred among 56% of respondents (Gordon et al., 2005). Moreover, unauthorized access to information occurred in over 30% of organizations in 2004 and cost over $31 million in losses in a sample of only 639 organizations (Gordon et al.). Virus attacks, however, are the greatest source of financial loss for organizations (Gordon et al.).

To avoid such attacks organizations may use anti-virus software, firewalls, intrusion detection systems, and instruction prevention systems (Gordon et al., 2005). In addition, organizations may utilize access control lists based on servers and data encryption. After intrusions occur, organizations use a number of strategies to prevent future intrusions, including hole patching (i.e., fixing vulnerabilities), reporting the intrusion to law enforcement, and informing legal counsel (Gordon et al.). When organizations do not report an intrusion to law enforcement it is typically due to fear of the negative publicity hurting public image or stock price. Other reasons for not reporting to law enforcement include concern that competitors could use the intrusion report to their advantage, the belief that a civil remedy is the best recourse, and simply being unaware that law enforcement is interested in such occurrences (Gordon et al.).

Nonproductive Activities

Nonproductive technology use at work includes those behaviors that are not directly productive for the organization and that often detract from accomplishing work tasks (Mastrangelo et al., 2006). Often, these behaviors involve social communication with others or engaging in personal tasks during work hours. Cyberloafing, cyberslacking, workplace Internet abuse, and online procrastination are types of personal, non-work-related uses of the Internet during working hours. Cyberloafing, for example, is "any voluntary act of employees using their companies' Internet access during office hours to surf non-work-related Web sites for non-work purposes and access (including receiving and sending) non-work-related e-mail" (Lim, Teo, & Loo, 2002, p. 67).

Cyberloafing is quite common in the workplace. One study found that employees spend a third of their time online procrastinating from work tasks (Lavoie & Pychyl, 2001). Another study found that over a quarter of the time spent online at work was non-work-related (Wyatt & Phillips, 2005). In a survey of Internet use in the workplace, 37% of respondents admitted surfing non-work-related websites a few times a day, and 16% admitted surfing non-work-related websites constantly throughout the day (Vault.com, 2005). Another study found that employees with Internet access at work spent 2.6 hours online each day, often on non-work-related and general news sites (Lim et al., 2002).

Among 25 categories of inappropriate websites that employees are likely to visit while working are websites containing hate speech, gambling, gruesome content, and nudity (Johnson & Chalmers, 2007). Moreover, surveyed employees admit to using the Internet to shop online, play games, conduct personal bank transactions, and chat with others online during work hours (Mastrangelo et al., 2006). Griffiths (2003) identified six different subtypes of workplace Internet abuse including cybersexual Internet abuse (e.g., visiting adult websites), online friendship or relationship abuse (e.g., communicating with friends online), Internet activity abuse (e.g., online shopping or travel booking), online information abuse (e.g., use of search engines and databases), criminal Internet abuse (e.g., online sexual harassment), and miscellaneous Internet abuse (e.g., digital image manipulation). Research suggests that males, younger workers, those with faster Internet connections at work than at home, and more impulsive and less conscientious workers engage in more personal use of work computers (Everton, Mastrangelo, & Jolton, 2005; Mastrangelo et al., 2006).

Despite the loss to organizations that these behaviors represent, employees rationalize such behaviors in several ways (D'Abate, 2005). Some employees believe they are able to handle work-related and non-work-related tasks simultaneously. Others consider workplace Internet abuse a justified reward once they have completed a work project. Some simply feel compelled due to convenience, since access to their computer, e-mail, and the Internet is readily available. Regardless, cyberloafing clearly utilizes company resources and diminishes allotted work time.

Inappropriate Activities

Destructive communication attacks receivers' self-esteem or reputation, or reflects indifference towards others' basic values (Redding, 1996). We expand this concept to include a range of "inappropriate" activities commonly facilitated by ECITs that can be deemed to be destructive. For example, sharing inappropriate jokes or confidential information via e-mail or "flaming" would be considered inappropriate activities. Inappropriate activities have in common a disregard for the appropriateness of communication content, form, and behaviors. As a consequence, these forms of communication can be harmful to individuals, groups, or the organization as a whole.

Flaming, or sending hostile and aggressive messages via text-based computer-mediated channels, is particularly destructive and can be shocking and deeply painful for those targeted. Several scholars have argued that specific characteristics of computer-mediated communication channels, including the potential for varying degrees of anonymity among users and the relative lack of accountability as compared to face-to-face interaction, contribute to high incidences of flaming in online interactions (Gurak, 2001; Kiesler, Siegel, & McGuire, 1984; Siegel, Dubrovsky, Kiesler, & McGuire, 1986; Sproull & Kiesler, 1991). Behaviors such as swearing, insults, name-calling, and the use of threats are typically considered evidence of flaming. In one study, 23% of flame-mail recipients reported receiving such destructive messages several times a week, and 48% said they receive them several times a month (Novell, 1997). Within an organization, such behaviors may occur in group discussion boards, online forums set up for organizational members, or in e-mail messages sent to others.

In spite of such potential, and accounts of flaming in organizations, some have questioned the prevalence of flaming (Lea, O'Shea, Fung, & Spears, 1992) and technologically deterministic explanations for it (O'Sullivan & Flanagin, 2003; Walther, Anderson, & Park, 1994). Moreover, alternative explanations for seemingly inappropriate online behavior have been offered that do not depend exclusively on channel characteristics (Postmes, Spears, & Lea, 2000). Consistent with Lea et al. (1992, p. 108), many argue that flaming should be viewed as "radically context-dependent" and recognized as group-specific and dependent on normative expectations, rather than as a feature of technologically-mediated communication (O'Sullivan & Flanagin, 2003). More than likely, flaming is only one aspect of a larger constellation comprised of aggressive or insulting messages (Crawford, 1999).

Sending or forwarding unsuitable e-mail jokes or messages is another form of inappropriate activity that is increasingly common due to the ease and speed of electronic communication channels. Inappropriate jokes containing sexist, sexual, or pornographic content are easily passed from one coworker to another. With e-mail programs' forward and carbon copy functions, large groups of people can be sent such inappropriate messages quickly, easily, and perhaps without sufficient consideration of the nature of the message or the full list of recipients.

Indeed, it appears that such transgressions are commonplace. Almost a quarter of surveyed users of instant messaging in the workplace reported sending jokes, gossip, rumors, and disparaging remarks, and 10% reported sharing pornographic, sexual, or romantic content (AMA/ePolicy, 2006). Harris Interactive found that nearly half their sample (48%) had sent or received joke emails, funny pictures/movies, or funny stories of a questionable tone (e.g., racy, sexual, or politically incorrect content) at work (Fortiva, 2005). The public e-mail archive from the Enron trial, for example, showed that one out of every 25 emails contained pornographic content, racially or ethnically offensive language, or dirty jokes or images (Matus, 2005).

A final type of inappropriate activity is the unauthorized transmission of confidential information, what Redding (1996) called using the "'truth' as a weapon [to…reveal] confidential information to unauthorized persons" (p. 28). This inappropriate use of communication channels also appears to be common. In one study, 23% of respondents admitted sending or receiving confidential company or client documents, and 20% admitted sending or receiving an e-mail that commented on confidential business (Fortiva, 2005). Another study found that 9% of users reported sharing confidential information about the company, a coworker, or a client via instant messaging (AMA/ePolicy, 2004).

This type of destructive electronic communication is not without risks. One study reported that more than 60% of surveyed companies disciplined employees for inappropriate use of the Internet, and more than 30% terminated employees for inappropriate Internet use (Greenfield & Davis, 2002). For example, in 2002 Hewlett-Packard fired two employees and suspended 150 more for sharing pornography via the company e-mail system (Conlin, 2002).

Deceptive and Equivocal Activities

The ubiquity of ECITs in contemporary organizations suggests they are also implicated in deceptive communication. Deceptive communication includes communication that is dishonest, involves lying, or is unfair (Redding, 1996), or that entails messages and information knowingly transmitted to create a false conclusion (Buller & Burgoon, 1996) by virtue of evasive or deliberately misleading messages, as well as euphemisms designed to cover up defects, conceal embarrassment, or make things appear better than they are. In nearly all cases, deceptive communication can be considered destructive for organizations.

Several features of computer-mediated communication (CMC) are relevant for both the production and detection of deception. As Carlson and colleagues (2004, p. 12) note, the "predominant form of electronic media is text, so that many but not all cues about status, position, and situational norms are missing ....This attenuation of cues ... may actually provide a fertile arena for norm breaking behaviors such as deception." For instance, symbol or language variety, which extends the options senders have when constructing messages, increases the likelihood of successful deception and reduces the likelihood of detecting deception (Carlson et al.). Moreover, messages from deceptive senders using CMC usually have a higher number of verbs, modifiers, and noun phrases than messages from truthful senders, although they also exhibit less lexical and content diversity (Zhou, Twitchell, Qin, Burgoon, & Nunamaker, 2003). And, individuals are more likely to give deceptive, though positive, portrayals of themselves to a communication partner thought to be physically distant from themselves (Bradner & Mark, 2002), potentially by virtue of electronic communication tools enabling misrepresentation.

Other CMC message features that increase the likelihood of successful deception and reduce deception detection include tailorability, reprocessability, rehearseability, and cue multiplicity (Carlson et al., 2004). Tailorability, or the customization of messages for particular recipients, can potentially enhance persuasion and thus deception. Low levels of reprocessability, or receivers' opportunity to revisit or reanalyze messages in the future in light of subsequent events, can similarly enhance deception. Rehearsability, or opportunities to plan and edit messages in order to portray content in a very specific manner, can also contribute to deceptive success. The hyperpersonal perspective (Walther, 1996), for example, argues that many forms of CMC provide opportunities to achieve specific self-presentation that might be particularly intentional and persuasive (Walther, 2007), and which can, in turn, contribute to successful online deception.

Cue multiplicity, or the number of channels supported by a medium, is also argued to affect deception via computer-mediated communication (Carlson et al., 2004). Indeed, research shows that modality can influence believability. Audio cues appear to enhance individuals' ability to detect deceit, particularly when compared to text-based communication where deceivers were actually judged as more truthful than those being honest (Burgoon, Stoner, Bonito, & Dunbar, 2003). Accordingly, receivers trying to detect deception place greater value on media with more channels (Carlson & George, 2004).

Electronic technologies have also been widely implicated in various instances of identity deception. Online identity deception includes category deception, impersonation, and identity concealment (Donath, 1999). Category deception is the intentional misrepresentation of identifying demographics (e.g., sex, age, status), and is often used in bulletin board systems or chat rooms. Impersonation, when one person pretends to be another, can be extremely destructive in organizations. For example, an employee may impersonate a high-level executive by sending an e-mail message from the executive's e-mail address. This, in turn, may damage the executive's reputation by spreading inaccurate information or causing unwarranted distress for receivers.

Identity concealment includes pure anonymity and pseudonymity. In a purely anonymous message, there is no link to any persona, thus few impressions can be formed about the actual sender. Anonymity implies a lack of identifiability, which could enable workers to engage in destructive activities without others knowing (Joinson, 2003). Nonetheless, purely anonymous technology use in organizational settings is rather rare. Based on an individual's e-mail address, username, a shared address book, or intranet directory, employees usually know with whom they are communicating.

Pseudonymity is communicating under a screen name (i.e., sending an e-mail to coworkers from a non-work e-mail account to mask identity) or using avatars (i.e., models, icons, or pictures) to represent one's identity. Research suggests that when using text-only online chat, those deceiving their partners experienced higher anxiety levels than those who were truthful, but using an avatar-supported chat environment reduced this anxiety (Galanzhi & Nah, 2007). Moreover, those who deceived their partners online tended to select avatars more unlike their real selves, suggesting potential benefits to masking one's true identity when being deceptive online (Galanzhi & Nah). Group Support Systems (GSS) leverage the potential openness of pseudonymity by allowing participants to partially conceal their identity in order to increase participation among group members (Postmes & Lea, 2000). Although pseudonymity can be a positive aspect of GSS by allowing group members the freedom to discuss and vote, group members can also communicate in hurtful, destructive ways, since they are not often fully identifiable.

In addition to deception, ECITs are particularly prone to increased equivocality and ambiguity that encourage multiple, often conflicting, interpretations (Daft & Lengel, 1986; Daft & Weick, 1984). Technologies both help and hinder organizational members' efforts to reduce equivocality and achieve shared understanding. In contrast to messages that intentionally and explicitly misrepresent information, equivocal messages are not false, but rather are unclear (Bavelas, Black, Chovil, & Mullett, 1990). Equivocation deviates from truthful communication in at least one of four ways: (a) the sender tries to deny ownership of the statement, (b) the message content is unclear, (c) the receiver is not addressed in the situation, or (d) the context is not directly answered by the reply (Bavelas, et al.). Technology choice and use can increase equivocality or fail to resolve it effectively. For example, when complex organizational tasks are mismatched with "lean" communication technology, oversimplification (i.e., overly lean media are used to resolve complex tasks) or over-complication (i.e., overly rich media are used to resolve simple tasks) can result.

Users can also employ technologies to create ambiguity intentionally, especially when they use ambiguity to accomplish goals (Eisenberg, 1984) and encourage divergent interpretations to coexist (Eisenberg & Witten, 1987). Strategic ambiguity serves four functions: it promotes unified diversity, preserves privileged positions, provides plausible deniability, and facilitates organizational change (Eisenberg & Goodall, 2005). Although in and of themselves these functions are not inherently destructive, plausible deniability, for example, can mask responsible parties' errors and contribute to deception, which can be destructive (Deetz, 1992).

Intrusive Activities

Intrusive activities include communication events that interrupt work tasks or workers' cognitive concentration and are, consequently, burdensome or destructive. Such activities cause a temporary cessation of the current flow of work, resulting in shifting focus from primary work activities to some secondary diversion (Van den Berg, Roe, Zijlstra, & Krediet, 1996). These distractions force employees to interrupt their planned activities to respond to the interruption (Solingen, Berghout, & Latum, 1998). Up to 20% of some employees' daily effort is spent dealing with interruptions (Solingen et al.), a phenomenon that results in considerable lost productivity for organizations and lost time for workers when switching tasks (Rubinstein, Meyer, & Evans, 2001). Several types of intrusive activities are associated with electronic technologies, including increased work interruptions, multitasking, information overload, work–life imbalance, and surveillance.

Although electronic communication and information tools are indispensable in helping workers perform critical tasks, they also present a major source of work interruption. Such interruptions include personal visits, telephone calls, and e-mail (Solingen et al., 1998), which in some studies account for nearly half of employees reporting distraction from their work (Burgess, Jackson, & Edwards, 2005). Indeed, surveys show that 81% of respondents reported that their e-mail program was always open (Williams & Williams, 2006), 70% of emails are viewed within six seconds of reception—faster than three telephone rings—(Jackson, Dawson, & Wilson, 2003), and 55% of those surveyed opened emails immediately or shortly after they arrived, regardless of what they were working on (Wallis & Steptoe, 2006). The loss of productive time due to e-mail interruptions can be significant. Up to 20% of an individual employee's daily effort is spent dealing with interruptions, often spending 15 to 20 minutes per interrupt (Solingen et al., 1998), and employees can spend over a minute recovering from each e-mail interruption in their efforts to refocus on previous tasks (Jackson et al.).

Instant messaging can also be highly intrusive, and some employees perceive instant messaging as negative and encroaching on time to complete their work (Herbsleb, Atkins, Boyer, Handel, & Finholt, 2002). Although instant messaging has not yet been studied extensively as an interrupt, interruptions are more likely in a virtual space than in a face-to-face environment (Fish, Kraut, Root, & Rice, 1993). Yet, instant messaging may be perceived as less of an interruption than a richer medium because an employee may negotiate his or her availability through instant messaging tools themselves (Nardi, Whittaker, & Bradner, 2000). The potentially destructive nature of e-mail, instant messaging, and other technologically-enabled interruptions is obvious, given the substantial work demands that must be met within limited periods of time.

Another intrusive activity is "multitasking," or the performance of several tasks simultaneously, which is increasingly more common with greater use of electronic technologies (Davenport & Beck, 2002; Zhang, Goonetilleke, Plocher, & Liang, 2005). Although workers often multitask to deal with work overload, this approach to work can be highly intrusive. Multicommunication, a form of multitasking, is engaging in more than one activity at one time or treating unplanned interruptions as equally important to planned activities (e.g., Bluedorn, 2002; Bluedorn, Kaufman, & Lane, 1992). Employees frequently participate in multiple, simultaneous interactions at work (Cameron & Webster, 2005), and research suggests that multiple conversations (using instant messaging) are common and possible. These became significantly less satisfying, however, as the number of multiple conversations in which one is engaged increases (Flanagin, 2005).

Multitasking may even be a norm for communication within some organizations that value the potential efficiencies created by accomplishing more than one interaction task at once (Turner, Grube, Tinsley, Lee, & O'Pell, 2006). For example, Joe Maggio, a senior executive at Raytheon, reportedly drives while conducting simultaneous telephone meetings and sending emails at red lights. Maggio, however, describes himself as not "all there" (Jackson, 2004), a state that can have dire consequences for his organization, and even worse consequences for his (and others') health. Maggio's comment illustrates the idea that "people imagine they can multitask, but sometimes people overestimate the extent to which they can do it" (Richtel, 2003, p. 1). Certainly there is also a public safety concern related to this type of multitasking; driving while using a mobile phone can reduce both reflex time and attention to driving (Salvucci, Chavez, & Lee, 2004). In fact, talking on a cell phone while driving is illegal in many states.

Information overload is also linked to ECIT use and occurs "when the information processing demands on time to perform interactions and internal calculations exceed the supply or capacity of time available for such processing" (Schick, Gordon, & Haka, 1990, p. 206). Put simply, information overload is receiving *too much* information. "Information technology and its use and misuse are a major reason why information overload has become a critical issue in many organizations in the 1980s and 1990s" (Eppler & Mengis, 2004, p. 331). The causes are a function of the information itself (i.e., quantity, frequency, quality); the person receiving, processing, or communicating the information; the individual, group, or organizational task that needs to be completed; the organizational structure (e.g., formal or informal work structures); and the information technology used in the organization (Eppler & Mengis).

A major cause of information overload includes new technologies such as groupware, the Internet, and intranets (Bawden, 2001). The same technologies that increase interruptions (e.g., IM, e-mail, mobile Internet devices) contribute to information overload. E-mail is particularly pernicious due to the proliferation of spam—unsolicited e-mail typically with commercial intent. Indeed, nearly 8% of emails sent worldwide are spam. In the United States, 75% of Internet users report receiving spam on a daily basis, and the estimated productivity loss associated with reviewing and deleting spam is $22 billion annually (Swartz, 2005). Moreover, even if employees avoid reading spam messages, they fill up inboxes and reduce system capacity.

Given the ubiquitous nature of ECITs in organizations, information overload will probably become more problematic with increased use. For example, over a third of an international sample of managers reported information overload on a daily basis (Farhoomand & Drury, 2002), a phenomenon that negatively affects performance as information levels increase (Eppler & Mengis, 2004). The destructive potential for information overload extends into many areas of work and can result in extended decision making time (Iselin, 1988) and reduced decision effectiveness (Ashton, 1974). Information overload negatively affects work by reducing both efficiency and productivity (Farhoomand & Drury) and is not without personal cost to employees. The increasing level of information via electronic media is often a source of stress, confusion, pressure, anxiety, and even reduced motivation, as one becomes increasingly overwhelmed (Eppler & Mengis, 2004).

Another negative effect of information overload is the encroachment on non-work life. Teleworking (or telecommuting)—working from home or outside the traditional workplace using a computer or telephone connection—connects workers to their jobs far beyond 40-hour work weeks and tips the scales of work/non-work balance away from personal lives. What is more, most employees are electronically tethered to their jobs not because of family commitments but because of employers' demands (Tremblay, Paquet, & Najem, 2006). With the increased availability of smaller mobile communication devices, these boundaries are further blurred. Indeed, 70% of mobile professionals are expected to use mobile e-mail by the end of this year (Visto, 2007), signaling further erosion of time exclusively set aside for workers' families and personal lives.

There are other negative effects associated with "taking your work home." For example, compulsive checking of e-mail and an inability to disengage from work can result from being electronically connected, which implies an expectation of availability and thus, immediate responsiveness (Mazmanian, Yates, & Orlikowski, 2006). Indeed, mobile e-mail users are expected to, and do, respond more quickly to e-mail than people who do not have access to a mobile device (Mazmanian et al.). What is more, some telecommuters display characteristics of "workaholism"— working compulsively at the expense of other pursuits (Olson & Primps, 1984).

Surveillance, or the use of technology to monitor employees, can also be seen as intrusive by employees (Allen, Coopman, Hart, & Walker, 2007). Surveillance is linked to increased stress, incidents of aggression, and destructive workplace conflicts (Liefooghe & MacKenzie-Davey, 2001). Moreover, it is widespread. In reports from a sample of organizations, 60% use software to monitor external incoming and outgoing e-mail, 27% monitor internal e-mail, and 11% use IM gateway or management software to monitor, purge, retain, and control IM risks and use (AMA/ePolicy, 2006). Although typically used as a mechanism of control and oversight, surveillance is also used for employee feedback and suggestions for improvement (Allen et al.).

Monitoring for control allows employers to gain compliance with rules and regulations (Urbaczewski & Jessup, 2002). Employees who are aware of electronic monitoring are more focused on their tasks, however they also report being less satisfied than employees unaware of electronic monitoring (Urbaczewski & Jessup). Employees view electronic monitoring systems not only as an invasion of privacy but also as unfair (Alge, 2001), and fairness plays a key role in attitude toward organizational processes (Ambrose & Alder, 2000). Even video conferencing has a surveillance connotation; some employees are reluctant to participate due to concerns about privacy invasion and the potential use of such systems for employee monitoring (Lee, Schlueter, & Girgensohn, 1997; Zweig & Webster, 2002). Overall, surveillance through electronic tools has the potential to be destructive if perceived as overly or inappropriately intrusive by employees.

Case Study Example

Saetre and Sornes' (2006) case study illustrates many aspects of the destructive communication behaviors described in this chapter and details employees' technology use at Dossier Solutions, a Norwegian high-tech company. Employees are young college graduates, largely working as computer programmers, whose first work experience is at Dossier. Employees are active users of the Internet, SMS (i.e., text) messaging, and

ICQ (i.e., chat), who are issued with high-end cell phones in order to conduct work tasks and communicate with one another.

In spite of their utility, the technologies Dossier Solutions uses are employed in a variety of destructive ways. For example, employees tend to cyberloaf by sending non-work-related SMS messages using their cell phones, as well as engage in non-work-related ICQ discussions during working hours. Each of these contributes to nonproductive technology use in the organization. In addition, the distribution of cell phones allows Dossier to keep employees constantly "on call" at all hours, thus blurring the boundary between work and time off.

Moreover, technologies are a constant source of interruption, thereby contributing to extensive and multiple intrusions into organizational activities. For example, employees are frequently interrupted by chat sessions and text messages. Saetre and Sornes (2006) recount:

> The use, and abuse of, these communication technologies interrupts the workday for people who sit and program relatively complex code. When they are interrupted every 15 minutes by an incoming e-mail or SMS, it has some consequences for how effective they are ... there's an incredible amount of hours wasted on ICQ and SMS every week at Dossier. (p. 78)

To illustrate, Kristian Mjoen, one of the company's co-founders, recalls a programmer at the company who was constantly interrupted by ICQ messages, on some days as often as every 30 seconds. Not only "did these constant interruptions consume time and disrupt her work process, but they also led her machine to crash quite frequently when she was chatting on ICQ" (p. 78). E-mail was another source of frequent interruptions at Dossier:

> Because everyone uses e-mail and tends to answer messages throughout the day, it ... interrupts work .... As people fail to take advantage of e-mail's asynchronicity, and continuously respond, e-mail becomes a distraction .... If you fall for the temptation of responding to all your emails as you receive them, then you are down to relatively short periods of effective work. (Saetre & Sornes, p. 79)

Kristian noted that these practices negatively affected the company's productivity. In fact, some of the tools enabled him to quantify the actual damage. The distribution of company cell phones, for example, allowed Kristian to monitor employee phone usage. Cell phone bills provided the quantifiable measures for employee time spent talking on the phone and sending SMS messages. In addition, Kristian could estimate that for each message sent, an equal number were likely returned. These measures allowed him to calculate how much work time may have been lost during the work day.

To address these destructive activities, Kristian took several actions. For example, he implemented a new policy asking employees to close their e-mail programs for periods of the day to limit the number of interruptions. In addition, he acknowledged that the company should show a greater respect for employees' personal time off and changed the cell-phone policy accordingly. In the end, his recognition of the destructive activities facilitated by ECITs enabled him to at least partially resolve them.

Preventing, Mitigating, or Resolving Destructive Organizational Technology Use

Despite their tremendous value, ECITs also have destructive potentials in organizations. They can facilitate counterproductive, nonproductive, inappropriate, deceptive and equivocal, and intrusive activities and potentially prompt or exacerbate destructive organizational outcomes. Yet, there are specific strategies that organizations can use to decrease the harmful possibilities of communication technologies.

Farhoomand and Drury (2002) propose several solutions to information overload at personal, technological, and organizational levels. Personal solutions include information filtering (i.e., selecting the appropriate information or consulting with coworkers), eliminating sources of extraneous information, delegating to subordinates, and prioritizing information and tasks. Accordingly, practical advice such as assigning oneself a "time out" from the mobile device in order to spend time with family or friends has become common (Cass, 2006).

Technological solutions involve using technology to reduce the amount of information encountered. For example, "push" technology, which works by alerting users to new and updated information based on pre-selected information sources (Edmunds & Morris, 2000), can reduce information overload. Another technological solution is the use of "intelligent agents," which can scan and comprehend text, and then summarize the information sent to users. Organizational solutions consist of devising new work processes and operations, consulting top management, and getting assistance from the information technology department. Employee training can significantly reduce the amount of e-mail defects, improve use of the e-mail subject line, and result in e-mail content that is clearer, more direct and to the point, and easier to read (Burgess et al., 2005).

Williams and Williams (2006) even suggest that companies require e-mail training before granting e-mail accounts and "create an 'e-charter,' a formal, companywide set of policies, rules and guidelines about e-mail use" (p. 40). They also recommend that senders (a) indicate in messages whether action is needed or if the message is informational only; (b) eliminate distribution lists containing more than five names; and, (c) if sending short messages, write the entire message in the subject line followed by "EOM" (end of message). Another possible solution is simply *ignoring* the information contributing to overload (Farhoomand & Drury, 2002).

To reduce destructive equivocality, managers should select communication technologies based on a match between the "richness" (versus leanness) of particular communication media and the complexity of organizational tasks (Daft & Lengel, 1984, 1986). Ideally, highly complex tasks should be matched with correspondingly rich media—those with high language variety (e.g., written, graphical, and verbal expression), immediate feedback ability, multiplicity of cues (e.g., body posture, facial expression), and capability for tailoring messages to personal circumstances.

Another approach to more constructive organizing around ECITs is developing technology-specific policies that can decrease several variants of destructive communication (Martin, 1999). Policies such as an e-charter, Internet Acceptable Use Policy, and other formal guidelines can reduce destructive electronic communication practices by specifying acceptable behavior, unacceptable behavior, and appropriate technology use. Additional remedies to reduce inappropriate technology include adjusting ongoing formal and informal socialization, coaching to improve communication skills, and crafting new employee orientation to explicitly address normative and acceptable communication behavior (O'Sullivan & Flanagin, 2003).

Training can reduce some of the destructive outcomes from technology use and has the potential to do so in a number of areas. First, training increases the workforce's awareness of appropriate communication technology use and associated organizational policies. Second, training briefs employees about the possible outcomes of technology use—both positive and negative. Third, education informs employees about their options regarding technology use in order to adhere to policy. Fourth, training enhances knowledge about resources to address or mitigate problems when they arise (e.g., counseling to help achieve work–life balance, technical solutions for decreasing spam emails). Finally, particularly for newer employees, group training and education enhance organizational socialization efforts, which can improve individuals' satisfaction within organizations, contributions to them, and commitment to the organization and its members (Jablin, 2001). Technologies themselves can even be used to advantage in this regard (Flanagin & Waldeck, 2004).

Creating a culture that allows for open communication is also important for ameliorating the destructive potential for communication technology abuses. Allowing for frank and open discussion of work–life balance issues, feelings of information overload, and other relevant issues can decrease negative possibilities. Overall, organizations can encourage a culture in which people are able to acknowledge, recognize, and address destructive technology use practices, ideally before they contribute to personal or professional problems.

Conclusion

Although the benefits of contemporary technologies in organizations are considerable, there also exist substantial destructive outcomes, which have received significantly less attention. In this chapter we have identified five types of destructive organizational activities—counterproductive activities, nonproductive activities, inappropriate activities, deceptive and equivocal activities, and intrusive activities—potentially connected to the use of communication technologies. We have elaborated on these in order to understand their causes, correlates, and prevalence. In addition, we have suggested ways for improving organizational technology use, thereby limiting their destructive potential.

As ECITs permeate ever greater proportions and aspects of our personal and professional lives, understanding the negative outcomes of these tools is increasingly important. Several groups of people are implicated in this endeavor, including researchers, managers, workers, and technology designers. The best solutions will almost certainly result from all of these groups working collectively to identify problems stemming from, and potentially even resolved by, the use of technologies.

References

Alge, B. J. (2001). Effects of computer surveillance on perceptions of privacy and procedural justice. *Journal of Applied Psychology, 86*(4), 797–804.

Allen, M. W., Coopman, S. J., Hart, J. L., & Walker, K. L. (2007). Workplace surveillance and managing privacy boundaries. *Management Communication Quarterly, 21*(2), 172–200.

AMA/ePolicy. (2004). *AMA/ePolicy Institute Research 2004 workplace e-mail and instant messaging survey results: Summary.* Columbus, OH: ePolicy Institute.

AMA/ePolicy. (2006). *AMA/ePolicy Institute Research 2006 workplace e-mail, instant messaging & blog survey results: Summary.* Columbus, OH: ePolicy Institute.

Ambrose, M. L., & Alder, G. S. (2000). Designing, implementing, and utilizing computerized performance monitoring: Enhancing organizational justice. *Research in Personnel and Human Resources Management, 18*(2), 187–219.

Ashton, R. H. (1974). Behavioral implications of information overload in managerial accounting reports. *Cost and Management, 48*(1), 37–40.

Barley, S. R. (1986). Technology as an occasion for structuring: Evidence from observations of CT scanners and the social order of radiology departments. *Administrative Science Quarterly, 31*(1), 78–108.

Bavelas, J. B., Black, A., Chovil, N., & Mullett, J. (1990). Truths, lies, and equivocations: The effects of conflicting goals on discourse. *Journal of Language and Social Psychology, 9*(1), 129–155.

Bawden, D. (2001). Information overload. *Library and Information Briefings, 92*(1), 1–15.

Beniger, J. R. (1996). Who shall control cyberspace? In L. Strate, R. Jacobson & S. B. Gibson (Eds.), *Communication and cyberspace: Social interaction in an electronic environment* (pp. 49–58). Cresskill, NJ: Hampton Press.

Bluedorn, A. C. (2002). *The Human organization of time*. Stanford, CA: Stanford University Press.

Bluedorn, A. C., Kaufman, C. J., & Lane, P. M. (1992). How many things do you like to do at once? An introduction to monochronic and polychronic time. *The Academy of Management Executive, 14*(2), 17–26.

Bradner, E., & Mark, G. (2002, November). *Why distance matters: Effects on cooperation, persuasion, and deception.* Paper presented at the ACM Conference on Computer Supported Cooperative Work, New Orleans, LA.

Brynjolfsson, E. (1993). The productivity paradox of information technology. *Communications of the ACM, 36*(1), 66–77.

Buller, D. B., & Burgoon, J., K. (1996). Interpersonal deception theory. *Communication Theory, 6*(2), 203–242.

Burgess, A., Jackson, T., & Edwards, J. (2005). E-mail training significantly reduces e-mail defects. *International Journal of Information Management, 25*(1), 71–83.

Burgoon, J. K., Stoner, G. M., Bonito, J. A., & Dunbar, N. E. (2003). Trust and deception in mediated communication, *36th Hawaii International Conference on Systems Sciences*. Hawaii.

Cameron, A. F., & Webster, J. (2005). Unintended consequences of emerging communication technologies: Instant messaging in the workplace. *Computers in Human Behavior, 31*(1), 85–103.

Carlson, J. R., & George, J. R. (2004). Media appropriateness in the conduct and discovery of deceptive communication: The relative influence of richness and synchronicity. *Group Decision and Negotiation, 13*(2), 191–210.

Carlson, J. R., George, J. F., Burgoon, J. K., Adkins, M., & White, C. H. (2004). Deception in computer-mediated communication. *Group Decision and Negotiation, 13*(1), 5–38.

Cass, A. (2006). There's too much information. *On Wall Street, 6*(November), 75–76.

Compton, D. C., White, K., & DeWine, S. (1991). Techno-Sense: Making sense of computer-mediated communication systems. *Journal of Business Communication, 28*(1), 23–43.

Conlin, M. (2002, September 30). Watch what you put in that office e-mail. *Business Week, 3801*(1), 114–115.

Crawford, N. (1999). Conundrums and confusion in organisations: The etymology of the word "bully." *International Journal of Manpower, 20*(1/2), 86–93.

Culnan, M. J., & Markus, M. L. (1987). Information technologies. In F. M. Jablin, L. L. Putnam, K. H. Roberts & L. W. Porter (Eds.), *Handbook of Organizational Communication: An Interdisciplinary Perspective* (pp. 420–443). London: Sage.

D'Abate, C. P. (2005). Working hard or hardly working: A case study of individuals engaging in personal business on the job. *Human Relations, 58*(8), 1009–1032.

Daft, R. L., & Lengel, R. H. (1984). Information richness: A new approach to managerial behavior and organization design. *Research in Organizational Behavior, 6*(2), 191–233.

Daft, R. L., & Lengel, R. H. (1986). Organizational information requirements, media richness, and structural design. *Management Science, 32*(4), 554–571.

Daft, R. L., & Weick, K. E. (1984). Toward a model of organizations as interpretation systems. *The Academy of Management Review, 9*(2), 284–295.

Davenport, T. H., & Beck, J. C. (2002). *The attention economy: Understanding the new currency of business.* Cambridge, MA: Harvard Business School Press.

Davidow, W. H., & Malone, M. S. (1992). *The virtual corporation.* New York: Harper Collins.

Deetz, S. A. (1992). *Democracy in an age of corporate colonization.* Albany, NY: State University of New York Press.

DeSanctis, G., & Poole, M. S. (1997). Transitions in teamwork in new organizational forms. *Advances in Group Processes, 14*(2), 157–176.

DOL. (2005). Computer and Internet use at work summary. *United States Department of Labor.* Retrieved August 16, 2007, from http://www.bls.gov/news. release/ciuaw.nr0.htm.

Donath, J. A. (1999). Identity and deception in the virtual community. In M. A. Smith & P. Kollock (Eds.), *Communities in cyberspace* (pp. 29–59). London: Routledge.

Edmunds, A., & Morris, A. (2000). The problem of information overload in business organisations: a review of the literature. *International Journal of Information Management, 20*(1), 17–28.

Eisenberg, E. M. (1984). Ambiguity as strategy in organizational communication. *Communication Monographs, 51*(3), 227–242.

Eisenberg, E. M., & Goodall, H. L., Jr. (2005). *Organizational communication: Balancing creativity and constraint* (4th ed.). Boston: Bedford-St. Martins.

Eisenberg, E. M., & Witten, M. G. (1987). Reconsidering openness in organizational communication. *The Academy of Management Review, 12*(3), 418–426.

Eppler, M. J., & Mengis, J. (2004). The concept of information overload: A review of literature from organization science, accounting, marketing, MIS, and related disciplines. *The Information Society, 20*(5), 325–344.

Everton, W. J., Mastrangelo, P. M., & Jolton, J. A. (2005). Personality correlates of employees' personal use of work computers. *Cyberpsychology & Behavior, 8*(2), 143–153.

Farhoomand, A. I., & Drury, D. H. (2002). Managerial information overload. *Communications of the ACM, 45*(10), 127–131.

Fish, R. S., Kraut, R. E., Root, R. W., & Rice, R. E. (1993). Video as a technology for informal communication. *Communications of the ACM, 36*(1), 48–61.

Flanagin, A. J. (2005). IM online: Instant messaging use among college students. *Communication Research Reports, 22*(2), 175–187.

Flanagin, A. J., & Waldeck, J. H. (2004). Technology use and organizational newcomer socialization. *The Journal of Business Communication, 41*(1), 137–165.

Fortiva. (2005, November 15). Risky business: New survey shows almost 10 percent of e-mail-using employees have sent or received e-mail that may pose a threat to businesses. *Fortiva, Inc.* Retrieved August 15, 2007, from http://www.fortiva.com/news/press-releases/archived05/harrissurvey.html.

Fulk, J., & DeSanctis, G. (1995). Electronic communication and changing organizational forms. *Organization Science, 6*(4), 337–349.

Galanzhi, H., & Nah, F. F. (2007). Deception in cyberspace: A comparison of text-only vs. avatar-supported medium. *International Journal of Human-Computer Studies, 65*(9), 770–783.

Gordon, L. A., Loeb, M. P., Lucyshyn, W., & Richardson, R. (2005). *CSI/FBI Computer crime and security survey*. San Francisco, CA: Computer Security Institute Publications.

Greenfield, D. N., & Davis, R. A. (2002). Lost in cyberspace: The web @ work. *CyberPsychology & Behavior, 5*(4), 347–353.

Griffiths, M. (2003). Internet abuse in the workplace: Issues and concerns for employers and employment counselors. *Journal of Employment Counseling, 40*(2), 87–96.

Gurak, L. J. (2001). *Cyberliteracy: Navigating the Internet with awareness*. New Haven, CT: Yale University Press.

Gurbaxani, V. (1990). Diffusion in computing networks: The case of BITNET. *Communications of the ACM, 33*(12), 65–75.

Herbsleb, J. D., Atkins, D. L., Boyer, D. G., Handel, M., & Finholt, T. A. (2002). *Introducing instant messaging and chat in the workplace*. Paper presented at the Conference on Human Factors in Computing Systems, Minneapolis, MN.

Howard, J. D. (1997). An analysis of security incidents on the Internet 1989–1995. Doctoral dissertation, Pittsburgh, PA: Carnegie Mellon University.

Iselin, E. R. (1988). The effect of information load and information diversity on decision quality in a structured decision task. *Accounting, Organizations and Society, 13*(2), 147–164.

Jablin, F. M. (2001). Organizational entry, assimilation, and disengagement/entry. In F. M. Jablin & L. L. Putnam (Eds.), *The new handbook of organizational communication: Advances in theory, research, and methods* (pp. 732–818). Thousand Oaks, CA: Sage.

Jackson, M. (2004, September 26). Pressured to multitask, workers juggle a fragmented existence. *The Boston Globe*, p. G1.

Jackson, T. W., Dawson, R., & Wilson, D. (2003). Understanding e-mail interaction increases organizational productivity. *Communications of the ACM, 46*(8), 80–84.

Johnson, J. J., & Chalmers, K. W. (2007). *Identifying employee Internet abuse*. Paper presented at the 40th Annual Hawaii International Conference on System Sciences, Hawaii.

Joinson, A. N. (2003). *Understanding the psychology of Internet behaviour: Virtual worlds, real lives*. New York: Palgrave Macmillan.

Kiesler, S., Siegel, J., & McGuire, T. W. (1984). Social psychological aspects of computer-mediated communication. *American Psychologist, 39*(10), 1123–1134.

Lavoie, J. A. A., & Pychyl, T. A. (2001). Cyberslacking and the procrastination superhighway: A web-based survey of online procrastination, attitudes, and emotion. *Social Science Computer Review, 19*(4), 431–444.

Lea, M., O'Shea, T., Fung, P., & Spears, R. (1992). Flaming in computer-mediated communication: Observations, explanations, implications. In M. Lea (Ed.), *Contexts of computer-mediated communication* (pp. 89–122). New York: Harvester Wheatsheaf.

Lee, A., Schlueter, K., & Girgensohn, A. (1997). *Sensing activity in video images.* Paper presented at the CHI'97 (International Conference for Human-Computer Interaction), Atlanta, GA.

Liefooghe, A. P. D., & MacKenzie-Davey, K. (2001). Accounts of workplace bullying: The role of the organization. *European Journal of Work and Organizational Psychology, 10*(3), 375–392.

Lim, V. K. G. (2002). The IT way of loafing on the job: Cyberloafing, neutralizing and organizational justice. *Journal of Organizational Behavior, 23*(5), 675–694.

Lim, V. K. G., Teo, T. S. H., & Loo, G. L. (2002). How do I loaf here? Let me count the ways. *Communications of the ACM, 45*(1), 66–70.

Lipnack, J., & Stamps, J. (1997). *Virtual teams: Reaching across space, time, and organizations with technology.* New York: John Wiley & Sons.

Markus, M. L. (1990). Toward a 'critical mass' theory of interactive media. In J. Fulk & C. Steinfield (Eds.), *Organizations and Communication Technology* (pp. 194–218). Newbury Park, CA: Sage.

Markus, M. L., & Robey, D. (1988). Information technology and organizational change: Causal structure in theory and research. *Management Science, 34*(5), 583–598.

Martin, J. (1999). Internet policy: Employee rights and wrongs. *HR Focus, 75* (March), 11–12.

Mastrangelo, P. M., Everton, W., & Jolton, J. A. (2006). Personal use of work computers: Distraction versus destruction. *CyberPsychology & Behavior, 9*(6), 730–741.

Matus, R. (2005). Monster in your mailbox. *InBoxer.* Retrieved June 22, 2007, from http://www.inboxer.com/downloads/Monsters_In_Your_Mailbox.pdf.

Mazmanian, M., Yates, J., & Orlikowski, W. (2006). *Ubiquitous e-mail: Individual experiences and organizational consequences of Blackberry use.* Paper presented at the 65th Annual Meeting of the Academy of Management, Atlanta GA.

Nardi, B. A., Whittaker, S., & Bradner, E. (2000). *Interaction and outeraction: Instant messaging in action.* Paper presented at the 2000 ACM Conference on Computer Supported Cooperative Work, Philadelphia, PA.

Nohria, N., & Berkley, J. D. (1994). The virtual organization: Bureaucracy, technology, and the implosion of control. In C. Heckscher & A. Donnellon (Eds.), *The post-bureaucratic organization: New perspectives on organizational change* (pp. 108–128). Thousand Oaks, CA: Sage.

Novell, U. K. (1997). *Shaming, blaming and flaming: Corporate miscommunications in the digital age.* London: Novell.

O'Sullivan, P. B., & Flanagin, A. J. (2003). Reconceptualizing "flaming" and other problematic messages. *New Media & Society, 5*(1), 69–94.

Olson, M. H., & Primps, S. B. (1984). Working at home with computers: Work and nonwork issues. *Journal of Social Issues, 40*(3), 97–122.

Postmes, T., & Lea, M. (2000). Social processes and groups decision making: Anonymity in group decision support systems. *Ergonomics, 43*(11), 1252–1274.

Postmes, T., Spears, R., & Lea, M. (2000). The formation of group norms in computer-mediated communication. *Human Communication Research, 26*(3), 341–371.

Redding, W. C. (1996). Ethics and the study of organizational communication: When will we wake up? In J. A. Jaksa & M. S. Pritchard (Eds.), *Responsible communication: Ethical issues in business, industry, and the professions* (pp. 17–40). Cresskill, NJ: Hampton Press.

Richtel, M. (2003, July 6). The lure of data: Is it addictive? *The New York Times,* p. 1.

Rubinstein, J. S., Meyer, D. E., & Evans, J. E. (2001). Executive control of cognitive processes in task switching. *Journal of Experimental Psychology: Human Perception and Performance, 27*(4), 763–797.

Saetre, A. S., & Sornes, J. O. (2006). Working at home and playing at work: Using ICTs to break down the barriers between home and work. In S. K. May (Ed.), *Case Studies in Organizational Communication: Ethical Perspectives and Practices* (pp. 75–85). Thousand Oaks, CA: Sage.

Salvucci, D. D., Chavez, A. K., & Lee, F. J. (2004). *Modeling effects of age in complex tasks: A case study in driving.* Paper presented at the 26th Annual Conference of the Cognitive Science Society, Hillsdale, NJ.

Schick, A. G., Gordon, L. A., & Haka, S. (1990). Information overload: A temporal approach. *Accounting, Organizations and Society, 15*(3), 199–220.

Siegel, J., Dubrovsky, V., Kiesler, S., & McGuire, T. (1986). Group processes in computer-mediated communication. *Organizational Behaviour and Human Decision Processes, 37*(1), 157–187.

Solingen, R. V., Berghout, E., & Latum, F. V. (1998). Interrupts: Just a minute never is. *IEEE Software, 15*(5), 97–103.

Sproull, L., & Kiesler, S. (1991). *Connections: New ways of working in the networked organization.* Cambridge, MA: The MIT Press.

Swartz, N. (2005). Deleting spam costs businesses billions. *Information Management Journal, 39*(3), 10.

Tremblay, D.-G., Paquet, R., & Najem, E. (2006). Telework: A way to balance work and family or an increase in work-family conflict? *Canadian Journal of Communication, 31*(3), 715–731.

Turner, J. W., Grube, J., Tinsley, C., Lee, C., & O'Pell, C. (2006). Exploring the dominant media: How does media use reflect organizational norms and affect performance? *Journal of Business Communication, 43*(3), 220–250.

Urbaczewski, A., & Jessup, L. M. (2002). Does electronic monitoring of employee Internet usage work? *Communications of the ACM, 45*(1), 80–83.

Van den Berg, P. T., Roe, R. A., Zijlstra, F. R. H., & Krediet, I. (1996). Temperamental factors in the execution of interrupted editing tasks. *European Journal of Personality, 10*(1), 233–248.

Vault.com. (2005). 2005 Internet use in the workplace survey results. Retrieved August 16, 2007, from http://www.vault.com/surveys/internetusesurvey/home. jsp.

Visto. (2007). The key drivers for mobile e-mail adoption. *Visto Corporation and Global Market InSite, Inc.* Retrieved August 16, 2007, from http://www.visto. com/news/releases/pdfs/Global_Market_InSite_Research.pdf.

Wallis, C., & Steptoe, S. (2006). Help! I've lost my focus. *Time, 167,* 72–77.

Walther, J. B. (1995). Relational aspects of computer-mediated communication: Experimental observations over time. *Organizational Science, 6*(2), 186–203.

Walther, J. B. (1996). Computer-mediated communication: Impersonal, interpersonal, and hyperpersonal interaction. *Communication Research, 23*(1), 3–43.

Walther, J. B. (2007). Selective self-presentation in computer-mediated communication: Hyperpersonal dimensions of technology, language, and cognition. *Computers in Human Behavior, 23*(5), 2538–2557.

Walther, J. B., Anderson, J. K., & Park, D. W. (1994). Interpersonal effects in computer-mediated interaction: A meta-analysis of social and antisocial communication. *Communication Research, 21*(4), 460–487.

Williams, T., & Williams, R. (2006). Too much e-mail! *Communication World, 23*(6), 38–41.

Wilson, C. (2005). *Computer attack and cyberterrorism: Vulnerabilities and policy issues for Congress:* CRS Report for Congress, Congressional Research Service, The Library of Congress.

Wyatt, K., & Phillips, J. G. (2005). *Personality as a predictor of workplace Internet use.* Paper presented at the OZCHI2005, Canberra, Australia.

Zhang, Y., Goonetilleke, R. S., Plocher, T., & Liang, S. F. M. (2005). Time-related behaviour in multitasking situations. *International Journal of Human-Computer Studies, 62*(4), 425–455.

Zhou, L., Twitchell, D. P., Qin, T., Burgoon, J. K., & Nunamaker, J. F. (2003). *An exploratory study into deception detection in text-based computer-mediated communication.* Paper presented at the 36th Hawaii International Conference on Systems Sciences, Hawaii.

Zweig, D., & Webster, J. (2002). Where is the line between benign and invasive? An examination of psychological barriers to the acceptance of awareness monitoring systems. *Journal of Organizational Behavior, 23*(5), 605–633.

Chapter 12

Virtual Groups

(Mis) Attribution of Blame in Distributed Work

Natalya N. Bazarova and Joseph B. Walther

A relatively new form of organizational collaboration—virtual groups whose members communicate primarily or entirely via e-mail, computer conferencing, chat, or voice—has become a common feature of twenty-first century organizations. Virtual groups operate within organizations that have members spread out among different locations, or are made up of individuals from the same location but who work in different departments. Virtual groups are formed among members of different organizations for short-term alliances, or they allow individuals who are on-site at clients' offices to coordinate with partners in their home organizations.

Although technologies bridge physical distances and enable virtual collaboration, they also pose certain challenges to which virtual team members must accommodate in order to be successful. The challenges that are endemic in virtual teams include temporal delays in communication, disruptions in shared context and workflow, context and culture differences, and a slower rate of information exchange because of the absence of nonverbal and environmental cues that must be made up for by more verbiage. Although organizations find much benefit from such teams, the efforts required to make virtual groups operate beneficially are significant. "Organizations profit from the diversity and reach such teams can encompass. Yet the costs in making such teams work effectively are borne by the team members themselves" (Walther, Boos, & Jonas, 2002, p. 1).

Successful virtual collaboration requires group members to adjust behavior and expectations accordingly, and failure to do so is likely to damage group performance and social relations. Yet much of communication behavior is deeply engrained, and individuals are seldom intuitively able to recognize and adapt to the sociotechnical challenges of virtual collaboration. As a result, for reasons that are often elusive to them, virtual teams frequently experience low levels of trust. Team members may experience increased discontent, conflict, and frustration directed at other team members, and reduced affection, cohesion, and team identity (Cramton, 2002; Hinds & Bailey, 2003; Mortensen & Hinds, 2001; Wilson, Straus, & McEvily, 2006). One might think that communicators would regard negatively the technology that brings with it such problems. As we will discuss, however, blame is often placed elsewhere, exacerbating the very problems virtual teams experience.

Successful adaptation to virtual teams depends to a large extent on how people construe the problems they encounter, particularly regarding the type of explanations they make about their own and their partners' performance. "The cognitive interpretation of a negative outcome is a primary driving force in determining whether or not an individual chooses to engage in counterproductive behavior" (Martinko, Gundlach, & Douglas, 2002, p. 43). One common cognitive response to negative outcomes is avoiding personal responsibility for problems by focusing blame on unrelated or uncontrollable causes, such as coworkers' behavior. Such attributions are likely to result in negative emotional and evaluative reactions (i.e., anger and frustration) towards team members.

Focusing on unrelated causes has additional negative consequences for the attributor. Although externalizing blame can seem face-saving and protective of self-esteem, it can be damaging in the long run. By deflecting attention from the real problem, individuals deprive themselves of opportunities to learn from mistakes and adapt to virtual group interaction requirements. Explaining dysfunctions in a biased, self-absolving manner can lead to chronic failure or "self-sealing non-learning" (Gemmill, 1989, p. 410) because team members fail to thoroughly examine the communication system or their communicative practices in order to avoid problematic reoccurrences. On the whole, negative *attributions* or judgments about others in virtual teams can create barriers to successful communication and collaboration, lead to conflict escalation, and become detrimental to team performance.

In this chapter we discuss the basic premises of *attribution theory* and follow this with an examination of the impact of distance (e.g., physical separation, proximity, remoteness) and technological constraints on maladaptive attributions in virtual teams. In particular, we outline the destructive potential for this type of attributions. The chapter concludes with suggestions for reducing maladaptive attributions, repairing social relations, and increasing performance in virtual groups.

Attribution Theory and Virtual Groups

Attribution theory describes how people typically generate explanations for outcomes and actions—their own and others'. Making sense of the causes of behavior is a fundamentally important human drive enabling people to manage themselves and their social environment effectively. "By explaining behavior, people make sense of the social world, adapt to it, and shape it" (Malle, 1999, p. 23). According to this theory, people generate two basic types of attributional explanations for events: internal and external. Internal or dispositional attributions explain behavior based on an individual's intrinsic personality traits, something innate to that person. External or situational attributions assign causality to an outside agent or force, usually environmental pressures or constraints, something outside of the person or the person's control. Attributions guide actors' attitudes and actions towards others but are susceptible to systematic biases (see for review, Kelley & Michela, 1980; Seibold & Spitzberg, 1982).

Various factors can affect attributions, including perceivers' motivations and expectations, knowledge or lack thereof about target persons, available cognitive resources, and cultural norms. All of these can operate on attributional judgments independently of the actual characteristics of persons about whom attributions are made. Certain factors facilitate situational attributions, even when behavior was, in reality, a volitional act, and other factors prompt dispositional attributions, even when behavior was, in reality, a result of environmental forces.

Attribution research has identified several biases that affect whether an individual is likely to assign dispositional versus situational explanations. The *fundamental attribution error* (Ross, 1977) is people's common penchant for exaggerating dispositional characteristics while ignoring situational constraints on the behavior. For example, inferring that a poor-performing group member is lazy and irresponsible, without regard to the situational factors affecting his or her participation (e.g., an approaching deadline for another project, illness, problems with technology, etc.), is an example of this error.

A kind of attributional bias, *the actor-observer bias* focuses on a difference in attributions people make for their own behavior (which tend to be situational) versus someone else's behavior they observe (which tend to be dispositional) (Jones & Nisbett, 1971). The *fundamental attribution error* overlooks this disparity. Relatedly, the *self-serving bias* occurs when people attribute their failure and success in a self-serving and ego-defensive manner by attributing failure to external factors, and success to internal factors. These distorted impressions can have potentially dire consequences for individuals' successful conduct at work, such as denial of one's contribution to the problem, avoidance of a conflict issue or a partner, blaming partners, withholding information, escalating conflict, and other aspects of relationship distress (see for review Manusov, 2007; Martinko, Douglas, & Harvey, 2006).

Attributional dynamics are well known in a variety of settings, from simple experimental tests to judgments by relationship partners. Their significance for virtual groups is critical, however, as several of the characteristics that epitomize virtual group interaction may lead in systematic ways to attribution biases. If the unique characteristics that accompany virtual collaboration are prone to systematic biases in attribution patterns, such biased attributions will hinder adaptation to virtual group work and become barriers to effective communication and collaboration.

Virtual group members face situational constraints unknown to one another because of physical separation and reliance on the limited communication cues in technologically-mediated communication. As a result, members usually have less than complete information about why their partners take or fail to take action, with respect to group activities. How these potentially influential factors—differences in remote versus local context and constraints, coupled with the use of computer-mediated communication (CMC)—affect attributions may be an underlying source of virtual team members' problems. That is, physical separation and mediated communication exacerbate the attributional biases, often self-serving and inaccurate, that people have about self and others in virtual working relationships. To date, two different perspectives have been proposed to account for the role of distance on attributions in virtual groups, attributions for other virtual team members and for one's own behavior in a virtual team. The next section summarizes recent research on attributions in virtual teams, ways to avoid maladaptive attributions, repair social relations, and improve performance in virtual teams.

Effects of Mutual Knowledge on Attributions

Despite a proclamation by a senior editor at the *Economist* that new communication technology can usher in *"The Death of Distance"* (Cairncross, 1997), digital technologies which bridge physical distances may not bridge *social* distances between people (Olson & Olson, 2000). "Distance will persist as an important element of human experience. Differences in local physical context, time zones, culture, and language all persist in spite of the use of distance technologies" (Olson & Olson, p. 2). Indeed, despite advances in technology, differences in physical context, time zones, culture, and language affect the communication and mutual knowledge collaborators must develop.

Communication through computer-mediated channels, in the absence of a shared physical space, requires greater effort. Additional energy must be expended to maintain the commonly shared frame of reference between partners that is necessary for communication efficiency and conversational cooperation (Clark & Marshall, 1981; Fussell & Krauss, 1992). Furthermore, the lack of a shared physical location makes oblique partners' nonverbal cues and some mutual knowledge (e.g., local events and schedules, members' presence or absence) that would normally be apparent in co-located, non-mediated settings (Cramton, 2002; Kraut, Fussell, Brennan, & Siegel, 2002).

In addition to the challenges of establishing mutual knowledge and common ground, a perception of communication partners' closeness or distance, in and of itself, affects cooperation, persuasion, and even decep-tion. For example, when participants in a CMC chat experiment believed that they were communicating with someone in a different part of the country, they gave more deceptive answers, were persuaded less, and were initially less willing to cooperate than when participants believed their partners were in the same city (Bradner & Mark, 2002).

Geographical distance between partners can also systematically affect attributions virtual partners make for one another. When compared to collocated partners, geographically distributed partners experience greater failures in mutual knowledge because of difficulties in accessing, communicating, and retaining remote partners' contextual information (Cramton, 2001). As a result, they committed greater fundamental attri-bution error, compared to their collocated counterparts (Cramton, 2001, 2002). That is, they blamed remote partners' personalities and characters, without acknowledging the role of situational factors in their partners' behavior, such as partners' local contexts and constraints.

As perceivers of others, remote communicators' *information deficits* and *cognitive preoccupation*—issues identified in psychological research that inflate the fundamental attribution error—are especially salient. Not only do remote partners have no immediate access to one another's con-text, but also information pertaining to multiple locations has to be inte-grated, updated, and shared via a text-based medium without nonverbal cues. Such communicative work requires more of individuals' cognitive resources and time than collocated work does. These demands often prompt negative dispositional inferences about remote partners. Without knowledge to the contrary, and without cognitive receptivity to competing explanations, virtual group members are frequently disposed to blame their remote partners' personalities for conflicts within the virtual group.

In Cramton's (2001) study, participant diaries and group records seemed to mirror many aspects of this attribution framework and has become a hallmark study of virtual groups. At the same time, Cramton herself admonished readers that the application demanded explicit hypothesis-testing and experimental confirmation. Indeed, results of other studies seeking to verify the fundamental attribution error in virtual groups have generated mixed empirical support and led to revisions or appropriation of other strains of attribution theory to account for the problems of virtual groups.

One empirical experiment, which found more dispositional attributions for physically distributed partners than collocated partners, examined pairs of subjects who worked together online from different rooms or in the same room (Cramton, Orvis, & Wilson, 2007). Dyad members worked together to answer a series of questions varying in difficulty, together or separately. In each case, one member was a confederate answering questions based on personal knowledge. The naïve dyad participant could use a booklet of questions and answers as an aid in the task. Whether dyad members were together or separate led to obvious differences in the collaboration conditions. Same-room subjects attributed their confederate partners' poor performance to situational factors (e.g., partner had no access to the booklet) rather than to inadequate ability or effort. In contrast, separated dyad members tended to explain their confederate partners' failing performance on the confederates' dispositions. Although this study establishes that physical proximity renders others' situational constraints more obvious to working partners, whether these patterns generalize to virtual working teams is less than clear. That is, these results may not generalize to the common knowledge issues that derive from geographic and institutional differences that Cramton (2001) originally considered in her application of attribution theory to virtual groups.

Our subsequent research expanding on Cramton's work tested the effect of collocation versus distribution on attributions using virtual teams (Bazarova & Walther, 2005). In this study we employed virtual groups, the members of which were either completely collocated (from the same college and the same geographical locale) or completely distributed (from different colleges and different geographical locales). After working for two weeks on a decision-making task via an asynchronous discussion board, group members reported whether their respective partners' behavior was due to dispositional or situational factors (e.g., geographical distances, generic situational factors, influence of other group members, communication medium).

Contrary to Cramton's (2001) earlier findings, the lack of a common location did not inflate dispositional attributions in our virtual teams. Rather, the collocated members made greater *dispositional* judgments about partners than did the distributed partners. There were no significant differences in *situational* attributions between distributed and collocated groups in this regard. In another study, this pattern held true for conflict in virtual teams (Mortensen & Hinds, 2001). The direct comparison between collocated and distributed teams examined the effect of distance on the teams' conflict dynamics and found similar levels of conflict in distributed and collocated groups.

These findings suggest that although collocated work provides greater knowledge about partners and situational factors than does distributed work, a lack of this knowledge does not necessarily inflate distributed team members' dispositional biases. Several explanations for the differences are possible. First, some empirical studies regarding attributions in collocated and distributed groups employed both collocated and distributed teams in their empirical studies and others did not. It is unclear whether attributional biases are unique to distributed collaborators and uncommon to collocated groups. Second, attributional patterns depend, to some extent, on whether the judged behaviors are evaluated as positive or negative (see, Malle, 2006). For example, some studies of mediated teams focus only on negative behaviors (e.g., conflict episodes, problematic performance) and others examine attributions for both positive and negative behaviors.

The virtual group setting stretches traditional attribution theory beyond its typical boundaries in several ways. The iterative and cumulative effects of communication with targets, the mediated nature of observations, and the active participation with the target (rather than passive observation) are uncommon in traditional attribution research. Nevertheless, these dynamics are common in virtual group work and have to be accounted for in understanding how virtual colleagues make attributions about one another and exchange situational information.

Effects of Distances on Attributions of Self

An alternative approach to exploring problematic attributions in virtual groups has focused on how distances between partners might affect attributions for one's own behavior, as opposed to attributions of others' behavior. This approach poses the question, "What if interactions with relatively unknown, distant partners systematically bias perceptions of our own behavior, rather than the judgments we make about our partners?" (Walther & Bazarova, 2007, p. 3). In contrast to how deficits in mutual knowledge affect attributions about virtual partners, self-attribution focuses on attributors' motivational concerns, and how those may be aroused differently in interactions with remote (versus collocated) partners.

In order to enhance or maintain self-esteem, individuals tend to overemphasize situational explanations for their own action and overlook situational explanations for others' behavior—the actor-observer bias (see also, Watson, 1982). Relatedly, a self-serving bias, which can serve to protect actors' egos, results in finding fault in something other than themselves for their own misdeeds. Since group communication involves interactions with numerous others, it provides additional targets for other-blaming attributions. Indeed, in any social interaction, actors can attributionally allude that others are the situational causes of their behavior, even when they could have attributed outcomes to the general situation or themselves (Robins, Mendelsohn, & Spranca, 1996). Participants often report that their partners made them act the way they did in an interactive setting. Potentially interactional partners are more dynamic, pertinent cues than the physical environment (Jones & Nisbett, 1971).

In virtual groups the self-serving bias might be more likely in the way people account for themselves, especially their own negative actions. "Partner blame may become the favored antidote to negative dispositional self-construals" (Walther & Bazarova, 2007, p. 4). Moreover, this tendency seems even more likely to occur when certain virtual group partners are less known and presumably dissimilar to the attributing actor. This suggests that remote partners are especially likely to shoulder attributional blame for individuals' own poor performance. This self-serving partner blame resembles scapegoating. "Scapegoats are created by others who are anxious to attach blame and absolve their personal responsibilities" (Bonazzi, 1983, p. 3). In virtual group settings, unknown and unseen partners can provide "a salient and less esteem-threatening target on which to blame one's own poor performance rather than acknowledge personal responsibility for problems in communication, coordination, and action" (Walther & Bazarova, 2007, p. 4).

In contrast, when virtual group members are collocated, the tendency to deflect blame towards partners may be curtailed. This is the case even if collocated members merely reside in the same locale, with similar local circumstances, and have not met or communicated face-to-face. If collocated members sense that their colleagues' situations are similar to their own, they may perceive that others' situational and contextual circumstances resemble theirs. Therefore, when an individual's behavior is discrepant from others, there is no faceless, distant target to blame, and the offending individual might be more likely to focus blame on him- or herself.

Blaming other group members is less likely when members know and like each other (e.g., Leary & Forsyth, 1987). It is also less likely when more risk is involved for doing so and greater accountability for inaccurate explanations. Communication partners' collocation, even when not face-to-face, makes partner-blaming riskier and raises accountability, as proximity increases the real and perceived likelihood of future interaction with people to whom we are likely to be accountable (Latane, Liu, Nowak, Benevento, & Zheng, 1995). Moreover, anticipated interaction increases interpersonal liking, a particularly potent effect in CMC groups that transcends context (Walther, 1994). Consequently, collocated group members often take more personal responsibility for poor performance in virtual communication than members of distributed groups.

These patterns were tested in a field experiment, in which individuals worked in three- and four-member groups on a funding allocation decision (Walther & Bazarova, 2007). Groups communicated strictly via the Internet, using an asynchronous bulletin group discussion facility, and had two weeks to arrive at a decision. Virtual groups were completely collocated, completely distributed, or geographically mixed (two members from the same school and the remaining two from two different schools). After the groups finished their task, group members answered open-ended questions about their worst and best behavior in the project and what they thought had caused these behaviors. ("Why do you think you did that?")

Distributed group members identified partners as the cause of their own negative behaviors more frequently than did the members of collocated virtual groups. That is, they made situational attributions that focused on their partners as the cause of their own actions. Members of collocated groups, on the other hand, more frequently acknowledged their own characteristics and deficiencies in identifying the cause of their poor performances than did members of distributed groups. Members of the geographically mixed groups, like those in the completely distributed groups, admitted little personal responsibility for performance problems. However, the degree to which they blamed partners was less extreme than in distributed groups (Walther & Bazarova, 2007).

Overall, this suggests that the rationalizations individuals offer for their own negative behavior in virtual groups are systematically influenced by collocation or dispersion of partners. Members of completely distributed groups less often acknowledge personal responsibility and instead more often blame their partners. When individuals work with unseen, unknown, remote partners in short-term distributed groups, those remote individuals can become scapegoats for individuals' own performance decrements. In contrast, when one's group partners feel closer, simply by virtue of being from the same geographical location or institutional affiliation—even when they have not met face-to-face—individuals less frequently scapegoat those partners. Rather, collocated group partners take more personal responsibility for their dysfunctional behavior, as shown in greater dispositional self-attributions (Walther & Bazarova, 2007).

Thus, empirical findings suggest that geographical distances between group members bias the attributions people make for their own and possibly for others' behavior in virtual groups. Biased attributions can disrupt the conduct of virtual groups and can be destructive for both current and future virtual collaboration. A failure to recognize one's own dispositional culpability and one's own need to adjust behavior and expectations to situational constraints of computer-mediated collaboration is likely to impede individual learning and development, especially when participants work in future virtual interactions (Walther et al., 2002). Furthermore, partner-focused attributions and blame create a negative group climate, with mistrust, frustration, hostility, and aspersions directed at remote partners' personalities (Cramton, 2001). Such groups are likely to experience performance losses because of the counterproductive behaviors that typically accompany maladaptive attributions and negative emotions: withholding information from remote partners, excluding remote partners from communication, pursuing of individual rather than group goals, and being unwilling to acknowledge and solve problems (see, Weiner, 1995).

In contrast, a psychologically safe communication climate can mitigate the negative effects engendered by virtual team interactions due to geography, electronic dependency, and dynamic structure (Gibson & Gibbs,

2006). A psychologically safe group communication climate is "characterized by support, openness, trust, mutual respect, and risk taking" (Gibson & Gibbs, p. 462), one that facilitates innovation, constructive discussion, information provision, openness to new perspectives, and suspension of judgment. In order to create such a climate, finding ways to reduce attributional biases directed at remote partners is essential. In the remainder of this chapter, we review the ways that research has found to deter attribution biases and repair social relations and performance in distributed groups.

Constructive Organizing to Repair Attributional Biases in Distributed Groups

Noting that, if attributions are the problem, attributions may be the solution, research has explored ways to mitigate attribution biases and help virtual group members constructively adjust their judgments and behaviors. That is, attribution judgments are malleable. "Inferences can ... be externally manipulated by cues and reminders as to the possible relation to the effect of certain plausible causes ... they lead the attributor to consider as he interprets the observed cause-effect evidence" (Kelley, 1971, p. 170).

One method to redirect virtual group members' attributions from partner-blaming is by having mediated practice sessions using collocated groups that focus on needed adaptations to technology. When there are no distant, unknown partners to scapegoat, virtual group participants are more likely to take personal responsibility for their misdeeds. Without a faceless distant partner upon which to attribute blame, team members can be more cognizant of their own performance. When actors learn to become aware of their mistakes and how to change them in practice sessions, this may trigger adaptations in subsequent distributed virtual work.

This strategy was tested in a study involving a sequence of collocated and geographically mixed online groups (Walther et al., 2002). After experiencing poor performance in mediated groups with collocated partners, participants admitted to procrastination and sporadic communication, but also displayed an inclination to approach things differently next time. In a second round of collaboration with both local and internationally-distributed partners, group members demonstrated superior interpersonal attraction and performance, compared to teams with no collocated sessions who worked in a sequence of distributed groups. This suggests at least one way to alter attribution biases.

A different and more direct method to reduce dispositional biases is by raising awareness about situational factors that affect behavior and communication in virtual groups. For instance, in Cramton et al.'s (2007) study, when isolated dyad members were made aware of the situational constraints on one partner's behavior (having no access to the answer list), the other partner's dispositional biases went away. Another strategy is to raise attention and awareness of the potential situational bases of behavior in virtual groups via the induction of inferential goals, a cognitive intervention adopted from psychological research. Instructions to participants establish the inferential goals of looking for certain dynamics during interactions with partners. Whereas people are generally predisposed to initially characterize events in dispositional terms (Gilbert, Pelham, & Krull, 1988), with the establishment of inferential goals, they may be successfully induced to redirect their sensemaking processes to focus on situational causes (Krull, 1993; Krull & Dill, 1996; Lee & Hallahan, 2001; Webster, 1993).

In our work we used an inferential goal induction to draw distributed members' attention to situational factors and thus encourage situational attributions to group issues (Walther & Bazarova, 2007). Some participants were told, "Different situational factors can explain how people behave and communicate. As you work on this project, please try to note what role different situational factors (e.g., geographical location, electronic medium, etc.) may play in your group discussion." Written instructions and e-mail participation reminders reinforced this goal. Although the goal statement was recalled by only half of the members to whom it was directed, for these members the goal statement raised their attention to the constraints associated with the computer-mediated channel. They commented on coordination difficulties in the mediated discussions: asynchronous nature of communication, "no set times to meet with the group," a technical problem with the system access, unfamiliarity with the online discussion boards, and the message directness because of the absence of nonverbal cues. All these were attributed to behavior and participation in the project. This suggests that although distances appear to bias attributions of blame toward remote partners, attributional biases can be repaired with an orientation inculcated through a situational inferential goal.

There are other constructive ways to repair social relations and increase performance in virtual groups that potentially deter attributional biases. Most are directed at facilitating group members' accommodations to the social and technical requirements of CMC. One method involves distributed team members in a relatively long-term collaboration. Biased attributions can dissipate in long-term groups as members of such groups are often motivated to seek and provide positive interpersonal information and relational communication. Over time, relationships in distributed teams can improve and become more harmonious as familiarity and shared context awareness increase (e.g., Mortensen & Hinds, 2001; Walther, 1995).

Other efforts to improve virtual group communication include providing behavioral guidance to the group through interaction procedures or "rules of virtual groups." Such rules aim at increasing interaction time and shared context among group members: starting early with the production phase of the work, communicating frequently, providing explicit verbal feedback, and observing deadlines (Walther & Bunz, 2005). Adherence to the rules appears to improve the groups' social climate and increase trust and liking, both of which can reduce biased attributions about remote members.

Research also suggests a beneficial effect from a virtual team's shared identity; such a group identity can mitigate the negative effects of distance and mediation. A shared social identity, shared context, and spontaneous communication can be associated with reduced conflict and improved group performance in distributed teams (Hinds & Mortensen, 2005). In experiments with offline groups, the recipe for creating a team identity can sometimes be as simple as developing a team name, identifying a common goal, fostering interdependence, and creating a feeling of ownership over a group project. There is much to be learned about whether these or other strategies work as well for virtual groups.

Conclusion

This chapter offers a review of recent attribution research regarding communication in virtual groups. When group members operate at disparate locations and use CMC to communicate and organize their efforts, which is increasingly common work configuration in contemporary organizations, they are prone to systematic biases in the judgments they make for the causes of group behavior. We have examined two different attributional frameworks in virtual teams—one attributing responsibility to others, the other attributing responsibility to oneself. This review underscores that perceivers' dispersion condition—their collocation or remoteness from virtual partners—affects how they interpret the causes of behavior. Along with distances, different situational characteristics of virtual group work—computer mediation, members' active participation, iterative and cumulative effects of communication with targets—may also influence attributions. These elements need to be integrated into conceptual thinking about attributions in virtual groups and the effects thereof.

Physical distances between partners emerge as a powerful situational factor shaping attribution patterns in virtual groups. The presence of a distant colleague provides a cognitively salient and convenient target for blame, which allows discounting of one's own personal responsibility in distributed collaboration. Unless corrected, misattribution of blame threatens a positive group climate by stirring negative emotions and counterproductive actions directed at distributed partners. Furthermore, it interferes with cognizance of one's own need for improvement or corrective action, leading to future adaptation failures to the situational demands of virtual group work.

Managers of virtual groups need to take into account these tendencies, which, if left unchecked, disrupt the groups and the work that distributed colleagues strive to complete. Moreover, these tendencies can occlude the possibility of improvement by the deflection of blame away from actors' faulty participation. Research in virtual groups should attend to new and improved methods of eliciting and redirecting the cognitive forces of virtual group members in a way that saves face for participants so partner-blame is not felt to be necessary. Group work is difficult enough, and virtual group work even more so, in part due to the innate but malleable tendencies that lead distant collaborators to focus blame where it may not belong.

References

Bazarova, N. N., & Walther, J. B. (2005, May). *Attributional judgments in virtual teams*. Paper presented at the International Communication Association Annual Conference, New York.

Bonazzi, G. (1983). Scapegoating in complex organizations: The results of a comparative study of symbolic blame-giving in Italian and French public administration. *Organization Studies, 4*(1), 1–18.

Bradner, E., & Mark, G. (2002, November). *Why distance matters: Effects on cooperation, persuasion, and deception*. Paper presented at the ACM Conference on Computer Supported Cooperative Work, New Orleans, LA.

Cairncross, F. (1997). *The death of distance: How the communications revolution is changing our lives*. London: Texere Publishing.

Clark, H. H., & Marshall, C. R. (1981). Definite reference and mutual knowledge. In A. K. Joshi, B. Webber & I. Sag (Eds.), *Elements of discourse understanding* (pp. 10–63). Cambridge: Cambridge University Press.

Cramton, C. D. (2001). The mutual knowledge problem and its consequences for dispersed collaboration. *Organization Science, 12*(3), 346–371.

Cramton, C. D. (2002). Attribution in distributed work groups. In P. J. Hinds & S. Kiesler (Eds.), *Distributed work* (pp. 191–212). Cambridge: MIT Press.

Cramton, C. D., Orvis, K. L., & Wilson, J. M. (2007). Situational invisibility and attribution in distributed collaborations. *Journal of Management, 33*(4), 525–546.

Fussell, S. R., & Krauss, R. M. (1992). Coordination of knowledge in communication: Effects of speakers' assumptions about what others know. *Journal of Personality and Social Psychology, 62*(3), 378–391.

Gemmill, G. (1989). The dynamics of scapegoating in small groups. *Small Group Behavior, 20*(3), 406–418.

Gibson, C. B., & Gibbs, J. L. (2006). Unpacking the concept of virtuality: The effects of geographic dispersion, electronic dependence, dynamic structure, and national diversity on team innovation. *Administrative Science Quarterly, 51*(4), 451–495.

Gilbert, D. T., Pelham, B. W., & Krull, D. S. (1988). On cognitive busyness: When person perceivers meet persons perceived. *Journal of Personality and Social Psychology, 54*(5), 733–740.

Hinds, P. J., & Bailey, D. E. (2003). Out of sight, out of sync: Understanding conflict in distributed teams. *Organization Science, 14*(6), 615–632.

Hinds, P. J., & Mortensen, M. (2005). Understanding conflict in distributed teams: An empirical investigation. *Organization Science, 16*(3), 290–307.

Jones, E. E., & Nisbett, R. E. (1971). The actor and the observer: Divergent perceptions of the causes of behavior. In E. E. Jones, D. E. Kanouse, H. H. Kelley, R. E. Nisbett, S. Valins & B. Weiner (Eds.), *Attribution: Perceiving the causes of behavior* (pp. 79–94). Morristown, NJ: General Learning Press.

Kelley, H. H. (1971). Causal schemata and the attribution process. In E. E. Jones, D. E. Kanouse, H. H. Kelley, R. E. Nisbett, S. Valins & B. Weiner (Eds.), *Attribution: Perceiving the causes of behavior* (pp. 151–174). Morristown, NJ: General Learning Press.

Kelley, H. H., & Michela, J. L. (1980). Attribution theory and research. *Annual Review of Psychology, 31*(4), 457–501.

Kraut, R. E., Fussell, S. R., Brennan, S. E., & Siegel, J. (2002). Understanding effects of proximity on collaboration: implications for technologies to support remote collaborative work. In P. J. Hinds & S. Kiesler (Eds.), *Distributed work* (pp. 137–163). Cambridge: MIT Press.

Krull, D. S. (1993). Does the grist change the mill? The effect of the perceiver's inferential goal on the process of social inference. *Personality and Social Psychology Bulletin, 19*(3), 340–348.

Krull, D. S., & Dill, J. C. (1996). On thinking first and responding fast: Flexibility in social inference processes. *Personality and Social Psychology Bulletin, 22*(9), 949–959.

Latane, B., Liu, J. H., Nowak, A., Benevento, M., & Zheng, L. (1995). Distance matters: Physical space and social impact. *Personality and Social Psychology Bulletin, 21*(8), 795–805.

Leary, M. R., & Forsyth, D. R. (1987). Attributions of responsibility for collective endeavors. *Review of Personality and Social Psychology, 8*(2), 167–188.

Lee, F., & Hallahan, M. (2001). Do situational expectations produce situational inferences? The role of future expectations in directing inferential goals. *Journal of Personality and Social Psychology, 80*(4), 545–556.

Malle, B. F. (1999). How people explain behavior: A new theoretical framework. *Personality and Social Psychology Review, 3*(1), 23–48.

Malle, B. F. (2006). The actor-observer asymmetry in causal attribution: A (surprising) meta-analysis. *Psychological Bulletin, 132*(6), 895–919.

Manusov, V. (2007). Attributions and interpersonal communication: Out of our heads and into behavior. In D. R. Rosko-Ewoldson & J. Monahan (Eds.), *Communication and social cognition: Theories and methods* (pp. 41–169). Mahwah, NJ: Lawrence Erlbaum Associates.

Martinko, M. J., Douglas, S. C., & Harvey, P. (2006). Attribution theory in industrial and organizational psychology: A review. In G. P. Hodgkinson & J. K. Ford (Eds.), *International Review of Industrial and Organizational Psychology* (Vol. 21, pp. 128–187). West Sussex: John Wiley & Sons.

Martinko, M. J., Gundlach, M. J., & Douglas, S. C. (2002). Toward an integrative theory of counterproductive workplace behavior: A casual reasoning perspective. *International Journal of Selection and Assessment, 10*(1), 36–50.

Mortensen, M., & Hinds, P. (2001). Conflict and shared identity in geographically distributed teams. *International Journal of Conflict Management,* 12(2), 212–238.

Olson, G. M., & Olson, J. S. (2000). Distance matters. *Human-Computer Interaction,* 15(1), 139–178.

Robins, R. W., Mendelsohn, G. A., & Spranca, M. D. (1996). The actor-observer effect revisited: Effects of individual differences and repeated social interactions on actor and observer differences. *Journal of Personality and Social Psychology,* 71(3), 375–389.

Ross, L. (1977). The intuitive psychologist and his shortcomings: Distortions in the attribution process. In L. Berkowitz (Ed.), *Advances in experimental social psychology* (pp. 173–220). New York: Academic Press.

Seibold, D. R., & Spitzberg, B. (1982). Attribution theory and research: Review and implications for communication. In B. J. Dervin & M. J. Voight (Eds.), *Progress in Communication Sciences* (Vol. 3, pp. 85–125). Norwood, NJ: Ablex.

Walther, J. B. (1994). Anticipated ongoing interaction versus channel effects on relational communication in computer-mediated interaction. *Human Communication Research,* 20(4), 473–501.

Walther, J. B. (1995). Relational aspects of computer-mediated communication: Experimental observations over time. *Organizational Science,* 6(2), 186–203.

Walther, J. B., & Bazarova, N. N. (2007). Misattribution in virtual groups: The effects of member distribution on self-serving bias and partner blame. *Human Communication Research,* 33(1), 1–26.

Walther, J. B., Boos, M., & Jonas, K. J. (2002). *Misattribution and attributional redirection in distributed virtual groups.* Paper presented at the 35th Hawaii International Conference on System Sciences, Hawaii.

Walther, J. B., & Bunz, U. (2005). The rules of virtual groups: Trust, liking, and performance in computer-mediated communication *Journal of Communication,* 55(4), 828–846.

Watson, D. (1982). The actor and the observer: How are their perceptions of causality divergent? *Psychological Bulletin,* 92(3), 683–700.

Webster, D. M. (1993). Motivated augmentation and reduction of the overattribution bias. *Journal of Personality and Social Psychology,* 65(2), 261–271.

Weiner, B. (1995). *Judgments of responsibility: A foundation for a theory of social conduct.* New York: The Guilford Press.

Wilson, J. M., Straus, S. G., & McEvily, W. J. (2006). All in due time: The development of trust in computer-mediated and face-to-face groups. *Organizational Behavior and Human Decision Processes,* 99(1), 16–33.

Chapter 13

Communication That Damages Teamwork

The Dark Side of Teams

David R. Seibold, Paul Kang, Bernadette M. Gailliard, and Jody Jahn

Teams are small groups of organizational members who possess comple-mentary characteristics, share a common goal, and are mutually account-able for their performance (Katzenbach & Smith, 1993). Organizational teams range from intact work units, through cross-functional groups (e.g., project teams), to ad hoc aggregates (e.g., discussion groups in high-involvement organizations). The latter two typically have a focused purpose and shorter lifecycle than other organizational teams (e.g., self-managing teams), which span multiple tasks and persist over time (Arrow, McGrath, & Berdahl, 2000).

Implementation of teams in U.S. organizations increased during the 1980s and 1990s, part of larger trends toward the modeling of such struc-tures from collectivistic cultures, the commitment to participation processes in the workplace, the "flattening" of traditional organizational hierarchies for reasons of cost reduction, and the potential for collabora-tion afforded by communication technologies (Seibold & Shea, 2001). The use of problem-solving groups in *Fortune* 1000 companies increased from 74% during 1987 to 91% in 1992, and self-managing teams in those organizations increased from 27% to 68% in the same six-year period (Lawler, Mohrmann, & Ledford, 1992). By 1999, 78% of U.S. companies relied upon self-managing teams of employees (Lawler, 1999). Although the percentage of self-managed teams remained constant through 2005, *Fortune* 1000 organizations utilizing employee participation programs, including discussion teams, increased to 90% (O'Toole & Lawler, 2006). A national random sample, as well as a survey of organizations known to use teams, concluded that over one-half of U.S. organizations use teams (Devine, Clayton, Philips, Dunford, & Melner, 1999). Ongoing project teams were the most commonly used type, ad hoc project teams second most common, and production teams existed in more that 20% of U.S. organizations. Most teams were cross-functional, and teams were most prevalent in nonprofit organizations.

As teams have become more pervasive, attention has focused on team effectiveness and success (Seibold, 2005). *Teamwork* is among the most examined topics, both in scholarly work and popular treatments (e.g., Bacon & Blyton, 2005; Larson & LaFasto, 1989). Phrases such as "Teamwork makes the dream work" and "There's no I in team" are increasingly championed by managers and trainers and intoned by members.

Despite the dramatic increase in teams, and correlative focus on teamwork, many American workers are disinclined to collaborate with others in team structures. Organization-wide structural problems undermine team efficacy and frustrate team members, including lack of goal clarity, inadequate resources, insufficient training, misaligned reward systems, coordination demands, and leaders who fail to model effective teamwork (Hackman, 1990). And a host of negative individual, relational, and subgroup relational dynamics (Fritz & Omdahl, 2006)—including gossip, incivility, retaliation, bullying, maladaptive coping strategies, negativity biases, style differences, role conflict and power struggles, and outright conflict—make the idea of teamwork ring hollow. Small wonder that potential members experience grouphate (Sorenson, 1981), the predisposition "to detest, loathe, or abhor working in groups" (Keyton & Frey, 2002, p. 109). Organizational members frequently cringe at the mention of teamwork, which they associate with lengthy, inefficient, emotionally-draining experiences that they endure with fake smiles and hope to escape without offending others.

We examine these and other issues regarding teams. To do so, we adopt a multilevel perspective in this chapter and review individual, dyadic, subgroup, group, organizational, and environmental factors contributing to the dark side of teams. We begin by describing teams *with teamwork*—the bright side—including the dimensions along which teamwork must be built to be effective. Next, we conceptualize the dark side and outline the multilevel framework for understanding this destructive potential in teams. We follow this by discussing factors at the subordinate (individual, dyad, subgroup), group, and superordinate (organization, environment) levels that constitute teams in particularly destructive ways. Prior to concluding with how teams might organize in more constructive ways, we explore a cross-level demonstration of dark-side dynamics to illustrate the complexity of issues that challenge constructive team communication.

Teams with Teamwork: The Bright Side

Teams *with teamwork* are those in which members share and can articulate a team vision that transcends short-term goals. Members with high levels of teamwork also have defined, valued, and accepted role expectations, and enjoy some degree of role-related autonomy. They set high standards for themselves (as opposed to having standards imposed by managers) and are self-disciplined. They develop a structure that is responsive to environmental demands, yet appropriate for the organization.

Members in teams with teamwork make important decisions within the team (in contradistinction to having decisions made for them from atop the unit). Members share leadership, have a formal team leader who emphasizes personally fulfilling activities and works to secure resources that the team needs to excel collectively, or both. High levels of teamwork are most evident in the quality of member interactions: they freely share information and interpretations with each other, acknowledge and reinforce others' contributions and support, and convey and display mutual respect and trust with one another (see Seibold, 1995 for an early formulation and discussion of four dimensions underlying teamwork—vision, roles, processes, and relationships).

Teams with strong and enduring teamwork tend to experience greater productivity, more innovation and creativity, and higher levels of member satisfaction (O'Toole & Lawler, 2006). However, not all teams develop effective teamwork in the first place, and many that do are unable to manage the challenges to sustained teamwork. Indeed, the confluence of individual, dyadic, subgroup, group, organizational, and environmental forces lead many teams to organize and communicate in ways destructive to individuals, subgroups, organizations, and the groups themselves. We address this aspect of teams, their "dark side," throughout this chapter. First, however, we clarify what we mean by the term "dark side."

Conceptualizing the Dark Side

The dark side of teams includes both intentional and unintentional forces and behaviors that impede effective, constructive teamwork and have the potential to harm organizations and their members. Dark-side team interactions can be intentional because some behaviors are enacted specifically to sabotage, undermine, violate, or disrupt teamwork (e.g., withholding information, mobbing). They also can be unintentional because some efforts are meant to facilitate teamwork but fail to do so as a result of unforeseen and incompatible circumstances (e.g., excessive group homogeneity, time pressures, geographical dispersion). In conceptualizing the dark side this way, we adopt a broad interpretation of the metaphor and extend the work of interpersonal communication scholars:

> First, the dark side is about the dysfunctional, distorted, distressing and destructive aspects of human behavior. Second, the dark side dallies with deviance, betrayal, transgression, and violation, which includes awkward, rude, and disruptive aspects of human behavior. Third, the dark side delves into the direct and indirect implications of human exploitation. Fourth, the dark side seeks to shed light on the unfulfilled, unpotentiated, underestimated, and unappreciated domains of human endeavor. Fifth, the dark side [studies] the

unattractive, the unwanted, the distasteful, and the repulsive. Sixth, the dark side seeks to understand the process of objectification—of symbolically and interactionally reducing humans to mere objects. Finally, the dark side is drawn to the paradoxical, dialectical ... aspects of life. (Cupach & Spitzberg, 2007, p. 5)

We embrace this view for two reasons. First, although scholars have studied the dark side of group processes (e.g., Janis, 1972; Stohl & Schell, 1991), they are the exception; researchers and practitioners predominantly concentrate on improving the functional aspects of groups (i.e., the bright side). Second, as we discuss below, although there are important differences between dyadic and group communication, much of group communication is dyadic: leader-member, team member-team member, team member-coworker from another team. Hence, some of the dark side dynamics revealed by interpersonal researchers also have resonance for teams and teamwork.

Multilevel Approach

The seemingly simple difference in size between dyads and groups as small as three members affects numerous dynamics among members: influence, affiliation, role differentiation, task factors, and communication factors (Parks, 1974). Indeed, Parks presents ten conceptual distinctions between dyads and groups of three or more persons. In groups (a) leadership is more pronounced, (b) formation of subgroups is possible, (c) power and authority is less constrained, (d) messages of disagreement are more frequent, (e) activity and involvement is both less intense and unequal, (f) satisfaction with other members is lower, (g) behavior is more predictable, (h) communication networks are possible, (i) feedback contains less self-disclosure and intimacy, and (j) unequal participation is more likely. These ten differences remind us that where and how dark side components may be formed or manifested is more varied and complex than simply dyadic-level communication. More generally, as we will show in the remainder of this chapter, the dark side of teams may occur at the level of the individual member, the dyad, subgroup(s) of members, or the entire group. Furthermore, in view of our introductory discussion of teams and teamwork, organizational and even environmental factors may contribute to dark side dynamics.

Group scholars have recognized the importance of a multilevel approach (Myers & McPhee, 2006; Poole, 1999). Conceptually committed to understanding groups as holistic systems, much group scholarship implicitly or explicitly includes more than one level. For example, a group leader and a deviant—a member who repeatedly deviates from important group standards of conduct—are two very different (individual) roles in terms of their effects on group processes and outcomes (e.g., Fiedler, 1967; Hogg, 2001). Investigations of friendship cliques within a larger group find that subgroup formation also affects group processes (Markovsky & Chaffee, 1995, see also Sias, Chapter 7 this volume). Myers and McPhee (2006) found related but differential effects of socialization interaction in firefighter crews on member-level assimilation and group-level dynamics.

At higher levels of system complexity, organizational structures and proximal embedding contexts also influence teamwork processes (Arrow et al., 2000). Beyond the organizational contexts, the *environment* in which organizations exist—distal embedding contexts—make up part of a multilevel approach to understanding the forces that contribute to dark side team interactions. Distal embedding contexts include environmental factors that indirectly affect the teamwork processes (e.g., sector practices, societal influences, technological constraints, etc.).

The utility of a multilevel approach for understanding the bright side of teams, as indicated by even the brief review above, also suggests the importance of including multiple levels in understanding the dark side of team interactions. Accordingly, we examine the factors that can constitute dark side team interactions from a multilevel perspective. We organize our treatment around dynamics at subordinate (individual, dyad, subgroup), group, and superordinate (organization, environment) levels. Table 13.1 summarizes these levels and associated contributors to dark side team dynamics.

The Dark Side of Teams

Subordinate Levels

At the individual, dyad, and subgroup levels, the dark side involves motives, predispositions, and behaviors created at each strata that—either intentionally or unintentionally—hurt, distract, or disrupt teamwork.

Individual Level

In addition to demographic (i.e., sex/gender, race/ethnicity, age, socio-economic status, religion) and cultural differences between individuals, members may have certain predispositions that contribute to destructive team interactions (Haslett & Ruebush, 1999; Keyton & Frey, 2002). Individual-level dynamics that can harm group processes include aggressive communication (Infante & Rancer, 1996), communication apprehension (McCroskey & Beatty, 1998), multiple identities (Oetzel & Robins, 2003) and role strain (Goode, 1960), grouphate (Sorenson, 1981), withholding information (Price, Harrison, & Gavin, 2006), and social loafing (Karau & Williams, 1993).

Table 13.1 Dark Side of Teams: A Multi-Level Perspective

Environment Level	Organization Level	Group Level	Subgroup Level	Dyad Level	Individual Level
↑ Geographic dispersion	↑ Inadequate resources	↑ Groupthink	↑ Majority/minority dynamics	↑ Close friendships	↑ Aggressive communication
↑ Virtual environment faultlines	↑ Timing problems	↑ Hazing	↑ Coalitions	↑ Deteriorating friendships	↑ Communication apprehension
	↑ Ambiguous goals	↑ Speed traps	↑ Tag-team influence blocks	↑ Romantic relationships	↑ Social loafing
	↑ Absence of managerial teamwork	↑ Group farrago	↑ Mobbing	↑ Face-threatening supervisor–subordinate relationships	↑ Individual farrago
	↑ Misaligned structures	↑ Concertive control	↑ Inappropriate humor	↑ Hurtful mentor–colleague relationships	↑ Grouphate
	↑ Flawed appraisal and reward systems	↑ Conformity pressures	↑ Dysfunctional competition	↑ "Difficult" coworkers	↑ Withholding information
		↑ Obedience to authority		↑ Distancing behaviors	↑ Multiple identities and role strain

To take just one of these as an example of the harmful effects on team-work, consider a member's propensity toward aggressive communication —the tendency to force another person to believe something or behave in a particular way (Infante & Rancer, 1996). Aggressive communication is linked to four individual traits: (a) assertiveness—a tendency to be inter-personally dominant, ascendant, and forceful; (b) argumentativeness—a trait marked by presenting and defending positions on controversial issues while attempting to refute the positions of other people; (c) hostility—symbolic expression of irritability, negativism, resentment, and suspicion; and (d) verbal aggressiveness—attacking the self-concept of people instead of, or in addition to, their positions. Verbal aggressiveness is negatively related to team members' satisfaction and group consensus (Anderson & Martin, 1999).

Dyad Level

Teamwork dysfunction can emerge from two-person relationships that negatively affect the team. Examples of potentially dysfunctional dyads include close or deteriorating friendships (Sias, 2006), romantic relationships (Mainiero, 1986; Pierce & Aguinis, 1997), face-threatening supervisor–subordinate relationships (Gardner & Jones, 1999), harmful mentor–colleague relationships (Kinney, 2006), and "difficult" cowork-ers (Duck, Foley, & Kirkpatrick, 2006). Negative work relationships such as these are associated with reduced job satisfaction, diminished commit-ment, and workplace cynicism (Fritz & Omdahl, 2006).

To be sure, workplace friendships are advantageous to the befriended because they provide emotional and social support, job enjoyment, enhanced creativity (Sias, 2006), and stress relief (Leiter & Maslach, 1988). Friendships also can enhance organizational commitment, increase morale, and decrease turnover. However, friendships at work may become destructive when they contribute to a dysfunctional work environment, when they result in inequality, and, at times, when they deteriorate (Sias). Moreover, as Sias notes, friendships can be a powerful form of unobtru-sive control that not only motivates people to accept an unsatisfactory sta-tus quo, but that binds workers to bad working environments because they do not want to abandon their friends. Workplace friendships also are sub-ject to dialectical tensions such as equality/inequality, impartiality/favoritism, openness/closedness, autonomy/connection, and judgment/acceptance (Bridge & Baxter, 1992). Some of these friendship tensions are problematic for other team members, especially when the partners in a dyad differ in formal status (supervisor versus subordinate roles) or infor-mal status (one is liked by all on the team, the other is not). Friendships also can become problematic—both for teamwork among all team mem-bers and for the close friends—when they perpetuate unequal distribution of rewards, when there is an inability to separate the expectations of the friendship from team expectations and procedures, when privacy boundaries are breached, and when daily interaction in the work environment damages the friendship (Sias).

When friendships at work deteriorate, it can be extremely uncomfortable for persons involved in the friendship, as well as for other team members. Emotion-management norms guiding the "appropriate" expression of authentic positive or neutral emotions and the masking of negative ones (Kramer & Hess, 2002) increase the discomfort in these situations if workers have to conceal felt emotions and "act as if" nothing is amiss. Once a friendship deteriorates, it becomes a non-voluntary relationship that may need to be maintained within the work environment, and in accordance with team norms concerning expression of emotion (e.g., "leave personal matters at home"). Hess (2000) describes three common distancing behaviors that can be destructive to the team when the awkwardness between parties bleeds over into task and informal interactions involving other team members. Distancing behaviors include expressing detachment, avoiding involvement, or displaying antagonism. These forms of destructive team communication take the form, respectively, of ignoring the other person and the relationship, being superficially polite, or expressing outward hostility by directly disclosing negative feelings.

Subgroup Level

The shared understanding of group identity and group norms bind together team members (Hogg & Tindale, 2005), but often in (sub)part rather than in whole. For example, Wit and Kerr (2002) found that when members think of themselves in terms of their subgroups they are more likely to act in the interest of the subgroup over that of the entire team. Potentially dysfunctional dynamics occurring at subgroup level include: (a) "tag-team" influence (Seibold & Meyers, 2007), in which influence occurs because one member (often of high status) competes with another's argument rather than the strength of their reasoning; (b) majority-minority dynamics (Meyers & Brashers, 1999), in which the disproportionate size of subgroups that hold different opinions leads to winners (the majority) and losers (the minority); and (c) inappropriate humor (Meyer, 1997), in which comments intended to be humorous but perceived by some other members as inappropriate divide the team.

Subgroups and coalitions threaten the group's unity, a disruption that can either facilitate positive change or completely divide the group (Wheelan, 2005). The formation of subgroups and coalitions are considered "growing pains" in the process of achieving organizational goals, and the divisive episodes may even be necessary for team development. Subgroups form in response to differing team member opinions about a leader (assuming a leader-directed team). Coalitions, on the other hand, are characterized by conflict and hostility and form when two or more members team up against others in the team, usually for a short period of time. Coalitions are clearly a part of the dark side of teams, and they harm teamwork on the relationships dimension noted earlier (Seibold, 1995).

"Mobbing," more frequently termed "harassment" (Brodsky, 1976) and "workplace bullying" (see Lutgen-Sandvik, Namie, & Namie, Chapter 2 this volume), can emerge from coalitions in teams. Mobbing and bullying are "hostile and unethical communication ... directed in a systematic way by one *or a few individuals* mainly towards one individual" (Leymann, 1996, p. 168; emphasis added). A form of emotional, psychological abuse, mobbing typically begins with small acts of disrespect and becomes blatant, harmful behavior when these acts are persistent and enduring (Zapf & Einarsen, 2005). When team members "gang up" on an individual, involvement in the team and performance suffer. Worse, the actions of the "mob" may be unnoticed, ignored, tolerated, or even encouraged by the organization—re-emphasizing the multilevel nature of forces contributing to dark side dynamics.

Group Level

Although the dark side of teams often is rooted in communication-related dynamics just noted at the individual, dyadic, and subgroup levels, the dark side is often caused or manifested primarily at the group level. The dark side of teamwork at the group level emerges from team processes such as groupthink (Janis, 1972), hazing (Nuwer, 1990), "speed traps" associated with members' false perceptions of time urgency (Perlow, Okhuysen, & Repenning, 2002), group farrago (Stohl & Schell, 1991), and concertive control (Tompkins & Cheney, 1985), among others. The latter two dysfunctional processes are grounded in an analysis of group communication, and we treat both in detail here.

Farrago, literally a mix of feed for cattle, figuratively refers to a confused, dysfunctional group fed by a dysfunctional individual member (often a bully or unusually dominant and vocal person) but whom group members enable and reinforce through their own behaviors (Stohl & Schell, 1991). Group farrago has the potential to destroy teamwork at the group level not only because of the characteristics of a focal, problematic individual, but also due to specific structural properties that sustain a farrago's existence at the group level (Stohl & Schell). These properties include the existence of an explicit policy encouraging participation by all members in decision making (including the problematic individual), lack of clear authority within the team, ambiguous rules of conduct, high task interdependence, and tolerance of members' unconventional and detrimental behaviors. These conditions then interact with group processes—before, during, and after meetings in which the dominant "jerk" frustrates other members—and add to the individual farrago's destructive potential. For instance, a tension emerges between the force of the individual and the resistance of the remaining team members. The participation norm, ill-defined rules and authority, and weak socialization enable the individual farrago's actions; the lack of official status for the individual supports the other members' resistance. Additionally, group norms tolerate the individual farrago's dominant and destructive behavior. Dysfunction thus breeds further dysfunction, and the cycle destroys relationships, procedures, performance, and essentially, teamwork.

Similarly, teams evidencing concertive control risk eroding teamwork. Tompkins and Cheney (1985) characterize concertive control systems as those where rules and regulations are enactments of the members' collective understanding of the values, mission, and goals of their organization and team. This form of control is unobtrusive and thus less apparent to the employee. Policies and procedures set forth by management continue to be part of the team's landscape, but the unit's "rules" are those interpretations and expansions that become an integral part of team structures and practices—and members' actions toward, and relationships with, each other. Unlike bureaucratic control, the locus of control rests within the team. The team develops premises that guide members' actions, and ultimately their decision making, based upon a negotiated consensus concerning the organization's (i.e., management's) overarching goals and objectives (Barker, 1993). Although such teams may fare positively in terms of performance, the control is ultimately detrimental for teamwork. Indeed, concertive control is part of the dark side to teamwork in autonomous and semi-autonomous work teams.

For example, Barker's (1993) ground-breaking study of concertive control in self-directed teams documents the evolution of attendance policies, among other things, for teams within an organization. Over time and given particular organizational requirements, teams' concertive control became as punitive and oppressive as any top-down system of overt control. What began as general norms that the whole team embraced eventually became stringent rules used to dictate specific members' actions. The rules created stress and pressure for new and old team members alike. Moreover, it was more difficult for newer members to accept the rules as they were imposed upon them rather than emerging as a natural outgrowth of their organizational identity. This fueled dysfunction among team members as a discrepancy in power grew between old and new members, and between full-time and temporary workers. If new or temporary members chose not to conform to the team's "policies," they were reprimanded and ostracized by the team until they were driven from the workplace.

Superordinate Levels

The dark side of teamwork also emerges due to forces from levels that transcend and encompass teams—the organization in which teams are situated (Seibold, 1998) and organizations' external environments (e.g., sector, cultural, social, political). As we noted in the introduction, the implementation of team structures has been driven by philosophical, cultural, economic, and technological forces in U.S. organizations and their environments. However, such factors and their consequences at the organization and environment levels can—intentionally or unintentionally—influence teams in a way that hurts, distracts, or disrupts teamwork. At the organization level, contextual factors can influence the roles, processes, and relationships dimensions of teamwork (Seibold, 1995). For instance, Stohl and Putnam's (1994) bona fide groups perspective suggests interconnections between a group and the organization in which it is embedded. This perspective also points to the role-related implications of multiple memberships (e.g., members' roles in one group to conflict with their roles in other groups) and permeable boundaries (e.g., flow of new members into a group) that can lead to intragroup role competition with existing members. At the environment level, larger contextual factors directly or indirectly affect group processes. For example, Oetzel's (2002) work on cultural diversity reveals the need to consider vertical differences, especially status, and cultural differences (e.g., individualism–collectivism) to understand how teams might become dysfunctional in culturally diverse settings. These issues are particularly important to groups globally collaborating (Stohl & Walker, 2002).

Organization Level

The dark side of teamwork is greatly influenced by the performance of administrators and managers who often serve as organizational-level representatives. Organizations have a responsibility to provide teams with the time, goals, guidelines, and resources required to complete their tasks effectively. The absence of these negatively affects team processes and performance. Indeed, the misappropriation of time, ambiguous goals or guidelines, and inadequate resources often lead to team dysfunction.

Managers' ability to provide adequate time and to organize work along a meaningful timeline are important contributors to team effectiveness and productivity. These guide the pace of work, and they provide benchmarks by which teams can determine when and how various parts of their work should be altered, as well as when that work should be completed (Hackman, 1990). Time limits and deadlines are among the most powerful temporal features observed in work teams (Ballard & Seibold, 2003). When these limits are in place and reinforced by managers, teams are able to develop rhythms and cycles that facilitate task completion. Conversely, teams without deadlines or those with confusing ones typically encounter problems. In such cases, pace is slower, work is completed sporadically, and members work on multiple projects simultaneously with poor coordination and little or no prioritization. The *communicative* bases of organizational temporality (i.e., what members intersubjectively understand time to mean in their organizations and units) are well documented (see Ballard & Seibold, 2003), as are the related coordination and conflict implications for teams (Ballard & Seibold, 2006).

Teams also require clear goals in order to use their autonomy and discretion to develop meaningful paths to those ends, to develop useful work structures, and to avoid socio-emotional problems (Seibold, 1998). Shaw's (1990) case study of mental health treatment teams in a hospital whose mission included therapy, training, and research illustrates the dysfunctional effects of conflicting organizational goals on teams. A tension between training and therapy made it difficult to provide adequate services to patients, particularly when team members changed and new ones were unaware of important and relevant information. Research and therapy were sometimes in conflict; using new and untested therapeutic techniques could potentially harm patients. Employees could not work effectively as a team because they had different (mission) motives as reasons for the choices they made in providing patient care. Providing effective patient care was even more difficult when new employees were unaware of the reasons certain policies were in place and chose to implement their own "better" way. The problems these conflicts created along the processes (operations-procedures-structures) dimension (Seibold, 1995) continued the destructive cycle in this team and shifted team interactions to the dark side.

Environment Level

Numerous challenges to teamwork emerge from the larger environment in which a modern team may be embedded. The increase in global commerce and global organizations presents new challenges to work teams whose members may be located across different time zones, operate in different countries, or interact and coordinate work via communication technologies without personal presence. The dark side of teams in complex organizations is often fueled by dispersed locations and the dynamics of virtual communication (see also Bazarova & Walther, Chapter 12 this volume). For example, a team of people from various locations within a multinational corporation must mitigate factors relating to *geographic dispersion* (separation in distance and time), as well as challenges that arise in the *virtual* team environment (e.g., nationality, trust, asynchronous communication, spontaneity, and social support). We consider each of these next.

Geographic dispersion refers to the objective, structural aspects of a team's composition, including varying dimensions and degrees of spatial distance, temporal distance, and configuration (O'Leary & Cummings, 2007). Although new technologies enable coordination and instant communication among geographically dispersed team members, there are dark side components in each of the three dimensions. *Spatial distance* is the physical distance between or among team members. With increased spatial distance, isolation of individuals or subgroups becomes more prevalent, and feedback is problematic for those who are "out of sight." As team members become more widely dispersed from one another, the number of time zones in the team becomes salient. This *temporal dimension* includes the degree to which team members' work schedules overlap. Work schedule incongruity can reduce synchronous interaction, spontaneous communication, and real-time problem solving. These coordination challenges may set the stage for *configurational* difficulties such as the development of dominant subgroups, power imbalances, and poor coordination with other groups.

Geographic dispersion of team members is endemic to virtual teams and is among their defining features, although virtuality is not the opposite of collocation (Gibson & Gibbs, 2006). Rather, virtuality has four components: geographic dispersion, dependence on technology, dynamic structure, and feelings of nationality. The more all four components characterize the team, the more it is considered to be a virtual team. The collocation of team members, on the other hand, allows for face-to-face communication, spontaneous interaction, and social support.

These four components of virtuality have unique effects on performance. For example, dependence on technology for basic communication tends to result in less innovation than is found in collocated teams with more information-rich, face-to-face interaction. Furthermore, the greater the extent to which a team is structurally dynamic (i.e., has fluid membership), the greater the uncertainty and risk that members feel about each other, especially with regard to sharing sensitive information. These dark side aspects of virtual teams are not surprising since team members also usually have a short history together and lack shared organizational memory. Increased feelings of nationality may increase the likelihood for subgroup social categorization, resulting in more salient divisions between subgroups of a work team. Such "faultlines" increase conflict, erode trust, and are most likely to be found between subgroups on teams characterized by geographic dispersion and greater degrees of virtuality (Poltzer, Crisp, Jarvenpaa, & Kim, 2006). They are prominent dark side dynamics in virtual teams, factors inherent in the environment level of those teams.

Crossing Levels

We have argued that the dark side of teams emerges as a complex function of multilevel dynamics that—singly and taken together—obstruct effective teamwork. We reviewed more than two dozen contributing dynamics at subordinate (individual, dyad, subgroup), group, and superordinate (organization, environment) levels. We have implied that these dark side dynamics operate not simply within levels but across them, although we have not illustrated that in great detail thus far. Our treatment of individual and group farrago (Stohl & Schell, 1991) crosses levels; like Stohl and Schell, we use the farrago phenomenon to underscore the mutually constitutive nature of communication at multiple levels affecting teams, including their dark side.

Zimbardo's (2007) explication of the Lucifer Effect, however, is a fully developed cross-level example of the dark side of teams that is especially instructive for our purposes. In one sense, Zimbardo deals with the individual level of dysfunction as he attempts to understand what compels ordinarily "good" people to do "evil" (e.g., prison guards' mistreatment of prisoners). Consistent with our conceptualization of the dark side, Zimbardo defines evil as "intentionally behaving in ways that harm, abuse, demean, dehumanize, or destroy innocent others—or using one's authority and systemic power to encourage or permit others to do so on your behalf" (p. 5). These behaviors can be explained from a dispositional, situational, or systemic point of view.

Many analyses invoke the dispositional view, which focuses on personality and psychological traits but does little to explain how two people with very different dispositions can commit the same evil act. However, a systemic perspective can help interpret evil actions by focusing on the conditions, circumstances, and situational factors that foster the deplorable behaviors. Two of the most important situational aspects that teams experience and that may encourage individual and collective evil behaviors are the *pressure to conform* and *obedience to authority*.

Zimbardo (2007) demonstrates conformity pressures with reference to Asch's (1958, cited in Zimbardo) line experiments. Participants were shown a line and asked to choose one of three other lines whose length matched the original. Among the three alternatives, one line was clearly longer, one shorter, and one exactly the same length. When alone, participants usually chose correctly; when part of a group, participants more often answered in accordance with the others even when they knew the answer was incorrect. This research suggests that people conform based on either informational needs or normative needs—the needs to belong or be accepted. Like Janis's (1972) analysis of groupthink, Zimbardo notes that conformity can be dysfunctional—in this case due to the "evil of inaction" (p. 317).

Similarly, when power differences exist within teams, Zimbardo (2007) asserts that individuals may become evil in exercising that power or, conversely, allow themselves to be subject to that power and be complicit in its illegitimate ends. In the Enron and WorldCom scandals, Zimbardo argues, certain members of those corporations' management teams used their power to commit egregious acts while numerous other team members were complicit in the dark side by their own inaction. Legitimate power differences also encourage dark side behaviors due to extreme obedience. Zimbardo demonstrates this phenomenon with reference to Hofling and colleagues' experiment involving 22 nurses. Each nurse received a call from an unknown physician who directed them to administer (a lethal amount of) medicine to a patient so that it would begin to take effect by the time the doctor arrived at the hospital. Although each nurse knew the prescribed dosage was lethal, all but one eventually deferred to the physician's perceived authority and attempted to carry out the doctor's orders until stopped by researchers.

What Zimbardo (2007) characterizes as the "evils" of inaction and extreme obedience are tangible examples of dark side behavior, and neither is necessarily rooted in an individual's personality or disposition. Instead, Zimbardo's "Lucifer Effect" suggests that the combined effects of predisposing individual and dyadic forces and the pressure to conform or the attribution of power at the group level jointly—and *across levels*—shed light on the dark side of teams with respect to their perpetration of despicable deeds. Together with Stohl and Schell's (1991) analysis of group farrago, Zimbardo's work offers compelling evidence for the mutually constitutive nature of the multiple levels we presented on the dark side of teams.

Dark Side *and* Bright Side Communication

Also apparent in our review is that the dark side in teams may be reflected in and constituted by the same medium as the bright side—communication. That is, members' interactions comprise both constructive and destructive organizing. On one hand, research has uncovered a plethora of dark side components. In order to achieve effective teamwork, a team necessarily must avoid these implied pitfalls (Burtis & Turman, 2006). But how does a work unit avoid falling victim to the dark side when achieving effective teamwork demands similar, if not the same, processes that quickly become problematic in teams with excessive concertive control?

Moreover, while pursuing task and maintenance activities, teams constantly negotiate simultaneous and multiple levels of communicative organizing—each of which is capable of manifesting dark side dynamics. Hence, the potential interactions among multiple dark side components, or dark side and bright side components, further complicate understanding dysfunctional teamwork. Can these interactions be beneficial to the unit? If so, in what ways? Addressing this multifaceted process may afford a deeper understanding of the dark side of teamwork and the complexity of group processes in general. On a related note, since the evaluation of team effectiveness is usually *post hoc*, the negotiation between the bright side and the dark side is minimized, if not completely ignored. Like team outcomes, communication is often truncated to a linear process and with dichotomous results—successful or flawed. Overlooked are underlying dynamics: whether a team preemptively dealt with the potential dark side, sensed the emergence of the dark side but effectively countered it, or suffered the effects of it but eventually came out of it.

As implied by our discussion, the dark side of teams is usefully juxtaposed against the bright side—teamwork. Teams must manage numerous dialectics or tensions (Kramer, 2004), most of which involve the bright side *and* the dark side like those associated with workplace friendships: equality/inequality, impartiality/favoritism, openness/closedness (Bridge & Baxter, 1992). For most team dialectics, the bright side is the positive manifestation (e.g., success) and the dark side is the negative manifestation (e.g., failure) of the tension. Decision-making group members, for example, must vigilantly examine various proposals to ensure proper evaluation before deciding on the best one (Hirokawa & Rost, 1992). Failing to exert such effort may result in groupthink-like symptoms (e.g., self-censorship). But if a member questions everything (even if his/her motives are for the overall good of the team), she or he may be seen as a farrago by other members. The dark side of team interactions, then, can also be seen as teamwork that is ill-fitting, given certain contexts and goals. As such, the necessity of the dark side invites further analysis and future research.

The dark side of team interactions is rich with investigative potential. In addition to better understanding the cross-level, dialectical, and inherently communicative dark side dynamics just noted, future research should consider a more developed model that considers additional dark side components from existing research as well as the potential of a more complex process involved in creating, maintaining, or perpetuating the dark side. Moreover, we see a need for prescription or intervention, in the forms of communicative strategies to (a) prevent potential dark side components, (b) deal with or manage enactments of the dark side, and (c) effectively cope with the aftermath of the dark side. As organizational work groups and teams continue to increase, so must our understanding of team processes—both bright and dark sides.

Constructive Organizing: Enabling the Bright Side, Dis(en)abling the Dark Side

In this final section we explore how teams can organize in constructive ways. We emphasize, first, the group level—especially the four dimensions underlying strong teamwork noted at the outset. Then we turn to other levels in the multilevel approach we have taken, examining ways that dynamics at the individual, dyad, organizational, and environmental levels can contribute to constructive, bright-side teamwork.

Group Level Organizing

Teams seeking enhanced teamwork must overcome challenges at the collective level along four dimensions (Seibold, 1995). These dimensions—*vision, roles, processes, and relationships*—reflect areas of significant member interaction that create and recreate teamwork. Communicative organizing along these dimensions is qualitatively different than organizing along related dimensions of groups and teams without teamwork—goals, jobs, structures, and interactions respectively. We consider them in turn, in each case juxtaposing typical group communicative organizing with that characterizing teams with high teamwork.

Organizational groups have goals, which typically are determined and demanded by managers atop those units or by the formal leaders within each group. However, teams with high levels of teamwork are distinguished by the vision members themselves also foster and embrace. *Vision* involves not only members' desired end state (i.e., the goals and objectives they may have internalized and their extensions), but also how the process of envisioning those ends and the result of attaining them affect the development of that unit and its unity, as well as the team's identity (for members and for outsiders).

Members of work groups have jobs, the formal duties associated with their assigned, defined position in the unit. However, members of teams characterized by high levels of teamwork also have roles that may be more or less than their jobs. Team leaders, for example, usually share their formal job duties through empowering other members and through semi-autonomous team management processes (while those leaders assume responsibility for activities outside the team—such as resource gathering, advocacy, and boundary spanning). Conversely, team members typically enact behaviors and functions that are more than their formal jobs—assisting others as needed, assuming responsibilities not included in their job descriptions, and providing needed informal functions necessary for maintaining team cohesiveness and ensuring task locomotion. *Role*-related communicative organizing leading to and recreating teamwork first entails whether and how each member comes to understand what other members expect of him or her. In turn, in units with high levels of teamwork, how does each member's role perception become consistent with others' expectations for her or him? Importantly, how does each member come to feel valued by others in the group for the role(s) she plays—especially when that may be less than the member can do or wishes to do, choosing instead to be "a team player" in the service of the team's vision?

Work units possess, indeed are characterized by, the operations and procedures that structure members and enable group performance and goal achievement. As with goals, these are often created by managers.

However, in units in which members attain strong teamwork with each other, the foundational task and maintenance *processes* that must be developed to ensure successful task accomplishment and to sustain teamwork tend to be substantially supplemented by the members themselves. Processes in teams with high levels of teamwork can be more flexible and responsive to the changing needs in the team, and challenges from its environment, than "standard operating procedures" that usually are implemented in top-down fashion by managers. Furthermore, in groups and teams that achieve high levels of teamwork, there are sufficient resources (financial, personnel, technology, and material) to sustain teamwork. There also are reward, training, and information systems that enable and facilitate members' strong teamwork. As Hackman (1990) observed, "Groups that have appropriate structures tend to develop healthy internal processes, whereas groups with insufficient or inappropriate structures tend to have process problems" (p. 498).

Finally, members of any group interact with each other directly and indirectly (through leaders and others in the team, and using multiple channels that vary in their richness). Members of groups or teams evidencing teamwork attain qualitatively different, and better, communication with each other, which in turn fosters stronger interpersonal relationships among team members than among members of units in which teamwork is not evident. This *relationships* dimension of teamwork refers to communication among members characterized by respectful and open sharing of information, by perspective taking and valuing difference, as well as the allowance for constructive communication of disagreement and striving for consensus. Though seemingly less central to task achievement and therefore often ignored, the communicative processes that build effective relationships among members are intrinsic to teamwork, the bright side of teams.

Multilevel Organizing

As indicated in Table 13.1 numerous factors, and at multiple levels, have the potential to darken team interactions. Teams that seek to enhance teamwork must therefore counteract them by disabling them or at least not enabling them—what we term dis(en)abling dark side forces. Many of the threats to teamwork we have identified will be dis(en)abled in direct proportion to the degree to which team members communicatively organize to foster teamwork on each of the four underlying dimensions just reviewed: unifying around a vision, negotiating and valuing all members' roles in the team, internally developing effective task and maintenance processes, and fostering stronger collegial relationships among members. Teams mediate individual, subgroup, and organizational influences (Seibold, 1998), and—as the nexus of teamwork—members' own communicative organizing can dis(en)able dark side forces. At the individual level, for example, aggressive communication, withholding information, and communication apprehension are neutralized, even remedied, in the process of members' learning and enacting communication that is open, respectful, and driven toward consensus. Similarly, social loafing, individual farrago, and grouphate have no bases nor spaces for development in teams in which members' communication is directed toward improved teamwork. The same is true of many dyad level forces (e.g., preventing or coping with dark side effects of close or deteriorating friendships, difficult coworkers, and distancing behaviors) and subgroup dynamics (e.g., majority-minority influence, coalitions, mobbing). And some dark side forces at the organizational level (e.g., ambiguous goals, misaligned structures) and environmental level (e.g., virtual team faultlines) will similarly be counteracted as part of, and as a consequence, of members' efforts to communicatively organize more effectively along vision, process, and relationship dimensions.

At the same time, in order to dis(en)able these dark side forces many things can be done on behalf of the team by management or human resources representatives, or by the team itself, and by outside members' efforts to develop teamwork noted above. Careful screening and selection of members for entry to the team, and socialization of them thereafter, can inoculate against the dark side at the individual level (by eliminating or developing potentially problematic members), the dyad level (by dealing proactively with problematic relationships), and the subgroup level (by confronting mobbing, dysfunctional competition, and inappropriate humor). Moving to the superordinate level, Lawler (1995) reports six organization level factors that improve the probability of successful teams when organizations are transitioning to team-based structures: (a) the existence of a company-wide philosophy that is consistent with teams; (b) organization of top managers in team structures themselves; (c) design or redesign of members' work in ways that require team structures; (d) an appraisal system tied, at least in part, to members' performance as a team; (e) a reward system partially allocated for team outcomes, not only for individual performance; and (f) training for all members in the skills needed to succeed in teams. Read in the context of our analysis of organizing initiatives outside a team that might inoculate against dark side forces on it and enable members within it to develop teamwork, any and all of these organization level initiatives by management or human resources have the potential to reduce superordinate constraints on the bright side of teams—teamwork.

References

Anderson, C. M., & Martin, M. M. (1999). The relationship of argumentativeness and verbal aggressiveness to cohesion, consensus, and satisfaction in small groups. *Communication Reports, 12*(1), 21–31.

Arrow, H., McGrath, J. E., & Berdahl, J. L. (2000). *Small groups as complex systems: Formation, coordination, development, and adaptation.* Thousand Oaks, CA: Sage.

Bacon, N., & Blyton, P. (2005). Worker responses to teamworking: Exploring employee attributions of managerial motives. *International Journal of Human Resource Management, 16*(2), 238–255.

Ballard, D. I., & Seibold, D. R. (2003). Communicating and organizing in time: A meso-level model of organizational temporality. *Management Communication Quarterly, 16*(3), 380–415.

Ballard, D. I., & Seibold, D. R. (2006). The experience of time at work: Relationship to communication load, job satisfaction, and interdepartmental communication. *Communication Studies, 57*(3), 317–340.

Barker, J. R. (1993). Tightening the Iron Cage: Concertive control in self-managing teams. *Administrative Science Quarterly, 38*(3), 408–437.

Bridge, K., & Baxter, L. A. (1992). Blended relationships: Friends as work associates. *Western Journal of Communication, 56*(2), 200–225.

Brodsky, C. (1976). *The harassed worker.* Lexington, MA: D.C. Health and Company.

Burtis, J. O., & Turman, P. D. (2006). *Group communication pitfalls: Overcoming barriers to an effective group experience.* Thousand Oaks, CA: Sage.

Cupach, W. R., & Spitzberg, B. H. (2007). *The dark side of interpersonal communication* (2nd ed.). Mahwah, NJ: Erlbaum.

Devine, D. J., Clayton, L. D., Philips, J. L., Dunford, B. B., & Melner, S. B. (1999). Teams in organizations: Prevalence, characteristics, and effectiveness. *Small Group Research, 30*(6), 678–711.

Duck, S., Foley, M. K., & Kirkpatrick, D. C. (2006). Uncovering the complex roles behind the "difficult" coworker. In J. M. H. Fritz & B. L. Omdahl (Eds.), *Problematic relationships in the workplace* (pp. 3–19). New York: Peter Lang.

Fiedler, F. E. (1967). *A theory of leadership effectiveness.* New York: McGraw-Hill.

Fritz, J. M. H., & Omdahl, B. L. (2006). Reduced job satisfaction, diminished commitment, and workplace cynicism as outcomes of negative work relationships. In J. M. H. Fritz & B. L. Omdahl (Eds.), *Problematic relationships in the workplace* (pp. 131–151). New York: Peter Lang.

Gardner, M. J., & Jones, E. (1999). Problematic communication in the workplace: Beliefs of superiors and subordinates. *International Journal of Applied Linguistics, 9*(2), 185–203.

Gibson, C. B., & Gibbs, J. L. (2006). Unpacking the concept of virtuality: The effects of geographic dispersion, electronic dependence, dynamic structure, and national diversity on team innovation. *Administrative Science Quarterly, 51*(3), 451–495.

Goode, W. J. (1960). A theory of role strain. *American Sociological Review, 25*(4), 483–496.

Hackman, J. R. (1990). *Groups that work (and those that don't): Creating conditions for effective teamwork.* San Francisco: Jossey-Bass.

Haslett, B. B., & Ruebush, J. (1999). What differences do individual differences in groups make? In L. R. Frey, D. S. Gouran & M. S. Poole (Eds.), *The handbook of group communication theory and research* (pp. 115–138). Thousand Oaks, CA: Sage.

Hess, J. A. (2000). Maintaining nonvoluntary relationships with disliked partners: An investigation into the use of distancing behaviors. *Human Communication Research, 26*(4), 458–488.

Hirokawa, R. Y., & Rost, K. M. (1992). Effective group decision making in organizations: Field test of the vigilant interaction theory. *Management Communication Quarterly, 5*(3), 267–288.

Hogg, M. A. (2001). Social categorization, depersonalization, and group behavior. In M. A. Hogg & R. S. Tindale (Eds.), *Blackwell handbook of social psychology: Group processes* (pp. 56–85). Oxford: Blackwell.

Hogg, M. A., & Tindale, R. S. (2005). Social identity, influence, and communication in small groups. In J. Harwood & H. Giles (Eds.), *Intergroup communication: Multiple perspectives* (pp. 141–164). New York: Peter Lang.

Infante, D. A., & Rancer, A. S. (1996). Argumentativeness and verbal aggressiveness: A review of recent theory and research. *Communication yearbook 19*, 319–351.

Janis, I. L. (1972). *Victims of groupthink.* Boston: Houghton Mifflin.

Karau, S. J., & Williams, K. D. (1993). Social loafing: A meta-analytic review and theoretical integration *Journal of Personality & Social Psychology, 65*(4), 681–706.

Katzenbach, J. R., & Smith, D. K. (1993). *The wisdom of teams.* Boston: Harvard Business School Press.

Keyton, J., & Frey, L. R. (2002). The state of traits. In L. R. Frey (Ed.), *New directions in group communication* (pp. 99–120). Thousand Oaks, CA: Sage.

Kinney, T. A. (2006). Should I stay or should I go now? The role of negative communication and relational maintenance in distress and well-being. In J. M. H. Fritz & B. L. Omdahl (Eds.), *Problematic relationships in the workplace* (pp. 179–201). New York: Peter Lang.

Kramer, M. W. (2004). Toward a communication theory of group dialectics: An ethnographic study of a community theater group. *Communication Monographs, 71*(2), 311–332.

Kramer, M. W., & Hess, J. A. (2002). Communication rules for the display of emotions in organizational settings. *Management Communication Quarterly, 16*(1), 66–80.

Larson, C. E., & LaFasto, F. M. J. (1989). *Teamwork: What must go right, what can go wrong.* Beverly Hills, CA: Sage.

Lawler, E. E. (1995). *Creating high performance organizations.* San Francisco: Jossey-Bass.

Lawler, E. E. (1999). Employee involvement makes a difference. *Journal of Quality and Participation, 22*(5), 18–20.

Lawler, E. E., Mohrmann, S. A., & Ledford, G. E. J. (1992). *Employee involvement and total quality management: Practices and results in Fortune 1000 companies.* San Francisco: San Francisco.

Leiter, M. P., & Maslach, C. (1988). The impact of interpersonal environment on burnout and organizational commitment. *Journal of Organizational Behavior, 9*(2), 297–308.

Leymann, H. (1996). The content and development of mobbing at work. *European Journal of Work and Organizational Psychology, 5*(2), 165–184.

Mainiero, L. A. (1986). A review and analysis of power dynamics in organizational romances. *Academy of Management Review, 11*(6), 750–762.

Markovsky, B., & Chaffee, M. (1995). Social identification and solidarity: A reformulation. In B. Markovsky & K. Heimer (Eds.), *Advances in group processes* (Vol. 12, pp. 249–270). Greenwich, CT: JAI Press.

McCroskey, J. C., & Beatty, M. J. (1998). Communication apprehension. In J. C. McCroskey, J. A. Daly, M. M. Martin & M. J. Beatty (Eds.), *Communication and personality: Trait perspectives* (pp. 215–231). Cresskill, NJ: Hampton Press.

Meyer, J. (1997). Humor in member narratives: Uniting and dividing at work. *Western Journal of Communication, 61*(2), 188–209.

Meyers, R. A., & Brashers, D. E. (1999). Influence processes in group interaction. In L. R. Frey, D. S. Gouran & M. S. Poole (Eds.), *The handbook of group communication theory and research* (pp. 288–312). Thousand Oaks, CA: Sage.

Myers, K. K., & McPhee, R. D. (2006). Influences on member assimilation in workgroups in high-reliability organizations: A multilevel analysis. *Human Communication Research, 32*(4), 440–468.

Nuwer, H. (1990). *Broken pledges: The deadly rite of hazing*. Atlanta, GA: Longstreet Press.

O'Leary, M. B., & Cummings, J. N. (2007). The spatial, temporal, and configurational characteristics of geographic dispersion in teams. *MIS Quarterly, 31*(3), 433–452.

O'Toole, J., & Lawler, E. E. (2006). *The new American workplace*. New York: Palgrave.

Oetzel, J. G. (2002). The effects of cultural diversity on communication in work groups: Synthesizing vertical and cultural differences with a face-negotiation perspective. In L. R. Frey (Ed.), *New directions in group communication* (pp. 121–137). Thousand Oaks, CA: Sage.

Oetzel, J. G., & Robins, J. (2003). Multiple identities in teams in a cooperative supermarket. In L. R. Frey (Ed.), *Group communication in context: Studies in bona fide groups* (2nd ed., pp. 183–206). Mahwah, NJ: Lawrence Erlbaum Associates.

Parks, M. (1974, April). *Dyadic communication from the perspective of small group research*. Paper presented at the Central States Speech Association Annual Conference, Milwaukee, WI.

Perlow, L. A., Okhuysen, G. A., & Repenning, N. P. (2002). The speed trap: Exploring the relationship between decision making and temporal context. *Academy of Management Journal, 45*(5), 931–955.

Pierce, C. A., & Aguinis, H. (1997). Bridging the gap between romantic relationships and sexual harassment in organizations. *Journal of Organizational Behavior, 18*(2), 197–200.

Poltzer, J. T., Crisp, C. B., Jarvenpaa, S. L., & Kim, J. W. (2006). Extending the faultline model to geographically dispersed teams: How collocated subgroups can impair group functioning. *Academy of Management Journal, 49*(5), 672–392.

Poole, M. S. (1999). Group communication methodology: Issues and considerations. In L. R. Frey, D. S. Gouran & M. S. Poole (Eds.), *The handbook of group communication theory and research* (pp. 92–112). Thousand Oaks, CA: Sage.

Price, K. H., Harrison, D. A., & Gavin, J. H. (2006). Withholding inputs in team contexts: Member composition, interaction processes, evaluation structure, and social loafing. *Journal of Applied Psychology, 91*(6), 1375–1384.

Seibold, D. R. (1995). Developing the "team" in a team-managed organization: Group facilitation in a new plant design. In L. R. Frey (Ed.), *Innovations in group facilitation techniques: Case studies of applications in naturalistic settings* (pp. 282–298). Cresskill, NJ: Hampton Press.

Seibold, D. R. (1998). Groups and organizations: Premises and perspectives. In J. S. Trent (Ed.), *Communication: Views from the helm for the twenty-first century* (pp. 162–168). Needham Heights, MA: Allyn & Bacon.

Seibold, D. R. (2005). Bridging theory and practice in organizational communication. In J. L. Simpson & P. Shockley-Zalabak (Eds.), *Engaging communication, transforming organizations: Scholarship of engagement in action* (pp. 13–44). Cresskill, NJ: Hampton.

Seibold, D. R., & Meyers, R. A. (2007). Group argument: A structuration perspective and research program. *Small Group Research, 38*(3), 312–336.

Seibold, D. R., & Shea, C. (2001). Participation and decision making. In F. M. Jablin & L. L. Putnam (Eds.), *The new handbook of organizational communication: Advances in theory, research, and methods* (pp. 664–703). Thousand Oaks, CA: Sage.

Shaw, R. B. (1990). Mental health treatment teams. In J. R. Hackman (Ed.), *Groups that Work (and those that dait): Creating conditions for effective teamwork* (pp. 330–348). San Francisco, CA: Jossey-Bass.

Sias, P. M. (2006). Workplace friendship deterioration. In J. M. H. Fritz & B. L. Omdahl (Eds.), *Problematic relationships in the workplace* (pp. 69–87). New York: Peter Lang.

Sorenson, S. (1981, May). *Grouphate.* Paper presented at the International Communication Association Annual Conference, Minneapolis, MN.

Stohl, C., & Putnam, L. L. (1994). Group communication in context: Implications for the study of bona fide groups. In L. R. Frey (Ed.), *Group communication in context: Studies of natural groups* (pp. 285–292). Hillsdale, NJ: Lawrence Erlbaum.

Stohl, C., & Schell, S. E. (1991). A communication-based model of a small group dysfunction. *Management Communication Quarterly, 5*(1), 90–110.

Stohl, C., & Walker, K. (2002). A bone fide perspective for the future of groups: Understanding Collaborating groups. In L. R. Frey (Ed.), *New directions in group communication* (pp. 237–252). Thousand Oaks, CA: Sage.

Tompkins, P. K., & Cheney, G. (1985). Communication and unobtrusive control in contemporary organizations. In R. D. McPhee & P. K. Tompkins (Eds.), *Organizational communication: Traditional themes and new directions* (pp. 179–210). Newbury Park, CA: Sage.

Wheelan, S. A. (2005). *Group processes: A developmental perspective.* Needham Heights, MA: Allyn and Bacon.

Wit, A. P., & Kerr, N. L. (2002). "Me versus just us versus us all" categorization and cooperation in nested social dilemmas. *Journal of Personality & Social Psychology, 83*(3), 616–637.

Zapf, D., & Einarsen, S. (2005). Mobbing at work: Escalated conflicts. In S. Fox & P. Spector (Eds.), *Counterproductive work behaviors* (pp. 237–270). Washington DC: American Psychological Association.

Zimbardo, P. (2007). *The Lucifer Effect: Understanding how good people turn evil.* New York: Random House.

Part V

Perspectives for Constructive Communication

Chapter 14

Responses to Destructive Organizational Contexts

Intersubjectively Creating Resilience to Foster Human Dignity and Hope

Patrice M. Buzzanell, Suchitra Shenoy, Robyn V. Remke, and Kristen Lucas

Organizational scholars often examine the ways in which workers communicate to deal with and surpass problematic workplace situations. Workers' communication may be situated at the microlevel as individuals productively frame and suggest interventions for bullying, incivilities, sexual harassment, and job loss (e.g., Fritz & Omdahl, 2006a; Lutgen-Sandvik, 2008; Sias, 2008). Communication also constitutes macrolevel processes as organizations anticipate or remedy the aftermath of terrorist attacks, tsunamis, mining disasters, student deaths by gunfire, and other situations (e.g., Gittell, 2008; Seeger & Ulmer, 2002). This chapter in particular focuses on workplace contexts and organizational members' communicative construction of resilience to retain dignity and hope in the face of destructive situations.

Resilience has been viewed in various ways: a trait that only certain people or families possess, a quality that emerges over time, a process of sustaining hardship, and the human capacity to recover from tragedy in personal and professional lives. Although there are potential neurobiological bases for the trait of resilience, we argue that context shapes and gives meaning and depth to such bases. Indeed, people from the same genetic pool may respond quite differently to the identical circumstances. As a quality, resilience is a "way of facing and understanding the world, that is deeply etched into a person's mind and soul" (Coutu, 2002, p. 55). As a process, it is a series of iterative attempts to locate meaning, normalcy, and productive identities and identifications in order to rebound or reintegrate from difficult life experiences. We maintain that resilience is a both a quality and a process constituted and reconstituted through interactions and intersubjective sensemaking. We align ourselves with the idea that resilience is a *"process of reintegrating from disruptions in life"* (Richardson, 2002, p. 309, emphasis added) and redirect attention to communicative constructions that enable people to rebound from destructive experiences.

This chapter describes how people living through destructive work-related experiences constructed resilience, those who faced job loss, irrational organizing processes, and long-term work–life tensions. Although the studies included may seem somewhat limited in scope, we argue that the underlying processes of constructing resilience are analogous to a wide array of contexts, individuals, and groups. We begin by providing an overview of resilience in general and the make-up of resilient people. Next, we describe data and findings from three workplace studies. We conclude with a synopsis of common discourses and practices that enabled people in these situations to endure what seemed to be, at the time, the bleakest or most difficult moments of their lives. We conclude with directions for future research.

Review of Literature on Resilience

In this review, we first provide a historical and interdisciplinary overview of resilience theory and research in diverse contexts. We specifically focus on the interactional level as people develop capacities for resilience with others. Second, we situate our attention on the workplace as one site whereby problematic conditions engender the construction of resilience.

Resilience Theory and Research in Diverse Contexts

The construct of resilience has been defined in several different ways without agreement regarding "(a) the age domain covered by the construct, (b) the circumstances where it occurs, (c) its definition, (d) its boundaries, or (e) the adaptive behaviors described" (Mandleco & Peery, 2000, p. 100). Most conceptualizations do, however, highlight the positive nature of outcomes in conditions perceived as adverse: "a dynamic process encompassing positive adaptation within the context of significant adversity" (Luthar, Cicchetti, & Becker, 2000, p. 543); "a phenomenon characterized by good outcomes in spite of serious threats to adaptation or development" (Masten, 2001, p. 227); a capacity or characteristic to maintain positive adjustment or even thrive under adverse conditions (Sutcliffe & Vogus, 2003); and "successful outcomes under conditions of adversity" (Gilgun, 1999, p. 41). Other conceptualizations focus on strategies for dealing with potentially destructive situations (e.g., coping mechanisms, adaptive responses, adjustment, negotiation) (Rutter, 2003), "positive adaptation in the context of significant risk or adversity" (Masten & Powell, 2003, p. 4), and "a process or phenomenon reflecting positive ... adjustment despite conditions of risk" (Luthar & Zelazo, 2003, p. 510).

Others refer to resilience as "an ongoing process of garnering resources that enables the individual to negotiate current issues adaptively and provides a foundation for dealing with subsequent challenges" (Yates, Egeland, & Sroufe, 2003, p. 249). These processes specify the negative triggering event or situation, mediating processes for dealing with it including remedial identity work (Lutgen-Sandvik, 2008), and positive outcome(s). From this perspective, actors intersubjectively construct resilience primarily when faced with significant threat, risk, or adversity. The resulting positive adaptation, recovery, or reintegration are hallmarks of resilience. An interdisciplinary community has adapted this basic model and explored the relationships among resilience and human development, stress responses, agency, and negotiation of self-definition.

Traditionally, resilience research focused on human development, or the nature of children's positive adaptations in adverse circumstances, particularly reasons why some children emerged stronger and relatively unaffected. Early research focused on risk and realized that a significant number of children not only were unimpaired but, in fact, flourished under conditions of adversity (Masten, 2001; Masten & Coatsworth, 1998). A key scholar in this early work, Norman Garmezy (e.g., 1974), sought to uncover the bases and characteristics of schizophrenia in his study of children at risk for psychopathology (e.g., children of schizophrenic parents). Garmezy concluded that resilience played a huge role in their ability to function, a conclusion that led to studies of competence, adversity, and resilience (Coutu, 2002; Masten & Powell, 2003).

In addition to human development, other studies attempted to ferret out the mind-body underpinnings of stress responses (e.g., sources and protective factors). This research centered on the psychological aspects of coping and the physiological aspects of stress (Tusaie & Dyer, 2004). The early studies of resilience sought to uncover associated intrapersonal factors (e.g., cognitive features, specific competencies) and environmental factors (Tusaie & Dyer). Intrapersonal factors included optimism, intelligence, creativity, ability to construct a cohesive life narrative, and an appreciation of one's uniqueness. Competencies included coping strategies, social skills, educational abilities, and memory above the average level.

Research linked a number of protective factors to building or maintaining resilience. Protective factors "moderate the effects of individual vulnerabilities or environmental hazards, so that a given developmental trajectory reflects more adaptation in a given domain than would be the case if protective processes were not operating" (Hauser, 1999, p. 4). Factors range from individual attributes to broader life experiences or conditions. Individual factors include person-specific differences in cognitive abilities and self-perceptions (of competence, worth, confidence); self-regulation skills (e.g., impulse control, positive outlook on life); relationships (e.g., parenting quality, closeness with competent adults), and connections to prosocial, rule-abiding peers and community resources and opportunities (e.g., good schools, neighborhood quality, health care; Masten & Powell, 2003).[1]

In the area of environmental factors, Heckhausen (2001) points to socioeconomic status as a protective factor, and Werner's (1995) ecological approach suggests that multiple protective factors exist at the individual, family, and community levels. These factors "appear to transcend ethnic, social class and geographic boundaries" (Werner, p. 82). Yet data fail to answer fundamental questions such as, "if one manipulates a particular protective factor in the child or in the environment, then what particular changes are likely to occur?" (Masten & Coatsworth, 1998, p. 214).

Others who study risk and resilience within the framework of developmental psychopathology (e.g., Gilgun, 1999) argue that resilience development is an act of human agency. For instance, Everall and colleagues (2006) view individuals as active agents who use various resources to assist them in rebounding from adversity. They define resilience as

> an adaptive process whereby the individual willingly makes use of internal and external resources to overcome adversity or threats to development. Resilient youth are defined not as individuals who possess a unique quality called "resilience" but rather as individuals who have overcome adversity through the resilience process. (p. 462)

Everall and colleagues delineated four domains of resilience in adolescent females including social processes or relationships; emotional processes or the awareness and expression of feelings; cognitive processes and feelings of personal control over their lives; and purposeful action, the perceptions of engaging in goal-directed behavior leading to greater independence, new behaviors, hope for their futures, and positive identities. Adolescents ostensibly developed and exerted agency from their growing recognition of control over their inner and outer worlds.

A constructionist approach to resilience, on the other hand, "reflects a postmodern interpretation of the construct and defines resilience as the outcome from negotiations between individuals and their environments for the resources to define themselves as healthy amidst conditions collectively viewed as adverse" (Ungar, 2004, p. 342). Ungar argues that the ecological model fails to accommodate the multiple meanings associated with resilience. On the other hand, the phenomenologically explored constructionist interpretation incorporates the different influencing factors and approaches to developing and maintaining resilience. As such, race, ethnicity, class, gender, ability, sexual social orientation, and other points of difference can be plumbed to determine not only "access to health resources but, at a more fundamental level, our definition of resilience itself" (Ungar, p. 360).

Some argue that biology can contribute to our understanding of successful adaptation to adversity (Curtis & Cicchetti, 2003; Luthar et al., 2000). Richardson's (2002) metatheoretical presentation, for example, describes resilience as a "force within everyone that drives them to seek self-actualization, altruism, wisdom, and harmony with a spiritual source of strength" (p. 313). He draws from physics, Eastern medicine, a belief in God or a creative force, as well as psychoneuroimmunology to develop this perspective. Others classify resilience and resilient qualities as issues within the domain of positive psychology, a field that seeks to foster life satisfaction, power sharing, community contributions, hope, and happiness (Seligman & Csikszentmihalyi, 2000). Resilience, then, is a yearning to lead meaningful lives replete with hope, dignity, and compassion. In sum, researchers have directed attention to human development, stress reactions, agency, person-environment negotiations, and biology.

Over time, criticism has arisen about the individual focus, unpredictability of adaptive phase models, and inattention to adults. Increasingly, scholars view resilience as a process or phenomenon and *not* an individual personality trait (Luthar & Zelazo, 2003; Richardson, 2002). Indeed, Luthar and Zelazo oppose classifying resilience as a personal trait because of its implication in situating blame for "failure" at the individual level. Put another way, when the individual is (or is not) resilient, then the individual is personally responsible for his or her ability or inability to bounce back. Rather, they are of the opinion that "resilient trajectories are enormously influenced by processes arising from the family and the wider environment" (Luthar & Zelazo, p. 513). They also object to the use of the term "resilient" as an adjective describing individuals and recommend its use only with regard to profiles or trajectories because of the difficulty of untangling causes and responsibilities of thriving in difficult circumstances. Moreover, the factors associated with lifespan resilience are insufficiently documented given that literature on adults, as opposed to children, is less extensive (with the exception of studies focusing on a "hardy personality" that copes successfully with stressful situations) (Daly, 1999).[2]

Resilience in the Workplace

Organizational members experience many workplace conditions that are adverse, destructive, and detrimental, as is evident in this volume. Since these destructive experiences are likely to engender resilient processes, either individually or collectively, then the workplace is an ideal site to explore the phenomenon. Workplaces are embedded in a global world marked by constant change, such as mergers, restructuring, reengineering, downsizing, and other factors that affect employment patterns and career directions (Brown, 1996; Hall & Mirvis, 1995; Sterns & Huyck, 2001). Individuals who are able to brand themselves in a distinctive and attractive fashion—as youthful, committed, mobile, and professional—and those who have the necessary career capital (e.g., resiliency) may survive and even flourish in this volatile contemporary marketplace (Buzzanell, 2000; Greller & Stroh, 1995; Lair, Sullivan, & Cheney, 2005).

Furthermore, workplaces may be populated with coworkers, bosses, and direct reports who are problematic or mildly uncivil at best, or as abusive, bullying, harassing, and extremely harmful at worst (e.g., Fritz & Omdahl, 2006b; Kreps, 1993; Lutgen-Sandvik, 2003, 2008; Sypher, 2004; Tracy, Lutgen-Sandvik, & Alberts, 2006). In these cases, the capacity to manage difficult people and situations depends on the degree to which targets of undesirable behaviors can analyze or reframe their experiences, make sense of and construct alternative narratives, and utilize different logics in their discourse, such as the language of care ethics or empowering metaphors (e.g., language of justice and ethics, metaphors of victimization; see Buzzanell, 2004; Clair, 1993; Liu & Buzzanell, 2004; Tracy et al., 2006). Those who rebound or reintegrate quickly may have developed strategies or processes of resiliency over their lifetimes but also appear capable of learning how to turn "disruptive changes and conflicts from potential disasters into growth opportunities" (Maddi & Khoshaba, 2005, p. 3; see also Hall, 2002; Inkson, 2007; London, 1998; Lutgen-Sandvik, 2008). Indeed, the conditions that trigger resilient processes might be considered career development insofar as resilience is positively related to actual career changes, such as job enrichment and enlargement (Grezda, 1999; McCall, Lombardo, & Morrison, 1988).

Considerable research (Brown, 1996; Coutu, 2002; London, 1998; Maddi & Khoshaba, 2005) foregrounds the importance of understanding how people handle changes in different aspects of their career, work, and family lives. This move to construct understandings of resilience in varied contexts parallels others' suggestions that inconsistencies in processes of resilience across children's experiences might warrant multiple definitions of resilience, such as social, academic, or emotional resilience (Everall et al., 2006; Olsson, Bond, Burns, Vella-Brodrick, & Sawyer, 2003). If one assumes that resilience is an intersubjective process that develops over time and has context-specific qualities, then multi-dimensional "resiliencies" make sense.

One area in which the term resilience has gained currency is career resilience, the "ability to adapt to changing circumstances, even when the circumstances are discouraging or disruptive" (London, 1998, p. 60; see also Brown, 1996; Gunz & Peiperl, 2007). Some of career resilience research harkens back to individual attributes and outcomes research on resilience. For instance, laid-off workers high in Type-A characteristics such as aggression and ambition were more likely than workers low in Type-A characteristics to be actively involved in job searches, despite labor market conditions (Leana & Feldman, 1992). In another study that surveyed layoff survivors about their responses to the continuing threat of job loss, workers who were optimistic and had a strong sense of self-efficacy tended to engage in control-oriented coping, while workers with low optimism and low self-efficacy had a stronger sense of powerlessness and were more likely to engage in escape strategies (Armstrong-Stassen, 1994, cited in London, 1998). These findings coincide with Siebert's (1996) observations that the most resilient people are those who balance self-esteem and self-criticism, blend confidence and doubt, and remain open to the idea that they have weaknesses.

Similarly, Coutu (2002) suggests there are three overlapping qualities in resilient individuals and organizations: a staunch acceptance of reality, a deep belief that life is meaningful, and the ability to improvise under pressure. Coutu recommends fostering a realistic, almost pessimistic, view of reality, as well as cognitive processes that encourage adapting, improvising, and imagining possibilities to myriad situations. Thus, studies on resilience in the workplace underscore Richardson's (2002) first two waves of resilience research. This research focuses primarily on the characteristics of resilient individuals and organizing and on the processes of developing resiliency, rather than on the processes of reintegrating, or recrafting new identities and lifestyles, after disruptions in life. It is the processes of developing resiliency to which we now attend.

Communicative Constructions of Resilience

As organizational members deal with the trauma, doubts, and challenges, they actively search for and give meaning to their worlds. This search involves intersubjective (re)shapings and (re)enactments of emerging and sometimes contradictory realities. In focusing specifically on the construction of resilience in the workplace, three overarching questions guide our analysis: (a) How do individuals discursively construct resilience in troubled times? (b) What do people perceive and describe as productive feelings, behaviors, and identity performances at these times? and (c) In what ways does communication play a role in the construction of resilience?

We examine three distinct cases. In each of these, we summarize the problematic process and highlight the communication processes involved in the construction of resilience. The first case deals with job loss and the emotion labor of regaining a sense of normalcy. The second case addresses day-to-day coping with stresses brought on by organizational irrationalities at Head Start. The third case looks at intersections of work and nonwork life, specifically, how people find and develop capacities for resilience when they also must deal with long-term disease and disability.

Job Loss

Individuals dealing with job loss lose not only their jobs but also their place in the world of work, families, and communities, as well as ways of organizing the spatio-temporal contours of their daily lives (Buzzanell & Turner, 2003). By all accounts, then, job loss—with its triggering event of involuntary termination and process of being unemployed—is exceedingly difficult. Despite individual differences in capacities to undergo stress (e.g., families' finances), the consequences of job loss are "generally detrimental to individuals by virtually any criteria a researcher chooses to examine" (Latack, Kinicki, & Prussia, 1995, p. 312). Negative outcomes are particularly obvious when a person is "let go" or "fired" because of individual performance or office politics rather than being part of a planned or large-scale downsizing. When persons believe they are to blame and that the organization has acted justly in the job loss process, they may experience even greater negative consequences.

The lens of emotion work, "the effort we put into ensuring that our private feelings are suppressed or represented to be in tune with socially accepted norms" (Fineman, 1993, p. 3), is useful for examining how individuals who have lost their jobs and how their family members deal with job loss. Another is identity work in which workers engage in efforts to invoke plausible and productive identities or life narratives from an array of possibilities (Gergen, 1994). These emotion and identity constructions are discursive, material processes akin, in many cases, to dialectics in which oppositional emotions and identities are entertained, recast, rejected, adapted, managed for self-presentation, and shaped into narratives for themselves and others.

The difficulty of emotion and identity work can be characterized in processes of sensemaking, discursive framing, and performance.

> [I]ndividuals who lost their jobs may have difficulty knowing what to relate, when and to whom to display concerns, and how to channel effort into creating acceptable displays. During these sensemaking processes, their emotion work may fall within the disquieting junctures of private-public and of raw feelings-acceptable feeling displays. (Buzzanell & Turner, 2003, p. 28)

The difficulty is that former, preferred, emerging, and current identities intersect in ways that may be problematic as individuals search for socially appropriate identity displays and descriptors. What may be appropriate at any given moment or location may not be so in the next.

Interviews with 24 persons from seven families (seven middle-class Caucasian men who involuntarily lost white-collar jobs and 17 family members) presented three interrelated themes: foregrounding/backgrounding of emotions, normalcy, and (re)instituting of traditional masculinities. These three themes suggested that *people intersubjectively create conditions for building on their capabilities for resilience and engaging in discourses of resiliency.* In the period of unemployment that followed involuntary job loss, those interviewed had different insights into and perspectives of the event and unemployment process. However, they typically engaged in discourses about (a) emotion, (b) normalcy, and (c) identity that provided them with a sense of stability, comfort, and even happiness about their abilities to maintain (and support others in) their most important roles in their lives.

With regard to *emotion*, individuals and their family members collectively worked toward talking about and performing positive feelings about their situations. If members failed to conform to these positive emotion performances at the time of job loss and afterwards, they disciplined themselves and also sought discursive control of others. For instance, one wife said that she originally blamed her husband for losing a great job but reconsidered what she was saying and revised it to be supportive of him. Individuals who incurred job loss chose, together with their families, to foreground feelings of hope, optimism about future job possibilities, gratefulness for that familial support and that the family could be provided for. At the same time, they acknowledged the legitimacy of feelings of anger, shock, betrayal, and hopelessness experienced at the time of termination and afterwards.

As families made sense of their situations, they deliberately foregrounded the positive and backgrounded the negative. They did not repress the negative, they simply portrayed these feelings as dysfunctional to their overall life goals. Families' emotion work centered on determining how and when they could or should enact certain feelings given the vast emotional repertoire they embodied as individuals. Perhaps the issue was not so much working to portray feelings that were appropriate to others, but constructing feelings that enabled them to regain a sense of normalcy.

Normalcy, creating a sense of familiarity and ordinariness, was pivotal to families' intersubjective construction of resilience. Participants said repeatedly that they tried to keep everything as normal as possible. Despite efforts to regain normalcy—to sustain important individual and family rituals and interactional patterns—they did not, and could not, return to the exact contexts in which they lived prior to job loss. So they worked to *talk normalcy into being* when their worlds were utterly chaotic and unpredictable. There was hope that things would become normal, and there were material adjustments (e.g., finances, living conditions, activities, resource allocations) that coincided with their new normalcy. Those things that were symbolically important to the families (e.g., Friday night dinners eaten outside of the home, shopping, vacations) were retained although the locations might be different (e.g., eating at a fast food rather than a more upscale restaurant).

Another theme centered on participants' *discursive constructions of identity anchors*. By crafting the term, identity anchor, we mean a relatively enduring set of identity discourses upon which individuals rely when explaining (to themselves and others) who they are and want to be. In the job loss study, managerial, professional, and masculine identities intersected to enhance formation of particular masculinities (e.g., heterosexual, white, managerial/professional), which meant being the breadwinner, household head or decision maker, and not being a "loser" on unemployment. Such a masculine identity was important to these men who discursively upheld these identity constructions, but partners and children similarly upheld these constructions. Others might use different discursive resources for identity anchors in times of chaos (e.g., trust in God to help see people through difficult times; see Black & Lobo, 2008).[3]

In short, people who experienced job loss constructed resilience by talking into being and performing positive emotions, a sense that their lives were normal, and anchoring identities. They discursively engaged and performed this resilience work in concert with others to construct a communicative context in which they could bounce back as individuals and as family systems. Thus, resilience was neither a fixed attribute of the individuals or family units nor a desirable outcome but was, instead, a dynamic intersubjective process.

Although the job loss case displays how individuals and families talk and interact in ways that encourage them to recover from a devastating work-related situation and create a new normalcy, resilience is also communicatively constructed in the workplace itself. In the next case underscoring organizational irrationalities, various stakeholders in organizational missions created resilience through everyday workplace interactions and the resulting structures dealt with the "craziness" of standard operating procedures (SOPs) and policies. Theirs is not a bouncing back from a specific event but an ongoing series of adjustments (setting and resetting of rules, metarules, and logics) to accomplish goals and live by overarching values, given a material context marked by irrationalities.

Irrationalities

Organizational irrationalities are everyday practices that pull organizational members in different, sometimes competing directions and include phenomena such as paradox, tension, contradiction, and irony (Trethewey & Ashcraft, 2004). Traditional approaches of organizational scholarship center on strategies and schemas to limit, constrain, and even erase the causes and consequences of organizational irrationality. However, organizational irrationality is not necessarily negative; in fact, it may actually be "the stuff of organizing" (Trethewey, 1999, p. 142). Because irrationality often constitutes organizational members' everyday understandings of situations, exploring contradictions and ironies of organizing illustrates another example of how organizational members construct resiliency. Workers faced with such irrationalities create intricate processes of "working around" the contradictions embedded in structures (e.g., reward), policies, procedures, and practices, while still adhering to central values and goals.

Head Start,[4] like many government-funded bureaucracies, at times presents members with contradictory, ironic, and seemingly nonsensical ways of organizing. Although such irrationalities could be perceived as destructive, Head Start teacher accounts suggest differently (Remke, 2006). Indeed, these teachers intersubjectively maintained resilience by continuously reintegrating themselves and others (i.e., teachers, students, administrators, community members, directors, visitors, and governmental experts) through their moment-by-moment talk, interactions, "rules" revisions or reinterpretations, policy redesigns, and adaptive structures. They did so despite regulations and SOPs they perceived impossible to meet. Teachers' ongoing communication flexibly framed conflicting demands so that they could bounce back from daily fissures in their values and goals, on one hand, and the Head Start mandates, on the other. Unlike resilience in the face of a singular event, resilient responses to organizational irrationality required an ongoing series of communicative strategies to respond to seemingly irrational phenomena that are embedded within organizing itself.

Participant-observation and in-depth interviews with the staff of ten Head Start classrooms suggested that Head Start teachers, like other public service workers, work within numerous irrationalities. They do so while navigating ideological and political systems and daily work practices that both hinder and create opportunities for client change and societal reform. For example, President Bush's "No Child Left Behind" initiatives required Head Start to develop more academic standards and measures for determining success. Many organizational members believed this moved Head Start from a program that helped the "whole" child's development (i.e., emotional, mental, physical, intellectual) to a program centered on instructing children in narrower (i.e., quantifiable, comparable) skills, often by sacrificing other more important competencies.

In addition, teachers reported subscribing to Head Start's rules and policies because they deferred to the expertise of government officials, but they routinely operated by "metarules"—overarching value-driven goals—that superseded all else. Metarules prioritized children's safety, developed parental expertise, and maintained Head Start's presence in the community. They deemed the completion of required paperwork and prescribed tasks as secondary to these more important goals. Teachers and administrators even devoted their family time and personal funds to ensure that children remained in the Head Start program and received needed materials.

Workers loosely followed Head Start requirements for lesson plans to be filed at least a week before implementation because of the constantly changing demands workers faced. As a result, teachers filed lessons according to schedule but operated with the idea that only a third of their planning could be implemented and they would amend filed lessons after the fact. Yet all teachers, staff, and administrators adamantly claimed that they adhered to the rules because these were the rules—maybe saying otherwise might jeopardize government funding. Belief in the rules might also provide a hedge against the chaos that awaited them every day.

Although teachers and administrators used rules and standards of Head Start to ensure the children were protected and treated fairly, rules sometimes prohibited those who really needed the help from obtaining assistance. Because Head Start is a voluntary program, Head Start relies on the parents or guardians to enroll their child in a local classroom. The parent must attend an orientation meeting, prepare numerous forms requiring signatures from several people (including a doctor), and then volunteer for the local classroom for a set number of hours each year. Although these tasks are not difficult for most parents, a majority of Head Start parents are dealing with numerous difficulties that can preclude completion of obligations. These difficulties often interrupted not only their lives, but also the lives of their children.

Head Start fills an important function by providing stability and safety to children who might not experience these in their personal lives. Despite familial pressures, parents enroll their child and volunteer to maintain the child's enrolled status. Children are removed from Head Start if the parents cannot meet all the requirements—there are no exceptions. For example, approved guardians must be waiting when the child gets off the bus; bus drivers must make visual contact with the guardian before the child is released. However, there is no mechanism to help parents who are unable to meet the bus and cannot appoint an alternative adult. The only alternative is for the child to be removed from Head Start, which might further endanger the child. Thus, the families that could profit the most from Head Start services are often those who cannot meet the minimum requirements to keep their child enrolled.

Although teachers acknowledged that there were some irrationalities at Head Start, they rationalized that the irrationality was fundamental to the organization—so fundamental to organizing their work and accomplishing their goals and relationships that, without the irrationality, Head Start could not exist. Unintentionally the teachers utilized irrationality for their benefit. They did not attempt to resolve the contradiction because irrationality was embedded in a system they knew, understood, circumvented, and believed they were unable to change. The teachers discourse embodied resilience because, to summarize their words, they were just doing what they had to do to get their jobs done. There was no need to change or transcend the irrationality because the teachers and staff workers operated in their own co-culture that legitimized their behavior and rationalizations. They did not try to transcend, which means they did not try to change the system—they knew the system and did not want it to change. Yet, they were constantly changing the system and modifying it to meet their needs on a day-to-day, moment-to-moment basis.

Their approaches to their work and their children countered traditional, standard structures. Traditional structures, such as education and the military, position people in categories and organize them based on their ability to accomplish standardized tasks. Head Start teachers resisted these taken-for-granted processes of bureaucracy (i.e., sameness, conformity, and rules accommodations) and challenged the foundational workings of this system. The teachers responded to the organizational irrationality by creating their own rationality, their own way of being and operating. They negotiated the logics of the dominant bureaucratic rationality and the chaotic, seemingly nonsensical reality of the Head Start children and families, which allowed the children and the organization to be successful in their own terms. For the Head Start teachers, *resilience became the communicative construction whereby they created their own organizing logics or conditions intersubjectively that enabled them to bounce back and reintegrate during and after especially "crazy" and potentially detrimental workplace experiences.*

Although the teachers and staff workers did not describe their communication as resistant, they articulated an alternative logic and embodied response rationality that did, in fact, resist the bureaucratically defined ways to accomplish work and allowed the participants to embrace the organizational irrationality, thus making it their own. By creating their own definitions for themselves and for their organization, their own expectations for themselves and their children, they devised an alternative system that rejected the dominant (inflexible) system. It was resilience that enabled them to pursue and sustain their alternative organizing logics. These logics were alternative insofar as they were not designed to displace the system but to coexist with the system, much as complementary medicines can co-exist with alternative and traditional medicines because they all accomplish different things (see Ellingson, 2004; for alternative organizing structures, see Buzzanell et al., 1997). It was through this alternative organizing that members continuously refashioned their work lives to construct new discursive and material realities.

In the final case, we move from specific incidents, such as job loss and alternative organizing logics, to the intersections of work–life issues. Here, actors constitute resilience through communication practices marked by accepting of harsh realities, adapting to the material meanings of those realities, holding onto identity anchors, and helping others develop the capacity for resilience to assist, reinforce, and encourage everyday work–life efforts.

Long-Term Work–Life Tensions

Whether people attempt to balance, negotiate, manage, accept, or juggle competing demands for their time, it is clear that work–life negotiations are a challenge for almost everyone at some point in their lives. These challenges can become even more difficult in the face of long-term disease or disability. In these cases, individuals and their family members co-created meanings that helped them with daily realities of long-term disability and requirements to be productive workers. Through such messages, they constructed resilience in order to reintegrate, fashion new normalcies, and utilize networks of support to help them to "bounce back." This resilience enabled them to develop a sense of efficacy, a belief that they could cope with and surmount difficulties, and a steadfast recognition of the reality with which they were faced.

Being diagnosed with a chronic illness or suffering a physical trauma that results in a physical disability can be devastating. Particularly in the case of diseases or disabilities that come later in life, it can require remaking self identity, repositioning into a new disability culture, and changing personal and familial relationships (Braithwaite & Braithwaite, 2005; Braithwaite & Thompson, 2000). Furthermore, the person with the disease or disability is not the only one affected. Entire family structures and community or workplace interactions change as people must learn to navigate their lives without what Frank (1997) would call their "healthy body-selves."

Bouncing back from disabling experiences and diagnoses requires considerable physical and psychological resilience. Things such as administering daily drug regimes and injections, learning to use a wheelchair or prosthetic limb, coping with chronic pain, and dealing with memory loss and personality changes due to brain injuries call for ongoing persistence and flexibility. To complicate these matters, the effects of such circumstances extend beyond the individuals and their personal relationships. The people with disabilities, as well as the people who love them, typically face career and employment (i.e., financial) consequences.

In interviews with 25 families (see Lucas, 2006), more than half of the families (n = 15) described a catastrophic health problem with an immediate family member. These included long-term diseases (e.g., rheumatoid arthritis, cancer, multiple sclerosis, diabetes, Parkinson's disease), brain injuries, paralysis, organ failure, debilitating on-the-job injuries (e.g., back pain, broken necks, broken backs), and developmental and physical disabilities. For these families, health and disability concerns were an important facet of everyday life and provided a poignant context for understanding the process of building resilience, resistance that often crossed the private domain into public (work) life.

Two interrelated processes dominated the way these families built resilience: accepting and adapting. Both appeared to be necessary for "accomplishing" resilience. *Accepting* was a crucial and ongoing component of resilience marked by the cognitive and emotional "facing down of reality" (Coutu, 2002, p. 50). In contrast to resignation, which carries connotations of defeat, accepting focused on holding realistic expectations and responding accordingly. For example, Frankl, (1959) explained that persons most likely to survive prisoner of war and concentration camps were those who envisioned their future as being prisoners looking forward to an imminent release. The latter died "of broken hearts," while the former survived by accepting the fate of themselves as a long-term, if not permanent, change (Frankl, 1959). An attitude of acceptance provided the advantage necessary to survive.

Likewise, in the case of long-term disease and disability, resilience-as-acceptance meant coming to terms with the condition (including the diagnosis, prognosis, degree, duration, etc.). For example, people with paralysis that accepted their paralysis as permanent often had the most successful recoveries. Instead of focusing their energies on walking, they were able to learn techniques that helped them make a successful transition back home (e.g., wheelchair use, proper lifting techniques, adaptive technologies). Family-member talk about their specific health-related problems evidenced resilience-as-acceptance. They frequently made comments such as, "This is how it is now;" "It ain't going away;" and "Every family has tragedy. I just had mine in a bunch."

The second necessary process was adapting, the process of making adjustments to respond productively to and rebound successfully from new life circumstances brought about by disruptions, tragedies, and crises. In this case, families found ways to adjust to their new circumstances of living with chronic illness or disability, or being a primary caregiver for a loved one. Participants worked intensive care-giving into their daily routines (e.g., feeding a disabled adult family member, providing long-term care for a child with severe disabilities), made strategic career decisions that enabled them to better meet work–life demands (e.g., opening a home-based business, staying in an unpleasant job to preserve insurance benefits), and integrated health care negotiations into their work–life priorities (e.g., dealing with insurance companies, managing sick leave time with their employers). These adaptations marked vivid ways in which long-term disease or disability blurred divisions between organizational lives and private lives.

Importantly, both processes appeared to be present and necessary for families to respond resiliently to the situations. Accepting without adapting amounted to resignation and defeat; and adapting without accepting represented denial and, perhaps, only short-term success. Moreover, in contrast to research that suggests a "transformational" element to life-traumas (see Bury, 1982; Crossley, 2000; Lutgen-Sandvik, 2008), "finding a silver lining" does not necessary lead to resilience. Positive outcomes were absent from these families' talk of work–life balance. They did not speak about being better, stronger people for the experience, nor did they discuss their improved abilities at multi-tasking and negotiating, or their increased knowledge of the human body and medicine as benefits of their own or family members' disability or disease. Instead, *they produced and performed a resilience that faced realities, socially constructed what those realities were, adapted to the situation while resisting unproductive commentary and policies by others, and found something worthwhile in their experiences*, such as their ability to do something that brought joy to the person with the disability and his/her family.

One case that speaks directly to the communicative nature of resilience is Matthew's; his wife had a medical emergency that left her with permanent vision loss and extensive paralysis (see Lucas, 2006). In addition to working full-time, Matthew had sole responsibility for housekeeping duties, as well as being the primary caregiver for his wife and two preteen children. Rather than pitying himself or fantasizing about a miracle cure, Matthew explained matter-of-factly, "Life is not fair." In addition to his description of his life circumstances in terms of resilience-as-accepting and resilience-as-adapting, Matthew's case also demonstrates how processes of resilience can be taught. He applied a closet-like metaphor to cope with his work–life demands, "I never bring work home. It stays right there. Don't bring it home. Don't talk about it. Leave it there. You got to be able to punch out and leave it *on the hanger* until you come the next day" (emphasis added). It took Matthew some time to learn how to master compartmentalizing his work this way. He explained, "after about four or five years, you can learn to *hang your hat there* for the day and go home. But it takes a while" (emphasis added).

He framed workplace routines to coincide with this metaphor and carried it forward with regard to his family-based responsibilities. Accepting that his wife's recovery was as complete as it would ever be. In what follows, he expressed how he handled the ongoing adaptation process:

> Live with it. Deal with it. That's what I always tell my daughters: "Deal with it." It's there. Deal with it. It ain't going to go away. If you can't deal with it, *put in on the shelf.* Then take it off later and deal with it. Just, it ain't going to go away. If something's got to be dealt with, it never goes away until you deal with it. (Emphasis added)

Not only did he draw upon his closet metaphor as a way to accept and adapt to the situation, his metaphor also was a vehicle for teaching lessons of resilience to his children. In this way, Matthew provided a vivid exemplar for understanding how individuals enact resilience and, simultaneously, encourage the development of resilience in others. Like those

experiencing job loss, his comments point to an ongoing creation and performance of a new normalcy in which the essence of important personal or
familial routines and identity anchors, such as being a good father and
worker, were preserved. In this regard, he served as a role model and
bearer of important socializing messages to his daughters so that they
could become resilient adults. Through it all, he managed his employment
responsibilities to the organization to sustain the material resources
needed to keep his family together.

Matthew and the other families in Lucas's (2006) study made significant
career adaptations consistent with the unique set of challenges they faced.
Implications of this case demonstrate *that resilience in work–life contexts
for which disruptions of a tenuous balance could occur at any moment
requires ongoing and complex communication with others in multiple
domains to reintegrate or bounce back on a regular basis*. As a research
opportunity for organizational communication scholars, perhaps instead
of focusing on work-to-family and family-to-work conflicts and the potentially negative career consequences of these workplace situations,
researchers might provide insight into the ways people intersubjectively
construct work–life resilience in ways that transcend domains.

Conclusion

Human actors intersubjectively construct resilience. That is, individuals
and collectivities literally talk and enact resiliency into being. Through
three empirical cases traversing individual through organizational levels,
we addressed the emotion and identity work, the organizing of irrationalities, and the messages, stories, and daily work–life performances that
enabled people to bounce back from potentially debilitating workplace
and work-related contexts. We also used these cases as springboards for
possible interventions to foster resilience. From the three cases, it is evident
that resilience is a collaborative effort, an exchange that encourages and
requires participation of family, workplace, and community members. As
a new story is crafted, there must be others who support and elaborate on
the version and its potential to remedy the destructive elements of the current situation. This co-crafting of narratives, identities, emotions, organizing logics, and other aspects relies on an acceptance of new realities.

This chapter is an initial exploration into the ways that ordinary people
create resilience through discourse and practices. Some pragmatic applications of our analyses suggest that members engage in sensemaking
processes to uncover that which they value most in their individual, familial, and organizational identities, routines, norms, values, or missions.
Communication and resilience are anchored around these features. Family, workplace, and community discussions—in co-located or virtual environments, blogs, and chatrooms—about central values around which

members can collaborate and how they prefer to participate could occur on a regular basis. These discussions would provide a context in which members could share information and strategies and mentor each other in resilience construction. Moreover, an acceptance of reality with desires to preserve the dignity of all involved in potentially debilitating situations provides foundations for collaboratively crafting new procedures, practices, identity stories, and work–life negotiations. Every couple of years, a task force of organizational members could revisit these practices and policies to see if they meet members' needs. This task force could bring in stakeholders from relevant collectivities, such as families, not-for-profit support associations, and healthcare personnel. Finally, there can never be a return to the previous situation after debilitating and destructive episodes have occurred. Assistance in containing, living with, and changing aspects along with the development of a new normalcy could help individuals deal with daily frustrations and identity challenges that contribute to stressors in difficult situations. Finally, workshops and focus groups that prompt conversations about the contradictions and ironies manifest in discourses, organizing practices, and associated material realities, such as specific tasks and consequences for well-being, can help sustain people and organizational systems and contribute to long-term innovative solutions.

In conclusion, the human resilience relies upon communication to develop capacities and strategies that enable people to bounce back or reintegrate from destructive situations. Communication facilitates acceptance of realities and construction of new normalcies that preserve that which participants hold dear (e.g., maintenance of family rituals, most important identities, continuation of the family unit, upholding the organizational mission, ability to provide and protect organization, family, or community members) to lend dignity and hope to human existence.

Notes

1 Resilience coaches and researchers (e.g., Reivich & Shatte, 2003; Siebert, 1996) have translated the concept of resilience into popular materials (e.g., trade publications, eBooks, workshops) by suggesting steps people can take and personality features that they can emulate to maximize their survival in dealing with certain types of people (e.g., angry, negative) and situations (e.g., emergencies, crises, and misfortunes) rather than being victimized. In both cases, notes on what to do—and not to do—are punctuated by vivid examples of Holocaust survivors, POW (prisoner of war) camp survivors, people who have experienced familial and workplace trauma, and so on.

2 Adult resilience has been studied in multiple contexts but most have focused on youth rather than adults per se in families, work culture, and communities (McCubbin, Thompson, Thompson, & Furtell, 1998). Glicken (2006) has looked at resilience in multiple contexts: culture; spirituality; areas of psychological difficulties such as substance abuse, mental illness, physical abuse, life

threatening illness, disabilities and bereavement; aging; gay, lesbian, bisexual and transgender individuals; loneliness, isolation and depression; family; acts of random violence; and communities.

So far the literature on adult resilience has paid more attention to people who "beat the odds, who avoid the negative trajectories associated with risks" (Schoon, 2006, pp. 8–9). These individuals were members of high risk groups, grew up in violent conditions, had major disabilities or illnesses, endured dysfunctional familial situations, or suffered abuse and trauma. Only recently has there been attention to resilience born of adverse workplace situations.

3 To continue identification with particular roles such as being student, mother, child, woman, and so on and with particular non-employment associations might contribute not only some feelings of stability and purpose in difficult times, but also might account for the contradictions in identity portrayals voiced and enacted by individuals not engaged in paid labor—stay-at-home mothers who refer to themselves by their prior job titles and professions, students describing themselves as doctoral students with the side note that they "used to be" IT troubleshooters or financial consultants. These linguistic choices and talk-in-interaction indicate that identity anchors are operating.

4 Head Start is a governmental program for disadvantaged preschoolers. In preparation for attending kindergarten at age five, qualified three- and four-year-olds attend the Head Start classroom four days a week and are taught age-appropriate reading and math skills. The children also participate in basic science projects and experiments and are exposed to diverse art styles and types of music. Parents and guardians of enrolled children are required to help in the Head Start classroom in the hope that the parents are able to improve their own social and parenting skills.

References

Black, K., & Lobo, M. (2008). A conceptual review of family resilience factors. *Journal of Family Nursing, 14*(1), 33–55.

Braithwaite, D. O., & Braithwaite, C. A. (2005). "Which is my good leg?": Cultural communication of people with disabilities. In L. A. Samovar & R. Porter (Eds.), *Intercultural communication: A reader* (11th ed., pp. 165–176). Belmont, CA: Wadsworth.

Braithwaite, D. O., & Thompson, T. L. (Eds.). (2000). *Handbook of communication and people with disabilities: Research and application.* Mahwah, NJ: Lawrence Erlbaum.

Brown, B. L. (1996). Career resilience. *ERIC Clearinghouse on Adult, Career, and Vocational Education (ERIC Digest Report #178).* Retrieved November 11, 2006, from http://www.cete.org/acve/docgen.asp?tbl=digests&ID=31.

Bury, M. (1982). Chronic illness as biographical disruption. *Sociology of Health and Illness, 4*(2), 167–182.

Buzzanell, P. M. (2000). The promise and practice of the new career and social contract: Illusions exposed and suggestions for reform. In P. M. Buzzanell (Ed.), *Rethinking organizational and managerial communication from feminist perspectives* (pp. 209–235). Thousand Oaks, CA: Sage.

Buzzanell, P. M. (2004). Revisiting sexual harassment in academe: Using feminist ethical and sensemaking approaches to analyze macrodiscourses and micropractices of sexual harassment. In P. M. Buzzanell, H. Sterk & L. H. Turner

(Eds.), *Gender in applied communication contexts* (pp. 25–46). Thousand Oaks, CA: Sage.

Buzzanell, P. M., Ellingson, L., Silvio, C., Pasch, V., Dale, B., Mauro, G., et al. (1997). Leadership processes in alternative organizations: Invitational and dramaturgical leadership. *Communication Studies, 48*(2), 285–310.

Buzzanell, P. M., & Turner, L. H. (2003). Emotion work revealed by job loss discourse: Backgrounding-foregrounding of feelings, construction of normalcy, and (re)instituting of traditional male masculinities. *Journal Applied Communication Research, 31*(1), 27–57.

Clair, R. P. (1993). The use of framing devices to sequester organizational narratives: Hegemony and harassment. *Communication Monographs, 60,* (1) 113–136.

Coutu, D. L. (2002). How resilience works. *Harvard Business Review, 80*(5), 46-55.

Crossley, M. L. (2000). Narrative psychology, trauma and the study of self/identity. *Theory & Psychology, 10*(4), 527–546.

Curtis, W. J., & Cicchetti, D. (2003). Moving research on resilience into the 21st century: Theoretical and methodological considerations in examining the biological contributors to resilience. *Development and Psychopathology, 15*(6), 773–810.

Daly, K. J. (1999). Crisis of genealogy: Facing the challenges of infertility. In H. I. McCubbin, E. A. Thompson, A. I. Thompson & J. A. Futrell (Eds.), *The dynamics of resilient families* (pp. 1–39). Thousand Oaks, CA: Sage.

Ellingson, L. L. (2004). Making meaning of chronic illness, disability, and complementary medicine. In P. M. Buzzanell, H. Sterk & L. H. Turner (Eds.), *Gender in applied communication contexts* (pp. 79–98). Thousand Oaks, CA: Sage.

Everall, R. D., Altrows, K. J., & Paulson, B. L. (2006). Creating a future: A study of resilience in suicidal female adolescents. *Journal of Counseling & Development, 84*(4), 461–470.

Fineman, S. (1993). An emotion agenda. In S. Fineman (Ed.), *Emotions in Organizations* (pp. 1–8). London: Sage.

Frank, A. W. (1997). *The wounded storyteller: Body, illness, and ethics.* Chicago: University of Chicago Press.

Frankl, V. E. (1959). *Man's search for meaning.* New York: Washington Square Press.

Fritz, J. M. H., & Omdahl, B. L. (2006a). Reduced job satisfaction, diminished commitment, and workplace cynicism as outcomes of negative work relationships. In J. M. H. Fritz & B. L. Omdahl (Eds.), *Problematic relationships in the workplace* (pp. 131–151). New York: Peter Lang.

Fritz, J. M. H., & Omdahl, B. L. (Eds.). (2006b). *Problematic relationships in the workplace.* New York: Peter Lang.

Garmezy, N. (1974). The study of competence in children at risk for severe psychopathology. In E. Anthony & C. Koupernik (Eds.), *The child in his family: Children at psychiatric risk, international yearbook* (Vol. 3, pp. 158–175). New York: Wiley.

Gergen, K. (1994). *Realities and relationships: Soundings in social construction.* Cambridge, MA: Harvard University Press.

Gilgun, J. F. (1999). Mapping resilience as process among adults with childhood adversities. In H. I. McCubbin, E. A. Thompson, A. I. Thompson & J. A. Futrell (Eds.), *The dynamics of resilient families* (pp. 41–70). Thousand Oaks, CA: Sage.

Gittell, J. H. (2008). Relationships and resilience: Care provider responses to pressures from managed care. *Journal of Applied Behavioral Science, 44*(1), 25–47.

Glicken, M. D. (2006). *Learning from resilient people: Lessons we can apply to counseling and psychotherapy.* Thousand Oaks, CA: Sage.

Greller, M. M., & Stroh, L. K. (1995). Careers from mid-life and beyond: A fallow field in need of sustenance. *Journal of Vocational Behavior, 47*(2), 232–247.

Grezda, M. M. (1999). Re-conceptualizing career change: A career development perspective. *Career Development International, 4*(6), 305–311.

Gunz, H., & Peiperl, M. (Eds.). (2007). *Handbook of career studies.* London: Sage.

Hall, D. T. (2002). *Careers in and out of organizations.* Thousand Oaks, CA: Sage.

Hall, D. T., & Mirvis, P. H. (1995). The new career contract: Developing the whole person at midlife and beyond. *Journal of Vocational Behavior, 47*(2), 269–289.

Hauser, S. T. (1999). Understanding resilient outcomes: Adolescent lives across time and generations. *Journal of Research on Adolescence, 9*(1), 1–24.

Heckhausen, J. (2001). Adaptation and resilience in midlife. In M. E. Lachman (Ed.), *Handbook of midlife development* (pp. 345–391). New York: John Wiley & Sons.

Inkson, K. (2007). *Understanding careers: The metaphors of working lives.* London: Sage.

Kreps, G. L. (1993). Promoting a sociocultural evolutionary approach to preventing sexual harassment: Metacommunication and cultural adaptation. In G. L. Kreps (Ed.), *Sexual Harassment: Communication implications* (pp. 310–318). Cresskill, NJ: Hampton Press.

Lair, D. J., Sullivan, K., & Cheney, G. (2005). Marketization and the recasting of the professional self. *Management Communication Quarterly, 18*(3), 307–343.

Latack, J. C., Kinicki, A. J., & Prussia, G. E. (1995). An integrative process model of coping with job loss. *Academy of Management Review, 20*(2), 311–342.

Leana, C. R., & Feldman, D. C. (1992). *Coping with job loss: How individuals, organizations, and communities respond to layoffs.* New York: Lexington.

Liu, M., & Buzzanell, P. M. (2004). Negotiating maternity leave expectations: Perceived tensions between ethics of justice and care *Journal of Business Communication, 41*(3), 323–349.

London, M. (1998). Resilience and hardiness: The basis for inner strength. In M. London (Ed.), *Career barriers: How people experience, overcome and avoid failure* (pp. 73–85). Mahwah, NJ: Lawrence Erlbaum.

Lucas, K. (2006). *No footsteps to follow: How blue-collar kids navigate postindustrial careers.* Doctoral dissertation. West Lafayette, IN: Purdue University.

Lutgen-Sandvik, P. (2003). The communicative cycle of employee emotional abuse: Generation and regeneration of workplace mistreatment. *Management Communication Quarterly, 16*(4), 471–501.

Lutgen-Sandvik, P. (2008). Intensive remedial identity work: Responses to workplace bullying and stigma. *Organization, 15*(1), 97–119.

Luthar, S. S., Cicchetti, D., & Becker, B. (2000). The construct of resilience: A critical evaluation and guidelines for future work. *Child Development, 71*(4), 543–562.

Luthar, S. S., & Zelazo, L. B. (2003). Research on resilience: An integrative review. In S. S. Luthar (Ed.), *Resilience and vulnerability: Adaptation in the context of childhood adversities* (pp. 510–550). New York: Cambridge University Press.

Maddi, S. R., & Khoshaba, D. M. (2005). *Resilience at work: How to succeed no matter what life throws at you.* New York: Amacom.

Mandleco, B. L., & Peery, J. C. (2000). Adolescent resilience: An evolutionary concept analysis. *Journal of Pediatric Nursing, 21*(3), 175–185.

Masten, A. S. (2001). Ordinary magic: Resilience processes in development. *American Psychologist, 56*(3), 227–238.

Masten, A. S., & Coatsworth, J. D. (1998). The development of competence in favorable and unfavorable environments. *American Psychologist, 53*(3), 205–220.

Masten, A. S., & Powell, J. L. (2003). A resilience framework for research, policy, and practice. In S. S. Luthar (Ed.), *Resilience and vulnerability: Adaptation in the context of childhood adversities* (pp. 1–28). New York: Cambridge University Press.

McCall, M. W., Lombardo, M. M., & Morrison, A. M. (1988). *The lessons of experience: How successful executives develop on the job.* New York: Lexington.

McCubbin, H. I., Thompson, E. A., Thompson, A. I., & Furtell, J. A. (Eds.). (1998). *Resiliency in African-American families.* Thousand Oaks, CA: Sage.

Olsson, C. A., Bond, L., Burns, J. M., Vella-Brodrick, D. A., & Sawyer, S. M. (2003). Adolescent resilience: A concept analysis. *Journal of Adolescence, 26*(1), 1–11.

Reivich, K., & Shatte, A. (2003). *Resilience factor: 7 keys to finding your inner strength and overcoming life's hurdles.* New York: Random House.

Remke, R. V. (2006). *(Ir)Rationalities at work: The logics, heart, and soul of Head Start.* Doctoral dissertation. West Lafayette, IN: Purdue University.

Richardson, G. E. (2002). The metatheory of resilience and resiliency. *Journal of Clinical Psychology, 58*(3), 307–321.

Rutter, M. (2003). Genetic influences on risk and protection: Implications for understanding resilience. In S. S. Luthar (Ed.), *Resilience and vulnerability: Adaptation in the context of childhood adversities* (pp. 489–509). New York: Cambridge University Press.

Schoon, I. (2006). *Risk and resilience: Adaptations in changing times.* Cambridge, UK: Cambridge University Press.

Seeger, M., & Ulmer, R. (2002). A post-crisis discourse of renewal: The cases of Malden Mills and Cole Hardwoods. *Journal of Applied Communication Research, 30*(2), 126–172.

Seligman, M. E. P., & Csikszentmihalyi, M. (2000). Positive psychology: An introduction. *American Psychologist, 55*(1), 5–14.

Sias, P. M. (2008). *Organizing relationships: Traditional and emerging perspectives on workplace relationships.* Thousand Oaks, CA: Sage.

Siebert, A. (1996). *The Survivor Personality: Why some people are stronger, smarter, and more skillful at handling life's difficulties and how you can be, too.* New York: The Perigree Books/Berkley Publishing Group.

Sterns, H. L., & Huyck, M. H. (2001). The role of work in midlife. In M. E. Lachman (Ed.), *Handbook of midlife development.* New York: John Wiley & Sons.

Sutcliffe, K. M., & Vogus, T. J. (2003). Organizing for resilience. In K. S. Cameron, J. E. Dutton & R. E. Quinn (Eds.), *Positive organizational scholarship* (pp. 94–110). San Francisco: Berrett-Koehler.

Sypher, B. D. (2004). Reclaiming civil discourse in the workplace. *Southern Communication Journal, 69*(2), 257–269.

Tracy, S. J., Lutgen-Sandvik, P., & Alberts, J. K. (2006). Nightmares, demons and slaves: Exploring the painful metaphors of workplace bullying. *Management Communication Quarterly, 20*(2), 148–185.

Trethewey, A. (1999). Isn't it ironic: Using irony to explore the contradictions of organizational life. *Western Journal of Communication, 63*(2), 140–167.

Trethewey, A., & Ashcraft, K. L. (2004). Practicing disorganization: The development of applied perspectives on living with tension. *Journal of Applied Communication Research, 32*(1), 81–88.

Tusaie, K., & Dyer, J. (2004). Resilience: A historical review of the construct. *Holistic Nursing Practice, 18*(1), 3–8.

Ungar, M. (2004). A constructionist discourse on resilience: Multiple contexts, multiple realities among at-risk children and youth. *Youth & Society, 35*(3), 341–365.

Werner, E. E. (1995). Resilience in development. *Current Directions in Psychological Science,, 4*(3), 81–85.

Yates, T. M., Egeland, B., & Sroufe, L. (2003). Rethinking resilience: A developmental process perspective. In S. S. Luthar (Ed.), *Resilience and vulnerability: Adaptation in the context of childhood adversities* (pp. 243–266). New York: Cambridge University Press.

Chapter 15

The Strange Case of the Farting Professor
Humor and the Deconstruction of Destructive Communication

Dennis K. Mumby

> By laughing at power we can expose its contingency, we can realize that what appeared to be fixed and oppressive is just the sort of thing that should be mocked and ridiculed. (Critchley, 2007, p. 18)

A few years ago when I was a faculty member at Purdue University, I attended a public lecture given by a renowned sociologist. I do not recall a whole lot about the substance of the lecture (I vaguely recall it being about Hegel, Marx, and Weber—who else?), but what I do vividly remember is that at regular intervals during the course of his lecture, this famous sociologist would let rip with some very loud, very sonorous farts. On each occasion he blithely lectured on, making no reference—apologetic or otherwise—to his "nonverbal asides" and, in eloquent validation of Goffman's (1959) thesis that an audience will work hard to protect the self an individual presents (in this case learned and revered scholar), the assembled faculty members and graduate students did not bat an eyelid either, pretending that nothing unusual was happening. Now, as a Brit raised on the subtleties and nuances(!) of toilet humor, I could barely contain myself. This was great, pungent (sorry) stuff! So, when, during the discussion period after the lecture, I asked a question about the juxtaposition of farting and sociological theory, I was sorely disappointed not to get any uptake, either from the famous sociologist or from my assembled colleagues.

Okay, so I did not ask that question (or at least only in my fantasy version of the event), but to me this incident is a fascinating example of how the sacred and profane co-exist in a quite intimate but often unacknowledged way. A public lecture on a university campus is a sacred event; it is a ritualistic enactment and embodiment of what we, as scholars, engage in—the creation and dissemination of original knowledge. In this public enactment we must all pay due obeisance to the solemnity of the event through our carefully circumscribed and reciprocal roles: the dutiful and engaged auditors, the reverential acolytes, the asker of the "smart" question, and so forth. But at such events the profane is never very far away.

It does not usually appear in the form of a famous farting sociologist, but nevertheless we are all aware of the extent to which we live in a house of cards that can come tumbling down with the slightest breeze (flatulent or otherwise). Institutions and organizations are precarious entities that rely on systems of norms, values, rituals, beliefs, and so forth, in order to be maintained and reproduced. And, of course, it is up to us—the social actors who are the communicative "stuff" of organizing—to engage in the face work necessary to make sure that the basic organizational fabric is not rent asunder when its fragility is momentarily exposed.

Lest you think that this "fart" story is simply a shameless and gratuitous way of getting you to read further, let me suggest that it is at the intersection of the fart and the solemn public lecture—or at least what they stand for—that we find some of the more interesting things that make organizations worth studying, particularly as that relates to finding ways to counter the more destructive features of workplaces and organizations in general.

This chapter, then, will be about humor and organizing, and in particular it will address the ways in which humor as a communicative practice can serve to puncture, undermine, and destabilize systems of organizational power. The fart story stands as an allegory for how humor can speak truth to power in institutional settings. As the above quote from Simon Critchley reminds us (and I do think we need to be reminded regularly of this), power is a contingent feature of organizational life—it is not fixed, stable, or god-given—and sometimes it does not take a whole lot (like a well-placed fart) to expose that power in all its ridiculousness and pomposity.

I do not have any evidence to back up this claim (except my own observations of and participation in organizational life), but I do think that much of what this book identifies as the "destructive side of organizational communication" exists in part because institutions and the people who run them take themselves far too seriously. Of course, organizations *have* to take themselves seriously, but that is also their great weakness. Beneath organizational power (both institutional and individual) lies a deep sense of insecurity—a fear that that power will disappear. In this context, destructive behaviors and toxic institutional forms are often desperate efforts to retain power and obscure (to oneself and others) those insecurities.

Academia is, of course, an institutional context that is rife with power plays and their attendant insecurities. We are all thrown into a system that brutally exposes any weaknesses and punishes us severely for it, with the dreaded denial of tenure being perhaps the most extreme instance of this brutality. But there is also the everyday pressure that makes us afraid to give any hint that we are not fully competent, completely driven, and spectacularly gifted. I have yet to meet a graduate student who does not at some point admit to the deep-seated fear of being publicly exposed as the charlatan they think they are, and who is not massively relieved to find out that, after almost 25 years as a professor, I still live in fear of that moment.

Such fear is well-captured in David Lodge's entertaining campus novel, *Changing Places*. Here, he writes about an after-dinner game called "humiliation," played by academics at "Rummidge University." Over dessert, each player takes turns in confessing to having not read something that is canonical in their research specialty. The winner is the scholar who confesses to the most scandalous omission. One evening a brilliant and rising young Shakespearean scholar from the English department admits to never having read *Hamlet*. The attendant academics are aghast, his career falls into a tailspin, and he is never heard from again. Now, how many of us could play this game with a clear conscience? How many of us would be willing to be as truthful as the poor young Shakespearean scholar? Not many of us, I think.

I use this illustration not to point out that we academics are all pretentious charlatans (we are all that to some degree—some more than others), but to draw attention to the ways in which we are constantly interpellated as academics who must present a particular and narrowly circumscribed persona. And we do a lot of identity work to maintain this persona. A few years back I gave a lecture at a university out west and talked about what I called the "ideology of busy-ness" in academia. By this, I meant that a significant part of the identity work in which academics engage involves constructing a self that projects and performs constant busy-ness, regardless of whether this is actually true or not. This ideology of busy-ness serves several functions: (a) It protects us from unwanted intrusion by pesky students ("Can I make an appointment to speak with you?" "Well, I am really busy right now—can you come back three weeks from Tuesday?"); (b) It protects us from unwanted intrusion by pesky colleagues ("I am trying to set up a meeting of the ad hoc committee on faculty parking—when are you available?" "Well, I can't come in Monday, Wednesday or Friday because they're my sacrosanct writing days, and Tuesday and Thursday I teach, and because I am so devoted to my students I spend many, many office hours helping them with their papers. I might have 30 minutes at 7:30 a.m. a week from Thursday"); and (c) It functions discursively to help us perform an identity that is consonant with what the institution demands of us—"busy-ness" is an ideological construct that reifies and naturalizes the image of the lone, garretted scholar feverishly working on "the next big idea" that will change the world as we know it. "Busy-ness" privileges the individual over the collective and disengaged isolation over community.

Again, none of this is intended to address and critique individual behaviors, but is meant to point rather to the structurational formations of academia—and, indeed, most other organizational forms—that privilege and reward certain forms of behavior and meaning construction over others. Academia rewards individualism over collectivism, and in the process constructs subjects who are constantly in search of a stable, ontologically secure subjectivity (Collinson, 2003); but this is a stability and security that is constantly deferred and illusory. Particularly in the context of post-Fordist organizational life (of which academia is increasingly a part), the stable professional identity has been replaced by the constant—but not necessarily progressive—movement of a culture of enterprise that privileges the new, the different, constant change, and so forth. In this sense, the ideology of "busy-ness" in academia fits well with this enterprise culture of self-branding and self-motivation.

My point in all this is that the "dark side" of organizational communication is not simply about those more explicit forms of destructive practice such as sexual harassment, workplace bullying, intimidating work environments, and so forth, but also involves the various forms of symbolic violence (Bourdieu, 1977) that institutions and their members perpetrate on each other. I would suggest that the dialectical tension between identities and insecurities (Collinson, 2003) is every bit as destructive to organizational members as those more obviously dysfunctional workplace practices. As such, when Collinson (2003) identifies three kinds of identity work that employees in post-Fordist organizations engage in (conformist, dramaturgical/performative, and resistant identities), he is highlighting the fact that not only is the constant search for a secure and stable professional identity illusory, but that it also does violence to the possibility of acting in more constructive ways that promote community, connection, democratic participation in decision-making, and so forth. I am not here trying to privilege a more authentic, genuine kind of organizing, but rather suggesting that the current system of organizing and its attendant "discourse of managerialism" (Deetz, 1992) forecloses even the consideration of other possibilities.

How, then, can we take up the relationships among humor, organizing, and power, given the above discussion? Following Critchley (2007), I suggest that humor is a "practically enacted theory" that, by virtue of its intersubjective character, provides unexpected insight into the human communicative condition:

> [H]umour reveals the depths of what we share. But crucially, it does this not through the clumsiness of a theoretical description, but more quietly, practically, and discreetly. Laughter suddenly breaks out in a bus queue, watching a party-political broadcast in a pub, when someone farts in a lift [again with the farting! He's a Brit, after all], or when listening to the false rhetoric of a self-aggrandizing CEO. Humour is an exemplary practice because it is a universal human activity that invites us to become philosophical spectators on our lives. It is a

> practically enacted theory .... To put it in a rather baroque formula-
> tion, humour changes the situation in which we find ourselves, or
> lights up the everyday by providing an *oblique phenomenology of
> ordinary life.* (2007, p. 28, emphasis in original)

I always like to describe critical theory to my students as "the enemy of
common sense" in that it provides a means to deconstruct and expose as
contingent that which has become taken-for-granted, reified, and hence
positioned beyond reflection, critique, and change. Complementing this
view, Critchley suggests that humor as a practically enacted theory
"returns us to common sense by distancing us from it" (p. 28). In other
words, good humor makes the familiar strange, and then refamiliarizes us
with the world in a slightly transformed condition—humor as "dissensus
communis" leads to a new "sensus communis."

Of course, not all humor works this way. Critchley distinguishes among
three different theories of humor: the superiority theory, the relief theory,
and the incongruity theory. In the first theory, laughter is said to emanate
from a recognition of superiority over others. Certainly, much of ethnic
humor is based on this principle and, generally speaking, it exploits a lack
of self-reflection, reifies "common sense" thinking, and leaves extant
structures of power untouched. In the second theory, humor is said to
function as a form of release of pent up psychic energy—energy that would
otherwise be used, in the Freudian sense, to repress feelings. Again, this
theory tends toward a conservative view of humor as a kind of safety valve
which allows for the maintenance of the status quo. However, it is in the
third theory of humor as incongruity that we can see its possibilities for
radical critique and social transformation.

Here, humor works by juxtaposing elements that do not normally
go together and that function in an irreverent way to undermine the
smooth functioning of institutional life—the habitus, if you will. This is
the form of humor that defamiliarizes the world for us and allows us
to experience a transformed sense of community. Certainly the fart
story that I began with would satisfy this principle of incongruity. The
idea of a famous academic blithely letting rip for all he is worth in a
solemn public context certainly destabilizes our "common sense" understandings of a public lecture and exposes the trappings of power to
ridicule. Ever since that event it is hard for me to take *any* academic talk
too seriously.

In the rest of this chapter, then, I want to address in more detail the relationships among humor, organizing, and power. Certainly in the last few
years the discursive turn has pushed everyday organizational discourse—
including humor—to the forefront of academic interest. Below I briefly
review the research on organizational humor, and then in the final part of
the chapter provide an analysis of E. L. Kersten's (2005) book, *The Art of*

Demotivation. I argue that its parodic and ludic intervention in management theory exists at the intersection of workplace humor and what Zoller and Fairhurst (2007) have recently referred to as resistance leadership. In sum, the intent of this chapter is to deal with an important topic in a somewhat irreverent and ironic manner, but in the hope that it makes a serious point.

Humor and Organizing

David Collinson (2002) observes that at the Ford Motor company in the 1930s and 1940s, laughter was viewed as a disciplinary offense. Quoting Sward (1948) he notes that "In 1940 John Gallo was sacked because he was 'caught in the act of "smiling," after having committed an earlier breach of "laughing with other fellows," and slowing down the line "maybe half a minute"'" (2002, p. 276). Anyone familiar with Henry Ford and his attempts to shape the moral fiber and behavior of his workers should not find this surprising. Ford's disciplinary efforts, including the creation of a short-lived "sociological department" to police his employees' behavior beyond the gates of his automobile plants, is perhaps an extreme (though not unusual) example of widespread attempts to rationalize work and eliminate the ungovernable human element from the production process.

In this sense, humor is an "excessive," ungovernable feature of organizational life that runs counter to the Protestant ethic that has undergirded western capitalism for much of its history. Bureaucratic organizational forms largely eliminate charisma in favor of rationalized systems of decision-making. In the right hands, humor reinserts the charismatic into organizational life in a way that can disrupt and derail the smooth functioning of the workplace.

It is not surprising, then, that with the critical and discursive turns in organization studies, workplace humor has become an important focus of study. Rather than view humor and joking as a trivial distraction from the "real" work of organizing, researchers have in recent years begun to treat humor seriously, as it were. Certainly, Donald Roy's (1959) "banana time" study is an early classic exemplar of this work, with its focus on how the four men in the "clicking room" used ritualistic forms of joking behavior to stave off alienation and the "beast of monotony" and hence "cling to the remnants of joy in work" (p. 160). Roy's classic study adopts a largely functionalist approach to workplace humor that reflects a strongly managerial perspective (does humor help or hinder workplace functionality?), but recent work has taken a decidedly critical turn with its efforts to systematically unpack the relationships among humor, power, resistance, and organizing (Collinson, 1988, 2002; Johnston, Mumby, & Westwood, 2007; Linstead, 1985; Lynch, 2002; D. M. Martin, 2004; Rosen, 1988; Taylor & Bain, 2003; Westwood, 2004).

In much of this work, humor is regarded as a powerful discursive mechanism for negotiating workplace meanings, shaping and asserting organizational identities, and intervening in the complex dialectic of control and resistance. As a mundane and remarkably ubiquitous feature of organizing, critical scholars have identified humor as an important point of entry into the everyday warp and woof of that dialectic. Moreover, the so-called postmodern turn has seen a distinct shift toward investigation of the ironic, parodic, and playful in organizational life, particularly as that relates to employees' efforts to deconstruct and destabilize dominant (typically managerial) meaning systems (Fleming & Spicer, 2002, 2003; Trethewey, 1999). In very broad terms, then, workplace humor has been identified as having interesting possibilities for destabilizing the increasingly totalizing disciplinary mechanisms of post-Fordist organizational life. Given the inherent ambiguity of organizational meaning systems, the tendency of humor to—by definition—play with that ambiguity through double entendre, contradiction, juxtaposition, and so forth, lends itself particularly well to investigation by critical researchers who are interested in the subversion of institutional norms and control mechanisms that are destructive in nature. Let me briefly take up some of the ways in which workplace humor has been examined.

Humor as Resistance Through Incongruity

A number of critical researchers have investigated the relationship between humor and workplace resistance to managerial control mechanisms. Much of this work has taken up class and gender as the organizing constructs around which humor is articulated as a significant sense-making practice. Willis's (1977) study of British working class male adolescents is an early attempt to explore the relationships among humor, class, and masculinity. Willis shows how the notion of "having a laff" is central to "the lads" construction of themselves as part of a resistant subculture that rejects the middle class culture of conformity of the school they "attend." "Having a laff" is simultaneously a marker of difference and identity for the lads; it both differentiates them from the "ear'oles" who passively conform to the dominant values of obedience and "getting ahead" through academic qualifications, and constructs a sense of masculine group solidarity that functions as a space of resistance against the dominant school culture. Here, the lads define humor non-discursively (the verbal is the domain of the dominant school culture) through action—stealing things, playing practical jokes, and so forth.

The most interesting and widely discussed feature of Willis's study is his claim that the lads' resistant subculture actually functions to prepare them for insertion into the capitalist labor process. By rejecting the equation of education with future success, they construct themselves as unskilled, undifferentiated labor, and hence foreclose any possibilities for genuine resistance and social transformation. In this sense, humor as a resistant expression of group solidarity and working class masculinity in effect acts as a mechanism through which capitalist relations of production are reproduced.

David Collinson's (1988, 1992) study of workplace humor can be viewed as an extension of Willis's work, focusing as it does on the social construction of working class masculinity on the shopfloor of a truck making factory. Collinson's research subjects are, for all intents and purposes, "the lads" in adulthood, although the culture of "having a laff" has effectively morphed into a shopfloor culture of "taking the piss" (British vernacular for mocking each other), in which the group solidarity of the adolescent years has become a rather Darwinian survival of the funniest (or more accurately, survival of the most malicious). Collinson illustrates how the everyday humor of the shopfloor operates in multiple and frequently contradictory ways to create a complex system of meanings and workplace identities. He shows, for example, how workers' collective resistance to managerial attempts to engineer workplace culture is often in tension with a rampant masculine individualism that pervades the shopfloor. Thus, the flip side of resistance to management (who are characterized as effeminate know-nothings running the company into the ground) is a shopfloor culture of extreme conformity where any sign of weakness is punished mercilessly.

Collinson's work on humor is important precisely because he highlights the radically contextual features of humor, identity, and power. Thus, workplace humor can be simultaneously resistant and conformist, challenging to the status quo and reproductive of extant power relations, community-oriented and highly individualistic. Most importantly, Collinson's analysis of workplace humor demonstrates how a significant part of workers' daily organizational lives is devoted to ongoing efforts to manage self-identities—since insecurities abound (promoted both by management and coworkers)—and other workers.

The incongruity theory of humor is also evident in the work of feminist researchers who explore the relationships among gender, power, and resistance. Bell and Forbes (1994), for example, provide a particularly compelling analysis of how female clerical workers at a university perform gendered identities through the use of "office graffiti" such as cartoons and parodies of office memoranda that are prominently displayed in their workspaces. These textual artifacts help construct an interstitial space of resistance for these women by challenging "the feminization of work and the reductionism of bureaucracy" (p. 195). Unlike the workers in Collinson's study who unreflectively enact hegemonic forms of working class masculinity, these women draw ironically on feminine stereotypes to simultaneously parody themselves and the institutional logic in which they

324 Dennis K. Mumby

find themselves. Thus, the women engage in a mode of appropriation and ironic reversal that draws directly on the institutional discourse that constructs them as particular gendered subjectivities. Indeed, the women do not attempt to simply reject the rationality and practices in which they are implicated (as is the case with Collinson's workers), but rather employ humor in the ambiguous, interstitial spaces of bureaucracy in order to create a subculture that is meaningful to them as women in that particular social location. Again, it is an interesting example of how the sacred and profane intersect in a way that enables the construction of alternative meaning systems and spaces of resistance.

Humor by incongruity is also deployed to deal with overt workplace oppression and abuse. For example, Bies and Tripp's (1998) study of coping strategies to manage tyrannical, abusive bosses found that some workers used humor that explicitly targeted bosses. Aptly named "carnival technique," this resistance strategy played out in celebratory, clandestine gatherings held to mock and disparage the boss. Workers used humor to ridicule and "demonize their bosses—that is, vent their frustrations, assign blame, call the bosses names (e.g., 'Beelzebub'), and generally bad-mouth their bosses" (p. 213). In one office, workers even created a ritual to initiate colleagues who had just experienced their first abusive interaction with the boss.

These studies suggest that humor often arises out of a combination of incongruity and transgression. Elements come together in unexpected ways that transgress the boundaries of what we typically think of as normal, acceptable, and appropriate. As Bies and Tripp (1998) note, good humor has something of the "carnivalesque" (Bakhtin, 1984) about it, where established hierarchies and power relations are suspended, if only temporarily. Of course, a necessary corollary to humor is laughter; humor without that reciprocal response is like one hand clapping. But laughter has not always been welcome in organizations, and for good reason—it marks a lack of control, a form of release, of jouissance, where one gives oneself up entirely to that fully embodied experience that is often beyond description.

This lack of control is not particularly compatible with managerial efforts to rationalize work and intensify the labor process. Where humor and laughter *are* permitted, it is often in the context of a carefully calculated effort on the part of management to engineer a "fun" corporate culture and use humor as a motivational tool. Such efforts are typically seen by employees for the transparent efforts at manipulation that they are. However, in thinking about humor and its resistant and transformational organizational possibilities in the face of destructive communication, the role of laughter and the connections among the body, humor, and laughter need to be carefully considered.

If we think of humor as potentially challenging existing organizational tropes and discourses, then laughter can be seen as the intersubjective recognition and uptake of that challenge. I am not suggesting here that making people laugh leads directly to organizational change, but rather that the sense of "communitas" (Turner, 1985) and bodily engagement produced by humor/laughter creates the possibility of thinking and doing otherwise, of pushing back against the status quo.

Humor as Transformative

In this context Angela Trethewey (2004) provides a powerful example of the transgressive and transformative possibilities that exist in the humor-laughter connection. Specifically, she addresses the intimate connections among laughter, eros, and pedagogy, suggesting that laughter is both a literal and metaphorical way to rethink the place of the erotic in organizational contexts. Although she is specifically addressing the classroom environment, her argument seems more broadly applicable to organizational life. Trethewey's argument goes something like this: Although sexuality (particularly women's sexuality) is typically excised from organizational life (except in its most fetishized and objectified forms), laughter is an embodied experience that provides a space for rethinking what the sexual and erotic might look like outside of a trope of (masculine) dominance and (feminine) subordination.

Trethewey makes the case, following Davis (1990, p. 12) that "the laughter metaphor redeems the experience of women's sexuality. Actively engaged laughter is contextual, emotional, physical, interactive, and by no means passive" (Davis, quoted in Trethewey, 2004, p. 37). She further argues that the erotic aspects of laughter are derived from humor's ability to make meaningful, energizing connections with others. In this sense, laughter becomes both medium and outcome of the exploration of, and reflection upon, organizational experience with engaged others. Trethewey provides the example of talking to her students about the experience of being a nursing mother in a professional environment. She discusses how she was both

> materially and ideologically positioned betwixt and between discourses of home and work, public and private, and struggled to negotiate an appropriate identity. As a class, we laughed together about my awkward experiences and identity(ies), but in so doing we began to critique taken-for-granted assumptions about work, family, sexuality and their relationship to current understandings of professionalism. (2004, p. 38)

Here we have a great example of how humor, the body, and laughter come together in an engaged and transgressive way to challenge understandings of the organizational status quo. The pregnant and nursing female body is an "excessive" element in organizational life that blurs the distinction between mind and body, rationality and emotionality; it messes with the smooth and efficient functioning of daily organizational life. Trethewey's humorous tales of workplace pregnancy and being a nursing mother provide a shared experience of a part of organizational life that is normally marginalized and treated as vaguely distasteful. Indeed, it is interesting to compare Trethewey's treatment of pregnancy and motherhood in a professional context with Joanne Martin's (1990) well-known deconstruction of a corporate CEO's story about a VP's caesarean birth that is timed to coincide with the launch of a new product. Martin reports that when the CEO related this story as an example of his company's "family-friendly" policies, a number of women in the audience booed and hissed to show their disapproval.

Read in the context of Trethewey's account, one wonders what might have happened if the audience had simply laughed at the hilariously wrongheaded and insensitive character of the CEO's story. One could speculate that the resulting sense of connection produced at such laughter speaking truth to power might have created an important space in which to address the deep contradictions between the ostensible moral of the story ("we are a family-friendly company") and its construction of employees as subordinated to company profits (when a baby is born is dictated by corporate needs). If nothing else, such laughter would have had the effect of deflating the offending CEO!

There is an important sense, then, in which humor (intended or otherwise!) and its attendant laughter create the possibility for organizational disorder and hence opens up spaces for thinking and action. I want to argue, however, that such possibilities are not the sole province of employees in their struggles against management. Yes, there is an important sense in which humor creates a "space of action" (Holmer Nadesan, 1996) within which dialectical struggles over competing meanings, identities, and organizational possibilities can unfold, but there is a strong tendency in the literature to dichotomize resistance as an employee activity and control as the exclusive domain of management. In the final section of this chapter I want to disrupt this dichotomy by taking up what Zoller and Fairhurst (2007) have termed "resistance leadership" and using this concept as a point of entry into an analysis of E. L. Kersten's (2005) groundbreaking management text, *The Art of Demotivation*.

Deconstructing Management Theory: Humor and *The Art of Demotivation*

In an interesting recent essay, Zoller and Fairhurst (2007) address the lack of dialogue between the two research domains of leadership studies and critical organization studies. They identify what they see as an unfortunate epistemological dichotomy that conceptualizes leadership almost exclusively as maintaining the organizational status quo and managing employee dissent, and that frames resistance practices as the privileged domain of the employee. What would happen, they argue, if we were to reframe what we think of as "resistance" and "leadership" in order to explore the possibilities of "resistance leadership?" Without recapitulating their entire argument here, they make a strong case that if social transformation is to occur, we must move beyond the "small wins" of the everyday destabilization of meanings through, for example, the enactment of irony and parody (i.e., little "d" discourse), toward more enduring, systemic social change in which new big "D" Discourses challenge the current dominant organizational and managerial discourses.

I hope I am not doing too much violence to the spirit of their argument to suggest that one way to practice such resistance leadership is through radical interventions in management theory, research, and practice itself. Given that management studies fundamentally shape the ways in which the process of organizing is enacted, it makes sense to argue that changes in management studies will, at least at some point, result in changes in organizing processes and the ways that people "manage" themselves and others. In this sense, I will make the case below that E. L. Kersten's (2005) *The Art of Demotivation* stands as an example of "resistance leadership" in that it radically intervenes in mainstream management theory by articulating its own theory of management that is simultaneously deeply parodic of "management thought" itself. As such, Kersten provides a space for critiquing and resisting the apparent omnipotence of managerial control in the post-Fordist workplace.

Characterizing the history of management thought in the context of social science more broadly, Charles Perrow (1986) has observed that "The problems advanced by social scientists have been primarily the problems of human relations in an authoritarian setting" (p. 53). In other words, the history of management research from Frederick Taylor forward has been framed around solving the problem of control; that is, how does one get employees to not only accept authoritarian work environments but to be happy—or at least sanguine—about giving up their democratic rights? Certainly in the last 40 years or so, management theory and research has addressed that problem by constructing a humanist discourse that functions ideologically to obscure the fundamentally authoritarian, anti-democratic relations upon which capitalist organizing is constructed.

Managerial discourses of motivation, self-actualization, empowerment, and so forth, construct a view of the workplace as a site of identity construction where a strong, vigorous subjectivity can be realized. Of course, this belies the corporate reality of re-engineering, downsizing, outsourcing, and leveraged buyouts, in which the corporate employee is a dispensable element in a complex economic equation. The juxtaposition of these discourses perhaps achieves its most bizarre realization in the popular corporate self-help book (available also on DVD for $600!), *Who Moved My Cheese?* (Johnson, 1998), in which the heart-warming story of two "littlepeople"—Hem and Haw—living in a rat maze is used to teach lessons about preparing for organizational change. No commentary is necessary.

E.L. Kersten's (2005) *The Art of Demotivation: A Visionary Guide for Transforming Your Company's Least Valuable Asset—Your Employees*, is a book that deserves to be taken seriously as a deeply ironic intervention in current management discourse. I would go so far as to suggest that Kersten's book stands as a "fart in the general direction" (Python, Monty, 1975) of management theory, peeling back the latter's humanist rhetoric to expose the authoritarian subtext that lies beneath. It is an undermining of the sacred by the profane. In fact, I do not think it is too big a stretch to argue that Kersten is the Stephen Colbert of management studies. The latter's Comedy Channel show, "The Colbert Report" (pronounced "reporr") has achieved cult status through Colbert's creation of a comic persona that parodies and exposes the hypocrisy of the bloviating, egotistical, dogmatic, bullying, hyper-masculine TV commentators exemplified by such figures as Bill O'Reilly. In a complementary manner, Kersten has created a work (and a company—Despair, Inc.) that uses management theory and practice against itself to reveal its dark underbelly and, in the process, opens up possibilities for humanizing work life. In this sense, it is an anti-humanist text that serves humanist ends.

Many of you reading this chapter are probably familiar with Despair, Inc.'s most popular products—the demotivational posters, mugs, and mousepads that parody those awful motivational posters that use "profound" sayings and warm, soothing images to "improve" workplace environments. Depair, Inc.'s posters have captions such as:

> Consulting: If you're not part of the solution, there is good money to be made prolonging the problem
>
> Get to Work: You aren't being paid to believe in the power of your dreams
>
> Mediocrity: It takes a lot less time and most people won't notice the difference until it is too late
>
> Nepotism: We promote family values here—almost as often as we promote family members

Once you've been exposed to these demotivational posters, it is impossible to look at the "real" posters in quite the same way again. I have one on my own office wall: *Power: Power corrupts. Absolute power corrupts absolutely. But it rocks absolutely, too* (appropriate, I think, for a critical theorist/department chair!).

The Art of Demotivation (*TAD*) articulates the management "philosophy" that lies behind these quotidian masterpieces of workplace cynicism. *TAD* is published in three editions: Manager, Executive, and Chairman. The manager edition, priced at $24.95, comes complete with an "undercover"—a fake dust jacket that portrays a fictional work titled, "Ethics, Integrity, and Sacrifice in the Workplace," by Clarke N. Westerne. As Kersten notes in the preface, "Given the controversial nature of this book and its ... potential to confuse and offend the non-managerial class, it is imperative that the reader exercise extreme caution when reading the book in the workplace" (p. viii). The executive edition, priced at $39.95, is described as a "statement of luxury and virility." Leather-bound, edged in gold leaf, and locked with a key to keep its secrets from the uninitiated, it is "a book that demands to be reckoned with—for a leader who expects the same." Finally, the chairman edition, priced at $1,195 (no joke!), comes bound in goatskin ("vegetarians, ask about our Tofu option") and is housed in its very own humidor. As the *Despair* website indicates,

> While the *hoi polloi* delight endlessly in disposable adornments and the *parvenu* in vulgar displays of new wealth, a reader of distinction holds oneself to a far more exacting standard. It is to those qualified to savor the luxuriating delights of handmade bookcraft that we offer this exquisite, limited-edition masterwork. (all quotes accessed at http://despair.com)

I describe the three editions because they give some sense of the managerial persona that Kersten constructs in the text. In the spirit of Stephen Colbert (though the book predates that show), Kersten conceives of management as rooted in hierarchy, class-based privilege, and a form of hegemonic masculinity that positions the leader as the embodiment of a virile, unquestioned authority. It is a "masters of the universe" view of corporate life that nicely parodies the excesses of the élite in a neo-liberal, globalized corporate environment with its leveraged buyouts, responsiveness to the short term share price, and massive executive bonuses.

The real substance of *TAD*, however, lies in its articulation of a theory of "radical demotivation" (RD). Rejecting several decades of "humanist" management research, Kersten claims that his new approach "is designed to disabuse employees of the narcissistic fantasies they cling to" (p. 3) regarding the nature of their organizational worth. In critiquing traditional management theory—and in particular the research that comes out of the human resource perspective—Kersten argues that there is an unhealthy and dysfunctional reciprocity between management and workers in which both groups buy into the "Myth of the Noble Employee."

In this myth, the success of corporations is erroneously premised on the ability of managers to motivate employees who are simply waiting for the right conditions for their untapped potential to be realized. Furthermore, this myth presupposes that employees are essentially good, hardworking, and responsible, and that the manager properly trained in human resource management will be able to harness this essential goodness (think "theory Y" here). The modern organization, Kersten, claims, is configured around the motivational needs of this "Noble Employee" with disastrous consequences for profit and productivity.

Kersten lays the blame for this state of affairs squarely at the feet of the "Motivational Educational Industrial (ME-I) Complex"—"a movement made up of a decentralized, constantly-evolving coalition of institutions that are intent on replacing the values of the Protestant Work Ethic with a 'culture of narcissism'" (p. 11). This ME-I Complex constantly reinforces the notion that "the good life" rests on self-fulfillment and the maintenance of self-esteem, achieved mainly through the "constant acquisition of goods and the unconditional affirmation of self" (p. 11). The continued reproduction of this Noble Employee myth, Kersten argues, has "disrupted the rational distribution and application of institutional power in modern organizations" (p. 16).

Kersten's answer to this problem is to lay out his revolutionary management theory of "Radical Demotivation" (RD)—an approach "that is rooted in the reality of human weakness rather than the fantasies of human potential …. It is designed to harness the dysfunction and toxicity inherent in your workforce and exploit it for your own financial gain" (p. 21). Significantly, Kersten ties RD and its successful implementation directly to issues of self and workplace identity discussed earlier in this chapter. His thesis is eerily redolent of Collinson's (2003) discussion of post-Fordist "identities and insecurities" when he argues that RD is

> a relatively simple way of controlling your employees by manipulating their identities, their very senses of self and the hopes and dreams that shape the goals they pursue throughout the day. It is a way of striking at the very root of the problem—your employees' beliefs that they are entitled to more than you, in your judicious position, have chosen to give them. (p. 22)

In his articulation of RD, Kersten gives full, unfettered voice to what Collinson and others have argued: Although management theory and practice ostensibly invokes a humanistic ethic of care, its subtext is the construction of corporate cultures that exploit the vulnerabilities and insecurities of the average employee and create a constantly shifting and unstable organizational environment. This is perhaps exemplified best by the "culture of enterprise" that currently characterizes the white-collar professional landscape and the "brand you" philosophy that defines it. Here, employees must not only be competent workers, but must also strive constantly to develop their individual "brand" that makes them stand out from their competitors (i.e., coworkers). This reminds me of one of Despair Inc.'s demotivational posters: *Individuality: Always remember that you are unique. Just like everybody else.*

From an RD perspective, then, employees are "a necessary evil" (p. 21), but when the RD philosophy is deployed successfully this necessary evil can be translated into a productive workforce that enables corporate executives to fulfill their charge: "to increase excess, discretionary capital [rather than] subsidize the ego-gratifying delusions of [their] employees" (p. 38). What, then, are the characteristics of the radically demotivated employee and how does such an employee enable the executive to enact his or her charge? Space limitations prevent me from exploring the nuances of these features, but Kersten (p. 27) lays out nine of them along with attendant organizational benefits (Table 15.1).

RD, then, strives to engender these features in employees with the goal of undermining self-worth and bending the will of employees to that of the corporation—all achieved for less money than under a traditional, humanistic management regime. Thus, Kersten takes Perrow's (1986) defining feature of industrial life—the problem of human relations in an authoritarian setting—and reworks that relationship to privilege the authoritarianism that always lies behind the velvet glove of humanism in the workplace.

Table 15.1 Demotivational Characteristics and Corresponding Benefits

Demotivational Characteristics	Demotivational Benefit
Feeling of powerlessness	Employee satisfied with less
Sense of victimization by fate	Feels desperate loyalty to company
Low self-esteem	Loses need for employee recognition
Acute defensiveness	Does extra work as means of ingratiation
Acute self-doubt	Works hard as a means of salvaging identity
Lack of emotional resilience	Works hard to avoid humiliation
Intense risk-aversion	Is satisfied being an extension of executive ambition
Chronic pessimism	Has better judgment; less money
Pervasive sullenness	Experiences accelerated acquiescence

I will not unpack Kersten's perspective any further, but suffice it to say that he develops chapters on core values, organizational storytelling, teamwork, self-narratives, and a number of others, all rooted in the management philosophy of Radical Demotivation. And the entire book is written in a deadpan, no-nonsense style that brooks no contradiction. It is funny because it turns management theory on its head by taking that theory seriously and using it to articulate a piece of "contrarian wisdom" with which we can identify, precisely because we recognize its features in our own places of work. To invoke Critchley again, it is a piece of "dissensus communis" that produces in its audience a "sensus communis" that profoundly shifts our perception of management theory and practice. In this sense, *TAD* provides an exquisite example of humor as practically enacted theory. It is an eloquent act of resistance against every management guru who thinks he or she (usually he) has the answer to how to "motivate" recalcitrant employees, and against the notion that if we just rationalize the workplace enough, then we can create the perfect (i.e., maximally productive) work environment. It is a book that exposes the irrational in the rational by taking the rational to its (il)logical conclusion.

Now, I would like to make my own little homage to Dr. Kersten and his theory of Radical Demotivation by extending its scope. Although he

Figure 15.1 Tenure: When your best just isn't good enough.

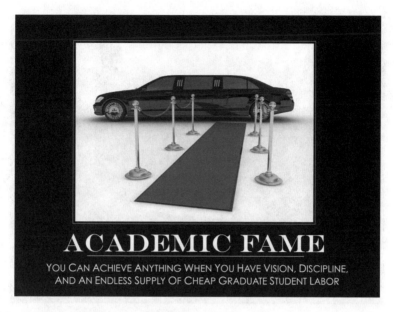

Figure 15.2 Academic Fame: You can achieve anything when you have vision, discipline, and an endless supply of cheap graduate student labor.

Figure 15.3 Faculty Meetings: So much heat, so little light.

Figure 15.4 Conference Travel: See the world, explore exotic places, bore people senseless.

Figure 15.5 Publish or Perish: Ninety-five percent of what gets published really should have perished.

Figure 15.6 Academic Publishing: When an audience of five means you're famous.

makes no such effort to develop this application, it seems to me that his philosophy would work well in an academic context. So, in the spirit of Radical Demotivation, I offer the following demotivational posters in the hope that they bring a little humor and laughter—and perhaps a little reflection—into our daily academic lives.

I am tempted to provide a commentary on each one, but I think that might be a little precious, and also grounds for accusations that I am rejecting my own advice and taking myself too seriously! And anyway, a joke explained is no longer a joke. Let me just say that each poster is intended to invoke at some level the politics of everyday academic life. Each tries to reflect in some way the struggles that we all face around everyday identity construction and the various forms of insecurity that academia as an institution invokes in us all. They are also intended as an act of resistance against the pressure that we are all under to take ourselves too seriously. If we give ourselves a little room to acknowledge and celebrate the farting professor and his ilk, then I think we will find ourselves rediscovering the pleasures of the academic life.

Conclusion

Humor is an important part of my life. I like to make people laugh, and I have a hard time taking much of anything too seriously (including myself).

Sometimes this gets me into trouble (and this chapter may be a case in point!), but a lot of the time it helps me create a strong sense of community and connection with the people around me. While it may not be a very sophisticated position to adopt, I am convinced that the dysfunctions and abuses of organizational life are frequently predicated on the desire of people and institutions to protect their identities at all costs. The problem is that those identities are not fixed and are constantly under threat, and so people must constantly work to protect those identities, often at the expense of other, less powerful coworkers and, by extension, a strong sense of community.

In a recent essay, Deetz (2005) has argued that engaging in critical theory as a way of life contains three moments: being filled with thought, being filled with care, and being filled with good humor. While the first moment invokes the need for careful analysis of systems of domination and the second recognizes the ways that others differ from self and thus challenge one's own situatedness, the third rejects simple cynicism and

> works toward the acceptance of the lack of certainty and the recognition that we make it up as we go. Vocabulary and answers are not final but rather are "resting places" ... as we move into worlds where they no longer work, where their partiality is shown, where a different response is needed. The righteousness and pretense are gone, and we must act without knowing for sure. The grand narratives are dead, but there is meaning and pleasure in the little ones. (2005, p. 105)

I hope that this chapter engages all three of these moments, but particularly the third. Humor is a practically enacted theory that, invoked in the right way, "outs" us all and makes explicit how we really do make it up as we go along. It seems to me that a more explicit recognition of this radical contingency of everyday life would undercut our ability to engage in the self-righteous enactment of fixed and bloated professional identities that so frequently create toxic organizational environments. Academia has its own unique cocktail of toxicity; as Henry Kissinger once said, "Academic politics are so vicious because the stakes are so low." There is often not much room for humor in the groves of academe, consumed as we often are with thinking "great thoughts," performing "busyness," acquiring acolytes, and protecting our own little fiefdoms. But in the spirit of the farting
professor, I'd like to suggest that we loosen our grip just a little bit on the Myth of the Noble Academic and pause to drink more deeply at the spring of good humor. I think we might like ourselves and others a little more.

References

Bakhtin, M. (1984). *Rabelais and his world* (H. Iswolsky, Trans.). Bloomington: Indiana University Press.

Bell, E. L., & Forbes, L. C. (1994). Office folklore in the academic paperwork empire: The interstitial space of gendered (con)texts. *Text and Performance Quarterly, 14*(2), 181–196.

Bies, R. J., & Tripp, T., M. (1998). Two faces of the powerless: Coping with tyranny in organizations. In R. M. Kramer & M. E. Neale (Eds.), *Power and influence in organizations* (pp. 203–220). Thousand Oaks, CA: Sage.

Bourdieu, P. (1977). *Outline of a theory of practice* (R. Nice, Trans.). Cambridge, UK: Cambridge University Press.

Collinson, D. (1988). "Engineering humor": Masculinity, joking and conflict in shop-floor relations. *Organization Studies, 9*(2), 181–199.

Collinson, D. (1992). *Managing the shop floor: Subjectivity, masculinity, and workplace culture.* New York: De Gruyter.

Collinson, D. (2002). Managing humour. *Journal of Management Studies, 39,* 269–288.

Collinson, D. (2003). Identities and insecurities: Selves at work. *Organization, 10*(4), 527–547.

Critchley, S. (2007). Humour as practically enacted theory, or, why critics should tell more jokes. In R. Westwood & C. Rhodes (Eds.), *Humour, work and organization* (pp. 17–32). London: Routledge.

Deetz, S. A. (1992). *Democracy in an age of corporate colonization.* Albany, NY: State University of New York Press.

Deetz, S. A. (2005). Critical theory. In S. K. May & D. K. Mumby (Eds.), *Engaging organizational communication theory and research: Multiple perspectives* (pp. 85–112). Thousand Oaks, CA: Sage.

Fleming, P., & Spicer, A. (2002). Workers' playtime? Unraveling the paradox of covert resistance in organizations. In S. Clegg (Ed.), *Management and organization paradoxes* (pp. 65–85). Amsterdam: John Benjamins.

Fleming, P., & Spicer, A. (2003). Working at a cynical distance: Implications for power, subjectivity, and resistance. *Organization, 10*(2), 157–179.

Goffman, E. (1959). *The presentation of self in everyday life.* New York: Anchor Books.

Holmer Nadesan, M. (1996). Organizational identity and space of action. *Organization Studies, 17*(1), 49–81.

Johnson, S. (1998). *Who moved my cheese?* New York: G. P. Putnam's Sons.

Johnston, A., Mumby, D. K., & Westwood, R. (2007). Representing the unrepresentable: Gender, humour, and organization. In R. Westwood & C. Rhodes (Eds.), *Humour, work and organization* (pp. 113–138). London: Routledge.

Kersten, E. L. (2005). *The art of demotivation.* Austin, TX: Despair, Inc.

Linstead, S. (1985). Jokers wild: The importance of humour in the maintenance of organizational culture. *The Sociological Review, 33*(6), 741–767.

Lynch, O. H. (2002). Humorous communication: Finding a place for humor in communication research. *Communication Theory, 12*(4), 423–445.

Martin, D. M. (2004). Humor in middle management: Women negotiating the paradoxes of organizational life. *Journal of Applied Communication Research, 32*(2), 147–170.

Martin, J. (1990). Deconstructing organizational taboos: The suppression of gender conflict in organizations. *Organization Science, 1*(3), 339–359.

Perrow, C. (1986). *Complex organizations* (3rd ed.). New York: Random House.

Rosen, M. (1988). You asked for it: Christmas at the bosses' expense. *Journal of Management Studies, 25*(4), 463–480.

Roy, D. (1959). "Banana time": Job satisfaction and informal interaction. *Human Organization, 18*(2), 158–168.

Taylor, P., & Bain, P. (2003). "Subterranean worksick blues": Humour as subversion in two call centres. *Organization Studies, 24*(9), 1487–1509.

Trethewey, A. (1999). Isn't it ironic: Using irony to explore the contradictions of organizational life. *Western Journal of Communication, 63*(2), 140–167.

Trethewey, A. (2004) Sexuality, eros, and pedagogy: Desiring laughter in the classroom. Women and Language, 27 (1), 34–39.

Turner, V. (1985). *The anthropology of experience*. Urbana, IL: University of Illinois Press.

Westwood, R. (2004). Comic relief: Subversion and catharsis in organisational comedic theatre. *Organization Studies, 25*(5), 775–795.

Willis, P. (1977). *Learning to labor: How working class kids get working class jobs*. New York: Columbia University Press.

Zoller, H. M., & Fairhurst, G. T. (2007). Resistance leadership: The overlooked potential in critical organization and leadership studies. *Human Relations, 60*(9), 1331–1360.

Chapter 16

Building a Constructive Communication Climate

The Workplace Stress and Aggression Project

Loraleigh Keashly and Joel H. Neuman

Over the past decade, there has been an enormous increase in empirical research pertaining to workplace aggression and bullying. The bulk of this work has focused, quite understandably, on the nature, prevalence, causes, and consequences of such behavior. Although a good deal of information has been gained in the process, there is little evidence that this accumulating knowledge has been systematically applied to the development, implementation, and evaluation of actual organizational interventions. With few exceptions, most of the literature relating to the prevention and management of workplace aggression and bullying has been conceptual or prescriptive in nature (e.g., Neuman & Baron, 1998; Rayner, Hoel, & Cooper, 2002) or has focused on workplace violence (e.g., Nicoletti & Spooner, 1996; Peek-Asa & Jenkins, 2003) and sexual harassment (e.g., Dougherty & Smythe, 2004; Keyton, Ferguson, & Rhodes, 2001). These approaches have paid little attention to less dramatic, but significantly more frequent, instances of psychological, emotional aggression, or persistent, enduring patterns of such abusive behavior typically associated with workplace bullying. Finally, much of what we know about bullying prevention comes from research on children in school settings (e.g., Carney & Merrell, 2001; Whitted & Dupper, 2005) and much less empirical work on bullying prevention has been done with adults in work settings. The Workplace Stress and Aggression (WSA) Project, a five-year grass roots initiative within the United States Department of Veterans Affairs (VA), was implemented, in part, to address this issue. In this chapter we will (a) summarize the need for such a program, (b) describe its basic elements, and (c) present preliminary assessment data demonstrating its effectiveness.

The Need for Workplace Aggression and Bullying Interventions

As noted above, most work in the area of intervention has focused on the prevention of workplace homicide and non-fatal physical assault. This includes, but is not limited to, workplace violence programs (Gates, Fitzwater, & Salazar, 2003), zero-tolerance initiatives (Casella, 2003), safe and secure workplace practices (Califano, 2000), training in how to defuse violence (Blythe & Stivarius, 2003), and self-defense courses (Sharpe, 1994). In terms of programs targeting non-physical (i.e., verbal, emotional, psychological) forms of aggression, there is considerable literature and practical applications related to conflict management in general (Fisher, Kopelman, & Schneider, 1994; Papa & Canary, 1995) and third-party techniques such as mediation, in particular (Domenici & Littlejohn, 2001; Keashly & Nowell, 2003; Moore, 2003).

Finally, in the area of employment law, there are a number of legal theories that have been suggested to discourage—or at least punish—certain forms of organizational misbehavior (Yamada, 2000). Most of these strategies are reactive, coming into play only once aggression has occurred and damage has been done. The research evidence indicates, particularly with persistent hostile treatment, that damage to both the individual and the organization is not easily ameliorated (see, Einarsen, Hoel, Zapf, & Cooper, 2003 for review). Thus, although such mechanisms will always be necessary, the more cost-effective and ethically responsible approach is a preventive one.

Although current approaches may prove useful in preventing or dealing with violence or conflict, they are less likely to be effective with workplace aggression and bullying, for several reasons. First, the vast majority of behaviors associated with workplace aggression and bullying are typically non-physical, subtle or covert (Hoel, Cooper, & Faragher, 2001; Keashly, 1998; Neuman & Baron, 1998), and rarely illegal (Yamada, 2000). Second, many of the behaviors associated with aggression and bullying are normalized as simply part of the job or expected outcomes in highly competitive, dog-eat-dog business climates (Frost & Robinson, 1999).

Third, harm-doing behaviors are often encouraged and rewarded by the organization or, at the very least, tolerated or ignored (e.g., willful blindness; Hulin, Fitzgerald, & Drasgow, 1996). To the extent that particular organizations reward aggression and bullying, recognition and prevention could actually challenge organizational structures of authority, values, and practices—efforts that will likely be resisted by management (Lewis & Orford, 2005). Fourth, more powerful others often perpetrate these behaviors, leaving the victim reluctant to use formal reporting mechanisms due to fear of retaliation or being disbelieved (Lutgen-Sandvik, 2006).

Fifth, unlike occasional acts of aggression, persistent aggression such as bullying is relational, and the nature and history of the relationship between parties contextualizes interpretations and subsequent behavior. From this perspective, bullying is viewed as an ongoing interaction in which messages are exchanged and appraised as to intent and appropriateness, factors that continually change (Kinney, 1993; Pörhölä, Karhunen, & Rainivaara, 2006). Thus, efforts to address bullying must focus on changing the nature and quality of the interactions. This requires the involvement of all parties to the interactions (actor, target, observers) rather than targeting only one or other party, as is more characteristic of traditional approaches. Indeed, the impact of the bullying interventions is often limited by focusing primarily on potential actors (e.g., management) and omitting other parties to these interactions (Hoel & Giga, 2006).

Finally, at a more macro level, the causes of workplace aggression and bullying are often systemic in nature and deeply rooted in the organizational culture and climate (e.g., Agervold & Mikkelsen, 2004; Lutgen-Sandvik & McDermott, 2008). In short, any potentially effective strategies must involve individuals at every level of the organizational hierarchy, consider contextual/systemic factors, and, ultimately, *produce culture change* within work units, departments, facilities, and, hopefully, the entire organization. Such strategies are implicitly prevention-focused.

The Workplace Stress and Aggression (WSA) Project

The WSA Project represents an attempt to reduce workplace aggression at an elemental level by changing the nature of conversations and relations between people in daily interaction and altering the values, beliefs, and assumptions driving those interactions. We grounded the approach in theories of interpersonal aggression, organizational justice, action research/learning, and organizational development and change. In this section, we describe the research methodology, intervention processes, and practices we developed and implemented. We also provide theoretical support for each element in this approach.

The Methodology

Formally begun in February 1999 and concluded in March 2004, the WSA Project was a grassroots initiative designed to better understand how stress and aggression impact individuals, work units, and the entire organization and to develop interventions to reduce the occurrence of disruptive behavior (for more detail see, Keashly & Neuman, 2005; Kowalski, Harmon, Yorks, & Kowalski, 2003; Yorks, Neuman, Kowalski, & Kowalski, 2007). The project used a quasi-experimental design in which 11 facilities served as pilot sites (the experimental condition) and 15 carefully matched facilities served as comparison sites ("control" condition). Within each of the 11 pilot sites, a joint management-labor Action Team was formed, and representatives from each of these teams participated as members of the main Project Team, the group coordinating the initiative. In addition to representatives from the Action Teams, the Project Team consisted of VA union and management leaders, academic researchers from four universities, and VA employees from several different functional areas. Unless stated otherwise, when using the word "teams," we are referring to the Action Teams and Project Team, collectively.

As a basic requirement of the project, both union and management leadership had to commit to participate in this venture. If either party withdrew its support, the project was terminated in that particular facility. This requirement was grounded in the belief and empirical evidence that organizational problems are often jointly created and, hence, resolution must be jointly created and implemented. The teams were educated about workplace aggression and bullying and received additional training in the Collaborative Action Inquiry (CAI) process (Kasl & Yorks, 2002), a data-driven, participative action research technique involving affected communities and their members and focusing on interpersonal communication and cycles of action and deep reflection (i.e., action learning).

As we will discuss in more detail, the Action Teams collected data about focal issues within their own facilities and prepared employees for the administration of the Workplace Intervention Project (WIP) Survey, which had questions concerning work environment qualities, employee attitudes, and experiences with aggression at work. We administered the survey at two points in time: November 2000 (baseline measures of workplace aggression) and November 2002 (post-intervention assessment). The 15 VA facilities that served as comparison (control) sites had no Action Teams or interventions. Instead, employees in these facilities simply completed the WIP Survey at the same two points in time.

Process and Underlying Theories

The basic philosophies of this initiative were grounded in research on interpersonal aggression, organizational justice, organizational learning, and theories of organization development and change. Processes involved (a) developing and using customized interventions, (b) changing the nature of the conversations and interactions among organizational insiders, (c) modeling expected and appropriate behaviors, (d) providing an educational component, (e) using data to uncover and test mental models and tacit assumptions, (f) having people on-the-ground take ownership of their problems, and (g) developing and implementing highly-targeted prescriptive solutions.

Customized, Prescriptive Interventions

Contemporary theories suggest a set of generic antecedents to aggression within and beyond work settings (e.g., Anderson, Anderson, & Deuser, 1996; Fox & Spector, 1999) including social, situational, and environmental factors that engender stress, frustration, perceptions of injustice, negative affect, and physiological arousal. Clearly, interventions that reduce these factors should be helpful in reducing the likelihood of aggression. Unfortunately, these antecedents are ubiquitous in work settings and attempts to eliminate them, while admirable, are unlikely to be completely (or even largely) successful because, depending on the work context, different factors drive aggression. For example, employees in one work unit may experience frustration due to the lack of promotional opportunities, while employees in another experience frustration associated with the lack of goal clarity (L. H. Peters & O'Connor, 1980). In other workgroups, the source of problems may involve abuses of power (Ashforth, 1994; Bies & Tripp, 1998). Thus, more effective strategies involve targeting interventions on specific social, situational, and environmental factors—especially those identified as being significant drivers of disruptive behavior within the specific work context. Successful interventions must be highly targeted, customized, and prescriptive to make the best use of available resources and ensure that the underlying problems of a specific work unit are addressed.

Another reason to customize interventions relates to motivation because people perform at higher and more sustained levels when asked to meet specific, rather than general, goals (Latham & Lee, 1986). As a practical matter, people must see the benefit of what they are doing if motivation is to be sustained. The importance of feedback (i.e., knowledge of results) is also important in the Job Characteristics Model of work motivation (Hackman & Oldham, 1976), and there is no way to obtain such feedback without identifying specific, measurable results. Customized interventions serve this purpose.

Using customized interventions may seem antithetical to the "best practices movement," so visible in organizational research in recent years. Although it is always useful to learn from the successes of others, each organization and individual work unit is unique and the "right" intervention must be empirically derived and tested in each distinct setting. This perspective has been described as data-driven decision making or, more recently, evidence-based management (Pfeffer & Sutton, 2006; Rousseau, 2006). At the same time, some generic processes and practices can provide a stable framework or structure within which flexibility, innovation, and individualized work can be accomplished. Peters and Waterman (1982) referred to this as being simultaneously "loose" and "tight." We will now discuss these elements.

Changing the Nature of the Conversations and Interactions

The "tight" or highly structured part of the approach we used involves the use of Collaborative Action Inquiry (CAI), "a systematic process [for the learning experience] consisting of repeated episodes of reflection and action through which a group of peers strives to answer a question of importance to them" (Bray, Lee, Smith, & Yorks, 2000, p. 6). In addition to this action-learning component, CAI is grounded in action research—an "application of the scientific method of fact-finding and experimentation to practical problems requiring action solutions and involving the collaboration and cooperation of scientists, practitioners, and laypersons" (French & Bell, 1999, p. 131). This is a generic process involving:

> data gathering, feedback to the client group, data discussion and work by the client group, action planning, and action. The sequence tends to be cyclical, with the focus on new or advanced problems as the client group learns to work more effectively together. (French, 1969, p. 26)

Within the project, the Action Teams represent the client groups with whom we worked to identify problems and then devise, implement, and evaluate interventions. This "tight" *process* provided the context within which each individual Action Team pursued its own individual *product* (one or more outcomes). When the project began, the Project Team members simply viewed the CAI process as a way of discovering successful interventions that might be applied to the prevention and management of workplace stress and aggression. Over time, the Project Team came to realize that the *process* was the *product*. That is, we recognized and embraced the idea that a good workplace aggression intervention requires changes in the very nature of the conversations that organizational members are having with each other, as well as the context in which these conversations occur (Kowalski et al., 2003; Walker, 2001). The essence of workplace aggression centers on the way people treat each other, both in actions and words. Using CAI, we began to see a dramatic change in the nature of interactions among team members and, pursuing the "grassroots" approach, worked to spread this change beyond the Action Teams to other employees within the 11 pilot facilities.

To accomplish this objective, within each of the teams, we did the following. First, we created a safe container or liberating structure—a supportive social space in which open and honest inquiry and collaboration could be possible (Fisher & Torbert, 1995; Nonaka, Toyama, & Byosiere, 2001). The process was grounded in theories of organizational justice and organizational learning (Yorks et al., 2007). In terms of organizational justice theories, we focused on fair process or procedural justice (Hubbel & Chory-Assad, 2005; Leventhal, 1980) and interactional/interpersonal justice (Bies & Moag, 1986; Greenberg, 1993). According to Leventhal, procedures are considered fair if they are made (a) in a consistent manner, (b) without self-interest (unbiased), (c) on the basis of accurate information, (d) with opportunities to correct the decision, (e) with the interests of all concerned parties being represented, and (f) following moral and ethical guidelines. Some examples of the CAI application that provide such fair process included initially implementing a process of "contracting," in which team members made each other aware of individual interests and expectations, and discussing how they would function as a team. This covered such issues as leadership responsibilities, logistics, individual and group roles, and accountability. These discussions provided the basis for the development of mutual understanding, openness, and trust by establishing and "codifying" the social contract.

Several learning tools provided practical mechanisms for giving expression to these theoretical ideals for procedural justice. For example, to ensure that everyone had a voice and was heard, we employed the version of the "talking stick," a Native American tradition. During team meetings, especially when confronting difficult issues, only one person was allowed to speak at a time—the person holding the "talking stick" (or a pepper shaker, as the first occasion to use this communication tool occurred in a restaurant). No one was permitted to take the floor from the person holding the talking stick; others could only ask questions for purposes of clarification. This ensured that everyone had an opportunity to speak and carefully frame his or her thoughts—rather than rush in an effort to hold the floor. The talking stick also facilitated much more active and deep listening on the part of other team members.

Other practices involved the use of periods of deep reflection in which individuals could share their thoughts, concerns, or suggestions. This also provided an opportunity for the group to assess its effectiveness, on any issue, at any point in time. Other learning tools involved the Learning Window (Senge, Kleiner, Roberts, Ross, & Smith, 1994), the Ladder of Inference (Argyris & Schön, 1993), and the Left-Hand Column.

The Learning Window consists of four quadrants, each containing a question or statement about information's validity. In the first quadrant, participants are asked, "What do you know and why do you know it?" That is, what facts do you possess about a given phenomenon or situation, and what data do you have to support those facts? The second quadrant requires participants to identify "what they *think* they know and what they need to discover to *actually* know it." The third and fourth quadrants involve, respectively, "obvious gaps in the knowledge" and a reminder to "be open to the unexpected." In essence, the Learning Window serves as a basis for evidence-based decision making based on the best possible data. Furthermore, it forces participants to surface and challenge untested (often erroneous) assumptions—a well-documented antecedent to aggression.

Similar to the Learning Window, the 'Ladder of Inference' (Argyris & Schön, 1993) is a mechanism for surfacing and testing tacit assumptions or attributions. It graphically describes the process by which individuals filter and selectively attend to data, add their own personal meaning to those data based on personal history and experience, draw conclusions, adopt beliefs, and act on those beliefs. In using the Ladder of Inference, participants are trained to avoid "jumping-up-the-ladder"—attending to certain data and prematurely acting on beliefs situations. Again, this learning tool is effective for reducing the likelihood that individuals will react to faulty and potentially biased attributions.

The Left-Hand Column exercise encourages people to surface "undiscussables," those things they may be thinking but are reluctant to share with others. This provides the parties with common understanding and an opportunity to avoid misunderstandings and adopt a problem-focused (v. emotion-laden) approach to their interactions.

Finally, we trained the participants in balancing advocacy and inquiry. In the case of advocacy, individuals take positions, make assertions, and engage in politicking and skillful discussion. With respect to inquiry, individuals seek to observe, hear, interrogate, clarify, and interview the parties with whom they are in dialogue. Both advocacy and inquiry are important in specific situations and at particular times. Being explicit when using each helps to clarify roles and appropriate role-related behavior.

Our experience suggests that the use of CAI leads to reduced aggression in a number of ways. First, perceptions of injustice are powerful antecedents to aggression (Geddes & Baron, 1997; Neuman, 2004) and mistrust (Bies & Tripp, 1998; Saunders & Thornhill, 2004). Consequently, promoting justice perceptions within the teams and the surrounding work units reduces the likelihood of aggression and mistrust and provides an opportunity to engage in open and honest communication. In essence, CAI helps create a safe container or collaborative social space for interpersonal interactions. Second, such communication reduces the likelihood of misattribution in the cognitive appraisal process, which is another well-known antecedent to aggression (Greenwell & Dengerink, 1973; Topalli & Oneal, 2003).

One criticism we heard initially from teams was that the type of communication we were promoting would suppress lively discussion and dialogue and subsequent creativity, while increasing pressures to conform. When addressing these concerns, we emphasized and demonstrated the distinction between constructive argumentation or challenging an idea, and verbal aggression or attacking an individual (Infante, Myers, & Buerkel, 1994). Teams came to see that it was the latter that disrupted creativity and forced conformity.

Third, the sharing of personal reflections (and Left-Hand Column thoughts) provides individuals with a better understanding of each team member's likes, dislikes, and sensitivities. Such an understanding facilitates the development of constructive relationships between members, which is the context within which all subsequent interactions will be evaluated. Fourth, the nature of CAI provides team members with a super-ordinate goal (i.e., shared problem, common threat) of recognized impor-tance that they are trying to resolve. Such unifying goals have proven to be very effective in reducing conflict and aggression (Sherif, Harvey, White, Hood, & Sherif, 1961). Finally, and central to the project, an important superordinate goal was the reduction of workplace aggression.

Behavioral Modeling

As part of the CAI process, members of the Project Team (and eventually the Action Teams) modeled the respectful and collaborative behavior they expected from others. There were, of course, occasions when teams failed to meet this ideal. These provided opportunities for learning in which peo-ple identified and named the inappropriate behaviors, expressed their feel-ings, and worked through problems.

To the extent that team members were successful in employing all of the learning practices, we saw evidence that the communication behaviors—and changing conversational styles—were, in fact, contagious and spread from team to team. Contagion became evident in each team's use of lan-guage. For example, Action Team members began referring to *Ladder of Inference, Left-Hand Column, what I think I know,* and *pepper shaker* in everyday conversation, even beyond formal team meetings. Several Action Team members who had become supervisors while working on the project stated that they used the practices as they worked with employees. Also, people began to comment on their own personal reflections and request the reflections of others. This is important for organizational communica-tion, since the behavior of others plays a significant role in social, vicarious learning in general and in the prevention and management of aggression in particular (Martinko & Zellars, 1996).

Education and Training

In addition to modeling, we also educated individuals about the nature of workplace aggression and bullying in an effort to sensitize them to these issues and increase awareness of their own assumptions and behaviors. We did this through formal training sessions with the Action Teams. Once trained, the Action Teams, in turn, passed this knowledge along in formal presentations to employees and managers in each of the pilot facilities, which increased employee and management awareness about workplace aggression and bullying. Awareness was also heightened when respon-dents completed the Workplace Aggression Research Questionnaire (WAR-Q), which, in part, required them to evaluate their exposure to 60 different aggressive behaviors (described below). Again, such a result is not surprising given the literature on training that identifies knowledge of a phenomenon as a key component in training for behavioral change (e.g., Schat & Kelloway, 2006).

Using Survey Data to Uncover and Test Mental Models and Tacit Assumptions

An important aspect of the WSA Project was its focus on the collection, analysis, and use of organizational data for problem identification and problem solving. WIP survey responses served as the primary (but not exclusive) data source. This questionnaire booklet consisted of three major sections arranged in the following order: (a) the Organizational Assessment Survey (OAS; a traditional workplace attitude questionnaire), (b) the Workplace Aggression Research Questionnaire (WAR-Q; Neuman & Keashly, 2004), and (c) a demographics information section. Consistent with the focus of this chapter, we discuss relevant portions of the WAR-Q and OAS (interested readers may contact either author for more detail about the WIP survey.)

Workplace Aggression Research Questionnaire (WAR-Q)

The main section of the WAR-Q lists 60 different examples of workplace aggression that were derived from existing research on types of negative workplace communication and behavior (see Table 16.1). Respondents indicated the extent to which they experienced each type of behavior and the person most responsible for subjecting them to that behavior.

Table 16.1 Workplace Aggression Research Questionnaire: Pilot-Comparison Pre-Post Change

Behavior	Pilots	Comparisons
1 Glared at in a hostile manner	X	
2 Excluded from work-related social gatherings	X	
3 Others storm out of the work area when you entered		
4 Others consistently arrive late for meetings that you called		
5 Sworn at in a hostile manner	X	
6 Subjected to negative comments about your religious beliefs		
7 Given the "silent treatment"	X	
8 Not given the praise for which you felt entitled	X	
9 Treated in a rude or disrespectful manner	X	
10 Your personal property defaced, damaged, or stolen		
11 Others fail to take action to protect you from harm		
12 Subjected to negative comments about a disability		
13 Subjected to obscene or hostile gestures	X	
14 Others refuse your requests for assistance		
15 Others fail to deny false rumors about you		
16 Given little or no feedback about your performance	X	

17 Others delay action on matters that were important to you	X	
18 Yelled at or shouted at in a hostile manner	X	X
19 Negative comments about your intelligence or competence	X	X
20 Others fail to return calls/memos/e-mail		
21 Your contributions ignored by others	X	
22 Someone interfered with your work activities		X
23 Subjected to mean pranks		
24 Lied to	X	X
25 Others fail to give you information that you really needed		
26 Threats/harassment for "blowing the whistle"		
27 Others fail to warn you about impending dangers		
28 Denied raise/promotion without being given a valid reason		
29 Signs or notes left that embarrassed you		
30 Subjected to derogatory name calling		
31 Blamed for other people's mistakes	X	
32 Target of rumors or gossip	X	
33 Shown little empathy/sympathy when having a tough time		
34 Coworkers fail to defend your plans or ideas to others		
35 Given unreasonable workloads or deadlines–more than others	X	
36 Others destroy or take resources that you need for job		
37 Accused of deliberately making an error		
38 Unwanted attempts to touch, fondle, kiss, or grab you	X	
39 Threats to reveal private/embarrassing info to others		
40 Subjected to temper tantrums when disagreeing	X	X
41 Prevented from expressing yourself	X	
42 Attempts made to turn other employees against you	X	
43 Someone flaunts status/treats you in condescending manner		
44 Subjected to excessively harsh criticism about your work		
45 Someone else take's credit for your work or ideas	X	
46 Kicked, bitten, or spat on	X	
47 Criticized for non-work (personal) life and activities	X	
48 Subjected to negative comments about your sexual orientation		
49 Subjected to racist remarks	X	
50 Reprimanded or "put down" in front of others	X	
51 Someone hit you with an object	X	
52 Subjected to ethnic or racial jokes or slurs	X	
53 Told how to spend your personal time when not at work		
54 Subjected to unwanted terms of endearment		
55 Subjected to suggestive or offensive stories	X	
56 Subjected to sexist remarks	X	
57 Threatened with physical harm	X	
58 Pushed, shoved, thrown, bumped into with unnecessary force	X	
59 Raped or sexually assaulted	X	
60 Assaulted with a weapon or other dangerous object		

Note: "X" indicates a significant reduction in mean aggression response ratings between Time 1 (2000, n = 4,801) and Time 2 (2002, n = 3,795).

The Organizational Assessment Survey (OAS)

A frequently suggested component of a workplace aggression prevention strategy is to have mechanisms in place for collecting data on key employee attitude variables that can be harbingers of issues of mistreatment in the workplace. For this purpose, we employed the Organization Assessment Survey (OAS), originally developed by the Office of Personnel Management (HSRD, 1993; Usala, 1996). This instrument captures 17 different dimensions (see Table 16.2). In addition to these dimensions that are composite variables, the questionnaire captures overall assessments of supervisor or team leader performance, and satisfaction with the organization, pay, physical working conditions, and their job overall, as well as intentions to leave the organization.

Table 16.2 Organizational Assessment Survey: Pilot-Comparison Pre-Post Change

Dimension	Pilots	Comparisons
Rewards and Recognition: Good performance is recognized and rewarded.	X	
Development/Guidance: Employees are given opportunities for development & adequate guidance and training.	X	X
Innovation/Improvement: Creativity is encouraged & managers embrace change.	X	
Customer Orientation: Organization is customer-focused.	X	
Management: Managers are responsive and engage in effective management practices.	X	
Respect/Fairness: People treat each other with respect and distribution of work and discipline is fair.	X	X
Information/Communication: Employees are kept informed.	X	
Involvement: Employees have a feeling of personal empowerment.		X
Conditions/Resources: Employees have adequate resources, training, and support.	X	
Work Environment: Physical conditions (e.g., noise, temperature, lighting) are good.	X	
Work-Family: Managers are responsive to work-family balance issues.	X	
Stress: Feelings of tension on the job and work is a source of stress.		
Cooperation/Teamwork: A spirit of cooperation and teamwork exists.	X	
Change Management: Programs help people deal with change and organization is making necessary changes.	X	X
Planning/Measurement: Procedures are in place for planning/ goal-setting and measuring progress.	X	
Diversity: Differences among people are respected and valued; zero tolerance for discrimination.	X	
Supervision: Trust between supervisors and employees and supervisors are seen as being fair.	X	

Note: "X" indicates a significant improvement in ratings between Time 1 (2000, n = 4,801) and Time 2 (2002, n = 3,795).

Data Collection, Analysis, and Feedback

The initial administration of the WIP Survey occurred in November 2000 (Time 1) and the post-test occurred in November 2002 (Time 2). In the pilot sites Action Teams distributed the questionnaires, and facility leadership provided time for employees to complete the surveys during work hours. The surveys included informed consent forms and a postage paid envelope addressed to a university-based researcher located outside of VA. All respondents were assured that non-VA, university-based researchers would maintain the raw data and never share data (in raw form) with VA personnel. At the comparison sites, the same procedure was used but, in the absence of Action Teams, internal mechanisms were created within each facility to assure proper distribution of the questionnaire. As in the pilot sites, VA management provided time for comparison site employees to complete the survey during working hours.

A large feedback meeting was held in February 2001, three months after the initial administration of the survey; all 11 pilot facilities received their data along with further training to assist them in working with the results. The reports each of the pilot sites received included mean response ratings for their facility on all of the individual questionnaire items and dimensions, along with comparable mean response ratings for the network in which they were affiliated—mean ratings across all 11 pilot facilities. In this way, each pilot site could review its own data and compare its standing on any variable to that of the entire network. In addition, the Project Team worked with each Action Team to run follow-up analyses, when requested by the Action Team. In short, the Project Team worked in collaboration with the individual Action Teams to help them make sense of the numbers, and this often involved drilling-down deeper into the data or looking for statistical relationships that might confirm specific hypotheses surfaced by the Action Teams. Such iterative sensemaking is representative of the action research process. At times, this process also involved obtaining additional data from other sources (interviews, focus groups, mini-surveys, organizational/archival data, etc.).

As part of the report prepared on the WAR-Q data, each facility was given a list of its "top 10" aggressive behaviors; that is, the aggressive behaviors with the 10 highest mean frequency ratings, along with a comparable "top 10" list for the entire network. This served as one basis for the development of interventions. Data from other sections of the WIP Survey assisted in better understanding the context within which aggression was occurring and also suggested potential causes (e.g., work-related stressors, perceptions of injustice, communication issues, etc.).

Over the months that followed, the Project Team worked with the Action Teams as they continued to interpret the data and test their mental models and tacit assumptions—why and how things happened in their workplaces using the Learning Window practice mentioned earlier (Senge et al., 1994). In this regard, members of the Project Team served as process consultants more than subject matter experts (Schein, 1990). For example, when an Action Team contacted the Project Team with a proposed intervention, liaisons from the Project Team, or the Project Team as a whole, would ask the Action Team for data in support of its operating assumptions and proposed interventions. In this way, the Action Teams developed an evidence-based, data-driven approach to improving their quality of work life as well as improving the communication and behavior associated with day-to-day interpersonal interactions. Although this process proved useful in all decision-making and problem-solving endeavors, it was particularly useful in the prevention and management of workplace aggression as it directly impacts the primary and secondary cognitive appraisal processes that precede behavior, while simultaneously influencing acceptable norms of interpersonal communication behavior.

Ownership of the Problems and the Solutions

The understanding that one must take personal ownership of problems as well as solutions is central to the CAI process and critically important in dealing effectively with aggression. The prevention of workplace aggression requires a change in the nature of the conversations and interactions between people in work settings. In essence, this involves a change in organizational culture and (hopefully) climate, initiatives that take time and a considerable amount of sustained effort (Beer, Eisenstat, & Spector, 1990; van de Ven & Poole, 1995).

The Job Characteristics Model (Hackman & Oldham, 1975, 1976) describes several "critical psychological states" that play an important role in the motivation process, and all of these variables are central to the CAI process. In particular, these states include experienced meaningfulness of the task (issues of importance as identified within each facility), experienced responsibility for the outcomes of the work (ownership of the problem-identification and problem-solving process), and knowledge of the actual results of the work activities (feedback of data and the associated sensemaking process) (Hackman & Oldham, 1980). Thus, effective use of CAI provides the motivation so central to a self-sustaining process. From this perspective, and as noted previously, the merits of this approach in addressing workplace aggression and bullying may have less to do with the particular issues the Action Teams seek to address and more to do with the process used to obtain those varied objectives (Walker, 2001).

Assessing Effectiveness and Impact

In this section, we discuss the effectiveness and impact of the WSA project in terms of the survey data and the nature of changes across time. Although we do not provide the details of the statistical analyses here, all the results we present here are statistically significant.[1]

Workplace Aggression Research Questionnaire Data

As shown in Table 16.1, at the pilot sites mean aggression response ratings for over half (32 out of 60) of the negative communication behaviors improved significantly between Time 1 and Time 2. The comparison sites, on the other hand, showed significant improvement in less than a tenth of those behaviors (5 out of 60). A closer inspection of Table 16.1 provides some support for the effectiveness of the interventions in obtaining the improvements. Of the five behaviors that improved at the comparison sites, three were identified (in the sample) as being most closely associated with the behavior of organizational outsiders (customers) as opposed to organizational insiders (superiors, coworkers, or subordinates). These improvements are more likely attributable to ongoing workplace violence programs (referred to within VA as the Prevention and Management of Disruptive Behavior) that focus on recognizing and defusing conflict situations arising with veterans (customers) seeking healthcare and other services.

In contrast, the majority of behaviors improved in the pilot sites involve primarily insider-initiated aggression. In particular, we note the statistical improvement in an array of passive forms of aggression (social exclusion, or the withholding of feedback, important information, or needed resources), expressions of hostility (glaring, hostile comments, rumors/gossip, put-downs), unfair treatment (rude and disrespectful behavior, unreasonable workloads, prevented from expressing oneself), and more extreme forms of aggression and violence (pushing, shoving, biting, kicking, and other sexual and non-sexual assaults).

Organization Assessment Survey (OAS) Data

The WSA project is an organizational change initiative in which interventions focus on the reduction of workplace aggression and bullying, as well as other work-related problems, many of which are work-related stressors. In short, the interventions were designed to improve the organizational culture, work climate, and work systems. To track the project's effectiveness in this regard, we analyzed data from the OAS, which captured 17 different aspects or dimensions of culture, climate, communication, justice perceptions, and work systems or processes. As with the aggression response ratings, the pilot sites showed significant improvement on 16 of these dimensions; the comparison sites showed significant improvement on only three.

Although we have not previously used this terminology, the project attempted to create a High Involvement Work Practices (HIWP) environment within the pilot sites (Guthrie, 2001; Lawler, 1992). Key measures of HIWP include appropriate levels of reward and recognition, goal clarity, providing feedback to and obtaining feedback from employees, a spirit of cooperation and of teamwork, and the existence of trust between employees and supervisors. Analysis of the data show a significant improvement in mean HIWP ratings at the pilot sites between pre- and post-tests, but there was no significant improvement for these measures at the comparison sites.

One might expect that interpersonal aggression is negatively related to assessments of employee satisfaction, and this appears to be the case. For the entire sample (across both time periods), mean aggression ratings were significantly, and inversely, related to mean ratings of job satisfaction, overall satisfaction with the organization, and intentions to quit. At Time 2, individuals at the pilot sites reported being more satisfied with their jobs and the organization and less likely to leave the organization than at Time 1. For comparison control facilities, there were no reliable differences for either job satisfaction or satisfaction with the organization, but there was a significant reduction in intentions to leave between Time 1 and Time 2.

Contextualizing the Results

It is important to consider the context in which data were collected. Although the effects described above are relatively small, the baseline measures were obtained in November 2000 and the post-intervention measures were collected in November 2002. In short, the terrorist attacks of September 11, 2001 occurred exactly midway though the study. Although this certainly had an enormous impact on people in general, it had a substantial and direct impact on work processes and workloads within the Department of Veterans Affairs. Consequently, we believe that the significant improvements in organizational culture, climate, work process, employee satisfaction and, most central to the issue at hand, the reduction in workplace aggression are even more impressive, given these circumstances.

Although the WSA Project concluded in March 2004, the Project Team continues to analyze data on various aspects of the project. In particular, as relates to the focus on changes in communicative climate, we continue to analyze a vast amount of qualitative data from Project and Action Team members (in the form of tape recordings, verbatim transcripts, and diaries of personal reflections). As such, more work is needed to fully assess and document the impact of the project. However, there are at least two additional pieces of evidence that suggest the project's contribution to the broader issue of constructive organizational communication.

First, the network director who originally sponsored this program contracted with some members of the Project Team to re-energize existing pilot facilities and expand the project into other facilities recently integrated (merged) into his network. Second, one of the original 11 pilot sites that had withdrawn from the WSA Project before its conclusion (for reasons unrelated to the project) has since re-engaged and is part of the new initiative currently underway. Considering the substantial costs associated with this new initiative, re-engagement suggests that that leadership (union and management) is convinced of the benefits of the WSA Project and, by extension, the CAI process that focused on the importance of communicative climate for employee experiences and behavior.

Discussion and Concluding Comments

Although the WSA Project was initially designed to ameliorate stress and aggression in VA, at its heart it increasingly focused on the nature and quality of interactions and communication among employees and between employees and management. And it is this focus and the process it represents that was the driver of the changes we have discussed. As a result of our experience and grounded in the data presented here and elsewhere (e.g., Kowalski et al., 2003; Yorks et al., 2007), we offer the following "lessons learned" as guidance for designing ways to develop constructive communication climates at work. First, since communication climate is co-created and propagated by all organizational members, any successful initiative to alter the climate requires the active participation and support of individuals at every level of the organization. Second, the initiative must change the nature of conversations in terms of content (what we attend to) and process (how we talk about it). Third, the process utilized must also be data-driven. That is, the identification of root causes and the formulation for actions to address them must be grounded in valid and reliable information about the work unit in question. Fourth, the notion of a safe container in which these activities and conversations are encouraged and supported is critical to effectively addressing communicative issues. Finally, this process must be continuously and rigorously monitored, evaluated, and adjusted as new data are obtained.

What is probably the most powerful lesson we learned was when you bring people together around an issue they care about and there is commitment to and support for engaging and working with these issues, relationships and climate changes for the better. Indeed, the process utilized in WSA Project and its attendant changes can become embedded in the organization's culture itself. An illustration of this is the implementation in the Veterans Health Administration of a new initiative referred to as CREW—Civility, Respect and Engagement in the Workplace—(see Osatuke, Ward, Dyrenforth, & Belton, 2007, for more detail). This initiative was developed in response to internal studies (including the WSA Project) that revealed (in)civility was a major factor in employee satisfaction. What is more, incivility was related to facility-level measures of sick leave, turnover, clinical care, patient satisfaction and EEO complaints. Employee experiences of incivility stand in sharp contrast to one of the VA's core values of fostering "a culture of respect, equal opportunity, innovation and accountability." Clearly, (in)civility was an issue of major importance to both management and labor, something people could come together to address. Civility in this context was defined as courteous and considerate workplace behaviors. The working model or theory-in-use that served to ground this initiative was that civility leads to respect which in turn leads to greater employee engagement in the mission of the VA. Ultimately, CREW is intended to increase both employee productivity and customer/patient satisfaction.

Consistent with the philosophy of the WSA project, and theories of organizational learning more generally, CREW assumes that perceptions of a civil climate will differ from one work setting to another as a function of local culture and other contextual factors. In fact, perceptions of fair and respectful treatment may differ among work units, as reflected in these unique organizational subcultures. Therefore, successful interventions must "meet people where they are" by responding to their perceptions, assumptions, and operational realities. Indeed, the process must result in changing the very nature of conversations people are having with each other. As such, the first step in the CREW initiative involves facilitating local conversations distinguishing civil behaviors ("How we want to be treated here"). This approach is grounded in the idea that the members of each work unit should be the subject matter experts as well as the decision-makers. Effective actions, then, are grounded in data-driven discussions and reflections by the people on-the-ground in each work unit. Furthermore, through systematic data collection, analysis, and sense-making activities, these people identify the root-causes of work-related problems. In the end, data serve as the basis for the development, implementation, and assessment of prescriptive interventions.

The VA is rolling out the CREW initiative in successive waves of pilot tests, each building on the findings and what was learned from preceding iterations of data collection and action. So far, the evidence is encouraging for organizational communication overall and supportive of the action-based approach. In addition to other positive outcomes outlined, the 32 pilot facilities participating in the CREW initiative also reported notable improvements in perceived civility. Longitudinal analysis currently under-way will examine whether these changes in perceptions of civility result in customer satisfaction and patient care improvements.

Although the WSA project and CREW share similar philosophies and processes, the WSA project began with a traditional problem-centered focus, and CREW has taken a more positive approach. That is, where the WSA project attempted to reduce or eliminate aggression, CREW has focused on increasing civility by envisioning how a civil workplace would (and should) look. This reflects the distinction between traditional problem-centered models and positive approaches such as appreciative inquiry (Cooperrider & Whitney, 1999) or, more generally, positive organizational scholarship (Cameron, Dutton, & Quinn, 2003). Regardless of the initial focus, both these initiatives reflect culture and climate change efforts aimed at fundamentally shifting how people communicate with each other and changing the values and norms that underlie these interactions.

We began this chapter by mentioning a number of legal and procedural approaches for dealing with workplace violence, conflict, sexual harassment, and bullying. All of these may prove useful. Furthermore, a truly effective strategy involves a fully integrated and systemic approach to dealing with the problem. Preventing workplace aggression and bullying and reducing incivility must involve changes in culture and climate. The CAI approach described herein provides a very practical and effective way to achieve that objective. Indeed, *any* meaningful intervention will depend on a self-sustaining, participant-driven, and context-specific process in which the journey is the destination.

Note

1 For more detailed results, please contact either of the authors.

References

Agervold, M., & Mikkelsen, E. G. (2004). Relationships between bullying, psychosocial work environment and individual stress reactions. *Work & Stress, 18*(4), 336–351.

Anderson, C. A., Anderson, K. B., & Deuser, W. E. (1996). Examining an affective aggression framework: Weapon and temperature effects on aggressive thoughts, affect, and attitudes. *Personality and Social Psychology Bulletin, 22*(4), 366–376.

Argyris, C., & Schön, D. A. (1993). *Knowledge for action: A guide to overcoming barriers to organizational change.* San Francisco, CA: Jossey-Bass.

Ashforth, B. E. (1994). Petty tyranny in organizations. *Human Relations, 47*(6), 755–778.

Beer, M., Eisenstat, R. A., & Spector, B. (1990). Why change programs don't produce change. *Harvard Business Review, 68*(6), 158–166.

Bies, R. J., & Moag, J. S. (1986). Interactional injustice: Communication criteria of fairness. In R. J. Lewicki, B. H. Sheppard & M. Bazerman (Eds.), *Research on Negotiation in Organizations* (Vol. 1, pp. 43–45). Greenwich, CT: JAI Press.

Bies, R. J., & Tripp, T., M. (1998). Two faces of the powerless: Coping with tyranny in organizations. In R. M. Kramer & M. E. Neale (Eds.), *Power and influence in organizations* (pp. 203–220). Thousand Oaks, CA: Sage.

Blythe, B. T., & Stivarius, T. B. (2003). Assessing and defusing workplace threats of violence. *AMA Management Update: Newsletter for AMA individual executive members.* Retrieved July 1, 2003, from http://www.amamember.org/hr/2003/aug_01.htm.

Bray, J., Lee, J., Smith, L. L., & Yorks, L. (2000). *Collaborative inquiry in practice: Action, reflection, and making meaning.* Thousand Oaks, CA: Sage.

Califano, J. (2000). Report of the United States Postal Service Commission on a Safe and Secure Workplace. *The National Center on Addiction and Substance Abuse at Columbia University.* Retrieved August 31, 2003, from http://www.casacolumbia.org/ usr_doc/33994.pdf.

Cameron, K. S., Dutton, J. E., & Quinn, R. E. (Eds.). (2003). *Foundations of positive organizational scholarship.* San Francisco: Berrett-Koehler.

Carney, A. G., & Merrell, K. W. (2001). Bullying in schools: Perspectives on understanding and preventing an international problem. *School Psychology International, 22*(3), 364–382.

Casella, R. (2003). Zero tolerance policy in schools: Rationale, consequences, and alternatives. *Teachers College Record, 105*(5), 872–892.

Cooperrider, D. L., & Whitney, D. (1999). *Collaborating for change: Appreciative inquiry.* San Francisco, CA: Berrett-Koehler.

Domenici, K., & Littlejohn, S. W. (2001). *Mediation: Empowerment in conflict management* (2nd ed.). Long Grove, IL: Waveland Press.

Dougherty, D. S., & Smythe, M. J. (2004). Sensemaking, organizational culture, and sexual harassment. *Journal of Applied Communication Research, 32*(2), 293–317.

Einarsen, S., Hoel, H., Zapf, D., & Cooper, C. L. (Eds.). (2003). *Bullying and emotional abuse in the workplace: International perspectives in research and practice.* London: Taylor & Francis.

Fisher, D., & Torbert, W. R. (1995). *Personal and organizational transformations: The true challenge of generating continual quality improvement.* London: McGraw-Hill.

Fisher, R., Kopelman, E., & Schneider, A. K. (1994). *Beyond Machiavelli: Tools for coping with conflict.* Cambridge, MA: Harvard University Press.

Fox, S., & Spector, P. E. (1999). A model of work frustration and aggression. *Journal of Organizational Behavior, 20*(6), 915–931.

French, W. L. (1969). Organization development objectives, assumptions, and strategies. *California Management Review, 12*(Winter), 23–34.

French, W. L., & Bell, C. H. J. (1999). *Organization development: Behavioral science interventions for organization improvement* (Vol. 6). Upper Saddle River, NJ: Prentice Hall.

Frost, P. J., & Robinson, S. (1999). The toxic handler: Organizational hero—and casualty. *Harvard Business Review, 77*(4), 96–107.

Gates, D., Fitzwater, E., & Salazar, M. K. (2003). Dealing with workplace violence: Strategies for prevention. *AAOHN Journal, 51*(6), 243–245.

Geddes, D., & Baron, R. A. (1997). Workplace aggression as a consequence of negative performance feedback. *Management Communication Quarterly, 10*(4), 433–454.

Greenberg, J. (1993). The social side of fairness: Interpersonal and informational classes of organizational justice. In R. Cropanzano (Ed.), *Justice in the workplace: Approaching fairness in human resource management* (pp. 79–102). Hillsdale, NJ: Lawrence Erlbaum.

Greenwell, J., & Dengerink, H. A. (1973). The role of perceived versus actual attack in human physical aggression. *Journal of Personality and Social Psychology, 26*(1), 66–71.

Guthrie, J. P. (2001). High-involvement work practices, turnover, and productivity: Evidence from New Zealand. *Academy of Management Journal, 44*(1), 180–190.

Hackman, J. R., & Oldham, G. R. (1975). Development of the job diagnostic survey. *Journal of Applied Psychology, 60*(2), 159–170.

Hackman, J. R., & Oldham, G. R. (1976). Motivation through the design of work: Test of a theory. *Organizational Behavior and Human Performance, 16*(2), 250–279.

Hackman, J. R., & Oldham, G. R. (1980). *Work redesign* (Vol. 16). Reading, MA: Addison-Wesley.

Health Services Research and Development (HSRD). (1993). OAS: Measurement Excellence and Training Resource Information Center. *VA Health Services Research & Development.* Retrieved January 1, 2000, from http://www.measurementexperts.org/instrument/instrument_reviews.asp?detail=34.

Hoel, H., Cooper, C. L., & Faragher, B. (2001). The experience of bullying in Great Britain: The impact of organizational status. *European Journal of Work and Organizational Psychology, 10*(4), 443–465.

Hoel, H., & Giga, S. I. (2006). Destructive interpersonal conflict in the workplace: The effectiveness of management interventions. Unpublished manuscript, Manchester Business School, University of Manchester, UK.

Hubbel, A. P., & Chory-Assad, R. M. (2005). Motivating factors: Perceptions of justice and their relationship with managerial and organizational trust. *Communication Studies, 56*(1), 47–70.

Hulin, C. L., Fitzgerald, L. R., & Drasgow, F. (1996). Organizational influences on sexual harassment. In M. Stockdale (Ed.), *Sexual harassment in the workplace* (Vol. 5, pp. 27–50). Thousand Oaks, CA: Sage.

Infante, D. A., Myers, S. A., & Buerkel, R. A. (1994). Argument and verbal aggression in constructive and destructive family and organizational disagreements. *Western Journal of Communication, 58*(1), 73–84.

Kasl, E., & Yorks, L. (2002). Collaborative inquiry for adult learning. *New Directions for Adult & Continuing Education, 94*(1), 3–10.

Keashly, L. (1998). Emotional abuse in the workplace: Conceptual and empirical issues. *Journal of Emotional Abuse, 1*(1), 85–117.

Keashly, L., & Neuman, J. H. (2005). Bullying in the workplace: Its impact and management. *Employee Rights and Employment Policy Journal, 8*(2), 335–373.

Keashly, L., & Nowell, B. L. (2003). Conflict, conflict resolution and bullying. In S. Einarsen, H. Hoel, D. Zapf & C. L. Cooper (Eds.), *Bullying and emotional abuse in the workplace: International perspectives in research and practice* (pp. 339–358). London: Taylor & Francis.

Keyton, J., Ferguson, P., & Rhodes, S. C. (2001). Cultural indicators of sexual harassment. *Southern Communication Journal, 67*(1), 33–50.

Kinney, T. A. (1993). An inductively derived topology of verbal aggression and its association to distress. *Human Communication Research, 21*(2), 183–222.

Kowalski, R., Harmon, J., Yorks, L., & Kowalski, D. (2003). Reducing workplace stress and aggression: An action research project at the U.S. Department of Veterans Affairs. *Human Resource Planning, 26*(2), 39–53.

Latham, G. P., & Lee, T. W. (1986). Goal setting. In E. A. Locke (Ed.), *Generalizing from laboratory to field settings* (pp. 100–117). Lexington, MA: Lexington.

Lawler, E. E. I. (1992). *The ultimate advantage: Creating the high-involvement organization.* San Francisco: Jossey-Bass.

Leventhal, G. S. (1980). What should be done with equity theory? In K. J. Gerneg, M. S. Greenberg & R. H. Willis (Eds.), *Social exchanges: Advances in theory and research* (pp. 27–55). New York: Plenum.

Lewis, S. E., & Orford, J. (2005). Women's experiences of workplace bullying: Changes in social relations. *Journal of Community and Applied Social Psychology, 15*(1), 29–47.

Lutgen-Sandvik, P. (2006). Take this job and ...: Quitting and other forms of resistance to workplace bullying. *Communication Monographs, 73*(4), 406–433.

Lutgen-Sandvik, P., & McDermott, V. (2008). The constitution of employee-abusive organizations: A communication flows theory. *Communication Theory, 18*(2), 304–333.

Martinko, M. J., & Zellars, K. L. (1996). *Toward a theory of workplace violence: A social Learning and attributional perspective.* Paper presented at the annual meeting of the Academy of Management, Cincinatti.

Moore, C. W. (2003). *The mediation process: Practical strategies for resolving conflict* (3rd ed.). San Francisco: Jossey-Bass.

Neuman, J. H. (2004). Injustice, stress, and aggression in organizations. In R. W. Griffin & A. M. O'Leary-Kelly (Eds.), *The dark side of organizational behavior* (pp. 62–102). San Francisco: Jossey-Bass.

Neuman, J. H., & Baron, R. A. (1998). Workplace violence and workplace aggression: Evidence concerning specific forms, potential causes, and preferred targets. *Journal of Management, 24*(3), 391–411.

Neuman, J. H., & Keashly, L. (2004, April). *Development of the Workplace Aggression Research Questionnaire (WAR-Q): Preliminary data from the Workplace Stress and Aggression Project.* Paper presented at the annual meeting of the Society for Industrial and Organizational Psychology, Chicago.

Nicoletti, J., & Spooner, K. (1996). Violence in the workplace: Response and intervention strategies. In G. R. VandenBos & E. Q. Bulatao (Eds.), *Violence on the job: Identifying risks and developing solutions* (pp. 267–282). Washington, DC: American Psychological Association.

Nonaka, I., Toyama, R., & Byosiere, P. (2001). A theory of organizational knowledge creation: Understanding the dynamic process of creating knowledge. In M. Dierkes, A. B. Antal, J. Child & I. Nonaka (Eds.), *Handbook of organizational learning and knowledge* (pp. 491–517). New York: Oxford University Press.

Osatuke, K., Ward, C., Dyrenforth, S., & Belton, L. (2007, August). *Civility, respect, engagement in the workforce (CREW): Conceptual model and organizational development intervention.* Paper presented at the annual meeting of the Academy of Management, Philadelphia.

Papa, M. J., & Canary, D. J. (1995). Conflict in organizations: A competence-based approach. In A. M. Nicotera (Ed.), *Conflict in organizations: Communication processes* (pp. 153–179). New York: State University of New York Press.

Peek-Asa, C., & Jenkins, L. (2003). Workplace violence: How do we improve approaches to prevention? *Clinics in Occupational and Environmental Medicine, 3*(4), 659–672.

Peters, L. H., & O'Connor, E. J. (1980). Situational constraints and work outcomes: The influences of a frequently overlooked construct. *Academy of Management Review, 5*(3), 391–397.

Peters, T. J., & Waterman, R. H., Jr.. (1982). *In search of excellence: Lessons from America's best run companies.* New York: Harper & Row.

Pfeffer, J., & Sutton, R. I. (2006). Evidence-based management. *Harvard Business Review, 84*(1), 62–75.

Pörhölä, M., Karhunen, S., & Rainivaara, S. (2006). Bullying at school and in the workplace: A challenge for communication research. In C. S. Beck (Ed.), *Communication yearbook* (Vol. 30, pp. 249–301). Mahwah, NJ: Lawrence Erlbaum.

Rayner, C., Hoel, H., & Cooper, C. L. (2002). *Workplace bullying: What we know, who is to blame, and what can we do?* London: Taylor & Francis.

Rousseau, D. M. (2006). Is there such a thing as "evidence-based management"? *Academy of Management Review, 31*(2), 256–269.

Saunders, M. N. K., & Thornhill, A. (2004). Trust and mistrust in organizations: An exploration using an organizational justice framework. *European Journal of Work and Organizational Psychology, 13*(4), 493–515.

Schat, A. C. H., & Kelloway, E. K. (2006). Training as a workplace aggression intervention strategy. In E. K. Kelloway, J. Barling & J. J. Hurrell (Eds.), *Handbook of workplace violence* (pp. 579–608). Thousand Oaks, CA: Sage.

Schein, E. H. (1990). A general philosophy of helping: Process consultation. *Sloan Management Review, 31*(3), 57–64.

Senge, P. M., Kleiner, A., Roberts, C., Ross, R., & Smith, B. (1994). *The fifth discipline fieldbook.* New York: Currency-Doubleday.

Sharpe, R. (1994, February 8). Self-defense classes go to the workplace, as fear of violence increases. *The Wall Street Journal,* p. 1.

Sherif, M., Harvey, O. J., White, B. J., Hood, W. E., & Sherif, C. W. (1961). *Intergroup conflict and cooperation: The Robbers Cave experiment.* Norman, OK: Institute of Group Relations.

Topalli, V., & Oneal, E. C. (2003). Retaliatory motivation enhances attributions of hostility when people process ambiguous social stimuli. *Aggressive Behavior, 29*(2), 155–172.

Usala, P. D. (1996). *Psychometric analysis of the Organizational Assessment Items: Work unit experiences and organizational experiences scales.* Washington, DC: U.S. Office of Personnel Management Employment Service, Personnel Resources and Development Center.

van de Ven, A. H., & Poole, M. S. (1995). Explaining development and change in organizations. *The Academy of Management Review, 20*(3), 510–540.

Walker, V. (2001). A proactive approach. In N. Tehrani (Ed.), *Building a culture of respect: Managing bullying at work* (pp. 117–134). London: Taylor & Francis.

Whitted, K. S., & Dupper, D. R. (2005). Best practices for preventing or reducing bullying in schools. *Children and Schools, 27*(3), 167–175.

Yamada, D. (2000). The phenomenon of "workplace bullying" and the need for status-blind hostile work environment protection. *Georgetown Law Journal, 88*(3), 475–536.

Yorks, L., Neuman, J. H., Kowalski, D. R., & Kowalski, R. (2007). Lessons learned from a five-year project within the Department of Veterans Affairs: Applying theories of interpersonal aggression and organizational justice to the development and maintenance of collaborative social space. *Journal of Applied Behavioral Science, 43*(3), 352–372.

Chapter 17

Working Alone
What Ever Happened to the Idea of Organizations as Communities?*

Jeffrey Pfeffer

Remember when everyone was talking about organizational culture and the idea of building strong cultures to achieve competitive advantage (e.g., Kotter & Leskett, 1992; O'Reilly, 1989; Tushman & O'Reilly, 1997, Chapter 5)? Remember *Theory Z* and Ouchi's (1981) argument that Williamson's (1975) description of possible organizing arrangements was incomplete? Ouchi maintained that in addition to achieving coordination and control through market-like mechanisms such as prices and contracts on the one hand, and hierarchies or bureaucracies on the other, there was yet another way of organizing and managing employees, and that was through clan-like relationships among people (e.g., Ouchi & Jaeger, 1978), characterized by high levels of trust and stability. More recently, Gittell's (2003) description of Southwest Airlines is consistent with the idea of achieving coordination through interpersonal trust and mutual adjustment of behavior (Thompson, 1967). Gittell argued that Southwest's extraordinary level of productivity and performance has come through high levels of coordination and control achieved through interpersonal relationships rather than simply through relying on either formal mechanisms or incentives.

Remember Japanese management, with its emphasis on the total inclusion of people in the company and long-term, even lifetime, employment, and the corollary idea that employees were important stakeholders in enterprises with claims equivalent in their importance to those of shareholders (e.g., Aoki, 1988)? Or to go even farther back, remember the welfare capitalism practiced by some large employers in the first three decades of the twentieth century? Many employers believed then that companies should take care of their employees and therefore offered benefits including company housing, paid vacations, healthcare, pensions, and, as in the case of Ford Motor Company, help from a "sociological department" in

---

* In E.E. Lawler II and J. O'Toole (Eds.). (2006). *America at work: Choices and challenges.* New York: Palgrave Macmillan.

setting up a household, saving and investing money, and keeping employees away from alcohol and hustlers (Lacey, 1986, pp. 131–134). Employers provided assistance to their workforce both out of a sense of civic duty and moral obligation—Henry Ford, for instance, claimed to be interested in building men, not just cars—and also as a way of potentially avoiding unionization efforts and more intrusive government intervention in the employment relationship (e.g., Jacoby, 1997).

Whatever the motivations, there were deeper connections between companies and their workers and more of a sense of communal responsibility than exists today. These ideas and the management practices associated with their implementation seem to have fallen by the wayside, at least in most organizations, and at least in the United States. As Cappelli (1999) has nicely shown, instead of building closer, more communal-like relationships with their workforce, over the past couple of decades most organizations in the United States have moved systematically to more market-like, distant, and transactional relationships with their people. Instead of taking care of and being responsible for their employees, companies have cut medical benefits for full-time employees and cut them even more aggressively for their retirees (Geisel, 2002; Hofmann, 2003). Meanwhile companies in large numbers have either changed defined-benefit pension plans to defined-contribution plans in which employees are more responsible for their own future economic security (Feinberg, 2004) or have abandoned offering pension benefits altogether.

This trend toward more market-like and distant connections has spread throughout the world as other companies in other countries such as Japan and Western Europe seek to emulate U.S. practices in managing the employment relation. The idea that shareholders are preeminent has also taken hold more strongly in other countries, even as some in the United States question the long-term consequences of adopting this shareholder-first perspective (Jacobs, 1991).

There are, of course, always important and noteworthy exceptions to these trends among both companies and countries, but the absence of much sense of community in most organizations is quite real and quite important for understanding the evolution of work in America, the relationship between organizations and their people, and the attitudes and beliefs of the workforce.

One consequence of the trend away from communal and caring relationships toward more arms-length, market-like transactions between organizations and their employees has been less trust and psychological attachment between employees and their employers. The evidence of job dissatisfaction, distrust, and disengagement is pervasive, as many surveys and studies from a number of industrialized countries tell the same tale: job satisfaction, employee engagement, and trust in management are all low and declining.

One survey by The Discovery Group reported that 62% of employees do not believe the information they receive from senior management (Katcher, 2004). A survey of the U.S. workforce found that one in six workers say they have withheld a suggestion for improving work efficiency, and fewer than 40% trust their company to keep its promises (Princeton Survey Research Associates, 1994). A 2003 survey by Korn Ferry found that 62% of global executives are unhappy with their current position of employment (Korn/Ferry, 2003). A Conference Board survey of 5,000 U.S. households conducted in August 2004 found that 67% of workers do not identify with or feel motivated to drive their employer's business goals, one quarter are just showing up to collect a paycheck, and almost half feel disconnected from their employers (Conference Board, 2005). That study concluded that "Americans are growing increasingly unhappy with their jobs, with the decrease in job satisfaction pervasive across all age groups and income levels" (Conference Board). Cappelli (1999, pp. 122–123) summarized numerous surveys of employee attitudes and commitment, noting that since the 1980s the measures were "in a virtual free-fall." Nor is this phenomenon confined to the United States. For instance, the Gallup organization "found that 80% of British workers lack commitment to their job, with a quarter of those being 'actively disengaged'" (Deloitte Research, 2004, p. 4).

The logic linking the less communal aspect of companies and the rise of distrust, disengagement, and diminished satisfaction, although not extensively empirically demonstrated, seems clear. Trust is enhanced through longer-term interactions and by believing that the other party is taking your interests into account. Both longer-term employment and time horizons and the belief that senior leadership is concerned about employee welfare characterize more community-like companies. Because people value workplace friendships and working with people they like and respect and are more willing to expend extra effort when they feel psychologically connected to their organizations—again the link between the extent to which companies are more community-like and outcomes such as job attitudes and willingness to invest more effort at work seems clear.

Another consequence of the diminished sense of community inside organizations has been more incivility defined as displaying a lack of regard for others in violation of norms of mutual respect (Pearson & Porath, 2005) and an increase in bullying in workplaces in which social ties and communal obligations are weaker. A study of 800 employees in the United States found that 10% reported witnessing incivility *daily* in their workplaces and one-fifth reported being the target of incivility at work at least once a week (Pearson & Porath). Furthermore, one-fourth of respondents who felt they were treated uncivilly intentionally cut back their work efforts, and one in eight left their job to escape the situation (Pearson & Porath).

The connection between community and workplace bullying and incivility seems evident. A sense of community and shared, mutual obligations and closer social ties among people would act to inhibit rude or nasty behavior. These inhibitions disappear in places characterized by more market-like and distant relationships among people and between people and their employers. Ironically and unfortunately all of these changes in employee attitudes and behavior are occurring—at the very moment when people's skills and discretionary effort are more important than ever for organizational success.

In this chapter, we briefly describe the evolution away from the conception of organizations as communities, what may have produced this change, as well as the opportunity provided to organizations that take a different approach and take the idea of the workplace as community more seriously. Putnam's (2000) description of the decline in many aspects of community in U.S. society more generally has been mirrored in work organizations, and few companies now embrace Theory Z or the many other books that recommend more inclusion of people in organizations and the creation of stronger social ties. We are not only "bowling alone," we are increasingly "working alone," even though there is important research that shows the importance of social capital for organizational success as well as individual success inside work organizations (e.g., Coff & Rousseau, 2000; Leana & Rousseau, 2000).

More communal relations among people and between organizations and their employees does seem to provide an advantage, but that many organizations nevertheless do not make decisions about managing their people consistent with this fact belies the common assumption that organizational leaders are rational, profit-maximizing decision-makers always choosing the best course of action. Instead, this discussion of the communal aspect of work in America makes clear, once again, the importance of values and beliefs in decisions that concern the relationships between companies and their employees. The importance of values has, in turn, implications for the education of managers both in school and inside companies as well as for the role of public policy in helping to shape the covenant between employers and their employees.

The Choices Companies Make

Organizations and their leaders make two fundamental and important decisions about their workforce, from which many other decisions and management practices naturally follow. The first basic decision is where to draw the organization's boundaries—which activities and people to include in an employment relationship and which activities and people to leave outside the company, to treat in more market-like and impersonal ways (e.g., Williamson, 1975). At the limit, of course, are virtual or almost-virtual companies with few or no actual employees. Thus, evidence suggests that more "externalized" work such as part-time employment and temporary and contract work is growing in importance and prevalence (e.g., Belous, 1989; Segal & Sullivan, 1997).

The second crucial decision, given that a company is going to have any employees at all, is what sort of relationship to forge with those employees, the people living inside the organization's boundaries, and, as a consequence, what kind of organizational culture to create. There are a number of interrelated dimensions that could be productively used to characterize this relationship between organizations and their people, including: (1) the expected duration of the relationship; (2) the degree of legalism and formalism that characterizes the employment relation; (3) related to the first and second dimensions, the extent to which the employment relation inside the firm is characterized by a market-like character (Cappelli, 1999) in which outcomes from the external labor market such as wage rates and benefit arrangements are directly imported into the company; and (4) related to the preceding three dimensions, how organizations treat the degree of inclusion of people in the company. Do organizations adopt a more community-like role, being concerned with nonwork aspects of people's lives, or do they adopt a more transactional and limited approach, essentially buying labor for money in an exchange that can be terminated by either side for any, or no, reason?

Forces Affecting the Community-Like Nature of Organizations

A number of explanations have been offered to account for the variation in the communal nature of companies both over time and across cultures, but none seems to be completely adequate or convincing, leaving an important topic for further research. The first and most obvious explanation for the decline in the degree and forms of attachment between companies and their employees is the greater competition or increased financial stringency faced by organizations. So, for instance, Jacoby (1997) argued that welfare capitalism was a casualty of the Great Depression. Cappelli (1999) maintained that the more market-like interactions between companies and their employees were a natural and logical response to increased competitive pressure and the consequent requirement for lower costs, including labor costs; explanations for changes in Japanese and European organizations toward a more American-like mode often point to increasing global competition and economic integration as a cause.

But the data are not completely consistent with an explanation stressing more competition as a cause of declining community-like ties in work organizations, nor does this account make logical sense. Barley and

Kunda's (1992) study of the rise and fall of regimes of normative and rational control in organizations provides some relevant evidence, if we assume that normative control is related to more communal relationships inside companies. Their study found that variations in economic conditions explained variation in control regimes over time. But as Barley and Kunda noted, neither the extent of competition nor the munificence or scarcity of the environment did or could explain the rise or fall of normative control. That's because both normative and rational control approaches promise enhanced efficiency and effectiveness. In other words, since communal-like relations presumably *increase* employee motivation and organizational performance, there is no logic to arguing that such organizing principles should decline in use just because companies face more competition.

Furthermore, welfare capitalism emerged in the late 1800s and early 1900s when economic competition was, if anything, fiercer than at any other time including the present. Griffin, Wallace, and Rubin (1986) noted that the average business failure rate during the period 1890–1928 was more than twice that of the post-World War II average. And so-called Japanese management practices such as single company unions and long-term employment relations actually emerged in full flower after World War II, when Japan was facing unprecedented levels of economic hardship.

Finally, many of the companies most noted for their communal nature (e.g., Southwest Airlines and the Men's Wearhouse) operate in industries (airlines and retailing) that are beset with competition and financial stringency. To the extent that stronger attachments and a less transactional relationship promote discretionary effort, reduced turnover, and, as a consequence, higher levels of productivity, it is far from logically clear why increased competitive pressure should not *increase* rather than decrease the communal nature of companies.

A second explanation for variation is national culture. Ouchi (1981), for instance, emphasized the difference between American agriculture with its dispersed (and presumably larger) farms and Japanese rice growing, where the farmers lived in closer proximity to each other. While not denying that there are important differences across countries, particularly in the extent to which nations seem to embrace individualistic competition or more collective and communal ways of interrelating (e.g., Hofstede, 1980), this explanation also has some problems. In the first place, there is a great deal of variation in management practices across organizations situated in similar industries within the same country. And even in single countries, such as Japan, and even in the same company, organizations often treat their women and part-time employees quite differently from the portion of the labor force that is considered to be core.

It is not clear whether national cultural values about how people ought to be treated and the communal nature of companies can readily account for this differential treatment of people inside the same organization. Moreover, the relatively rapid change in management practices experienced, for instance, in the United States, which went from the organization man of the 1950s to the fee agents of the 1980s and 1990s, makes lodging an explanation in something as stable as national values and culture problematic.

A third explanation is institutionalization and imitation. There is no doubt that companies play "follow-the-leader," and consulting organizations and benchmarking practices are among the forces that encourage imitation and the spread of management ideas. Even a study of downsizing, which one might think is one of the most economically driven decisions, found strong evidence of mimicry (Brudos, 1997). There is also no doubt that management approaches such as welfare capitalism and more inclusion or more market-like relationships with employees come into and go out of fashion, and that management practices are at least to an extent driven by fads and fashions (Abrahamson, 1996). The difficulty with this explanation is that not only does it leave much contemporaneous variation across companies unexplained, but it also leaves largely unexplored the causes or sources that determine what comes into fashion and what goes out, and which ideas are in vogue.

Yet another explanation lodges the source of variation in the values and experiences of the CEO. Southwest Airlines will be forever identified with its long-term CEO, Herb Kelleher, and the company's culture and style, as well as the management practices and associated values that reflected Kelleher's philosophy, including putting employees first, customers second, and shareholders third. The sense of the company as a community or even a family is part and parcel of the company's way of operating, as Colleen Barrett, president and chief operating officer, explained:

> We've talked to our employees from day one about being one big family. If you stop and think about it for even 20 seconds, the things we do are things that you would do with your own family. We try to acknowledge and react to any significant event in our brothers' or sisters' lives, whether it's work-related or personal. We do the traditional things, like sending birthday cards and cards on the anniversary of their date of hire. But if employees have a child who's sick or a death in the family, we do our best to acknowledge it. We celebrate with our employees when good things happen, and we grieve with them when they experience something devastating. (Shinn, 2003, p. 19)

George Zimmer, founder and CEO of the Men's Wearhouse, was very much a child of the 1960s, and he talked about doing things to ensure he remained spiritual enough. Again, the humanistic values that emanated from Zimmer permeated the company and infused its specific management practices such as offering loans to employees having financial difficulties and giving employees second and third chances even when they had stolen a pair of socks or put a customer's deposit in their pocket for several days.

DaVita, a large operator of kidney dialysis centers, reborn under CEO Kent Thiry, reflected Thiry's values and orientation toward community. It is not every CEO, particularly a nonfounding CEO with fewer than 10 years of service, who would set up a family foundation to provide educational benefits to company employees' children, something that Thiry did. The company was referred to as a village, Thiry was the "mayor," and the ethos was very much one of community that emanated from Thiry and his close associates.

There is no question, particularly in America, at a time of strong, even dominant, CEOs, that the tone set at and by the top permeates much of the organization, and this is true whether that tone consists of the ethical lapses of Ken Lay at Enron and the abusive, take-no-prisoners ethos of "Chainsaw" Al Dunlap (e.g., Byrne, 2003; McLean & Elkind, 2003) or the humanistic, community-oriented tone of Thiry, Zimmer, and Kelleher. But what this explanation lacks, of course, is an account of precisely how these CEOs' values get formed and, perhaps as importantly, in the case of CEOs who were not the founders of their companies, how and why boards of directors selected them in the first place and then subsequently retained them and accepted their cultural values and management approach. Although leaders and their beliefs matter, an exclusively leader-centric account seems to leave out the explanation for how these leaders formed their particular view of what organizations should be and how they come to get selected and are able to remain in power.

An important additional factor, not often addressed in either research or theorizing, that may help explain the variation in the communal nature of organizations over time and across locales is the set of social values and norms that get embedded in particular theories and perspectives about people and organizations, perspectives that do not simply "arise" but that are promulgated by interest groups with particular agendas and beliefs. So, for instance, when George Zimmer gave a talk to a class of Stanford MBAs, the most frequently asked question was what other retail CEOs said about his unique and different philosophy and approach to running a retail business. Zimmer's response was that he did not spend much time talking to other retail CEOs (nor, one would suspect, listening to or benchmarking their ideas).

The question reflects the correct belief that there are socially accepted and valued ways of running a company, that these beliefs influence how leaders behave, and that in current times, such ways of managing do not much include thinking of organizations as communities or employees as important. A new question then arises as to how CEOs and companies with this approach are able to withstand the various pressures, including pressures from peers in business and pressures from the capital markets. But another equally important question is how social expectations and ideas about appropriate models of organization get established in the first place. As Zimmer also made clear in his talk, there were two ways of thinking about business and society: as places facing the need to allocate scarce resources and compete, or as places existing in a world filled with infinite love, compassion, and expandable resources. He remarked, with a smile, that he could predict which of the two views of the world the MBA program inculcated.

At the societal level, the waxing and waning of ideology that informs management practice is not exogenous but is, instead, driven by the political agendas of affluent groups with an ideology that they would like to advance (e.g., DeParle, 2005). Therefore, management practices reflect general trends in beliefs about people, their responsibilities, and how they relate to each other, as well as what makes organizations effective. The rise of neoclassical economics with its assumptions of methodological individualism, the pursuit of self-interest (e.g., Miller, 1999), individual choice and responsibility, and the importance of market-mediated exchanges (Kuttner, 1996) is at once inconsistent with a view of organizations as communities of mutual responsibility and shared obligation and also helps to explain why a communal organizing model may be particularly scarce at times such as the present and in places, such as the United States, where such an ideology has gained ascendance.

Therefore, culture matters—not just or perhaps even primarily the national culture, but more particular social values embedded in people's implicit assumptions about human behavior and organizations and what makes each effective. As extensively documented elsewhere (e.g., Kuttner, 1996), such beliefs and ideologies about human behavior are neither simply subject to empirical proof of their validity nor emergent from society, but instead, these points of view are promulgated by foundations and organizations that are active in the political discourse precisely to influence not only specific policies but also, more importantly, the language and assumptions that shape how people see the world, including the organizational world (Ferraro, Pfeffer, & Sutton, 2005). In that sense, the waxing and waning of an organization as community model is a consequence of more general changes in views of human and organizational behavior that are the result of political action by advocates favoring a particular conception and point of view.

Needless to say, these explanations for variations in the prevalence of a communal model of organizing are not mutually exclusive. Moreover, their influence on organizing models ought to be studied rather than, as is almost invariably the case, simply asserted (e.g., Ouchi, 1981). Most importantly, the explanations should be considered, to the extent possible, simultaneously in studies of management practices, to assess their joint and separate effects.

Some Dimensions of Organizations as Communities

To talk about or to study the idea of organizations as communities, it is essential to develop some dimensions or indicators that might measure the extent to which organizations are, or are not, communal. A reading of the literature and a consideration of some companies that explicitly have adopted communal-like language and management practices suggest at least the following aspects for consideration in such a definition.

Helping Employees in Need

One element of community is that people look out for and take care of one another. At DaVita, formerly Total Renal Care, one of the largest operators of dialysis centers in the United States, the CEO dresses up as one of the Three Musketeers to reinforce the idea of "one for all and all for one." Very much like Southwest Airlines, which has a similar arrangement, DaVita collects contributions from employees to help other employees facing unanticipated medical expenses or other family emergencies that strain their financial resources. At SAS Institute, the company provides much the same sort of assistance. There are no sick days at SAS, but employees who fall ill get sympathy, concern, and a paycheck. Employees who violate the company's trust in them and abuse their perquisites get removed from the organization. When an SAS employee drowned in a boating accident, leaving his two young children no longer eligible to continue in company-subsidized, high-quality day care, SAS did the humane and concerned thing and let the children remain until they were no longer eligible by reason of age. At the Men's Wearhouse, because most retail employees are fairly low paid, there are funds available to provide no- or low-interest loans to people who need help, for instance, financing automobile repairs so they can have transportation to and from their workplace.

The presence and extensiveness of this sort of mutual aid and company-provided resources to help employees through difficult and unanticipated life events is a hallmark of companies that feel like communities and that connect employees more closely to each other and to the corporation.

Employee Benefits and Assistance

Another element of community is that the community, society, or organization takes care of people and their needs throughout the course of their life and not just in emergency situations. So, in cities there are schools for children and, presumably, social services and healthcare for the ill and the aged. In a similar fashion, more communal organizations typically offer a wider and more generous range of assistance and benefits to employees. SAS Institute is famous for its on-site subsidized daycare, on-site medical and recreational facilities, and the eldercare and adoption advice services it provides for its people and their dependents. SAS offers access to its cafeterias to families of employees so that, for instance, children in the on-site daycare can eat lunch with their parents. DaVita also offers medical benefits that are generous, considering its industry type and workforce composition, and provides ongoing training and education so that employees can develop their skills and progress in their careers. The Men's Wearhouse, the $1.4 billion retailer of tailored off-price men's clothing, uses a relatively small number of part-time employees so a higher proportion of its workforce is eligible for its relatively generous benefits, including profit sharing.

Unlike the assumptions of the neoclassical economic model in which people receive money and benefits for their labor and are expected to optimize the associated trade-offs between the various components of pay as well as among the different employment opportunities they could choose, organizations operating under a more communal approach seek to provide for employees' anticipated needs such as health-care and retirement. There are obvious tax advantages to providing assistance in this way, but the primary motivating factor seems to be a sense of obligation to provide benefits to help employees in significant aspects of their lives. Companies with a communal orientation do not abandon these programs at the first sign of financial stringency or when others in their industries do.

Nepotism and Dating Policies

In communities, people meet each other and form close interpersonal ties. In communities, neighborhoods, and ethnic enclaves, people become close friends and sometimes fall in love. Although only a small minority of employers have formal policies forbidding workplace dating, most discourage intimate relationships in the workplace in order to avoid "conflicts of interest, ethical trespasses and leaks of proprietary information," as well as time spent flirting (rather than working) and dealing with sexual harassment suits (Feeney, 2004, p. 37).

Not so in Southwest Airlines, where, of the company's 35,000 employees, about 2,000 are married to each other (Feeney, 2004). Nor SAS Institute, where both the current and the past head of human resources were married to other SAS employees, where people often meet at work, fall in love, get married, have children that they then send to SAS daycare, while both continue to work for the company. When I wrote a case on SAS, I interviewed a male programmer who responded to the question as to why he did not leave SAS at the height of the Internet frenzy to make more money elsewhere with the comment "my wife [a fellow SAS employee] would have left me."

Company-Sponsored Social Events

Communities have community activities—fairs, parades, holiday displays—that bring people together to celebrate accomplishments, mark the passage of time, and share significant milestones. One element of strong culture organizations is holding company-sponsored and -encouraged social events and other activities that bring people together (e.g., Deal & Kennedy, 1982), and organizations that seek to build a more community-like atmosphere therefore do things to create opportunities for informal social interaction.

The Men's Wearhouse has about 30 Christmas parties around the country where employees and their significant others come to celebrate with music, good food, and an awards ceremony. The company encourages its store managers to organize social outings and basketball or baseball games throughout the year so that employees enjoy recreation with each other. DaVita sponsors DaVita academies that offer not only learning and training but also games and socializing. SAS Institute encourages employees and their families to use the company's facilities and has numerous celebrations, including ones for new product releases. In the on-site recreational facilities, such as basketball and tennis courts, employees not only get their exercise but also literally "play" with each other. Southwest Airlines, too, is famous for its fun atmosphere and for the many celebrations and ways in which people get to interact informally with each other and with senior management.

The purpose of all of this is to encourage people to build deeper ties to each other and to create relationships fostered on mutual liking and interaction, not just on work-related interdependence. The idea is that by building a community feeling through informal social interaction, the company creates social capital that can be relied upon to build trust and to encourage people to work together to accomplish common goals.

Resolving Work-Family Issues

Inter-role conflict—the inconsistent demands of both being a family member and an employee—is pervasive in the U.S. workplace. Galinsky, Bond, and Friedman (1993) reported that 40% of employed parents experienced problems in combining work and family demands, and Frone, Russell, and Cooper (1992) found work interferes with home life three times as frequently as home or family responsibilities interferes with work. Bakker and Geurts (2004, p. 360) noted that "[e]mployees particularly experience negative interference between work and family life when they are exposed to a high workload and demanding interactions with clients."

Communal organizations try to resolve these issues in numerous ways, but most importantly by creating a culture and environment in which the activity of employees taking care of those outside of work for whom they are responsible is accepted and expected. The evidence is clear that the mere existence of formal policies permitting flexibility are insufficient, because employees are reluctant to take advantage of programs such as flexible work hours, maternity or paternity leave, the opportunity to work from home, or the opportunity to work part-time or job share (e.g., Evans, Kunda, & Barley, 2004). That's because "managers and peers interpret the use of flexibility programs as evidence of a lack of commitment, motivation, and productivity" and supervisors frequently deny requests for more flexible and family-friendly work schedules (Evans, et al., p. 3). What matters are not formal policies but the organization's culture and its orientation and values about work-family issues.

SAS Institute is frequently on the list of the best places to work and has won many plaudits for its family-friendly environment. SAS employees can adjust their work hours to accommodate family needs, and more importantly, the company has a workweek of 35 to 40 hours, not the long days and weeks more typical of the software industry. The company recognizes that the people most important to its employees are those that they care for and are responsible for, such as their husbands and wives, children, domestic partners, and parents, and it makes available both benefits and work arrangements that make it feasible to have both a job and a life. As a consequence, SAS has been able to attract a large number of talented women employees into professional and managerial roles as well as people from families with children, much greater than the average for companies in the software industry. Accessing talented women gives SAS a competitive advantage in the challenging task of recruiting and retaining talent in an industry that is in the end all about intellectual capital.

Long-Term Employment

One is presumably a member of a community for a long and indefinite period. Similarly, the idea of long-term employment is fundamental for those organizations that operate in a more communal fashion. Following September 11, 2001, Southwest Airlines, even as it prepared for the anticipated downturn, stayed clean of the knee-jerk reaction of immediately laying off workers, even as all of its industry competitors reduced their schedules and their workforces. SAS Institute tells its employees that it expects to see them have numerous careers and pursue various professional interests during the course of their work life, but it hopes that these changes will all occur at SAS. EADS, the large European defense and space agency that owns 80% of Airbus, also laid off no one following September 11, even though orders for new air-craft plummeted. Their head of human resources maintains that the goodwill engendered through that action has been instrumental in their overtaking Boeing and in avoiding the union conflicts and various production and quality programs that have plagued Boeing.

One reason this idea of long-term employment is so fundamental is that many of the other dimensions of community make sense only in the context of long-term mutual commitments. It is difficult and probably not very sensible, for example, to provide for employees over their life courses through pensions, medical benefits, and adoption and long-term care if the employees are not going to be in the company very long. But another reason for the emphasis on long-term employment is that it is fundamental to building a sense of permanence and attachment that communal-like organizations seek.

The irony is that although there is a pervasive sense of instability, fear of job loss, and increasing impermanence in the workplace, as Jacoby (1999) has argued, there is actually less evidence than one might expect that job tenures have actually shortened very much for most of the adult workforce or that career jobs are disappearing. In some sense, then, many companies have obtained the worst of both worlds—on the one hand, the costs and presumed disadvantages of long-tenured workforces such as higher benefit costs, and, on the other hand, people fearful of losing their jobs and not taking a long-term perspective on their commitment and attachment to the company.

Table 17.1 summarizes the dimensions and management practices that could form the basis for characterizing organizations in terms of their community-like nature.

The Advantages and Disadvantages of Managing Organizations as Communities

Understanding the logic behind managing organizations as communities compared to managing the employment relationship in a more market-like fashion can help us understand how these models vary over time, across organizations, and across cultures, as well as the factors leaders must consider working on, should one or the other model come to be perceived as desirable.

The Argument for Managing Organizations as Communities

The problem with the market-oriented, free agency-like model described by Cappelli (1999) as growing in prominence can be nicely seen by

Table 17.1 Dimensions that might be Used for Characterizing the Degree to which Organizations are Communities

Helping Employees in Need
  "Rainy day" fund
  Low-interest or no-interest loans to employees having financial difficulties
  Maintaining salary or benefits when not required to do so

Employee Benefits and Assistance
  Pensions, including defined-benefit pensions
  Health insurance or healthcare
  Adoption and eldercare assistance
  Tuition reimbursement and educational assistance
  Recreational facilities or health club membership

Nepotism and Dating Policies
  Are employees married to each other allowed to work in the company?
  Are there formal or informal policies precluding dating?

Company-Sponsored Social Events
  Holiday parties
  Travel and trips for recreation
  Games and sports teams and leagues
  Celebrations of accomplishments and milestones

Resolving Work/Family Issues
  Use of parental leave
  Maternity policies
  Flexible work hours
  Part-time work as an employee option, including job sharing
  On-site childcare

Long-Term Employment
  Voluntary turnover
  Layoffs

considering professional sports or investment banking, two labor markets that are probably the closest to the model in their operation. In each instance, the arrangement works well for the free agents, particularly those favored in the competition by their performance, but the employers tend not to do so well. When Warren Buffett stepped in to run Salomon Brothers after a bond trading scandal, one of the things he talked about was how the individual investment bankers were getting rich even though the returns to shareholders, measured by indicators such as return on shareholder equity, were quite poor for the firm. Most baseball teams lose money, at least in the absence of collusion to restrict players' salaries (e.g., Helyar, 1991).

These results are scarcely surprising. In the absence of any form of attachment other than money, people will continually be assessing their alternative market opportunities, will always be at risk of leaving, and because of the social comparison aspect to the salary determination process, the upward pressure on salaries will often be relentless. Salaries are invariably set with respect to some market level, but almost all consider themselves to be above average in their skills and performance (e.g., Brown, 1986). Consequently, there will be a tendency for average salaries to trend upward, unless there are severe downturns in the economy or enough foreign competition to fundamentally change the salary structure. This process accounts for the upward pressure on salaries in professional sports as well as the CEO labor market.

Moreover, turnover will be higher than it might otherwise be—again baseball, and for that matter other sports in the era of free agency, and investment banking provide good examples of this—imposing extra costs on the organization. These costs include the direct costs entailed in replacing the people leaving, costs in customer retention and satisfaction that come from having clients dealing with a perpetually inexperienced workforce, and the losses due to coordination failures or increased investment in the coordination and control required when people are working interdependently with others who are strangers.

Consequently, some companies seek to transform the employment relationship from one based strictly on money or other extrinsic incentives to one based on other things such as social relationships, purpose, and cultural fit as well. So, for instance, Apple Computer, in its heyday early in its history, recruited people, including former CEO John Sculley, by talking about its mission to change the world of computing.

Yet another way of deemphasizing the solely economic aspects of the employment relationship is to create a more communal-like feeling in the company, increasing the strength and importance of social bonds among people as well as the emotional connection between employees and the company. This is precisely the human resource strategy pursued by the MTW Corporation (now the Innovation Group), a Kansas City-based information technology contractor and developer of software for the insurance industry. By taking care of its people—providing more benefits and culture that signaled that people were valued and expected to be part of the company and contribute to decision-making—turnover fell to about 7% even in the height of the labor market frenzy, and the company was consistently profitable and growing.

Because of the norm of reciprocity, commitment is mutual. To expect employees to be loyal to the company, the company needs to be loyal to them. To expect employees to see themselves as citizens or members of a community that they find attractive enough to work for, exert discretionary effort on its behalf, and remain in the company, organizations must do the various things already discussed to create a sense of community that would warrant such attitudes and actions.

There are some additional important advantages of building organizations as communities. In the market-like arrangements characteristic of many contemporary employers, negotiation over everything is frequent.

These negotiations take time and effort and divert attention from developing products and services and serving customers. Trust, as it turns out, is much more efficient as a coordinating mechanism than to have to specify and haggle over every detail of work and the employment contract. Moreover, by incorporating more of the employee's life, including the parts outside of work, into the organization, employees are freed from external distractions and can focus on doing their work and making the company successful.

One of the reasons SAS Institute claims it can operate effectively with a shorter work week is that when its people are at work, they face no distractions. They do not have to worry either about their benefits or their children in daycare. They do not have to worry whether the company is exploiting them and whether they need to be out looking at employment alternatives. Frictions and wasted energy are reduced, albeit never completely eliminated, in organizations that are more communal-like and are thereby able to build deeper and more trusting relationships with their people.

The Arguments against Managing Organizations as Communities

There are, of course, many reasons why companies are reluctant to embrace, or at least fully embrace, a community-oriented perspective. One explanation comes from many executives' reactions when my colleagues and I teach cases such as Southwest Airlines or SAS Institute—the executives feel that the organizations are too "cult-like" and are uncomfortable with their strong cultures, even though those strong cultures have contributed in important ways to their success. The norm of individualism runs strong in the United States in particular, and in the West in general (e.g., Morris & Peng, 1994), and community, at least in some of its aspects and implications, is almost by definition group-oriented and group-centered. The clash with general social values looms large in explaining companies' reluctance to adopt this management approach.

Another aspect of the same phenomenon of managerial discomfort with community can be seen in a *Fortune* television interview with James Goodnight, cofounder and CEO of SAS. The interviewer accused Goodnight of being "paternalistic," which both the interviewer and, at least initially, Goodnight took to be a pejorative term. Upon reflection, however, Goodnight responded that if paternalism meant that he cared about his employees and their well-being, then he just might be paternalistic.

The point is that paternalism, or caring about the total person throughout his or her life course, is something expected of family members and friends, but somehow we have gotten the idea that business is, and should be, different from the rest of life, operating using different norms, values, mores of interaction, and rules. Ethics and honest behavior, for example, are important in interacting with family, friends, neighbors, and in religious and civic organizations, but ethical behavior has to be defended on occasion at work, with special workshops and training to inculcate behavior that is more completely natural in other settings. As another example, internal competition and forced curve ranking is often lauded in business, but sibling rivalry, although a reality, is seldom held out to be a desirable state of affairs, and few child-rearing experts argue that pitting family members against each other in a competition for status leads to good outcomes.

This attempt to keep work and business separate and distinct from other domains creates problems and is, in the end, impossible. As Libby Sartain, former head of HR at Southwest and now running HR at Yahoo, noted, how can work be separate from the rest of life when, with cell phones, e-mail, PDAs, and so forth, one can hardly escape from work?

A second reason for avoiding more communal and inclusive relationships with employees is potential legal issues. For instance, to offer a pension plan makes the employer responsible for ensuring the integrity of the plan and its administration, and, in the case of defined-benefit plans, financially responsible for ensuring that promised benefits are, in fact, paid. Offering on-site daycare may make the employer responsible for what goes on in the daycare center, even if it in operated by a contractor, and legally liable for problems caused by the daycare employees. Talking about organizations as communities and about continued association or membership may create an implied promise of long-term employment and get the employer into trouble for violating implicit contracts if layoffs occur. All benefit plans impose reporting requirements. In an increasingly litigious world, labor lawyers basically tell employers to promise as little as possible to expressly limit and to put in writing any obligations they do incur and, in general, to delimit the implicit and broad promises implied by the idea of organizations as communities.

Interestingly, there is little evidence that all of this legal maneuvering actually curtails the amount of employment litigation. In fact, by creating formalistic, legalistic, and distant relations between employers and their people, it is likely that legal action on the part of employees who feel they are wronged is actually encouraged, because there are no positive sentiments they hold toward the company to cause them to hold back. Anecdotally companies such as SAS Institute or the Innovation Group (formerly MTW Corporation) that have deeper and less formal relationships with their people actually face fewer employee suits than comparable organizations. Nonetheless, the advice of labor lawyers looms large as an explanation for why a more communal model of organizations has not diffused.

Separate from, but ideologically related to, the legal issues, many organizations seek to delimit their obligations to their employees and, to the extent possible, devolve responsibility for nonwork aspects of employees' lives back to the employees. That's because organizations do not want to open the Pandora's box by beginning to be responsible for more than they absolutely need to order to get the work accomplished. As part of the move toward a market-like employment relationship, organizations seek to delimit their sphere of involvement in the life and well-being of their workforce—by the way, at the same time feeling free to monitor people's behavior at work, including their Internet and e-mail behavior, and to make demands on people even during their off hours. Nonetheless, the idea of a limited transaction carries over and thus limits what companies feel they are responsible for.

So the advantages of greater involvement and inclusion are balanced with social expectations, norms of separateness, transactional relationships, and concerns about legal liability and assumption of responsibility. Different companies at different times and in different countries balance these conflicting pressures to reach different decisions about what kind of organization to construct.

The Role of Public Policy, Values, and Management Education

What should be clear from the foregoing discussion is that there is some degree of equifinality in employment models—different ways of organizing can be economically effective for organizations as long as they are implemented in an internally consistent fashion and fit the organization's business model and strategy (e.g., Cappelli & Crocker-Hefter, 1996). In other words, to use a contemporary example, one can be either Wal-Mart or Costco and be economically successful (Maier, 2005). However, different organizational models have different costs for employees and the broader society. After all, many of the functions assumed by organizations operating more as communities must be performed by other institutions such as government or private charities, or else these functions are left undone for employees who work in more market-like organizations.

To take just two examples, if employers do not provide medical coverage or pensions for their employees, those employees must somehow either acquire health insurance and retirement income on their own or, as is often the case, rely on the government to provide at least a limited safety net. And with respect to job satisfaction and commitment, employees who can rely on and trust their employers to look after more of their welfare are more likely to be satisfied with their employment—witness the difference in turnover levels, for instance, between Costco with its greater wages and benefits and Wal-Mart, which pays as little as possible given the local labor market, uses a higher percentage of part-time employees, and therefore provides benefits to fewer of its people (Shuit, 2004).

Throughout the history of the modern industrial age, there has always been choice in how companies structured their relationship with their employees, from the time of welfare capitalism at the beginning of the twentieth century, to the era of the "organizational man" (Whyte, 1956) in the 1950s, to the time of Theory Z and Japanese-style management in the 1980s, to the present-day emphasis on markets and labor market flexibility. As already noted, these choices are affected by values and beliefs, and also by public policy with its direct effect on management practices through law and regulation and its indirect effect through shaping norms about appropriate management behavior. Recent trends in values and beliefs and public policy regimes make the idea of organizations as communities less likely, regardless of the virtues of such an approach.

Management practice is affected by what is taught in business schools (Ghoshal, 2005), in part because schools in the United States now turn out more than 100,000 MBAs per year, business education based in large measure on the U.S. model and U.S. literature is expanding rapidly around the world, and in addition to the people enrolled in formal degree programs, many other executives come into contact with business school through executive programs. As documented by Ghoshal (2005) and others (e.g., Ferraro et al., 2005), business school curricula are heavily influenced by economics and the assumptions and language of economics, including assumptions of self-interest, agency problems, and the virtues of markets as ways of allocating resources (see also, Kuttner, 1996). Although there are obviously other points of view—and one can find human resource management courses that offer organizational models emphasizing commitment, strong culture, and community (e.g., O'Reilly & Pfeffer, 2000)—economics remains the mother discipline and an important influence on managerial thought, language, and practice.

The consequences of this economic orientation need not just be logically inferred but can be empirically seen in studies that explore how business school students' values and behavior change while in school. The Aspen Institute's (2001) study of values shows that over the course of their education, students come to place less emphasis on customers and employees and more emphasis on shareholders and creating shareholder value. McCabe and his colleagues (e.g., McCabe & Trevino, 1995) have shown in numerous studies that business school students are more likely to report having cheated than students from other majors. And a study of corporate malfeasance found that while organizational size was positively related to the likelihood of corporate malfeasance, this relationship was even stronger for companies with a higher proportion of senior management with MBA degrees. Ghoshal (2005) has argued that all these consequences mean that business education and its language and theoretical foundations need to be fundamentally rethought and redesigned. Until this task is accomplished, however, business education and the dominant economic logic make building organizations as communities less likely.

Government, under the banner of an "ownership society" and making the economy more efficient by reducing regulation, has also invoked economic language, assumptions, and practices, thereby serving as a model to other organizations. Public employees, such as nurses and teachers, feel under attack and are called "special interests" as various states and cities try to introduce more variation in pay, less job seniority, and less generous staffing ratios. Ironically, government's relaxation of regulations that might constrain the choices of companies often does not encourage companies to behave responsibly toward their people.

So, there are no proscriptions on abandoning healthcare insurance for either employees or retirees, and competitive dynamics will virtually force companies to do so when enough others in their industry do, leaving those who want to maintain more generous communal benefits at a competitive disadvantage. The result is that 45 million Americans now have no health insurance, an increase of more than five million in the last five years, and the National Academy of Sciences estimates that 18,000 people die each year because they have no insurance and thus reduced access to care (Pear, 2005). Companies are also free to change or abandon pension plans, again putting pressure on competitors to do likewise. This dynamic is currently playing out in the airline industry where companies in bankruptcy can renegotiate the terms of employment and can jettison pension obligations, almost forcing other companies not yet in bankruptcy to match these actions for competitive survival.

The irony is that government regulation, or its absence, lets companies off the hook for promises, but then government itself, through guarantees of minimum pension benefits and the need to provide healthcare to those who otherwise cannot afford it, winds up shouldering the costs offloaded by private sector employers. In fact, faced with their own pension obligations that strain their budgets, city and state governments have begun to contemplate changing their own retirement practices to move away from defined-benefit plans that guarantee a certain percentage of income based on years of service, and instead to have their employees assume more responsibility for their own retirement income through defined-contribution plans. Thus, it is questionable whether public policy and public organization examples encourage the development of a more communal orientation toward the workforce.

Although the current zeitgeist is very much contrary to the idea of organizations as communities of shared fate, and much more consistent with an ethos of every person for him- or herself (get what you can when you can and how you can), this actually leaves an amazing competitive opportunity for the companies that operate differently. Just as in product markets, competitive advantage in labor markets comes from offering a better—and different—value proposition. Doing what everyone else does basically produces the same results as everyone else. Variation in performance, either positive or negative, comes from being different. So, the competitive advantage in attracting employees enjoyed by SAS Institute, Southwest Airlines, and DaVita, for example, only grows to the extent that their cultures and communal orientation are increasingly unique.

Missed Opportunities

Work in America continues to be problematic in many dimensions, and maybe even more so than when the original volume was published. My reading of that original work is that in the 1970s, people were largely concerned about whether or not work itself had sufficient variety and autonomy—whether jobs were sufficiently enriched to motivate and engage the workforce (e.g., Hackman & Oldham, 1980), the effects of alienating jobs on physical and mental health, and the need for worker training. Alienation from and boredom with work—often routine and deskilled work—was an important focus of attention.

The good news is that work requiring no skill, work that can be outsourced or off-shored, has been, or soon will be. The work that remains in advanced industrial economies is increasingly intellectual or knowledge work, requiring innovation and skill—except, of course, for personal services that cannot be provided at a distance. The bad news is that what seems to be more problematic is not just people's work, although autonomy and control over work remains a critical issue, but also employees' connections to their employers and each other.

> People are now spending more time at work than ever before:
> The Japanese do not feel rich, Imada (1997) argued, because an over-emphasis on work and long hours has made it difficult for many Japanese to enjoy family life ... . U.S. workers now work more hours per year than do workers in any other industrialized country ... . Middle-class parents in dual-earner households worked a total of 3,932 hours in 2000, equivalent to more than two full-time jobs in most European countries. (Berg, Appelbaum, Bailey, & Kalleberg, 2004, pp. 332–333)

Not only are people spending lots of time at work, but work roles also remain central to social identity and status, and the conflict between work and nonwork time and responsibilities remains pervasive (e.g., Barnett, 1994; Bolger, DeLongis, & Kessler, 1989; Gareis & Barnett, 2002). So the fundamental question is, what sort of relationship is forged between people and their employers within the workplace, the place where people spend so much time? There is certainly evidence that people want to do meaningful work, work that has purpose and that they find fulfilling in the sense of accomplishing something they believe contributes to achieving some important goal (Ashmos & Duchon, 2000), as well as work that permits them to realize their full potential as a person (Mitroff & Denton, 1999).

But people also desire a sense of belonging and community at work. People are social creatures and social interaction at work is important. For people spending more time and making more personal sacrifices for their work, not only what they do but also the relationship with their employer is psychologically important.

For a number of reasons briefly reviewed here, most organizations are not providing the sense of community and psychological attachment that most people seek. This leaves many people dissatisfied and reasonably uncommitted to their employers, which results in less discretionary effort and providing fewer ideas and innovation than might otherwise be the case. In sum, the story of work in America today, with respect to the communal nature of organizations, is a story of missed opportunities. There are many factors and forces at play in creating this situation, ranging from public policy to what we teach in business schools to general social norms, values, and expectations about the appropriate relationship between people and organizations. For work in America to change, each and all of these factors and forces will need to be both better understood and a target for intervention.

References

Abrahamson, E. (1996). Management fashion. *Academy of Management Review, 21*(2), 254–285.

Aoki, M. (1988). *Information, incentives, and bargaining in the Japanese economy.* Cambridge, MA: Cambridge University Press.

Ashmos, D. P., & Duchon, D. (2000). Spirituality at work: A conceptualization and measure. *Journal of Management Inquiry, 9*(1), 134–145.

Aspen Institute. (2001). *Where will they lead? MBA students attitudes about business and society.* New York: Aspen Institute for Social Innovation Through Business.

Bakker, A. B., & Geurts, S., A. E. (2004). Toward a dual-process model of work-home interference. *Work and Occupations, 31*(3), 345–366.

Barley, S. R., & Kunda, G. (1992). Design and devotion: Surges of rational and normative ideologies of control in managerial discourse. *Administrative Science Quarterly, 37*(3), 363–399.

Barnett, R. C. (1994). Home-to-work spillover revisited: A study of full-time employed women in dual-earner couples. *Journal of Marriage and the Family, 56*(3), 647–656.

Belous, R. S. (1989). *The contingent economy: The growth of the temporary, part-time, and subcontracted workforce.* Washington, D.C.: National Planning Association.

Berg, P., Appelbaum, E., Bailey, T., & Kalleberg, A. (2004). Contesting time: International comparisons of employee control of working time. *Industrial and Labor Relations Review, 57*(3), 331–349.

Bolger, N., DeLongis, A., & Kessler, R. C. (1989). The contagion of stress across multiple roles. *Journal of Marriage and The Family, 51*(2), 175–183.

Brown, J. D. (1986). Evaluation of self and others: Self-enhancement biases in social judgments. *Social Cognition, 4*(3), 353–376.

Brudos, A. (1997). The new capitalism and organizational rationality: The adoption of downsizing programs, 1979–1994. *Social Forces, 76*(2), 229–250.

Byrne, J. A. (2003). *Chainsaw: The notorious career of Al Dunlap in the era of profit-at-any-price.* New York: HarperCollins.

Cappelli, P. (1999). *The new deal at work: Managing the market-driven workforce.* Boston: Harvard Business School Press.

Cappelli, P., & Crocker-Hefter, A. (1996). Distinctive human resources are firms' core competencies. *Organizational Dynamics, 24*(Winter), 7–22.

Coff, R., W., & Rousseau, D. M. (2000). Sustainable competitive advantage from relational wealth. In C. R. Leana & D. M. Rousseau (Eds.), *Relational wealth: The advantages of stability in a changing economy* (pp. 27–48). New York: Oxford University Press.

Conference Board. (2005, February 28). U.S. job satisfaction keeps falling, the Conference Board reports today. *News release.*

Deal, T. E., & Kennedy, A. A. (1982). *Corporate cultures: the rites and rituals of corporate life.* Reading, MA: Addison-Wesley.

Deloitte Research. (2004). *It's 2008: Do you know where your talent is?* New York: Deloitte Research.

DeParle, J. (2005, May 29). Goals reached, donor on right closes up shop. *New York Times.*

Evans, J. A., Kunda, G., & Barley, S. R. (2004). Beach time, bridge time, and billable hours: The temporal structure of technical contracting. *Administrative Science Quarterly, 49*(1), 1–38.

Feeney, S. A. (2004). Love hurts. *Workforce Management, 83*(2), 36–40.

Feinberg, P. (2004). Defined benefit pension plans falling out of favor. *Business Insurance, 38*(20), 46.

Ferraro, F., Pfeffer, J., & Sutton, R. I. (2005). Economics language and assumptions: How theories can become self-fulfilling. *Academy of Management Review, 30*(1), 8–24.

Frone, M. R., Russell, M., & Cooper, M. L. (1992). Antecedents and outcomes of work-family conflict: Testing a model of the work-family interface. *Journal of Applied Psychology, 77*(1), 65–78.

Galinsky, E. J., Friedman, D. E., & Bond, J. T. (1993). *The changing workforce: Highlights of the national study.* New York: Families and Work Institute.

Gareis, K. C., & Barnett, R. C. (2002). Under what conditions do long work hours affect psychological distress? *Work and Occupations, 29*(4), 483–497.

Geisel, J. (2002). Retirees to face higher costs for employer health care plans. *Business Insurance, 36*(September), 3.

Ghoshal, S. (2005). Bad management theories are destroying good management practices. *Academy of Management Learning and Education, 4*(1), 75–91.

Gittell, J. H. (2003). *The Southwest Airlines way: Using the power of relationships to achieve high performance.* New York: McGraw-Hill.

Griffin, L. J., Wallace, M. E., & Rubin, B. A. (1986). Capitalist resistance to the organization of labor before the New Deal: Why? How? Success? *American Sociological Review, 51*(2), 147–167.

Hackman, J. R., & Oldham, G. R. (1980). *Work redesign.* Reading, MA: Addison-Wesley.

Helyar, J. (1991, May 20). Playing ball: How Peter Ueberroth led the Major League in the "collusion era." *The Wall Street Journal.*

Hofmann, M. A. (2003). Employers attempt to keep health care costs under control. *Business Insurance, 37*(September), 4.

Hofstede, G. H. (1980). *Culture's consequences: International differences in work-related values.* Newbury Park, CA: Sage.

Jacobs, M. T. (1991). *Short-term America: The causes and cures of our business myopia.* Boston: Harvard Business School Press.

Jacoby, S. M. (1997). *Modern manors: Welfare capitalism since the New Deal.* Princeton, NJ: Princeton University Press.

Jacoby, S. M. (1999). Are career jobs headed for extinction? *California Management Review, 42* (Fall), 123–145.

Katcher, B. (2004). *How to improve employee trust in management,* from www.amanet.org.

Korn/Ferry International. (2003, September 30). *62% of global executives dissatisfied with current positions.* Retrieved from http://www.kornferry.com/Library/Process.asp.

Kotter, J. P., & Leskett, J. L. (1992). *Corporate culture and performance.* New York: Free Press.

Kuttner, R. (1996). *Everything is for sale: The virtues and limits of markets.* Chicago: University of Chicago Press.

Lacey, R. (1986). *Ford: The men and the machine.* New York: Little, Brown and Company.

Leana, C. R., & Rousseau, D. M. (2000). Relational wealth. In C. R. Leana & D. M. Rousseau (Eds.), *Relational wealth: The advantages of stability in a changing economy.* New York: Oxford University Press.

Maier, M. (2005). How to beat Wal-Mart. *Business 2.0, May,* 108–114.

McCabe, D. L., & Trevino, L. K. (1995). Cheating among business students: A challenge for business leaders and educators. *Journal of Management Education, 19*(2), 205–218.

McLean, B., & Elkind, P. (2003). *The smartest guys in the room: The amazing rise and scandalous fall of Enron.* New York: Penguin Group.

Miller, D. T. (1999). The norm of self-interest. *American Psychologist, 54*(12), 1053–1060.

Mitroff, I. I., & Denton, E. A. (1999). A study of spirituality in the workplace. *Sloan Management Review, 40*(4), 83–92.

Morris, M. W., & Peng, K. (1994). Culture and cause: American and Chinese attributions for social and physical events. *Journal of Personality & Social Psychology, 67*(6), 949–971.

O'Reilly, C. A. (1989). Corporations, culture, and commitment: Motivation and social control in organizations. *California Management Review, 31*(1), 9–25.

O'Reilly, C. A., & Pfeffer, J. (2000). *Hidden value: How great companies achieve extraordinary results with ordinary people.* Boston: Harvard Business School Press.

Ouchi, W. G. (1981). *Theory Z: How American business can meet the Japanese challenge.* Reading, MA: Addison-Wesley.

Ouchi, W. G., & Jaeger, A. M. (1978). Type Z organization: Stability in the midst of mobility. *The Academy of Management Review, 3*(2), 305–314.

Pear, R. (2005, May 29). Health leaders seek consensus over uninsured. *New York Times.*

Pearson, C. M., & Porath, C. L. (2005). On the nature, consequences, and remedies of workplace incivility: No time for "nice"? Think again. *Academy of Management Executive, 19*(1), 7–18.

Princeton Survey Research Associates. (1994). *Worker representation and participation survey: Report on the findings.* Princeton, NJ: Princeton Survey Research Associates.

Putnam, R. D. (2000). *Bowling alone: The collapse and revival of American community.* New York: Simon and Schuster.

Segal, L. M., & Sullivan, D. G. (1997). The growth of temporary services work. *The Journal of Economic Perspectives, 11*(2), 117–136.

Shinn, S. (2003). Luv, Colleen. *Bized, March/April,* 18–23.

Shuit, D. P. (2004). People problems on every aisle. *Workforce Management, 83*(2), 26–34.

Thompson, J. D. (1967). *Organizations in action.* New York: McGraw-Hill.

Tushman, M. L., & O'Reilly, C. A. (1997). *Winning through innovation: A practical guide to leading organizational change and renewal.* Boston: Harvard Business School Press.

Whyte, W. H. J. (1956). *The company man.* New York: Simon and Schuster.

Williamson, O. E. (1975). *Markets and hierarchies.* New York: Free Press.

Glossary

Action research (participatory action research) application of the scientific method of fact-finding and experimentation to practical problems requiring action solutions and involving the collaboration and cooperation of scientists, practitioners, and laypersons

Active careerist those who unabashedly pursue advancement in the workplace and primarily seek self-worth through their work

Aggressive communication tendency to attack others' self-concepts in order to deliver psychological pain or force others to believe something or behave in a particular way

AIDS acquired immune deficiency syndrome; a collection of symptoms and infections resulting from the specific damage to the immune system caused by the human immunodeficiency (HIV) in humans

Art of Demotivation, The book by E. L. Kersten that takes up and applies management theory in a parodic and humorous fashion; argues that employees are not an untapped human resource, but a problem to be overcome through processes of demotivation

Attribution focus of causation that an individual projects on someone in the process of judging why someone behaved as she or he did; in classical attribution theory, attributions are dispositional (focused on a characteristic of the person) or situational (focused on some feature of the physical or social environment)

Bounded emotionality balancing individual needs for authentic and spontaneous emotional expression with relational requirements, and organizational control

Burnout a general "wearing out" from the pressures of work characterized by (1) emotional exhaustion; (2) depersonalization or a negative shift in responses to others, particularly clients; and (3) a decreased sense of personal accomplishment

Busyness, ideology of A discourse and meaning system, often produced and invoked by academics, that serves to obscure their daily activities from the scrutiny of others

Careerism devotion to a successful career, often at the expense of one's integrity, personal life, and ethics

Category deception　the intentional misrepresentation of an identifying demographic category such as one's sex, age, or status

Civility　the act of showing regard, respect, restraint, and responsibility for the social demands of the situation

Clique　narrow exclusive circle or group of persons held together by common interests, views, or purposes

Collaborative action inquiry　a systematic process for the learning experience consisting of repeated episodes of reflection and action through which a group of peers strives to answer a question of importance to them

Consumer culture　a social culture in which one's sense of identity is tied up with what he or she owns and the consumption of material goods becomes a primary focus

Cooperative interruptions　a form of turn-taking that can engender identification, affirmation, and convey listening; less likely to be competitive and most often shows agreement, support, and enthusiasm for others' contributions and voice

Cordial hypocrisy　the strong tendency of people in organizations, because of loyalty or fear, to pretend that there is trust when there is not; being polite in the name of harmony when cynicism and distrust are the norm

Corporate colonization　draws attention to the ways that the instrumental interests and aims of corporations have disproportionately shaped the outlooks, interests, and aims of individuals, communities, and governing bodies

Counterproductive technology use　behaviors related to the use of communication technology that conflict with organizational goals and place employers at risk either legally or financially

Critical race theory　an area of scholarship that characterizes race as ongoing site of struggle in the United States, and seeks to eliminate racial oppression by unmasking everyday structures and practices that perpetuate race-based subordination

Culture-centered approach　examines the ways in which mainstream discourses silence cultural communities, using reflexive dialogue to create possibilities for listening to the voices of these communities, explores the role of communication at the intersections of structure, culture and agency

Cyberloafing　abusing Internet privileges at work by performing non-work related tasks; any voluntary act of employees using their companies' Internet access during office hours to surf non-work-related Web sites for non-work purposes and access (including receiving and sending) non-work-related e-mail; also known as cyberslacking, workplace Internet abuse, and online procrastination

Dark side of teams　confluence of individual, dyadic, subgroup, group, organizational, and environmental forces that lead many teams to organize and communicate in ways destructive to individuals, subgroups, organizations, and the groups themselves

Deceptive communication communication that is dishonest, involves lying, or is unfair, or that entails messages and information knowingly transmitted to create a false conclusion, by virtue of evasive or deliberately misleading messages, as well as euphemisms designed to cover up defects, conceal embarrassment, or make things appear better than they are

Demotivational posters workplace posters, produced by *Despair, Inc.*, that parody the ubiquitous office motivational posters that use "profound" sayings and warm, soothing images to improve workplace morale

Destructive communication intentional or unintentional communication that attacks receivers' self-esteem or reputation, or reflects indifference towards others' basic values, and is harmful to organizational members, groups within organizations, or organizations as a whole

Dimensions of teamwork vision, roles, processes, and relationships—areas of significant member interaction that create and recreate teamwork within the group

Discrimination the discernment of qualities and recognition of the differences between things and the subsequent prejudicial treatment of those who are different based on certain characteristics

Discursive framework understanding communication as shaping and framing social realities

Distrust a cognitive and emotional process in which actors are suspicious of motives, doubt the veracity, and have a lack of confidence in organizations or their members

Diversity the ideology of including people with different backgrounds and beliefs

Emotional contagion transfer of moods among people, tendency to express and feel emotions that are similar to and influenced by those of others; can involve caregiver taking on client emotions or organizational members assuming other members' feeling states; when employees move to polar extremes of emotional contagion (complete emotional involvement), they are more likely to burn out

Emotional labor a process whereby workers manage their emotions in response to organizational and occupational prescriptions, expectations, and display rules; largely inauthentic emotional display used by organization as a commodity

Emotional tyranny use of emotion by powerful organization members in a manner that is perceived to be destructive, controlling, unjust, and even cruel

Empathic concern an emotional stance in which the caregiver experiences concern about the welfare of the other without feeling parallel emotions of the other; correlated with employee satisfaction

Entrepreneurialism (or entrepreneurial culture)   an economic and social shift that favors enterprise

Entrepreneurial self   an autonomous, reflexive being who steers his or her life, taking initiative and assuming responsibility for his or her own success

Ethnicity   an aspect of social identity based on cultural phenomena such as place of origin, language, rituals, and traditions

Face-work   a common conversational want and need that compels people to act in ways that preserve their own and others' public self-images

Fart   an explosion of noxious body gasses from the anal sphincter

Flaming   hostile and aggressive interactions via text-based computer-mediated communication

Fundamental attribution error   a biased judgment about the cause of someone's behavior, in which an individual makes a dispositional attribution without considering likely situational factors; see *attribution*

Gender identity   a person's own sense of sex identification as male or female

Glass ceiling   a barrier so subtle that it is transparent, yet so strong that it prevents women and minorities from moving up in the management hierarchy

Grouphate   individuals' predisposition to detest, loathe, or abhor working in groups

Heteronormativity   processes that perpetuate situations wherein variations from heterosexual orientation are marginalized, ignored, or persecuted by social practices, beliefs or policies (e.g., social notions that human beings fall into two distinct and complementary categories: male and female; sexual/marital relations are normal only between people of different sexes; each sex has certain natural roles in life)

Homophobia   hatred, hostility, disapproval, or prejudice toward homosexuals or homosexual behavior

Hostile work environment   when an employee experiences workplace harassment and fears going to work because of the offensive, intimidating, or oppressive atmosphere generated by the harasser based on race, religion, sex, national origin, age, disability, veteran status, or, in some jurisdictions, sexual orientation, political affiliation, citizenship status, marital status, or personal appearance

Humor as resistance   body of research that examines workplace humor as an everyday discursive strategy through which employees construct identities and meanings that challenge hegemonic managerial discourse

Humor by incongruity   theory of humor arguing that humor resides in the juxtaposition of incompatible or contradictory elements (e.g., a renowned professor farting during a solemn public lecture); provides possibilities for resistance and social transformation

Identity anchors   a relatively enduring set of identity discourses upon which individuals rely when explaining who they are and want to be to themselves and others

Incivility   rude, offensive, and demeaning behaviors that vary in intensity and intention to harm others; behaviors that demean, demoralize, and degrade others; can be a subtle or overt attempts to disarm, distance, disrespect, or silence another in ways that privilege one's own views, position, and possibilities

Information overload   when an individual receives too much information; when information-processing demands exceed the supply or capacity of time available for such processing

Interpersonal trust   level of reliance on the integrity, strength, ability, or surety existing between individuals

Interpersonal trust, foundations of

> **Cognitive foundations of interpersonal trust**   trust based on evidence and judgments about the competence and reliability of a person
>
> **Affective foundations of interpersonal trust**   trust based on the emotional bonds that develop care, concern, and emotional investments in relationships

Intrusive activities   communication events that interrupt work tasks or workers' cognitive concentration and are, consequently, burdensome or destructive

Isolate   individual who is separated or cut off from others by physical or social barriers

Love-is-blind hypothesis of trust   when prior trust softens blow of betrayal; people granted the benefit of the doubt because of an accumulated history of otherwise benign and positive experiences

Love-is-forgiveness hypothesis of trust   people tolerate incivility and other potential trust-violating acts because they feel they have little choice or because they want to maintain a level of decorum with their bosses and coworkers

LGBT   abbreviation for "lesbian, gay, bisexual, transgendered"

Malware   malicious computer software that interferes with normal computer functions or sends personal data about the user to unauthorized parties over the Internet

Marginalization   a process through which one is relegated to an unimportant or powerless position within a society or group

Marginalized   the exclusion of groups of people from meaningful participation in society generally because of a minority status

Micro-affirmations   seemingly small gestures that can enhance another's self image or reduce uncertainty about his or her worth and contributions

Micro-inequities   seemingly minor unpleasantries or small differences in how people are treated that can have negative effects on employees

Minority   a sociological group that does not constitute a political plurality of the total population

Moral emotions   affective reactions to violations or affirmations of moral obligations governing the conduct of individuals, relationship partners, or larger communities

Multicommunication   a form of multitasking, defined as engaging in more than one activity at one time or treating unplanned interruptions as equally important to planned activities; polychronicity

Multitasking   the performance of several tasks simultaneously

Mutual knowledge   shared awareness among communicators of a situational context, such as a physical space, situational distractions, local events, or competing schedules; easier to attain when communicators share a physical location than when they are geographically separated

Negative face   desire or want for autonomy and freedom from imposition; acts or behaviors that compromise this desire

Network attacks   actions directed against computer systems to disrupt equipment operations, change processing control, or corrupt stored data

Nonproductive technology uses   behaviors that are not directly valuable for the organization and that often detract from accomplishing work tasks

Opportunity costs   what it takes to regain or produce anew something lost or valued; cost incurred (sacrifice) by choosing one option over the next best alternative (which may be equally desired)

Organizational irrationalities   everyday practices that pull organizational members in different and sometimes competing directions (e.g., paradox, tension, contradiction, irony)

Organizational trust   members' faith in or reliance on the integrity, strength, ability, and surety of organizations and their leaders; confidence and belief in the uprightness of organizational actions and actors

Organizational Trust, Bases of

> **Dispositional trust**   the tendency to trust without trust being earned
>
> **History-based trust**   the willingness to trust based on past relationships
>
> **Third-parties as conduits of trust**   trust based on influential colleagues' views or experiences with person trusted

Category-based trust   trust based on shared membership in a common group

Rule-based trust   trust based on shared understandings about appropriate behavior

Organizational Trust, Dimensions of

Competence   perceived leadership and organizational effectiveness

Openness   the level of honesty and transparency demonstrated by organization leaders

Concern   the degree to which members feel organization is concerned about their well-being

Reliability   the degree to which members feel others' behavior is consistent and dependable

Identification   the degree to which organizational members are connected to organization's goals, values, norms, and beliefs

Ostracism   the act or process of banning or excluding an individual from a larger group

Outcast   individual intentionally separated from or shunned by others

Passive careerist   those who would not otherwise position work as the central element of their identities but are forced into this position within the competitive entrepreneurial context

Polychronicity   see Multicommunication

Positive face   desire or want for connection with others; acts or behaviors that threaten one's desire and need to be viewed positively by and connected to others

Postcolonialism   the study of global processes in the backdrop of colonial and neocolonial configurations; explores the intersections of the politics of international divisions of labor and resources, and the global processes through which these disparities are maintained and reinforced

Presenteeism   slack productivity from ailing workers; workers in hostile environments may be at work, but they are not producing at their peak potential

Pseudonymity   communicating under a screen name instead of one's actual name; can also be achieved by the use of avatars (e.g., models, icons, or pictures) used to represent one's real self in computer-mediated communication

Psychologically-safe group communication climate   working environment that is characterized by support, openness, trust, mutual respect, and risk taking; one that facilitates innovation, constructive discussion, information provision, openness to new perspectives, and suspension of judgement

Race   an artificial construction of human differences based on physical characteristics such as skin color, facial features, and hair texture

Racial animus   a perspective that racism consists of explicit, overt, often violent acts that white individuals or groups perpetuate against people of color to assert white superiority

Racial harassment   unwelcome conduct engendered by racism that unreasonably interferes with an individual's work performance or creates an intimidating, hostile, or offensive work environment

Racism   any theory or belief that a person's inherited physical characteristics associated with racial designations (e.g., skin color, hair texture or facial features) determine human intellectual capacity and personality traits

Racism, types

> **Institutional (structural) racism**   systemic, collective patterns and practices that help to entrench racial inequality in organizations and institutions
>
> **Internalized racism**   a belief among persons of color that white persons are superior and persons of color are inferior

Radical demotivation   E. L. Kersten's management theory arguing that the key to corporate success is to disabuse employees of the narcissistic fantasies they harbor about their intrinsic worth to the company; designed for managers to enable them to harness the dysfunction and toxicity inherent in their workforce and exploit it for their own financial gain

Resilience   intersubjectively   and   communicatively   constructed process(es) of rebounding from or reintegrating after disruptions, tragedies, crises, and destructive organizational relationships and situations

Resilience, types

> **Accepting (or resilience-as-acceptance)**   the cognitive and emotional process of "facing down of reality" necessary for resilience; acceptance does not contain the connotations of defeat found in "resignation"
>
> **Adapting (or resilience-as-adaptation)**   the process of making adjustments to respond productively to or rebound successfully from new life circumstances brought about by disruptions, tragedies, crises, and destructive organizational relationships and situations

Resistance leadership   term coined to transcend the dichotomy of worker resistance and management control that characterizes critical organization studies; involves leaders engaging in behaviors that resist rather than reproduce organizational status quo

Scapegoating   assigning blame or failure to another to absolve one's wrongdoing or responsibility and deflect attention away from oneself; taking out frustrations out on a weaker, more vulnerable organizational or group member

Sexual harassment   unwelcome sexual advances, requests for sexual favors, and other verbal or physical conduct of a sexual nature when this conduct explicitly or implicitly affects an individual's employment, unreasonably interferes with an individual's work performance, or creates an intimidating, hostile, or offensive work environment

Sexual harassment, types

Hostile-environment sexual harassment situations where employees are subject to unwanted sexual behavior from persons other than a direct supervisor in which authorities fail to take steps to discourage or discontinue such behavior; unwanted sexual attention so prevalent or so severe that workplace becomes destructive or damaging

Quid pro quo sexual harassment situations where employees are subject to unwanted sexual behavior from a person in a hierarchically-superior position that makes employment, promotion, or raise contingent on the receipt of sexual favors

Third-person sexual harassment victim not directly harassed but negatively affected by witnessing or hearing about others' sexual harassment

Sexual harassment as discursive process   sexual harassment as a form of communication that shapes social realities in the workplace

Sexual harassment-prone organizations   organizational cultures that promote and encourage sexually aggressive behavior

Sexual orientation   broadly understood as enduring emotional, romantic, sexual, or affectional attraction towards others; distinguished from other components of sexuality including biological sex, gender identity (psychological sense of being male or female), and social gender role (adherence to cultural norms for feminine and masculine behavior)

Social stigma   severe social disapproval of personal characteristics or beliefs that are contrary to cultural norms

Social support   physical and emotional comfort given by family, friends, co-workers, and others; helpful interactions that can ameliorate stress, burnout, and emotional pain

Social support, types

> **Emotional support** providing empathy, caring, acceptance, and assurance
>
> **Informational support** helping others define their role, providing general facts about a job or issue, and offering skills training
>
> **Instrumental support** giving time, resources, or labor

Stress a process of (1) alarm reaction, (2) resistance, and (3) exhaustion; difference between worker satisfaction (as represented by individual need fulfillment) and realities of the work situation as experienced by individuals

Subaltern members of marginalized groups outside the structures of political representation; general attribute of subordination (e.g., in class, age, gender)

Surveillance use of technology to monitor employees

Swift trust the propensity to make quick, unevaluated, yet lasting, decisions to trust

Team small group of organizational members who possess complementary characteristics, share a common goal, and are mutually accountable for their performance

Teamwork cooperative or coordinated effort on the part of a group of persons acting together in the interests of a common cause

Telework(ing) working from home or outside the traditional workplace using a computer or telephone connection; also called telecommuting

Toxin handlers the managers, secretaries, or intermediaries who address, eliminate, and assuage the conflicts, stressors, problems, abuse, and hurt feelings common in organizations

Victim schema mentally preparing for the possibility of being the target of sexual harassment by creating realistic roadmaps for how to respond

Virtual groups interdependent partners who communicate primarily or exclusively using electronic communication technology such as computer-mediated communication, may connect from completely different geographic locations or institutions, the same location or institution, or some combination of geographic dispersion

White-supremacist ideology a belief that white persons are superior to members of other racial groups

Workaholism working compulsively at the expense of other pursuits, especially work encroaching into all areas of one's non-work life (family, friends, hobbies, etc.)

Workplace aggression efforts by individuals to harm others with whom they work or the organizations in which they are employed

Workplace bullying   persistent verbal and nonverbal acts directed toward one or more workers that cause humiliation, offense, distress, or interference with work and create a hostile, counterproductive environment; typically involves power disparity between targets and bullies

Workplace bullying, types of

Authoritative bullying   the persistent abuse of power granted through organizational position; most commonly reported type

Discriminatory bullying   abusing someone out of prejudice, usually workers who differ from or refuse to accept the norms of the rest of the workgroup or belong to a certain outsider group

Displaced bullying   scapegoating or aggressing against someone other than the source of strong provocation because aggressing against the source of such provocation is too dangerous

Dispute-related bullying   bullying sparked by interpersonal disagreements that build into extremely escalated, entrenched conflicts

Organizational bullying   organizational practices that are oppressive, exploitive, over-controlling and seed abuse (e.g., corporate downsizing, outsourcing jobs, forcing uncompensated overtime work, closing entire plants to relocate for low-cost labor)

Serial bullying   many workers are bullied, usually one after the other by an authoritative bully

Index